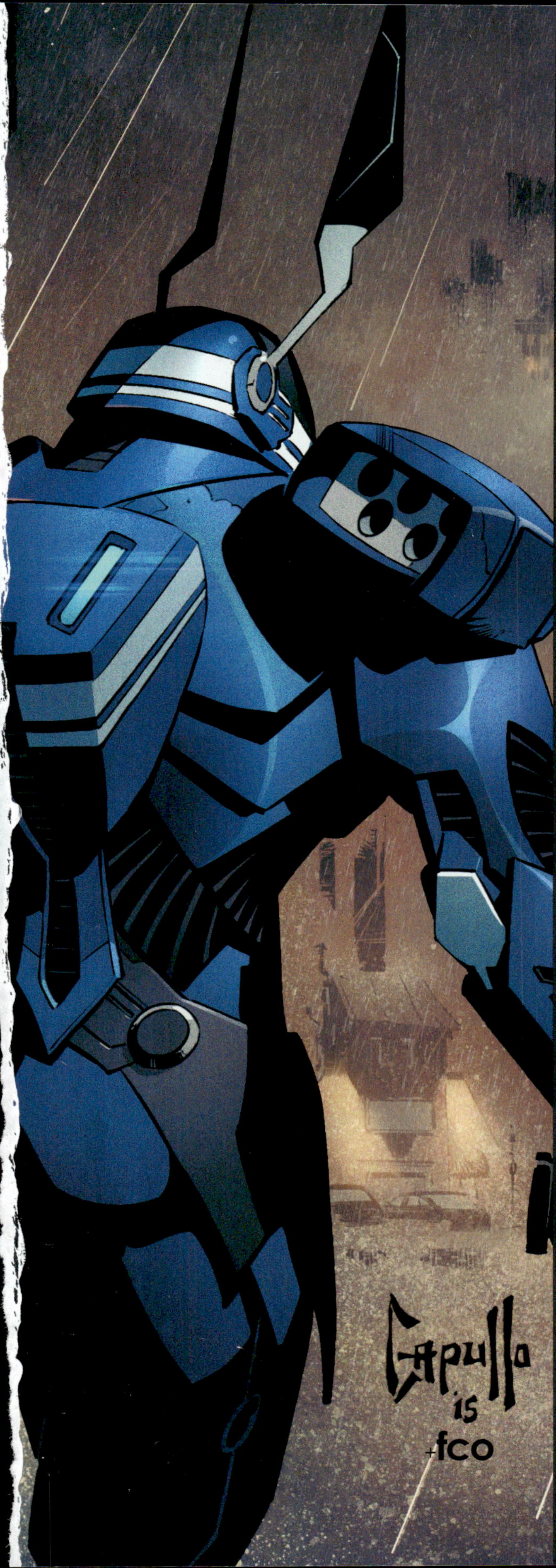
Capullo
15
+fco

VOLUME 8

SUPERHEAVY

BATMAN

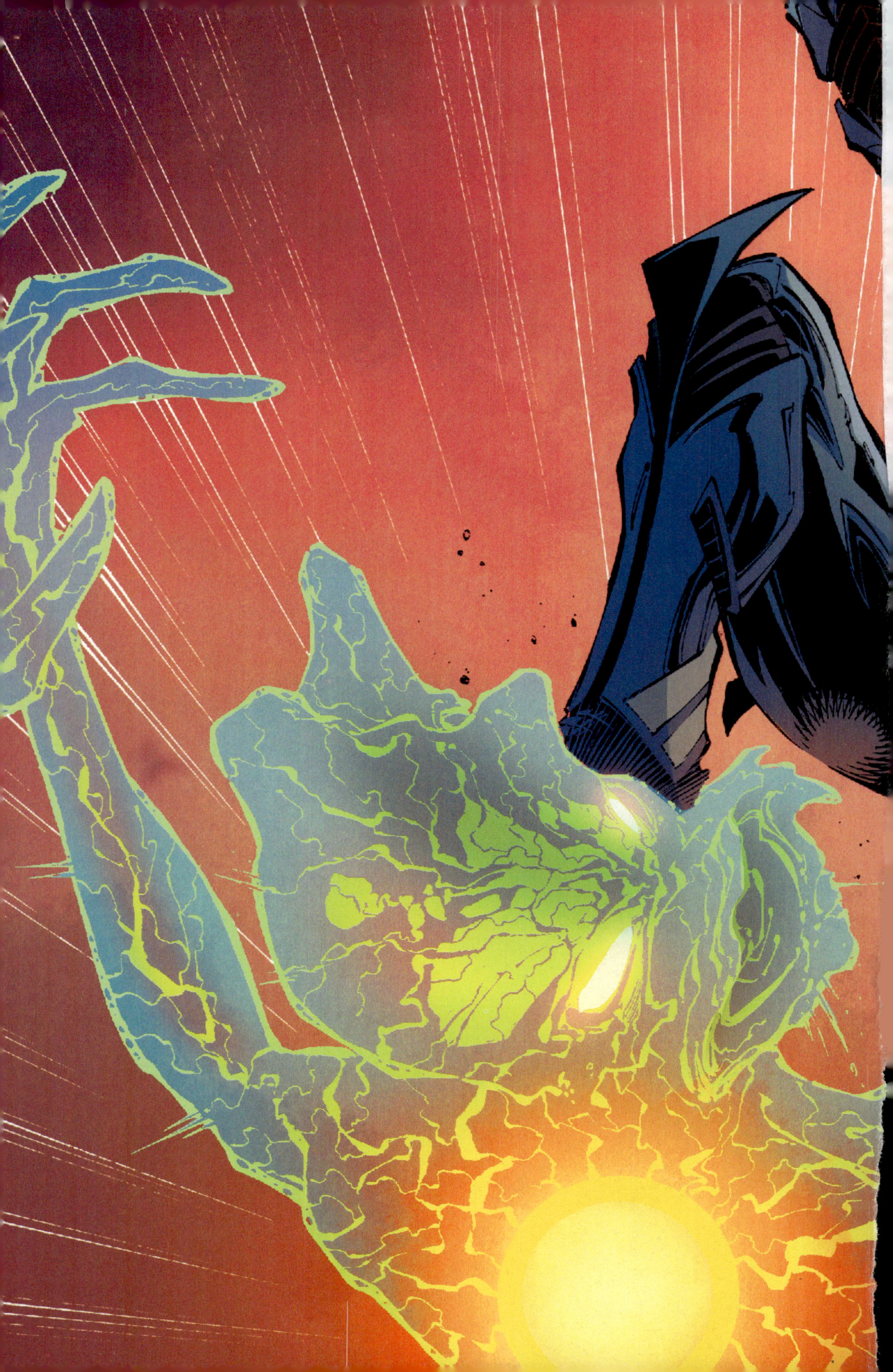

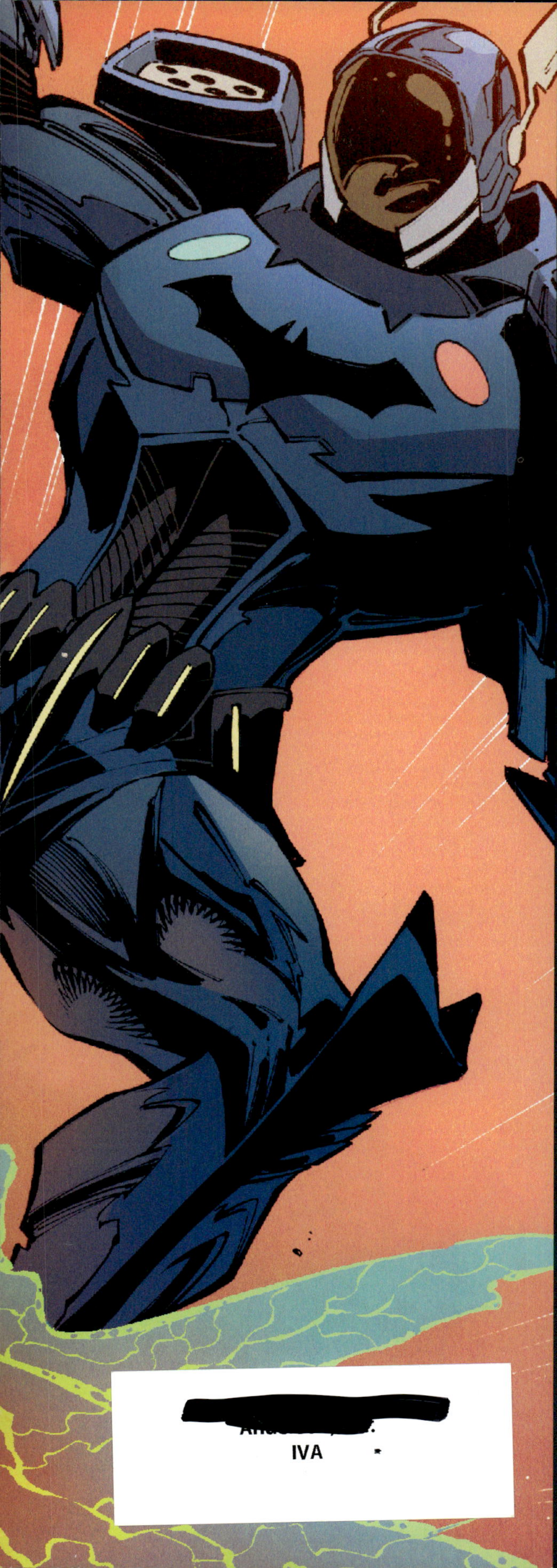
[redacted]
IVA

BATMAN

VOLUME 8
SUPERHEAVY

WRITTEN BY
SCOTT SNYDER

PENCILS BY
GREG CAPULLO

INKS BY
DANNY MIKI

COLOR BY
FCO PLASCENCIA

LETTERS BY
STEVE WANDS

INTERLUDE
WRITTEN BY
SCOTT SNYDER
& BRIAN AZZARELLO

ART BY
JOCK

COLORS BY
LEE LOUGHRIDGE

LETTERS BY
DERON BENNETT

COLLECTION COVER ARTISTS
GREG CAPULLO
& DANNY MIKI

BATMAN CREATED BY
BOB KANE with **BILL FINGER**
SUPERMAN CREATED BY
JERRY SIEGEL & JOE SHUSTER
BY SPECIAL ARRANGEMENT WITH
THE JERRY SIEGEL FAMILY

MARK DOYLE Editor – Original Series
REBECCA TAYLOR Associate Editor – Original Series
DAVE WIELGOSZ MATT HUMPHREYS Assistant Editors – Original Series
JEB WOODARD Group Editor – Collected Editions
ROBIN WILDMAN Editor – Collected Edition
STEVE COOK Design Director – Books
DAMIAN RYLAND Publication Design

BOB HARRAS Senior VP – Editor-in-Chief, DC Comics

DIANE NELSON President
DAN DIDIO and JIM LEE Co-Publishers
GEOFF JOHNS Chief Creative Officer
AMIT DESAI Senior VP – Marketing & Global Franchise Management
NAIRI GARDINER Senior VP – Finance
SAM ADES VP – Digital Marketing
BOBBIE CHASE VP – Talent Development
MARK CHIARELLO Senior VP – Art, Design & Collected Editions
JOHN CUNNINGHAM VP – Content Strategy
ANNE DEPIES VP – Strategy Planning & Reporting
DON FALLETTI VP – Manufacturing Operations
LAWRENCE GANEM VP – Editorial Administration & Talent Relations
ALISON GILL Senior VP – Manufacturing & Operations
HANK KANALZ Senior VP – Editorial Strategy & Administration
JAY KOGAN VP – Legal Affairs
DEREK MADDALENA Senior VP – Sales & Business Development
JACK MAHAN VP – Business Affairs
DAN MIRON VP – Sales Planning & Trade Development
NICK NAPOLITANO VP – Manufacturing Administration
CAROL ROEDER VP – Marketing
EDDIE SCANNELL VP – Mass Account & Digital Sales
COURTNEY SIMMONS Senior VP – Publicity & Communications
JIM (SKI) SOKOLOWSKI VP – Comic Book Specialty & Newsstand Sales
SANDY YI Senior VP – Global Franchise Management

BATMAN VOL. 8: SUPERHEAVY

DC Comics, 2900 West Alameda Avenue, Burbank, CA 91505
Printed by RR Donnelley, Salem, VA, USA. 2/12/16. First Printing.
ISBN: 978-1-4012-5969-3

Library of Congress Cataloging-in-Publication Data is Available.

PEFC Certified

Printed on paper from sustainably managed forests and controlled sources

PEFC/29-31-75   www.pefc.org

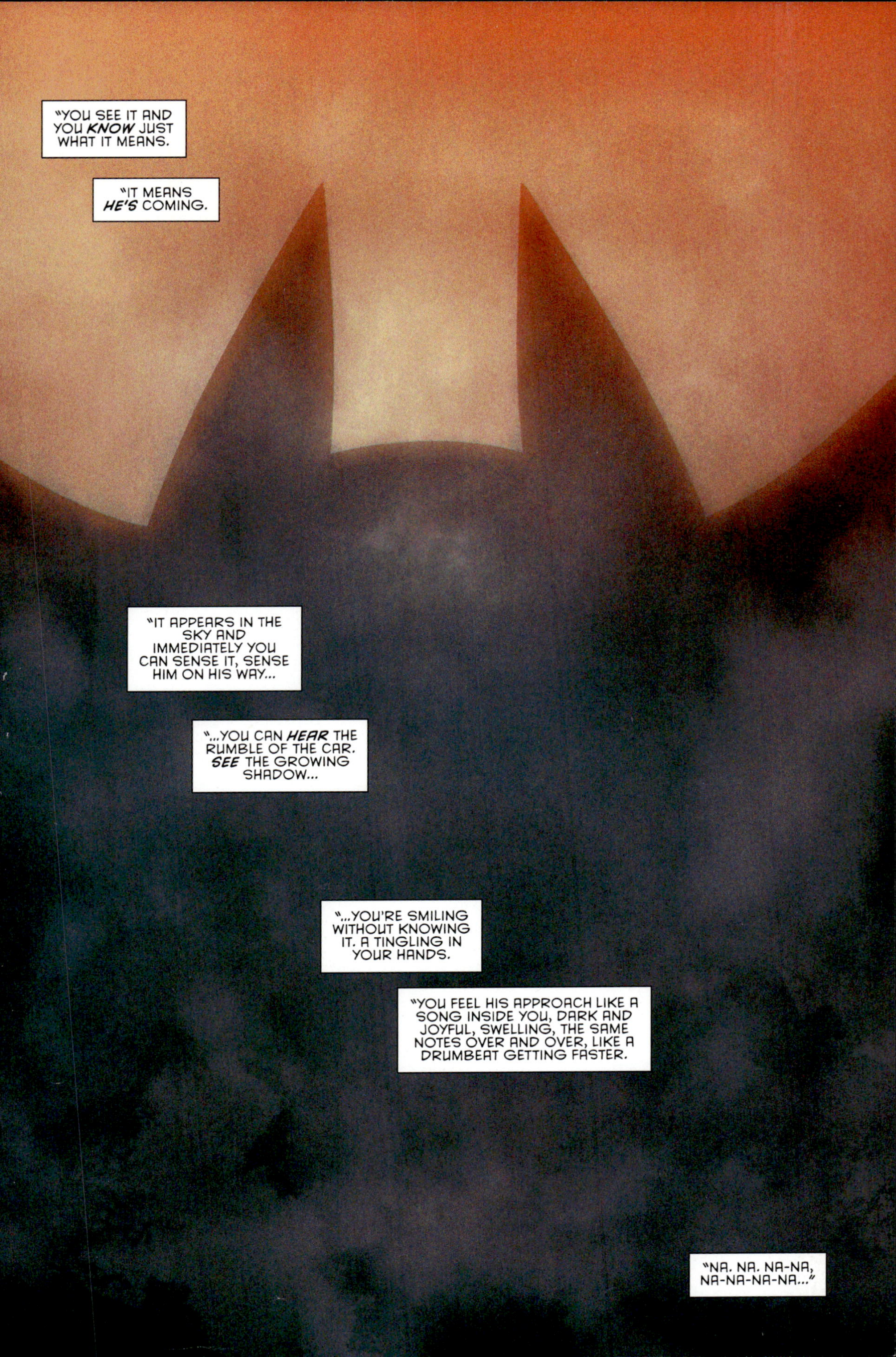
"YOU SEE IT AND YOU *KNOW* JUST WHAT IT MEANS.
"IT MEANS *HE'S* COMING.
"IT APPEARS IN THE SKY AND IMMEDIATELY YOU CAN SENSE IT, SENSE HIM ON HIS WAY...
"...YOU CAN *HEAR* THE RUMBLE OF THE CAR. *SEE* THE GROWING SHADOW...
"...YOU'RE SMILING WITHOUT KNOWING IT. A TINGLING IN YOUR HANDS.
"YOU FEEL HIS APPROACH LIKE A SONG INSIDE YOU, DARK AND JOYFUL, SWELLING, THE SAME NOTES OVER AND OVER, LIKE A DRUMBEAT GETTING FASTER.
"NA. NA. NA-NA, NA-NA-NA-NA..."

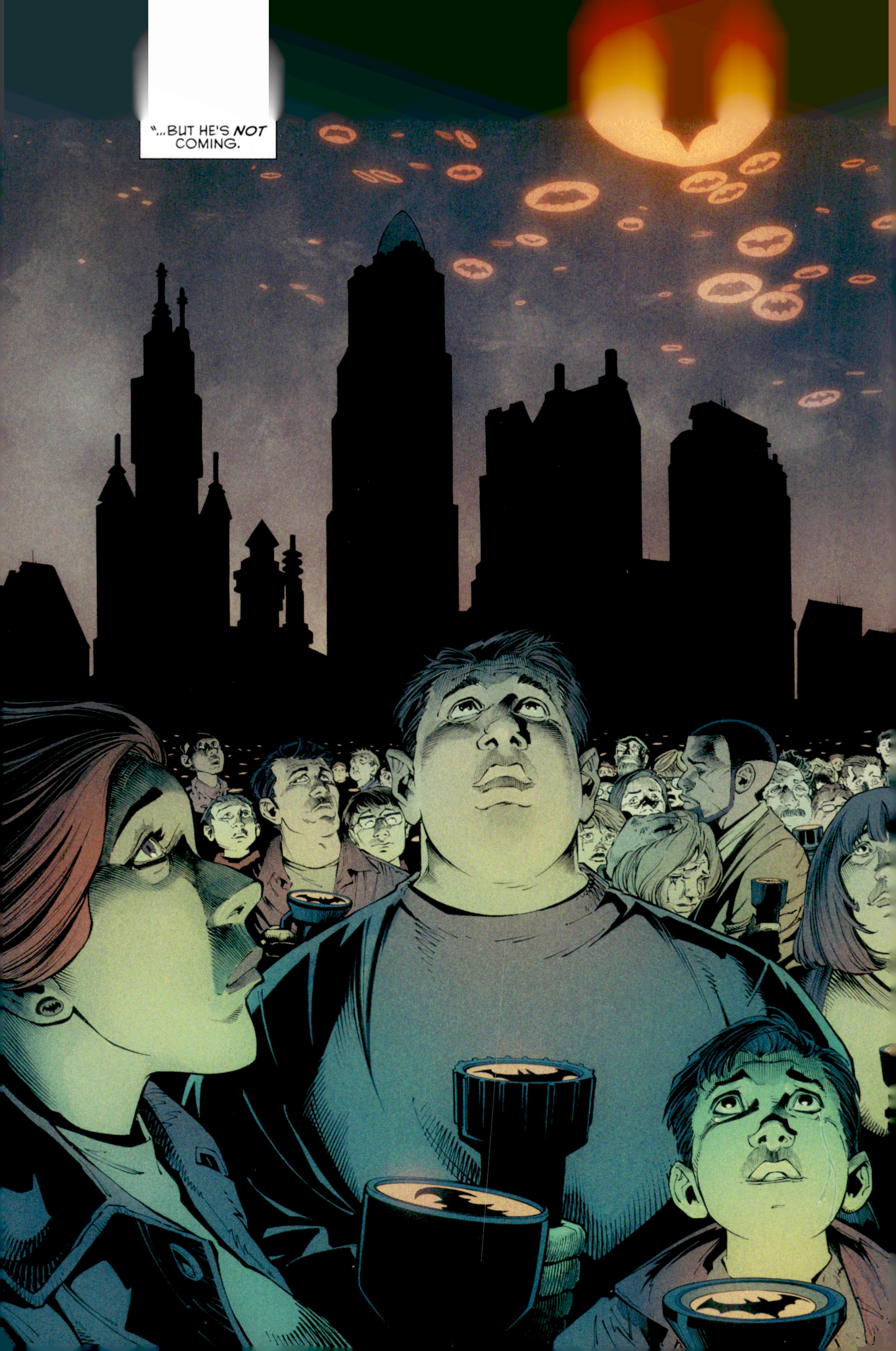
"...BUT HE'S *NOT* COMING.

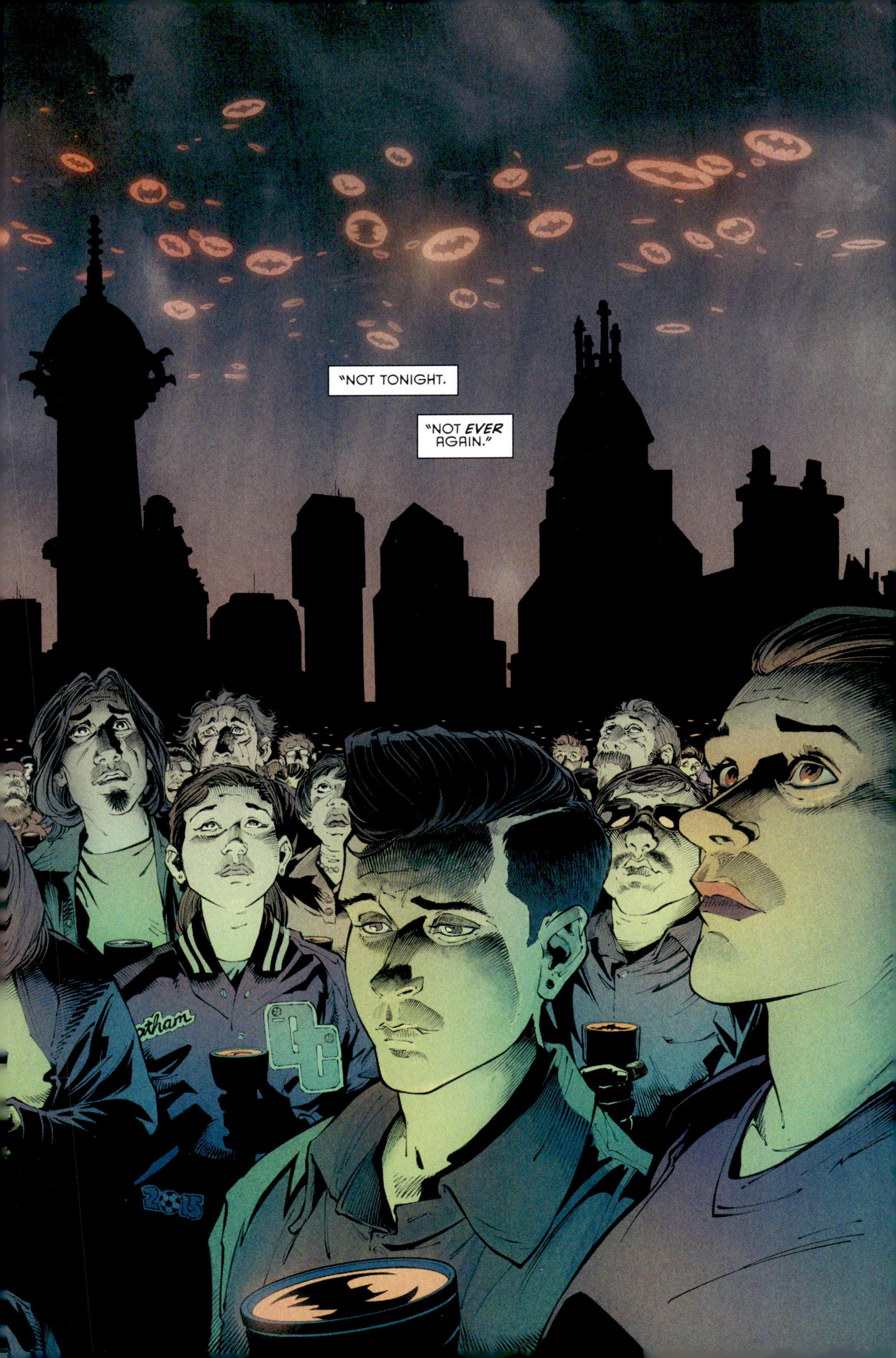
"NOT TONIGHT.
"NOT *EVER* AGAIN."

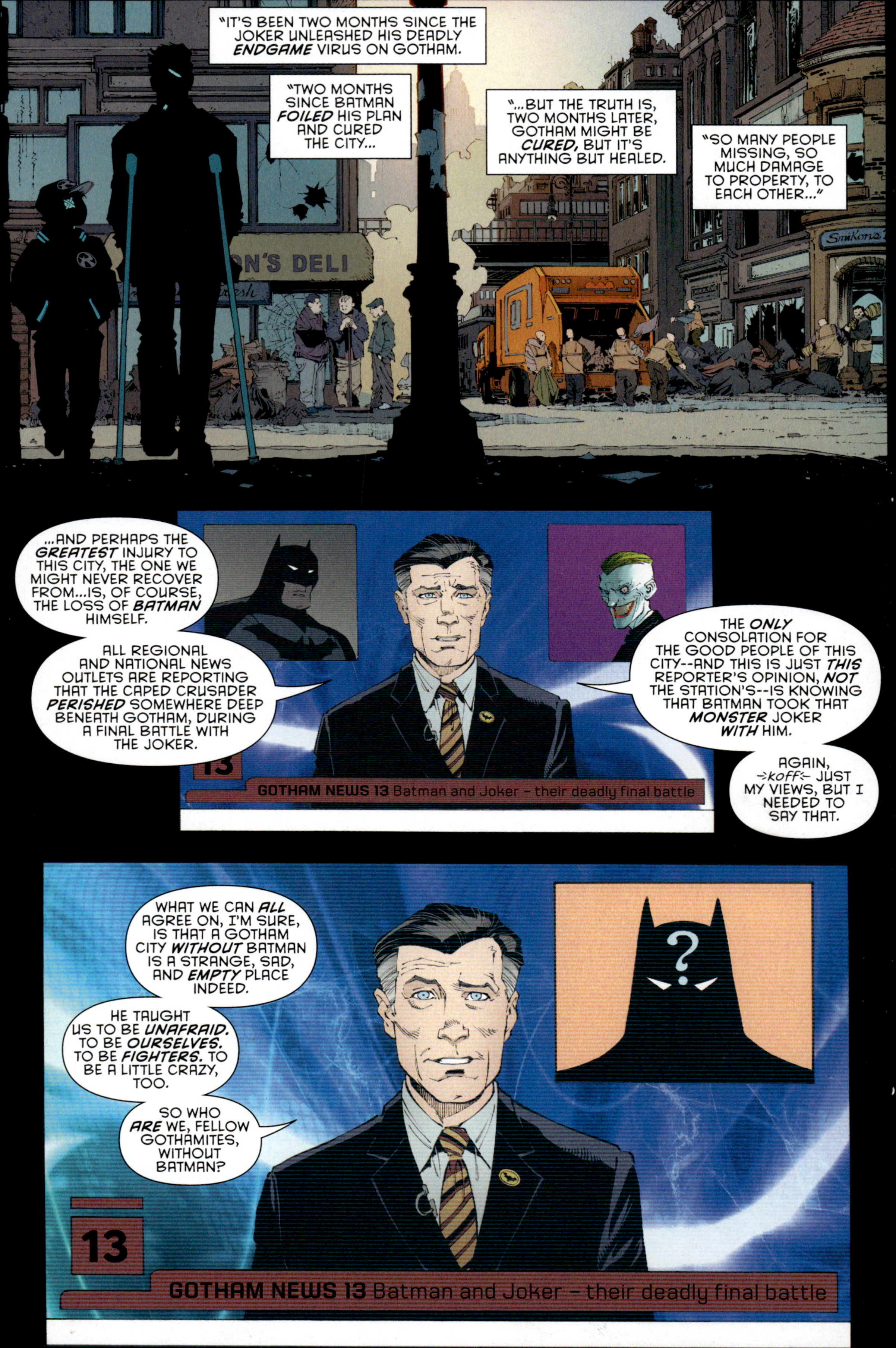
"IT'S BEEN TWO MONTHS SINCE THE JOKER UNLEASHED HIS DEADLY *ENDGAME* VIRUS ON GOTHAM.
"TWO MONTHS SINCE BATMAN *FOILED* HIS PLAN AND CURED THE CITY...
"...BUT THE TRUTH IS, TWO MONTHS LATER, GOTHAM MIGHT BE *CURED,* BUT IT'S ANYTHING BUT HEALED.
"SO MANY PEOPLE MISSING, SO MUCH DAMAGE TO PROPERTY, TO EACH OTHER..."
ON'S DELI
...AND PERHAPS THE *GREATEST* INJURY TO THIS CITY, THE ONE WE MIGHT NEVER RECOVER FROM...IS, OF COURSE, THE LOSS OF *BATMAN* HIMSELF.
ALL REGIONAL AND NATIONAL NEWS OUTLETS ARE REPORTING THAT THE CAPED CRUSADER *PERISHED* SOMEWHERE DEEP BENEATH GOTHAM, DURING A FINAL BATTLE WITH THE JOKER.
THE *ONLY* CONSOLATION FOR THE GOOD PEOPLE OF THIS CITY--AND THIS IS JUST *THIS* REPORTER'S OPINION, *NOT* THE STATION'S--IS KNOWING THAT BATMAN TOOK THAT *MONSTER* JOKER *WITH* HIM.
AGAIN, ➛*KOFF*⬿ JUST MY VIEWS, BUT I NEEDED TO SAY THAT.
GOTHAM NEWS 13 Batman and Joker – their deadly final battle
WHAT WE CAN *ALL* AGREE ON, I'M SURE, IS THAT A GOTHAM CITY *WITHOUT* BATMAN IS A STRANGE, SAD, AND *EMPTY* PLACE INDEED.
HE TAUGHT US TO BE *UNAFRAID.* TO BE *OURSELVES.* TO BE *FIGHTERS.* TO BE A LITTLE CRAZY, TOO.
SO WHO *ARE* WE, FELLOW GOTHAMITES, WITHOUT BATMAN?
13
GOTHAM NEWS 13 Batman and Joker – their deadly final battle

"WELL, PERHAPS-- MERCIFULLY--THANKS TO *ONE* GOTHAM INSTITUTION, WE *WON'T* HAVE TO FIND OUT.

"FOR NEARLY THREE CENTURIES, *POWERS INTERNATIONAL* HAS BEEN ONE OF THE MOST *PROMINENT* CORPORATE CITIZENS OF GOTHAM CITY, AND THE NATION.

"NOW, WITH THEIR *ACQUISITION* OF THE RECENTLY *DEFUNCT* WAYNE ENTERPRISES, THE POWERS FAMILY IS LOOKING TO *BROADEN* THEIR ROLE IN THE CITY'S RECONSTRUCTION. FROM RESIDENTIAL PROJECTS TO MUNICIPAL SITES...

GOTHAM NEWS 13 Powers International: "Time to start over"...**GOTHAM NEWS 13**

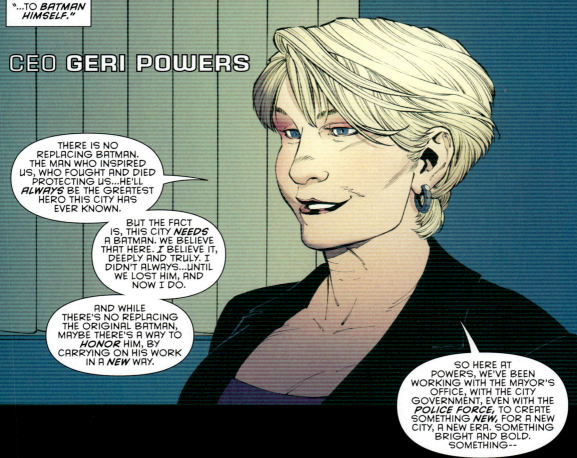

"...TO *BATMAN* HIMSELF."

CEO GERI POWERS

THERE IS NO REPLACING BATMAN. THE MAN WHO INSPIRED US, WHO FOUGHT AND DIED PROTECTING US...HE'LL *ALWAYS* BE THE GREATEST HERO THIS CITY HAS EVER KNOWN.

BUT THE FACT IS, THIS CITY *NEEDS* A BATMAN. WE BELIEVE THAT HERE. *I* BELIEVE IT, DEEPLY AND TRULY. I DIDN'T ALWAYS...UNTIL WE LOST HIM, AND NOW I DO.

AND WHILE THERE'S NO REPLACING THE ORIGINAL BATMAN, MAYBE THERE'S A WAY TO *HONOR* HIM, BY CARRYING ON HIS WORK IN A *NEW* WAY.

SO HERE AT POWERS, WE'VE BEEN WORKING WITH THE MAYOR'S OFFICE, WITH THE CITY GOVERNMENT, EVEN WITH THE *POLICE FORCE,* TO CREATE SOMETHING *NEW,* FOR A NEW CITY, A NEW ERA. SOMETHING BRIGHT AND BOLD. SOMETHING--

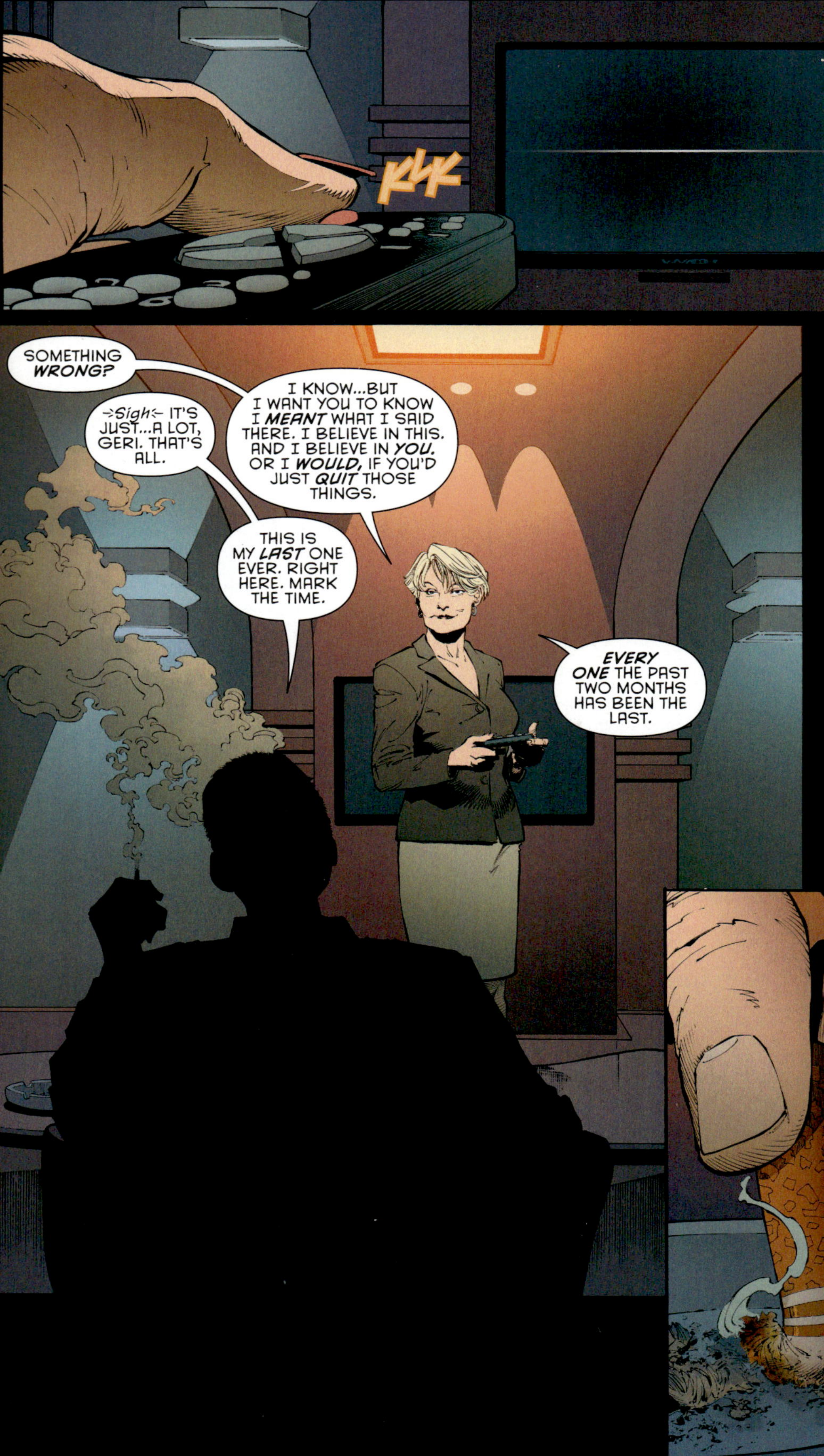
KLK
SOMETHING WRONG?
I KNOW...BUT I WANT YOU TO KNOW I MEANT WHAT I SAID THERE. I BELIEVE IN THIS. AND I BELIEVE IN YOU. OR I WOULD, IF YOU'D JUST QUIT THOSE THINGS.
⇒Sigh⇐ IT'S JUST...A LOT, GERI. THAT'S ALL.
THIS IS MY LAST ONE EVER. RIGHT HERE. MARK THE TIME.
EVERY ONE THE PAST TWO MONTHS HAS BEEN THE LAST.

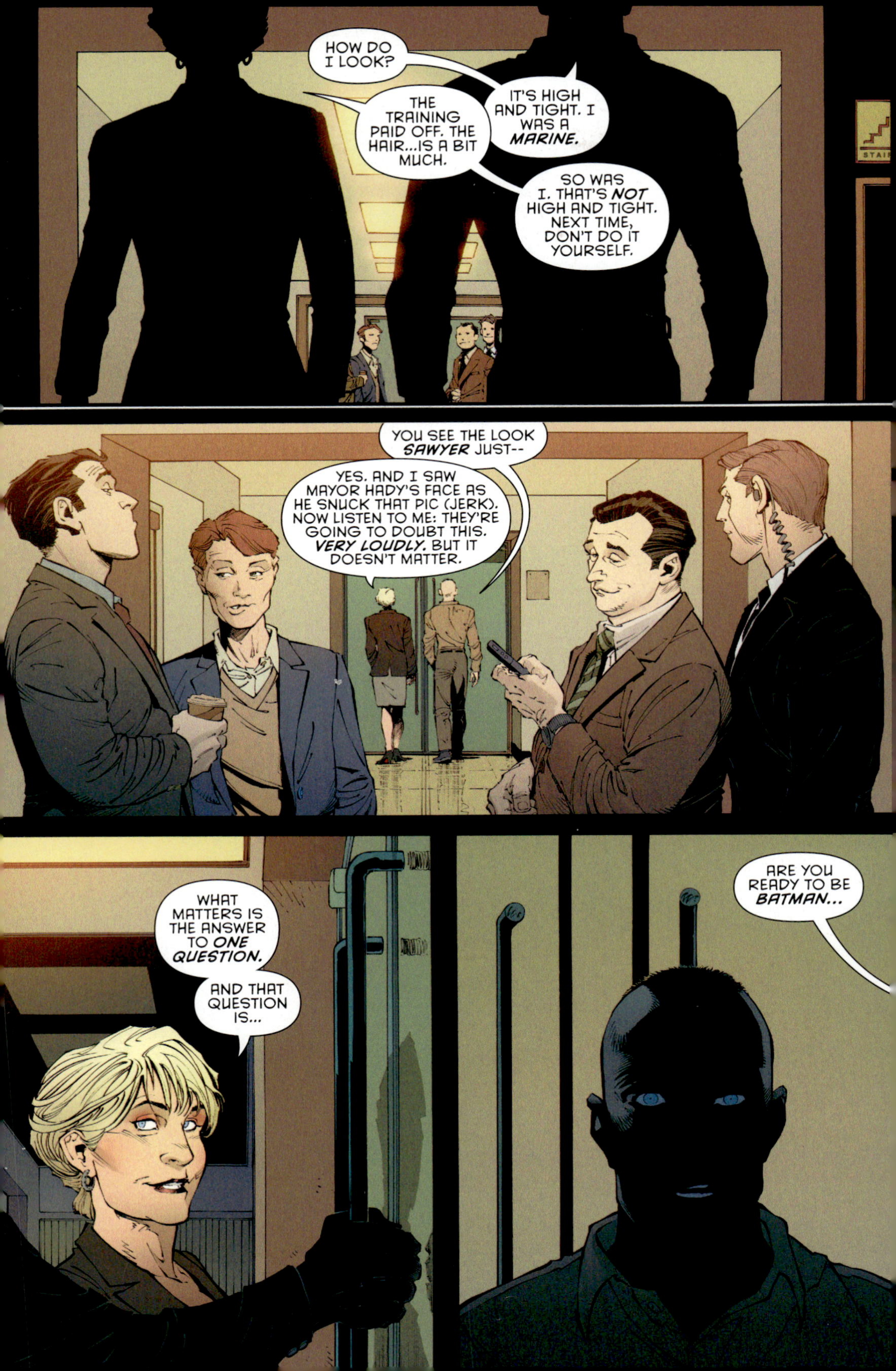
HOW DO I LOOK?
THE TRAINING PAID OFF. THE HAIR...IS A BIT MUCH.
IT'S HIGH AND TIGHT. I WAS A *MARINE.*
SO WAS I. THAT'S *NOT* HIGH AND TIGHT. NEXT TIME, DON'T DO IT YOURSELF.
STAIR
YOU SEE THE LOOK *SAWYER* JUST--
YES. AND I SAW MAYOR HADY'S FACE AS HE SNUCK THAT PIC (JERK). NOW LISTEN TO ME: THEY'RE GOING TO DOUBT THIS. *VERY LOUDLY.* BUT IT DOESN'T MATTER.
WHAT MATTERS IS THE ANSWER TO *ONE QUESTION.*
AND THAT QUESTION IS...
ARE YOU READY TO BE *BATMAN...*

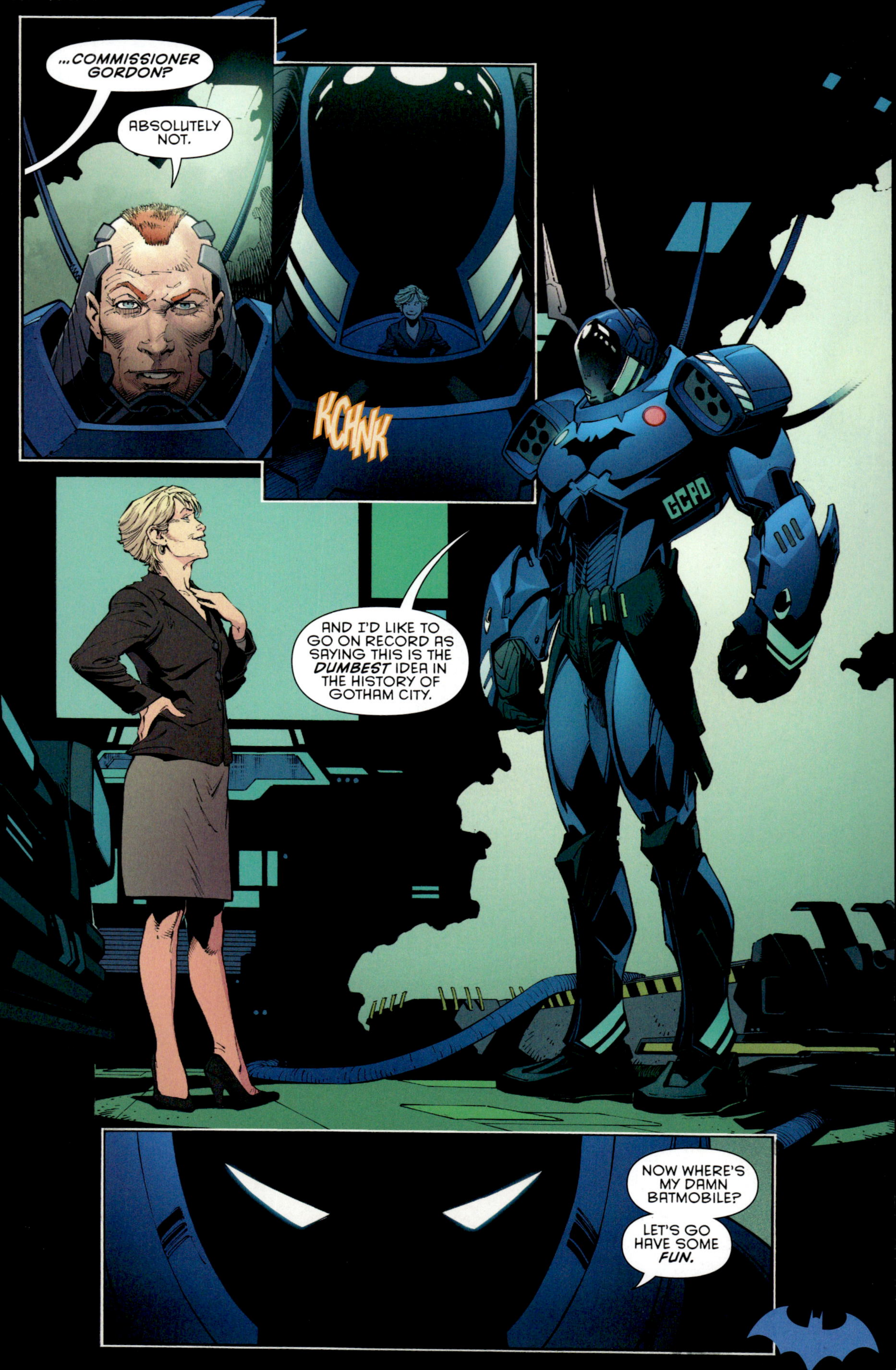

...COMMISSIONER GORDON?
ABSOLUTELY NOT.
KCHNK
GCPD
AND I'D LIKE TO GO ON RECORD AS SAYING THIS IS THE DUMBEST IDEA IN THE HISTORY OF GOTHAM CITY.
NOW WHERE'S MY DAMN BATMOBILE?
LET'S GO HAVE SOME FUN.

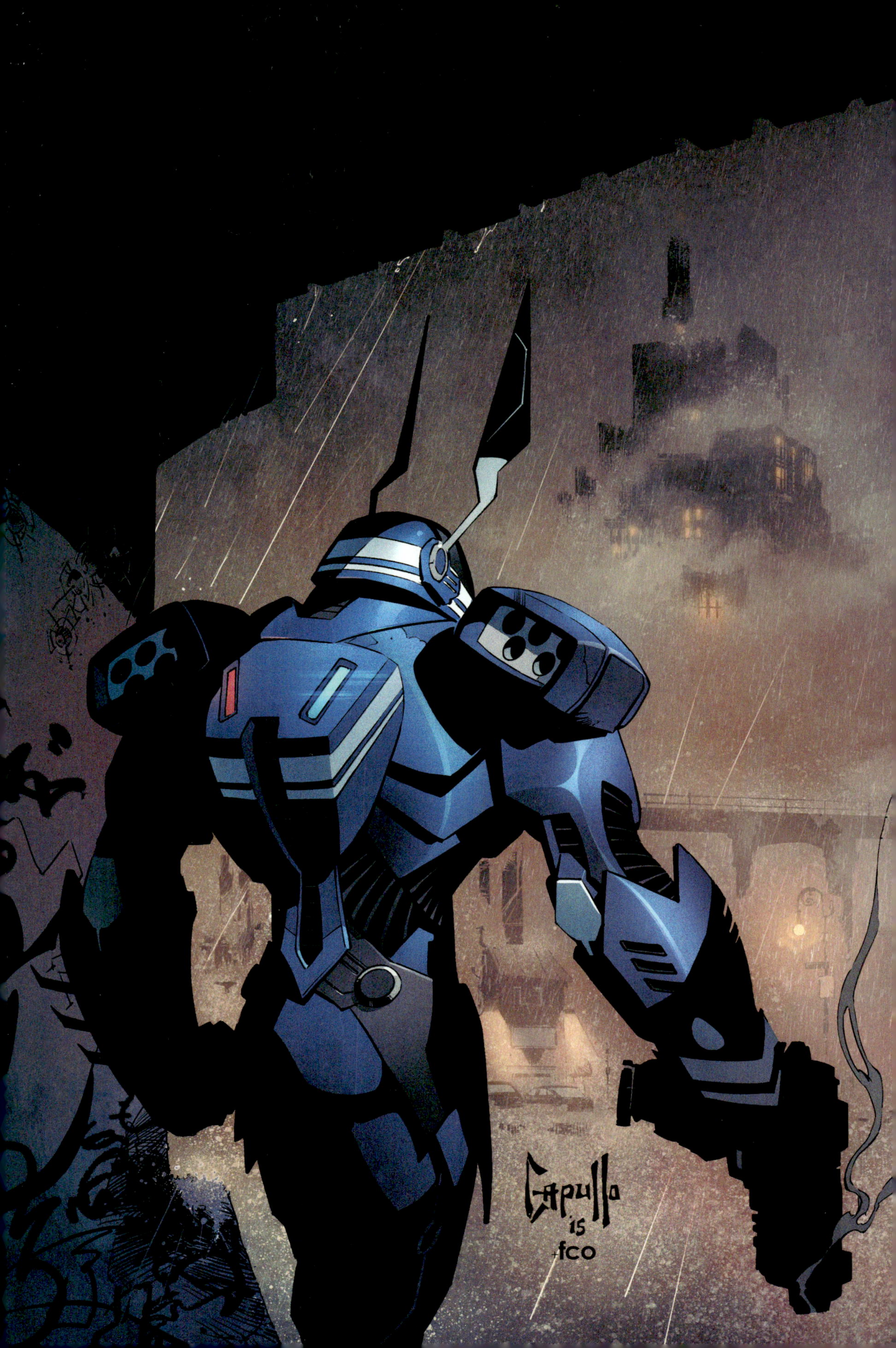
Capullo
15
+fco

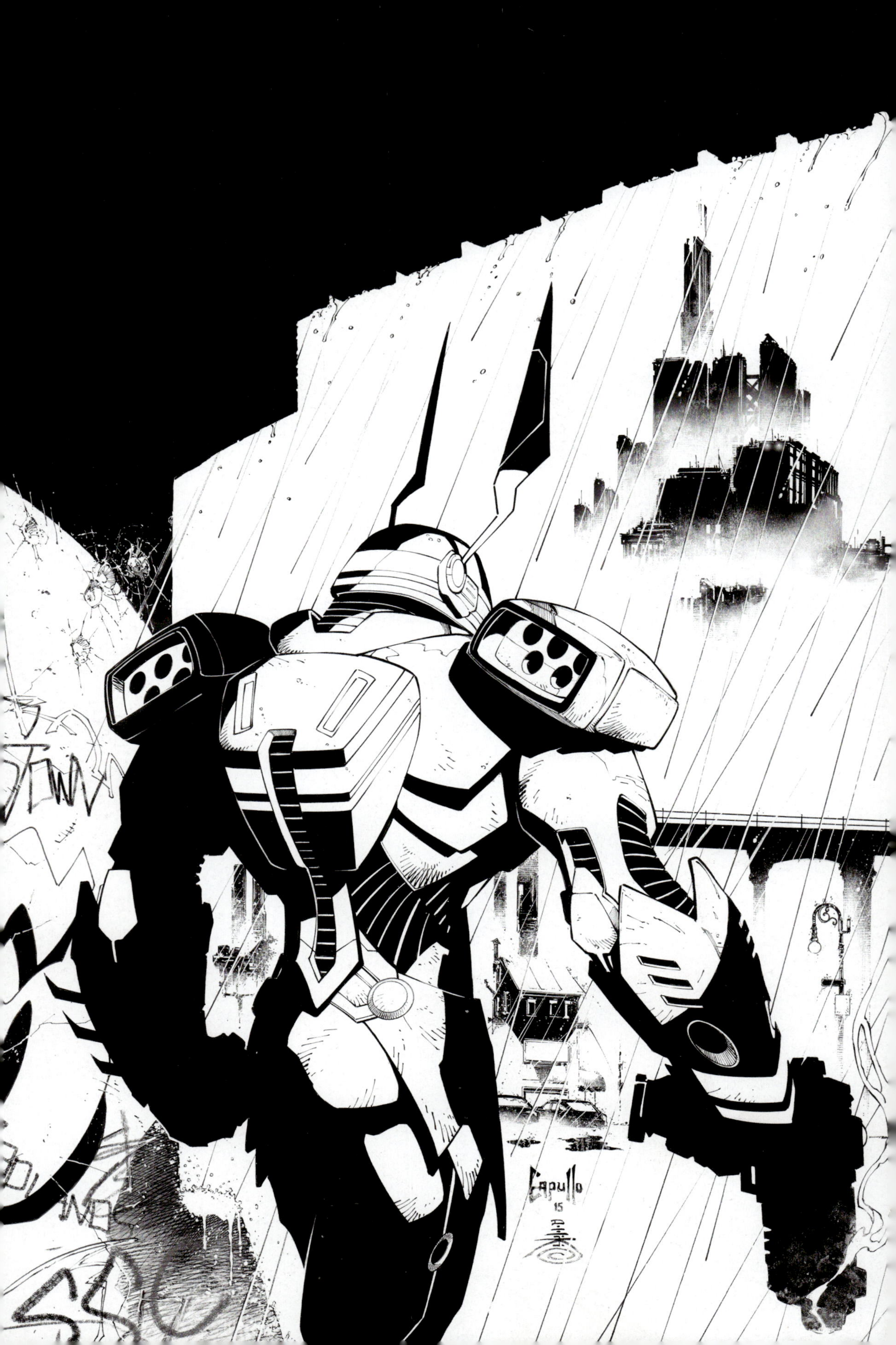
Capullo
15

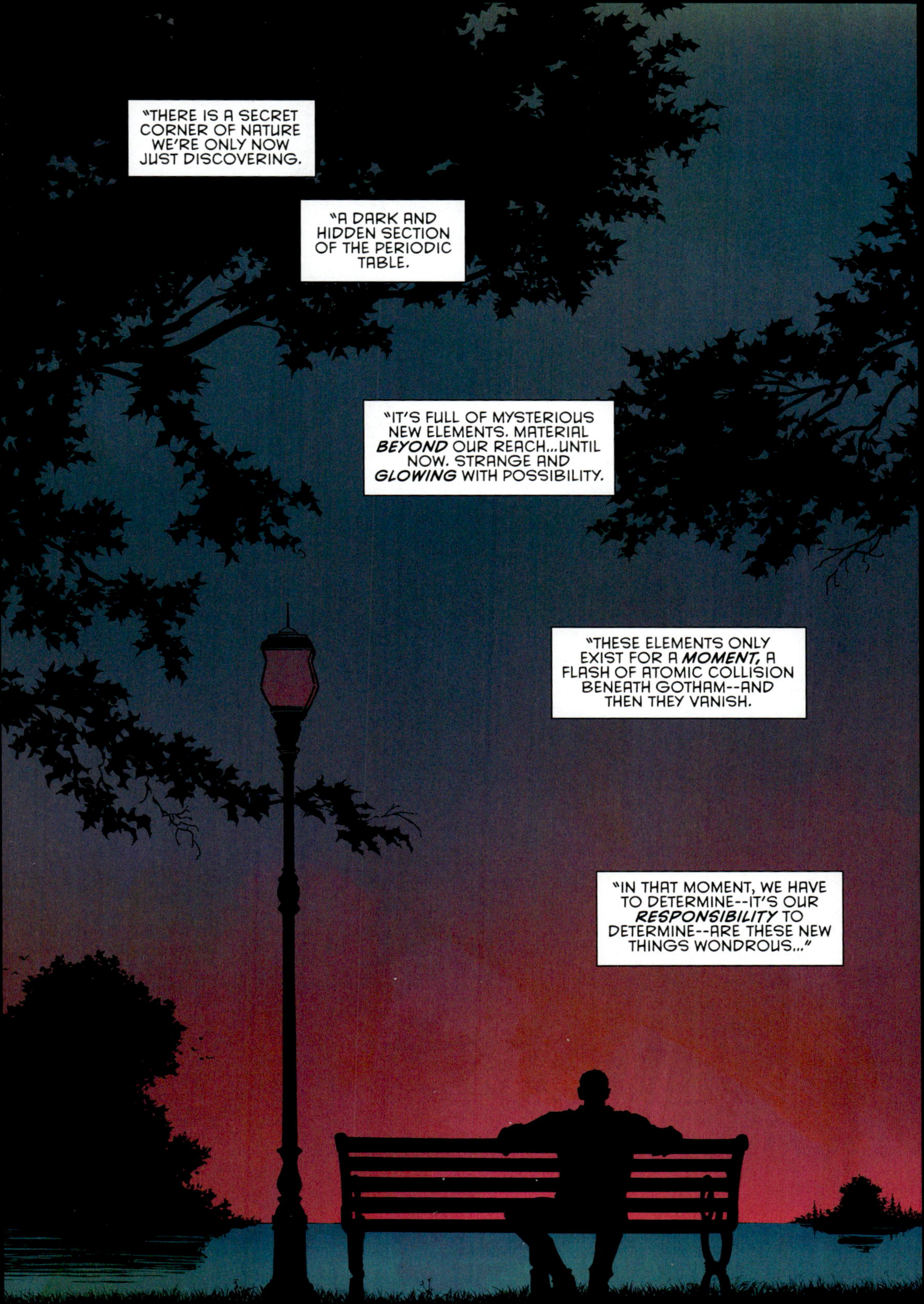
"THERE IS A SECRET CORNER OF NATURE WE'RE ONLY NOW JUST DISCOVERING.
"A DARK AND HIDDEN SECTION OF THE PERIODIC TABLE.
"IT'S FULL OF MYSTERIOUS NEW ELEMENTS. MATERIAL *BEYOND* OUR REACH...UNTIL NOW. STRANGE AND *GLOWING* WITH POSSIBILITY.
"THESE ELEMENTS ONLY EXIST FOR A *MOMENT,* A FLASH OF ATOMIC COLLISION BENEATH GOTHAM--AND THEN THEY VANISH.
"IN THAT MOMENT, WE HAVE TO DETERMINE--IT'S OUR *RESPONSIBILITY* TO DETERMINE--ARE THESE NEW THINGS WONDROUS..."

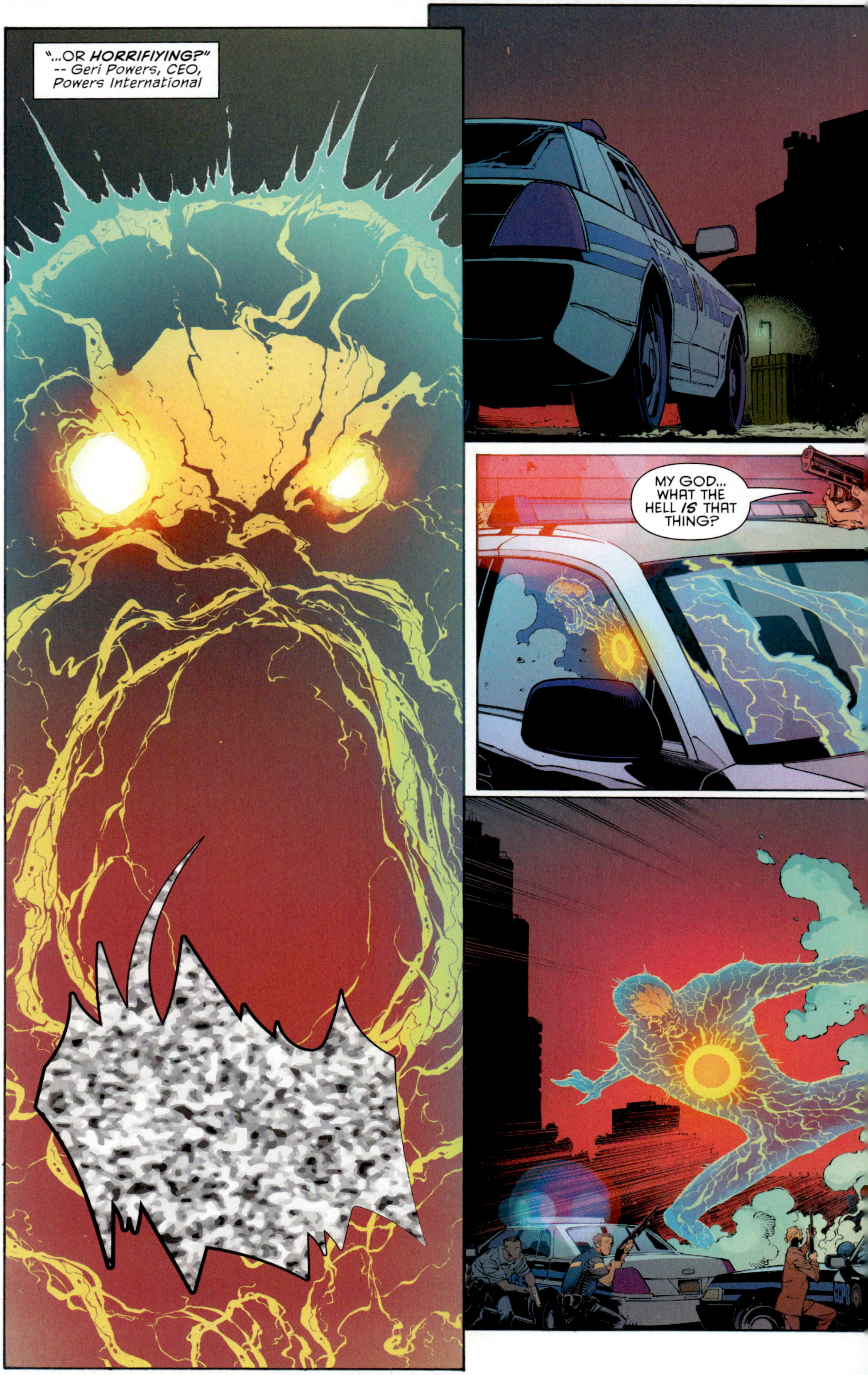
"...OR HORRIFIYING?" -- Geri Powers, CEO, Powers International
MY GOD... WHAT THE HELL IS THAT THING?

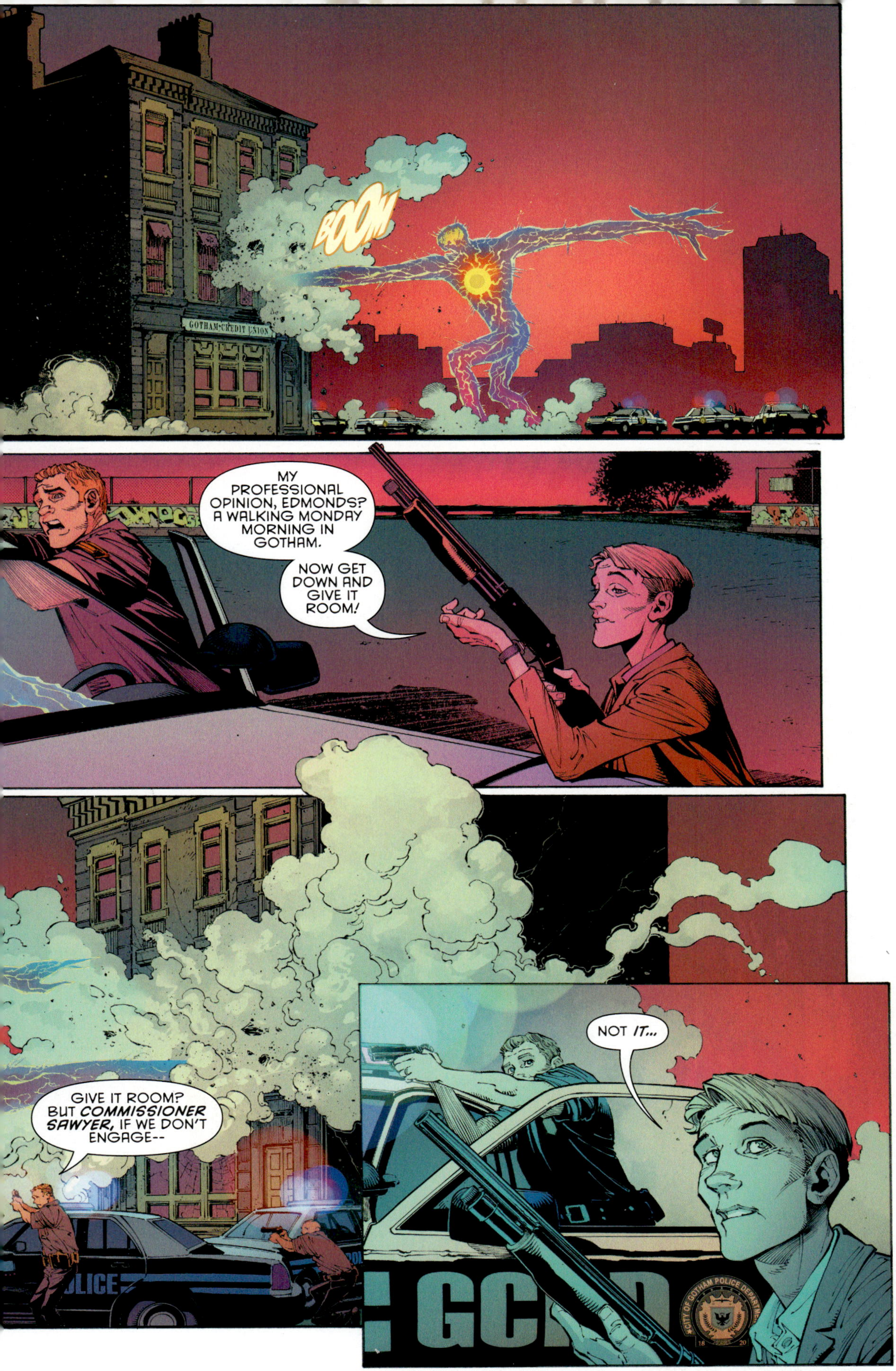
BOOM
GOTHAM CREDIT UNION
MY PROFESSIONAL OPINION, EDMONDS? A WALKING MONDAY MORNING IN GOTHAM.
NOW GET DOWN AND GIVE IT ROOM!
GIVE IT ROOM? BUT COMMISSIONER SAWYER, IF WE DON'T ENGAGE--
NOT IT...
POLICE
GCPD
CITY OF GOTHAM POLICE DEPARTMENT
18 20

"...IT."

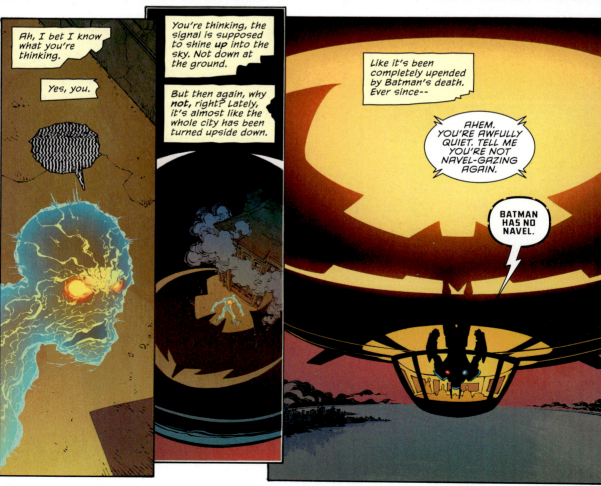

Ah, I bet I know what you're thinking.

Yes, you.

You're thinking, the signal is supposed to shine **up** into the sky. Not down at the ground.

But then again, why **not,** right? Lately, it's almost like the whole city has been turned upside down.

Like it's been completely upended by Batman's death. Ever since--

AHEM. YOU'RE AWFULLY QUIET. TELL ME YOU'RE NOT NAVEL-GAZING AGAIN.

BATMAN HAS NO NAVEL.

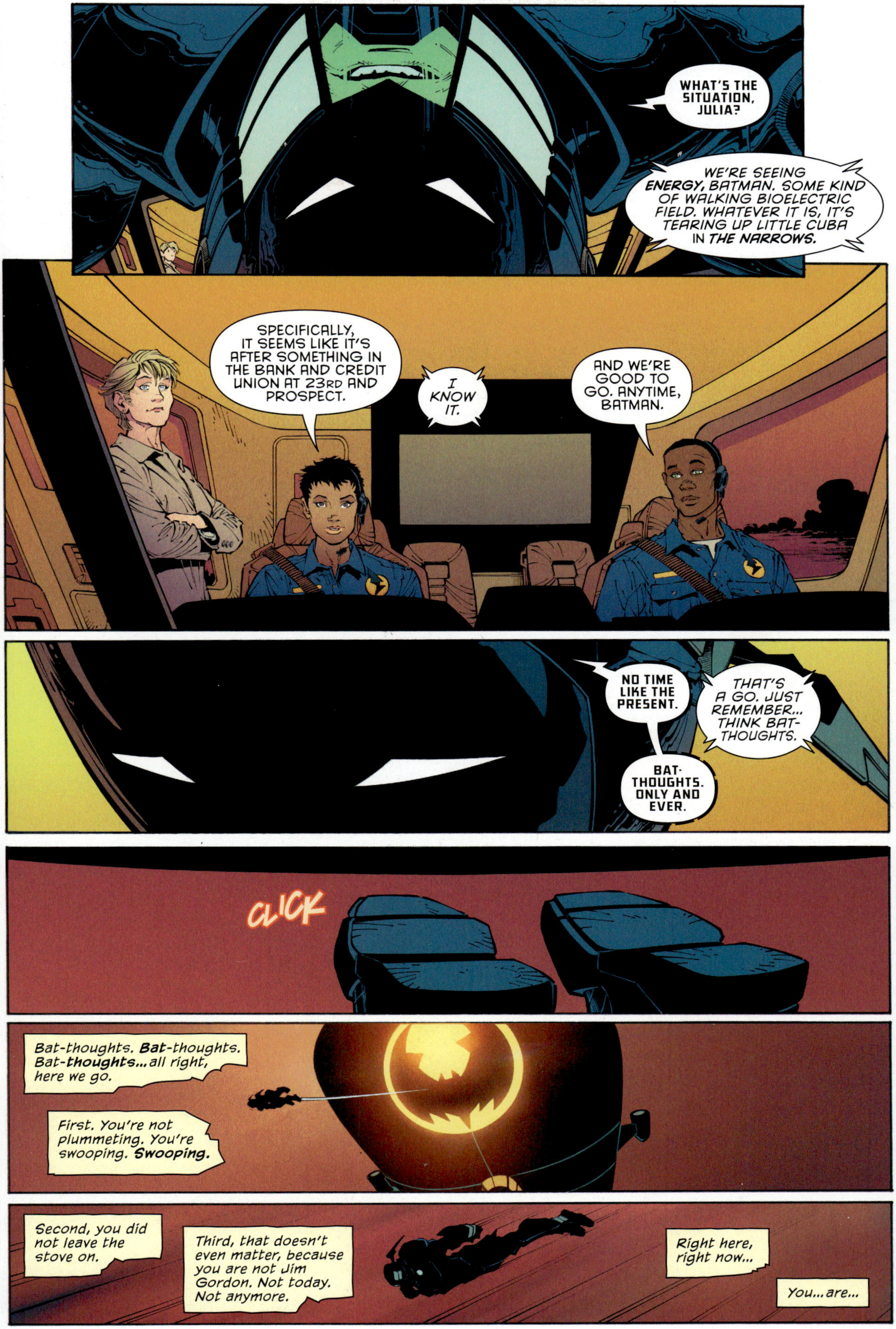

WHAT'S THE SITUATION, JULIA?
WE'RE SEEING ENERGY, BATMAN. SOME KIND OF WALKING BIOELECTRIC FIELD. WHATEVER IT IS, IT'S TEARING UP LITTLE CUBA IN THE NARROWS.
SPECIFICALLY, IT SEEMS LIKE IT'S AFTER SOMETHING IN THE BANK AND CREDIT UNION AT 23RD AND PROSPECT.
I KNOW IT.
AND WE'RE GOOD TO GO. ANYTIME, BATMAN.
NO TIME LIKE THE PRESENT.
THAT'S A GO. JUST REMEMBER... THINK BAT-THOUGHTS.
BAT-THOUGHTS. ONLY AND EVER.
CLICK
Bat-thoughts. Bat-thoughts. Bat-thoughts... all right, here we go.
First. You're not plummeting. You're swooping. Swooping.
Second, you did not leave the stove on.
Third, that doesn't even matter, because you are not Jim Gordon. Not today. Not anymore.
Right here, right now...
You... are...

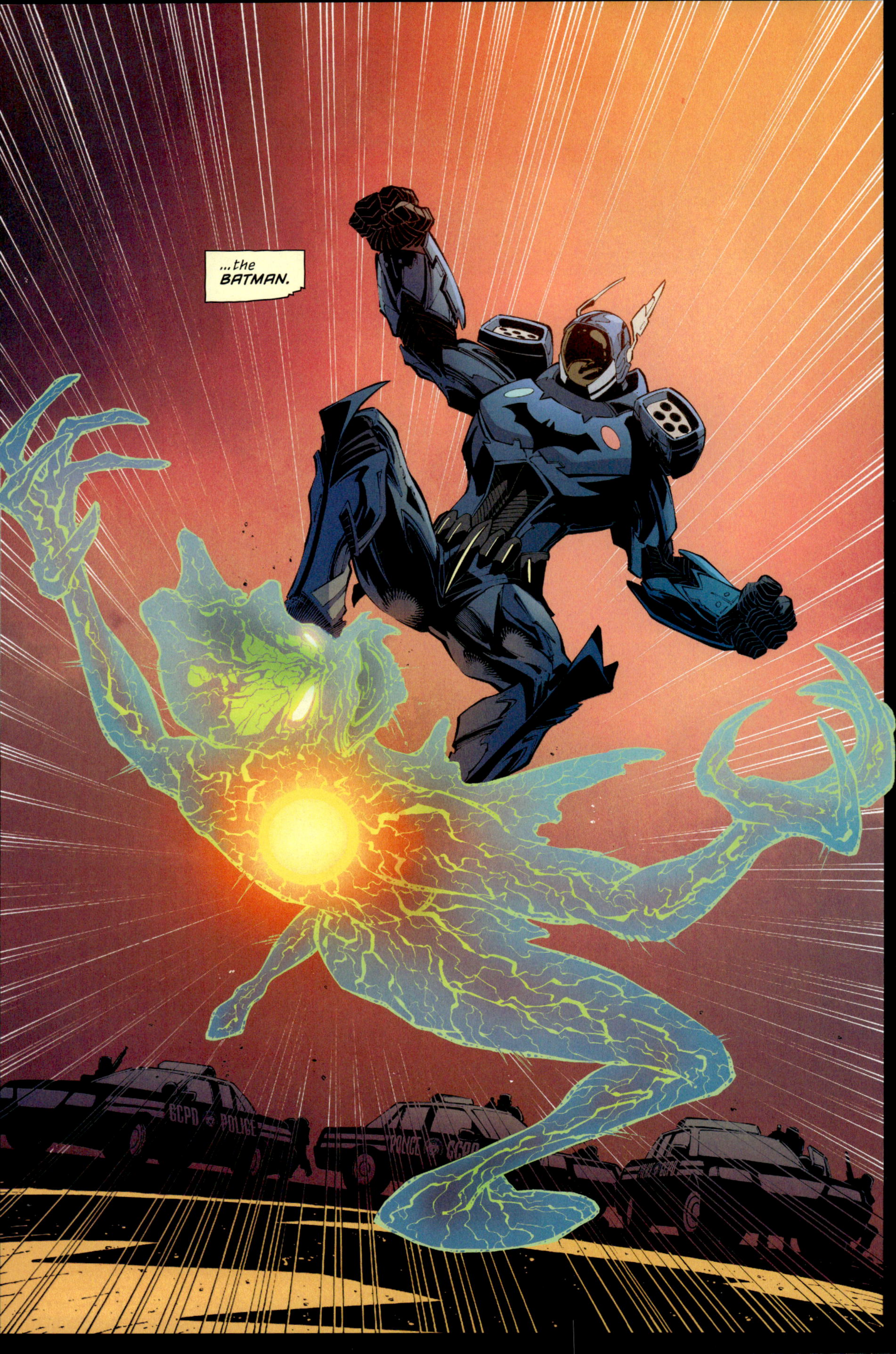
...the BATMAN.
GCPD POLICE

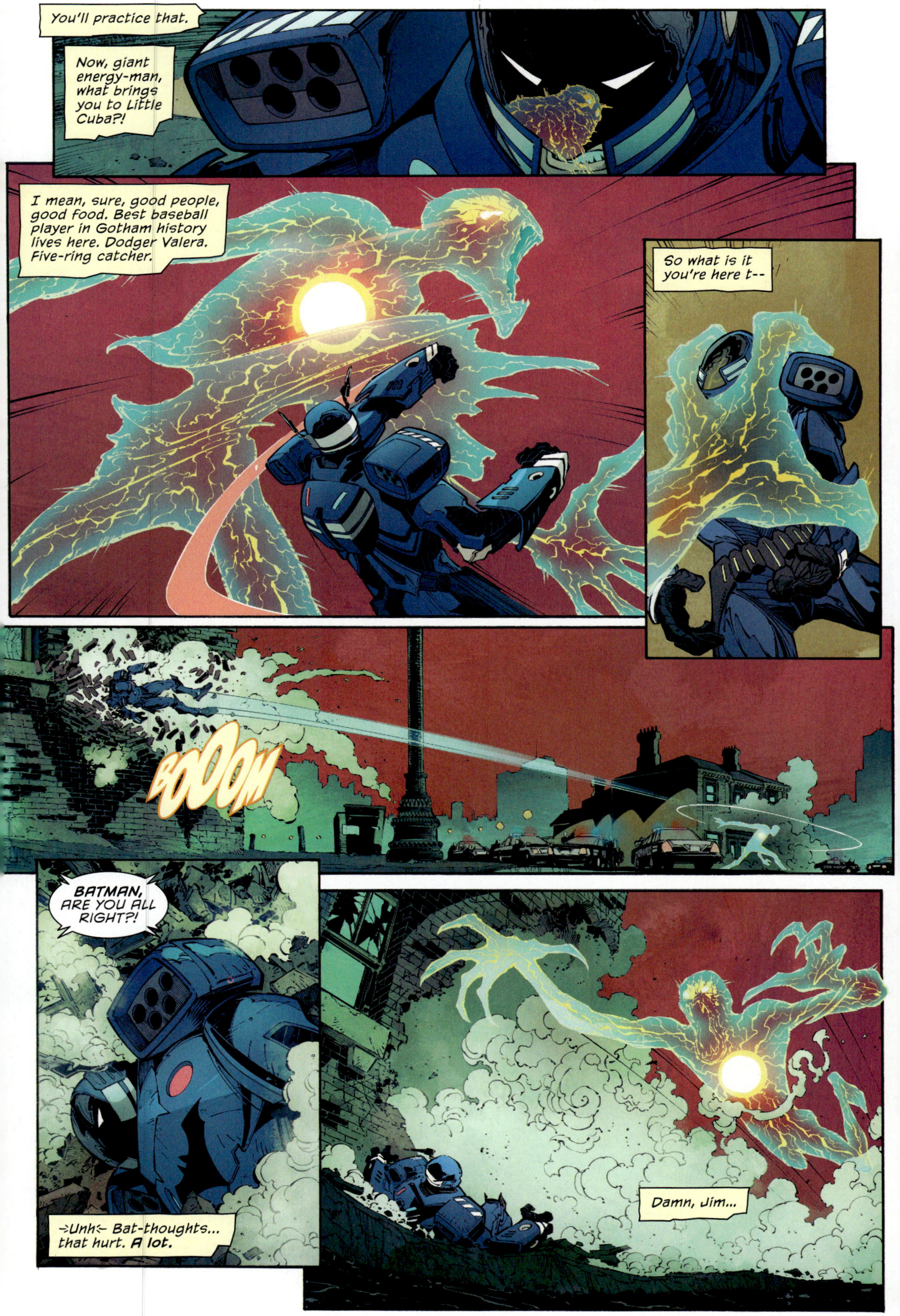
You'll practice that.
Now, giant energy-man, what brings you to Little Cuba?!
I mean, sure, good people, good food. Best baseball player in Gotham history lives here. Dodger Valera. Five-ring catcher.
So what is it you're here t--
BOOOM
BATMAN, ARE YOU ALL RIGHT?!
-Unh- Bat-thoughts... that hurt. A lot.
Damn, Jim...

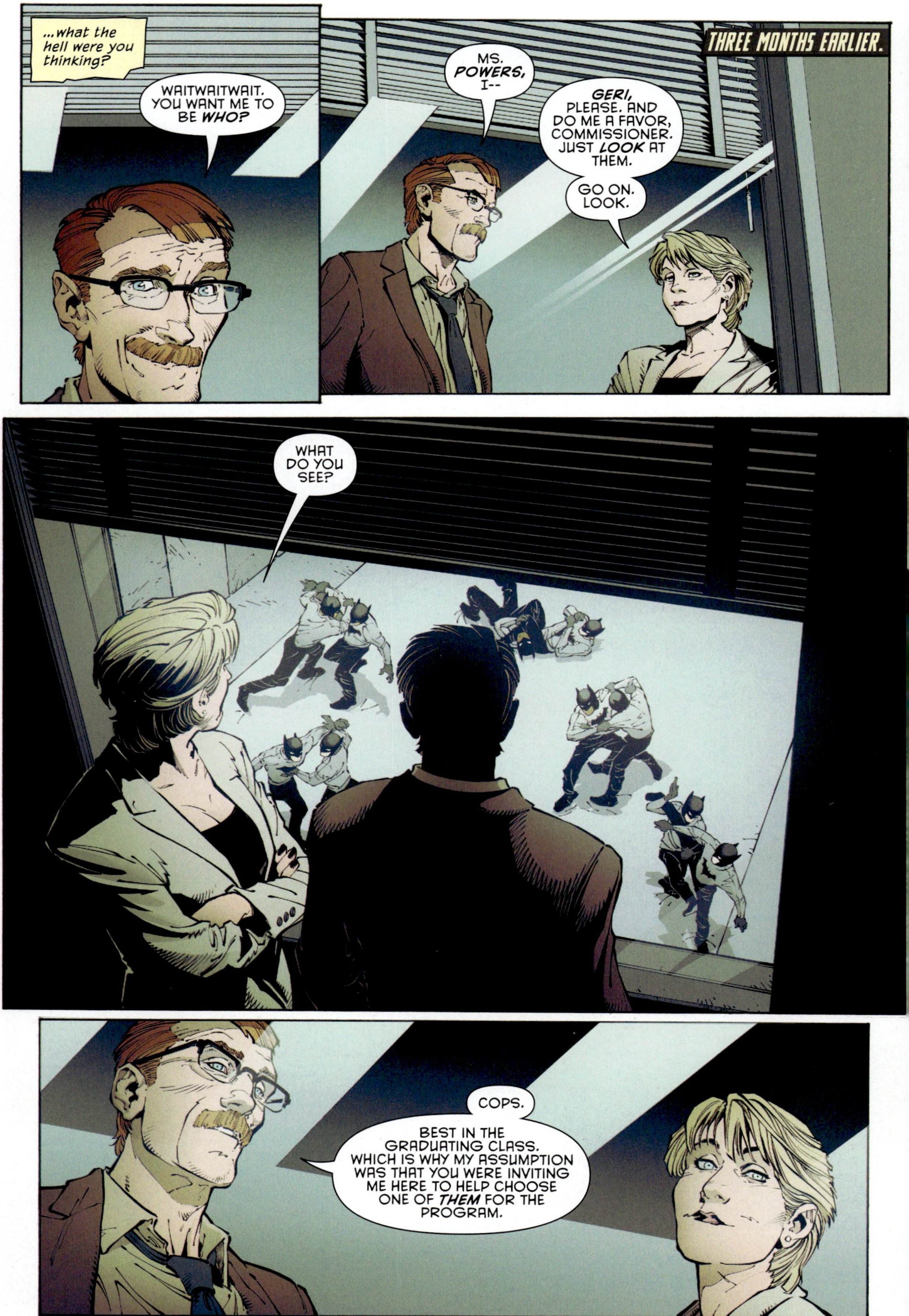
...what the hell were you thinking?
THREE MONTHS EARLIER.
WAITWAITWAIT. YOU WANT ME TO BE WHO?
MS. POWERS, I--
GERI, PLEASE. AND DO ME A FAVOR, COMMISSIONER. JUST LOOK AT THEM.
GO ON. LOOK.
WHAT DO YOU SEE?
COPS.
BEST IN THE GRADUATING CLASS. WHICH IS WHY MY ASSUMPTION WAS THAT YOU WERE INVITING ME HERE TO HELP CHOOSE ONE OF THEM FOR THE PROGRAM.

I MEAN, THAT'S *WILLIAMS.* THE GUY IS QUICK AS A WHIP. TOP OF HIS CLASS...

YES. AND HE'D MAKE A MUCH *SMARTER* BATMAN THAN YOU, JIM.

RIGHT. OF COURSE HE WOULD. OR *HUANG.* LOOK AT HER. SHE PRACTICALLY *LIVES* AT THE STATION.

YES. AND SHE'D MAKE A MUCH *TOUGHER* BATMAN THAN YOU.

HELL, THEY'D ALL BE *PRETTIER* BATMEN THAN YOU, I'LL SAY THAT.

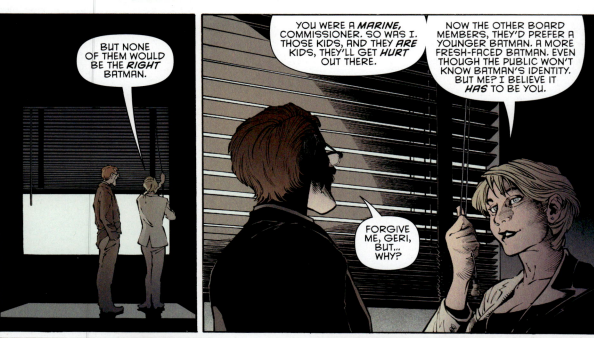

BUT NONE OF THEM WOULD BE THE *RIGHT* BATMAN.

YOU WERE A *MARINE,* COMMISSIONER. SO WAS I. THOSE KIDS, AND THEY *ARE* KIDS, THEY'LL GET *HURT* OUT THERE.

NOW THE OTHER BOARD MEMBERS, THEY'D PREFER A YOUNGER BATMAN. A MORE FRESH-FACED BATMAN. EVEN THOUGH THE PUBLIC WON'T KNOW BATMAN'S IDENTITY. BUT ME? I BELIEVE IT *HAS* TO BE YOU.

FORGIVE ME, GERI, BUT... WHY?

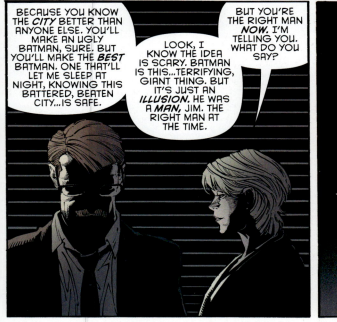

BECAUSE YOU KNOW THE *CITY* BETTER THAN ANYONE ELSE. YOU'LL MAKE AN UGLY BATMAN, SURE. BUT YOU'LL MAKE THE *BEST* BATMAN. ONE THAT'LL LET ME SLEEP AT NIGHT, KNOWING THIS BATTERED, BEATEN CITY...IS SAFE.

LOOK, I KNOW THE IDEA IS SCARY. BATMAN IS THIS...TERRIFYING, GIANT THING. BUT IT'S JUST AN *ILLUSION.* HE WAS A *MAN,* JIM. THE RIGHT MAN AT THE TIME.

BUT YOU'RE THE RIGHT MAN *NOW.* I'M TELLING YOU. WHAT DO YOU SAY?

...

I'M SORRY...

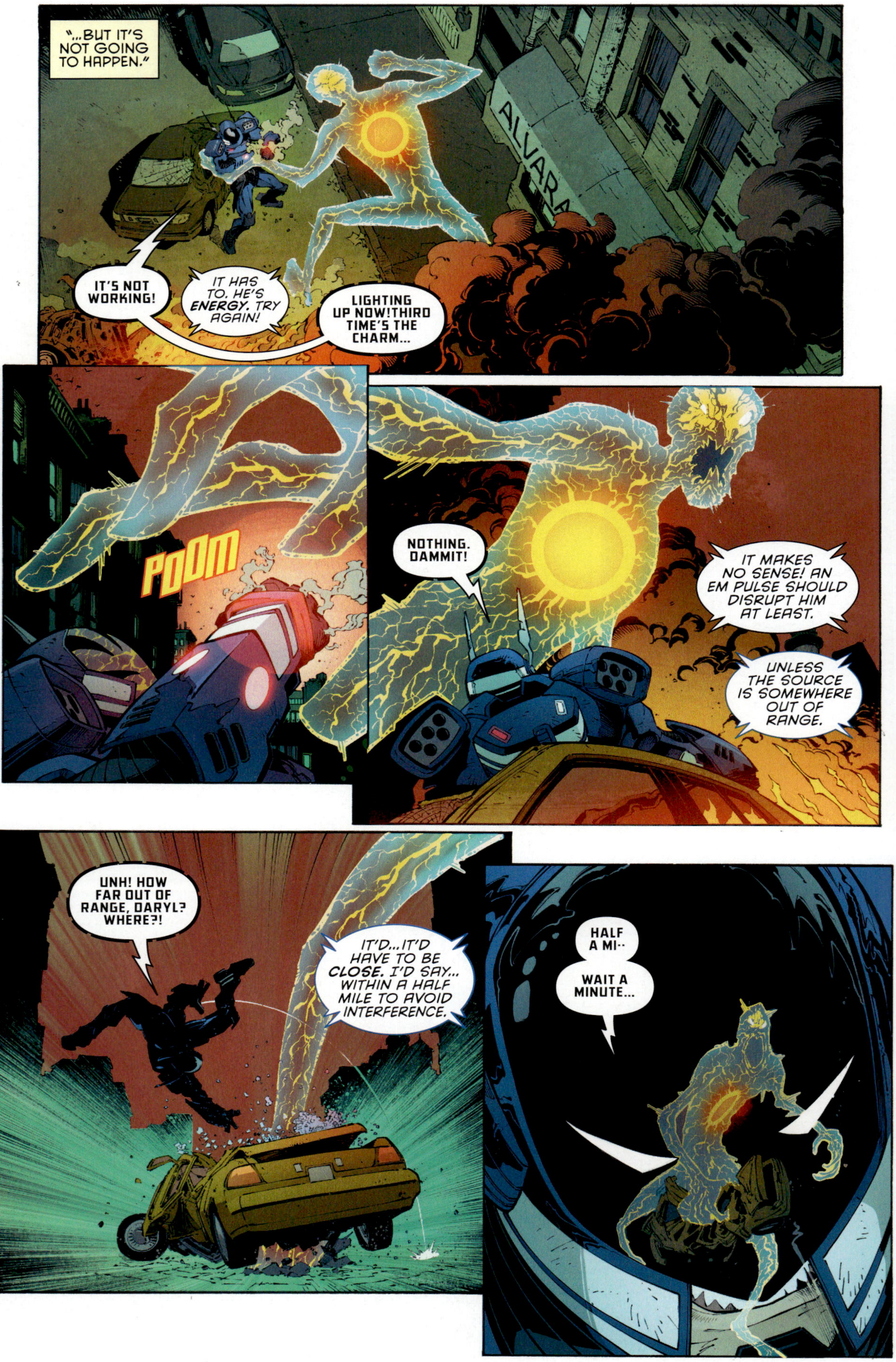
"...BUT IT'S NOT GOING TO HAPPEN."
ALVARA
IT'S NOT WORKING!
IT HAS TO. HE'S ENERGY. TRY AGAIN!
LIGHTING UP NOW! THIRD TIME'S THE CHARM...
POOM
NOTHING. DAMMIT!
IT MAKES NO SENSE! AN EM PULSE SHOULD DISRUPT HIM AT LEAST.
UNLESS THE SOURCE IS SOMEWHERE OUT OF RANGE.
UNH! HOW FAR OUT OF RANGE, DARYL? WHERE?!
IT'D...IT'D HAVE TO BE CLOSE. I'D SAY... WITHIN A HALF MILE TO AVOID INTERFERENCE.
HALF A MI--
WAIT A MINUTE...

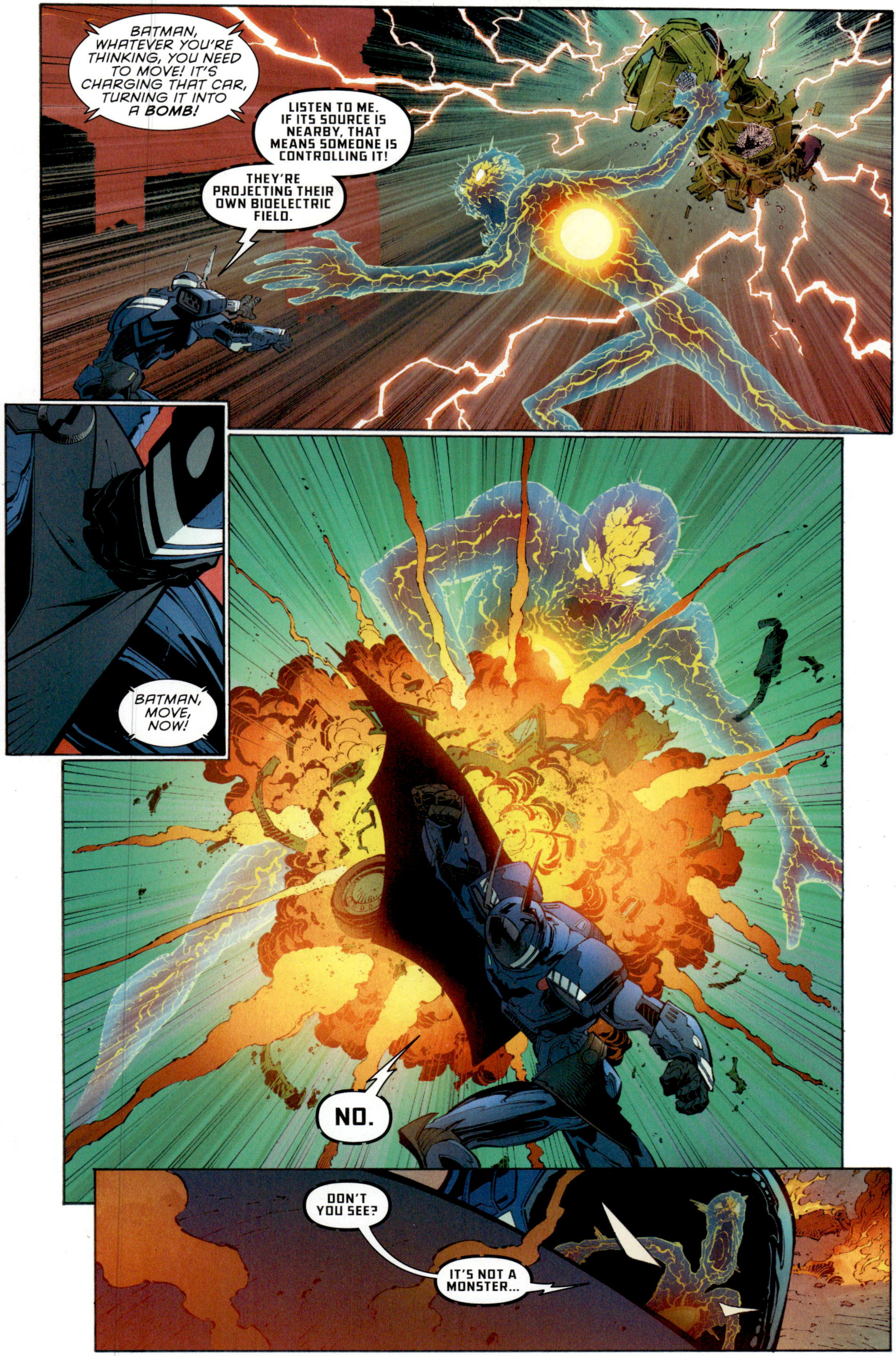
BATMAN, WHATEVER YOU'RE THINKING, YOU NEED TO MOVE! IT'S CHARGING THAT CAR, TURNING IT INTO A BOMB!
LISTEN TO ME. IF ITS SOURCE IS NEARBY, THAT MEANS SOMEONE IS CONTROLLING IT!
THEY'RE PROJECTING THEIR OWN BIOELECTRIC FIELD.
BATMAN, MOVE, NOW!
NO.
DON'T YOU SEE?
IT'S NOT A MONSTER...

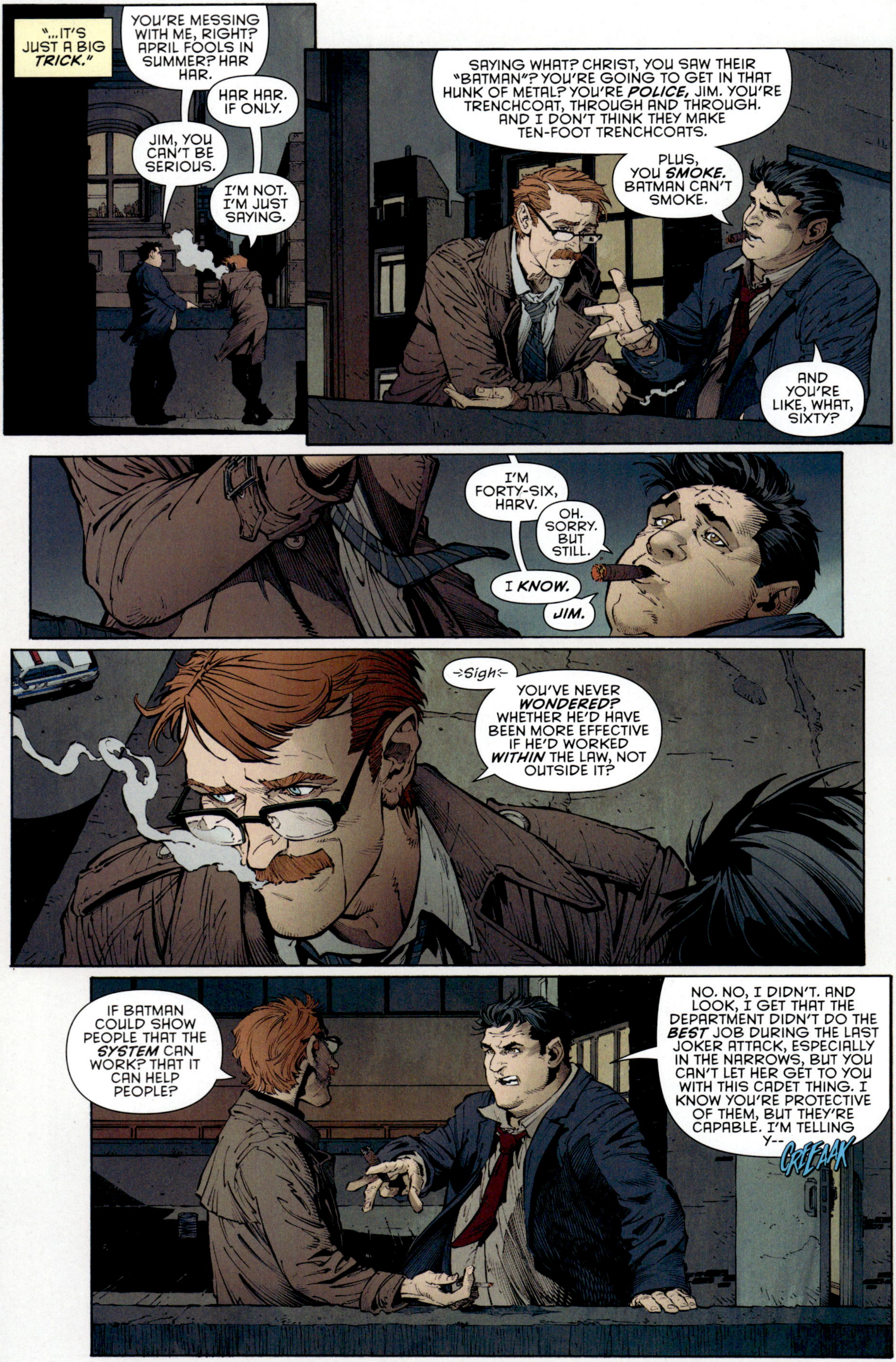
"...IT'S JUST A BIG TRICK."
YOU'RE MESSING WITH ME, RIGHT? APRIL FOOLS IN SUMMER? HAR HAR.
HAR HAR. IF ONLY.
JIM, YOU CAN'T BE SERIOUS.
I'M NOT. I'M JUST SAYING.
SAYING WHAT? CHRIST, YOU SAW THEIR "BATMAN"? YOU'RE GOING TO GET IN THAT HUNK OF METAL? YOU'RE POLICE, JIM. YOU'RE TRENCHCOAT, THROUGH AND THROUGH. AND I DON'T THINK THEY MAKE TEN-FOOT TRENCHCOATS.
PLUS, YOU SMOKE. BATMAN CAN'T SMOKE.
AND YOU'RE LIKE, WHAT, SIXTY?
I'M FORTY-SIX, HARV.
OH. SORRY. BUT STILL.
I KNOW.
JIM.
Sigh
YOU'VE NEVER WONDERED? WHETHER HE'D HAVE BEEN MORE EFFECTIVE IF HE'D WORKED WITHIN THE LAW, NOT OUTSIDE IT?
IF BATMAN COULD SHOW PEOPLE THAT THE SYSTEM CAN WORK? THAT IT CAN HELP PEOPLE?
NO. NO, I DIDN'T. AND LOOK, I GET THAT THE DEPARTMENT DIDN'T DO THE BEST JOB DURING THE LAST JOKER ATTACK, ESPECIALLY IN THE NARROWS, BUT YOU CAN'T LET HER GET TO YOU WITH THIS CADET THING. I KNOW YOU'RE PROTECTIVE OF THEM, BUT THEY'RE CAPABLE. I'M TELLING Y--
CREEAAK

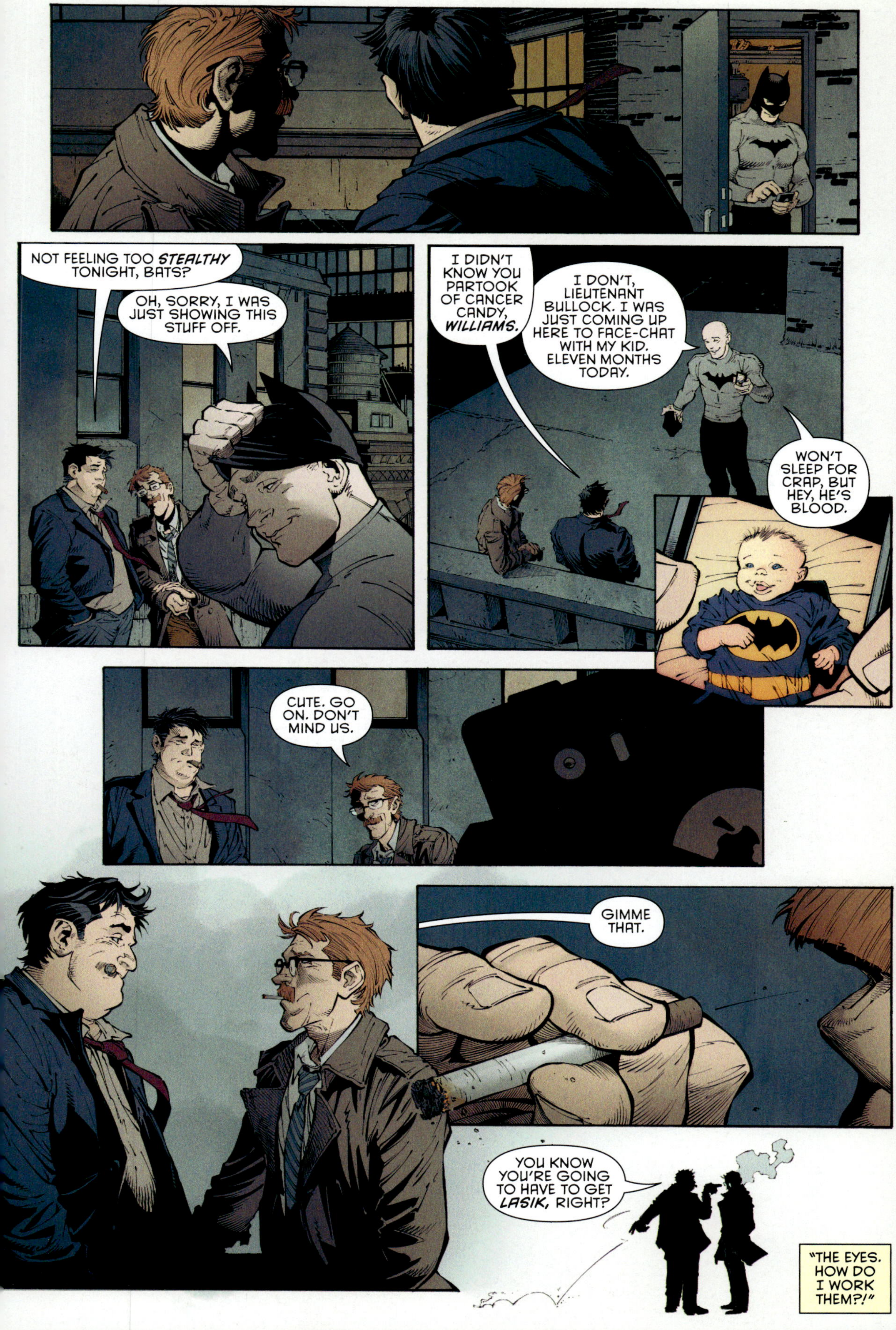
NOT FEELING TOO *STEALTHY* TONIGHT, BATS?
OH, SORRY, I WAS JUST SHOWING THIS STUFF OFF.
I DIDN'T KNOW YOU PARTOOK OF CANCER CANDY, ***WILLIAMS.***
I DON'T, LIEUTENANT BULLOCK. I WAS JUST COMING UP HERE TO FACE-CHAT WITH MY KID. ELEVEN MONTHS TODAY.
WON'T SLEEP FOR CRAP, BUT HEY, HE'S BLOOD.
CUTE. GO ON. DON'T MIND US.
GIMME THAT.
YOU KNOW YOU'RE GOING TO HAVE TO GET *LASIK,* RIGHT?
"THE EYES. HOW DO I WORK THEM?!"

ON IT. WHAT ARE WE LOOKING FOR?

UNH! SOMEONE STEALING HOME!

I DON'T UNDERSTAND, IF--

THE MONSTER IS AN EXTENSION OF A PARTICULAR CRIMINAL. AND WHAT DO WE KNOW ABOUT THEM?

THEY WERE ATTACKING A BANK.

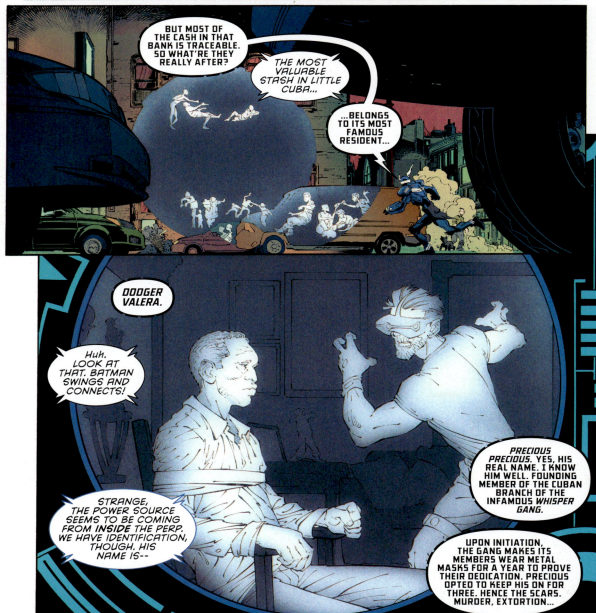

BUT MOST OF THE CASH IN THAT BANK IS TRACEABLE. SO WHAT'RE THEY REALLY AFTER?

THE MOST VALUABLE STASH IN LITTLE CUBA...

...BELONGS TO ITS MOST FAMOUS RESIDENT...

DODGER VALERA.

Huh. LOOK AT THAT. BATMAN SWINGS AND CONNECTS!

STRANGE, THE POWER SOURCE SEEMS TO BE COMING FROM INSIDE THE PERP. WE HAVE IDENTIFICATION, THOUGH. HIS NAME IS--

PRECIOUS PRECIOUS. YES, HIS REAL NAME. I KNOW HIM WELL. FOUNDING MEMBER OF THE CUBAN BRANCH OF THE INFAMOUS WHISPER GANG.

UPON INITIATION, THE GANG MAKES ITS MEMBERS WEAR METAL MASKS FOR A YEAR TO PROVE THEIR DEDICATION. PRECIOUS OPTED TO KEEP HIS ON FOR THREE. HENCE THE SCARS. MURDER, EXTORTION...

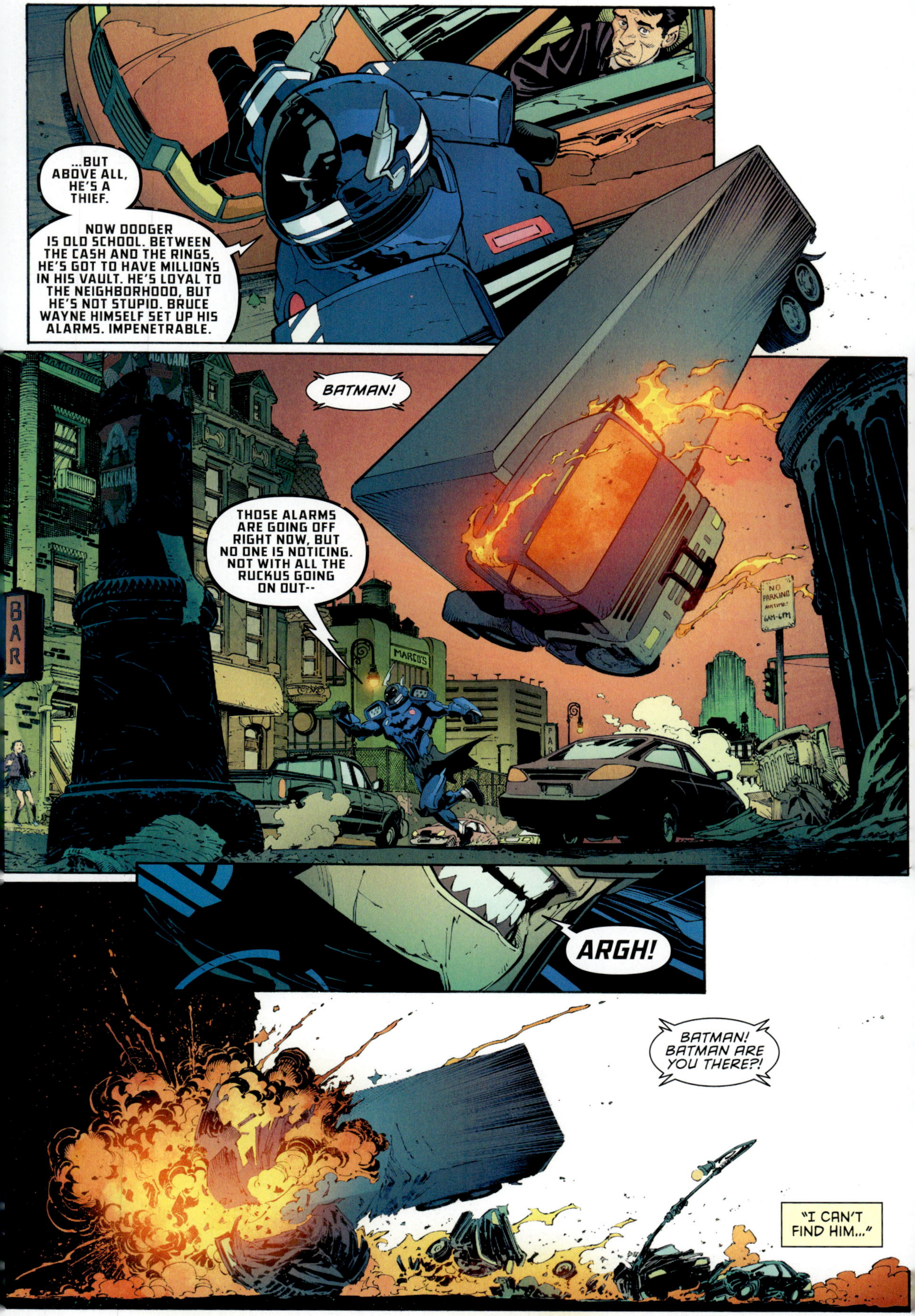
...BUT ABOVE ALL, HE'S A THIEF.
NOW DODGER IS OLD SCHOOL. BETWEEN THE CASH AND THE RINGS, HE'S GOT TO HAVE MILLIONS IN HIS VAULT. HE'S LOYAL TO THE NEIGHBORHOOD, BUT HE'S NOT STUPID. BRUCE WAYNE HIMSELF SET UP HIS ALARMS. IMPENETRABLE.
BATMAN!
THOSE ALARMS ARE GOING OFF RIGHT NOW, BUT NO ONE IS NOTICING. NOT WITH ALL THE RUCKUS GOING ON OUT--
BAR
MARCO'S
NO PARKING ANYTIME 6AM-6PM
ARGH!
BATMAN! BATMAN ARE YOU THERE?!
"I CAN'T FIND HIM..."

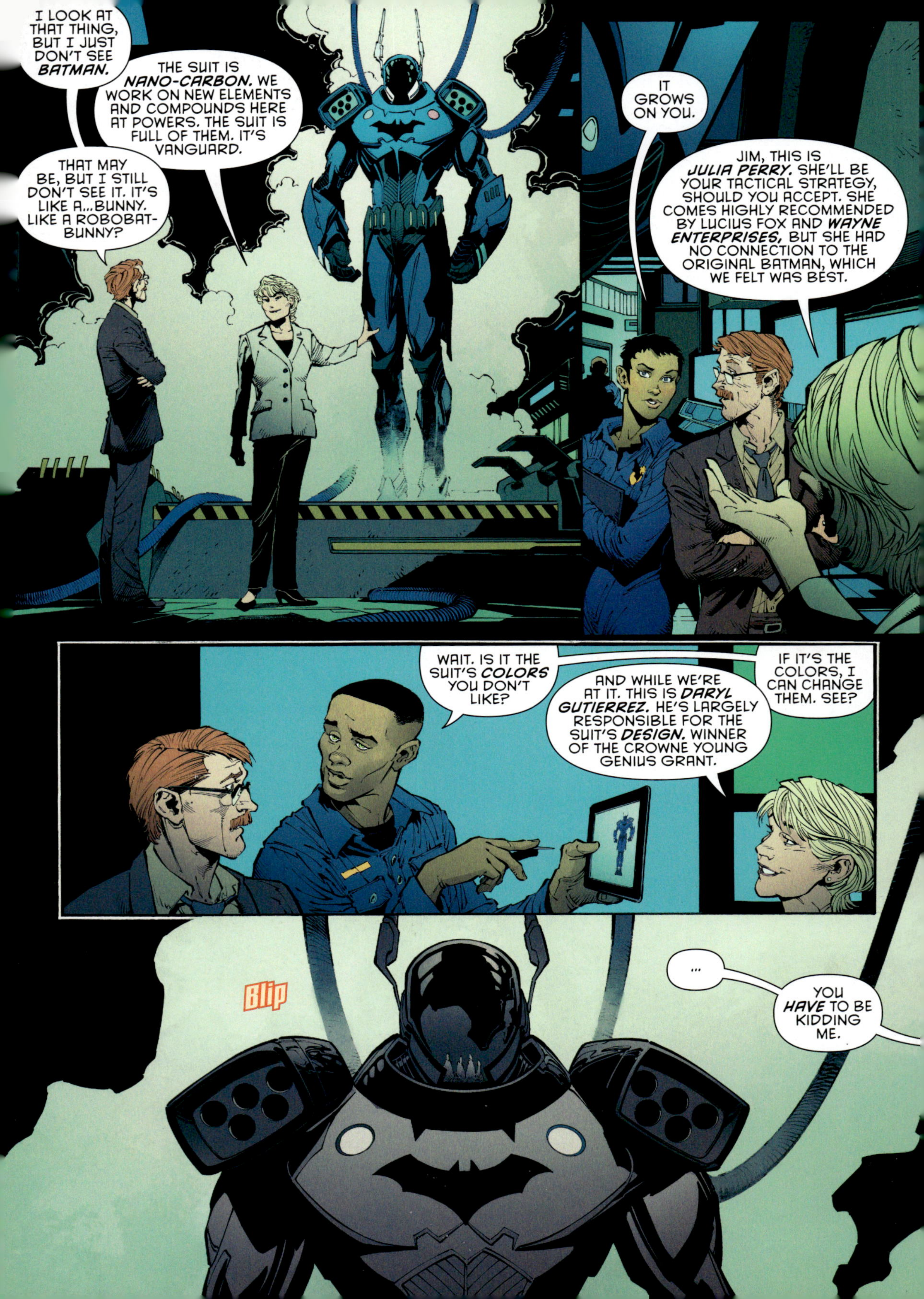
I LOOK AT THAT THING, BUT I JUST DON'T SEE BATMAN.
THE SUIT IS NANO-CARBON. WE WORK ON NEW ELEMENTS AND COMPOUNDS HERE AT POWERS. THE SUIT IS FULL OF THEM. IT'S VANGUARD.
THAT MAY BE, BUT I STILL DON'T SEE IT. IT'S LIKE A...BUNNY. LIKE A ROBOBAT-BUNNY?
IT GROWS ON YOU.
JIM, THIS IS JULIA PERRY. SHE'LL BE YOUR TACTICAL STRATEGY, SHOULD YOU ACCEPT. SHE COMES HIGHLY RECOMMENDED BY LUCIUS FOX AND WAYNE ENTERPRISES, BUT SHE HAD NO CONNECTION TO THE ORIGINAL BATMAN, WHICH WE FELT WAS BEST.
WAIT. IS IT THE SUIT'S COLORS YOU DON'T LIKE?
IF IT'S THE COLORS, I CAN CHANGE THEM. SEE?
AND WHILE WE'RE AT IT. THIS IS DARYL GUTIERREZ. HE'S LARGELY RESPONSIBLE FOR THE SUIT'S DESIGN. WINNER OF THE CROWNE YOUNG GENIUS GRANT.
BLIP
...
YOU HAVE TO BE KIDDING ME.

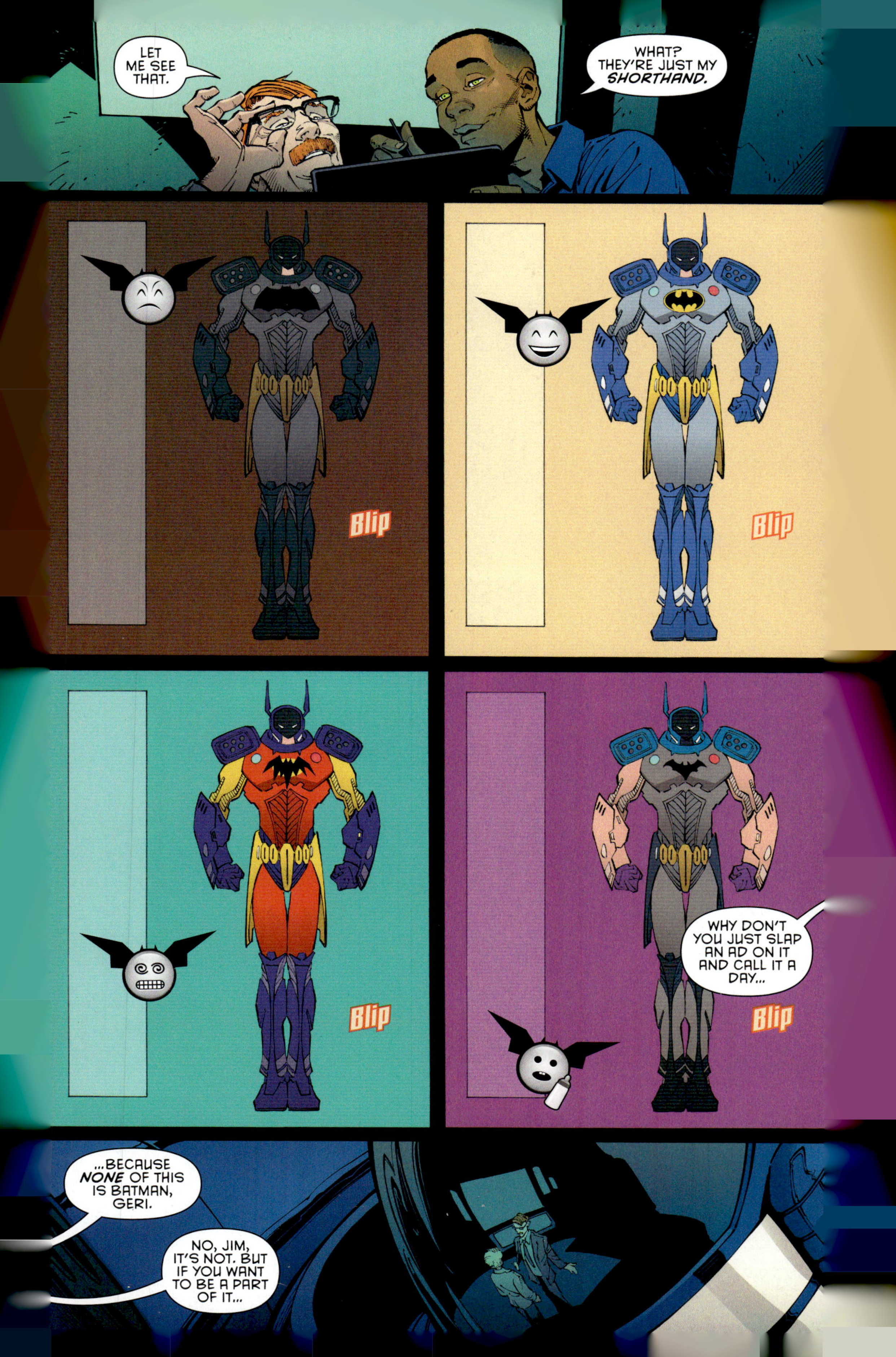
LET ME SEE THAT.
WHAT? THEY'RE JUST MY *SHORTHAND.*
Blip
Blip
Blip
WHY DON'T YOU JUST SLAP AN AD ON IT AND CALL IT A DAY...
Blip
...BECAUSE *NONE* OF THIS IS BATMAN, GERI.
NO, JIM, IT'S NOT. BUT IF YOU WANT TO BE A PART OF IT...

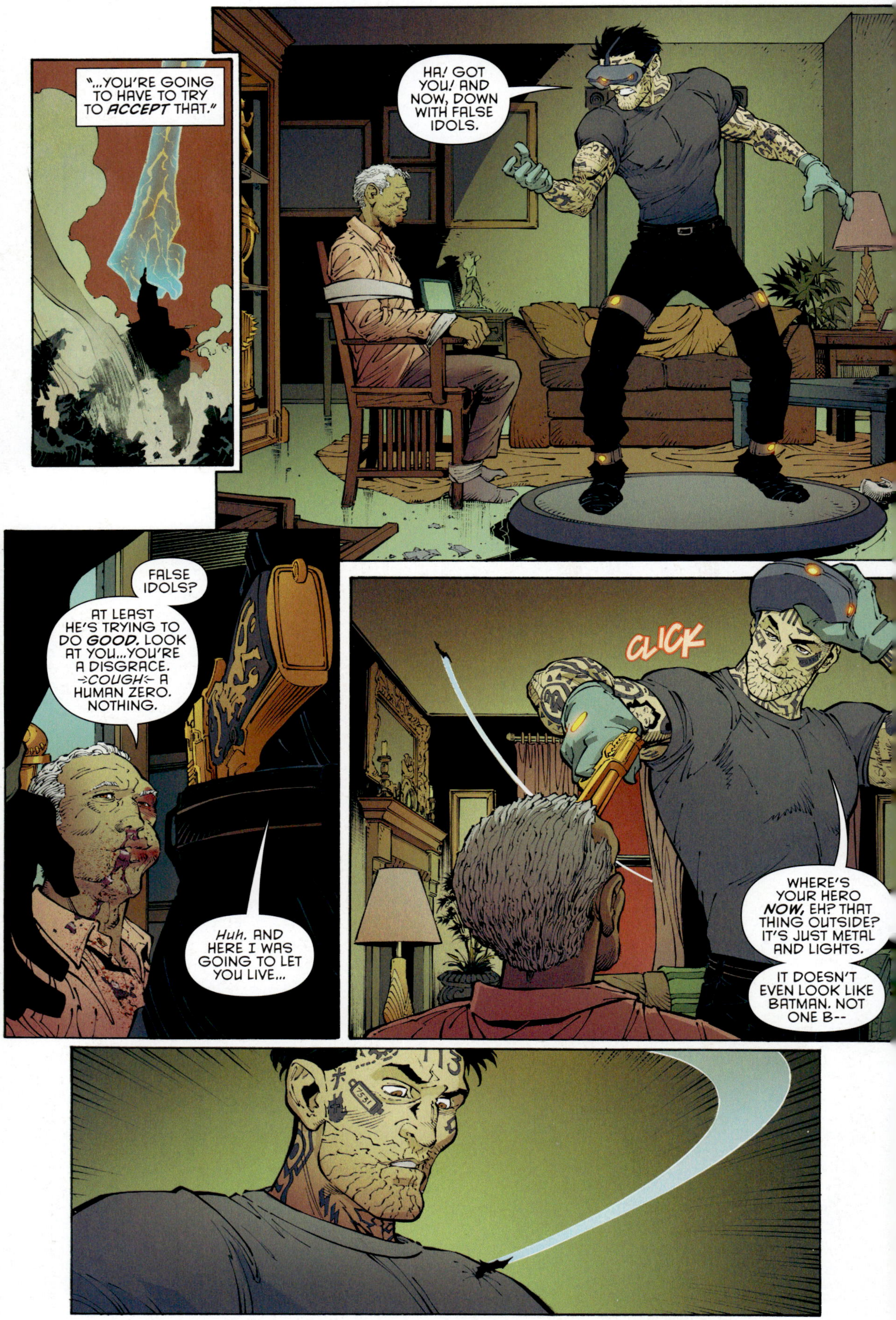
"...YOU'RE GOING TO HAVE TO TRY TO ***ACCEPT*** THAT."
HA! GOT YOU! AND NOW, DOWN WITH FALSE IDOLS.
FALSE IDOLS?
AT LEAST HE'S TRYING TO DO ***GOOD.*** LOOK AT YOU...YOU'RE A DISGRACE. ⇒*COUGH*⇐ A HUMAN ZERO. NOTHING.
Huh. AND HERE I WAS GOING TO LET YOU LIVE...
CLICK
WHERE'S YOUR HERO ***NOW,*** EH? THAT THING OUTSIDE? IT'S JUST METAL AND LIGHTS.
IT DOESN'T EVEN LOOK LIKE BATMAN. NOT ONE B--

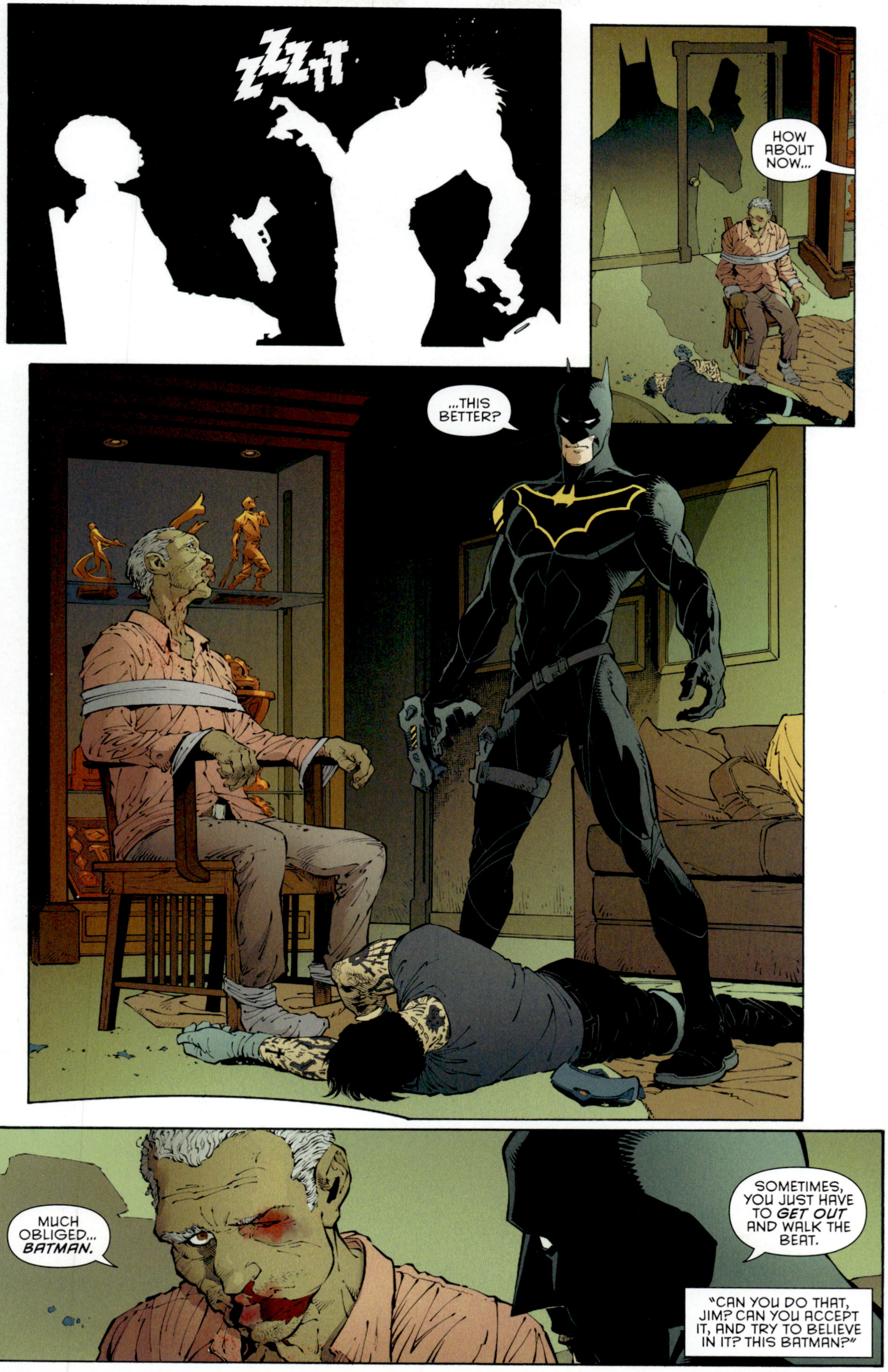
ZZZZTT
HOW ABOUT NOW...
...THIS BETTER?
MUCH OBLIGED... BATMAN.
SOMETIMES, YOU JUST HAVE TO GET OUT AND WALK THE BEAT.
"CAN YOU DO THAT, JIM? CAN YOU ACCEPT IT, AND TRY TO BELIEVE IN IT? THIS BATMAN?"

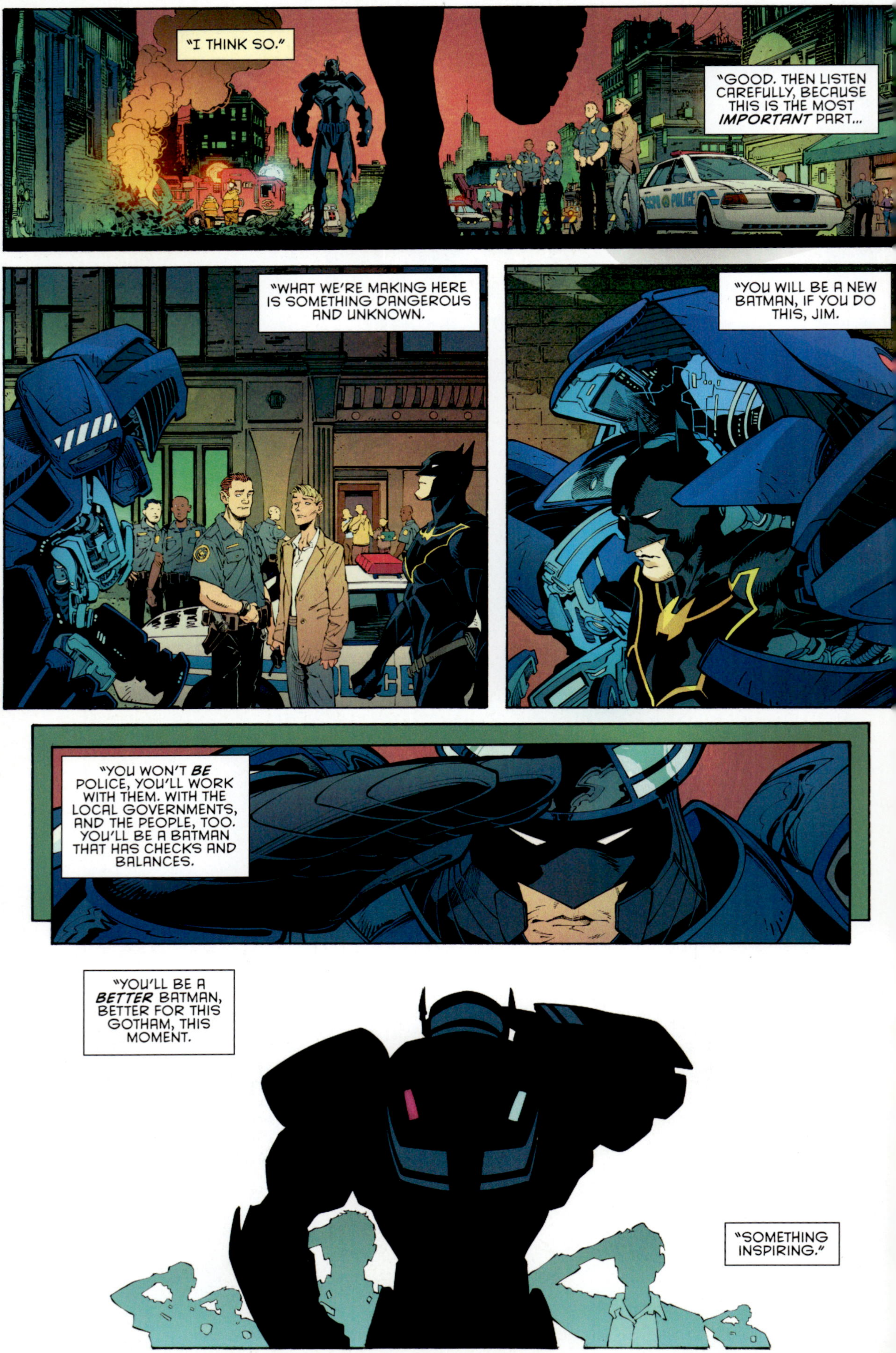
"I THINK SO."
"GOOD. THEN LISTEN CAREFULLY, BECAUSE THIS IS THE MOST IMPORTANT PART...
"WHAT WE'RE MAKING HERE IS SOMETHING DANGEROUS AND UNKNOWN.
"YOU WILL BE A NEW BATMAN, IF YOU DO THIS, JIM.
"YOU WON'T BE POLICE, YOU'LL WORK WITH THEM. WITH THE LOCAL GOVERNMENTS, AND THE PEOPLE, TOO. YOU'LL BE A BATMAN THAT HAS CHECKS AND BALANCES.
"YOU'LL BE A BETTER BATMAN, BETTER FOR THIS GOTHAM, THIS MOMENT.
"SOMETHING INSPIRING."

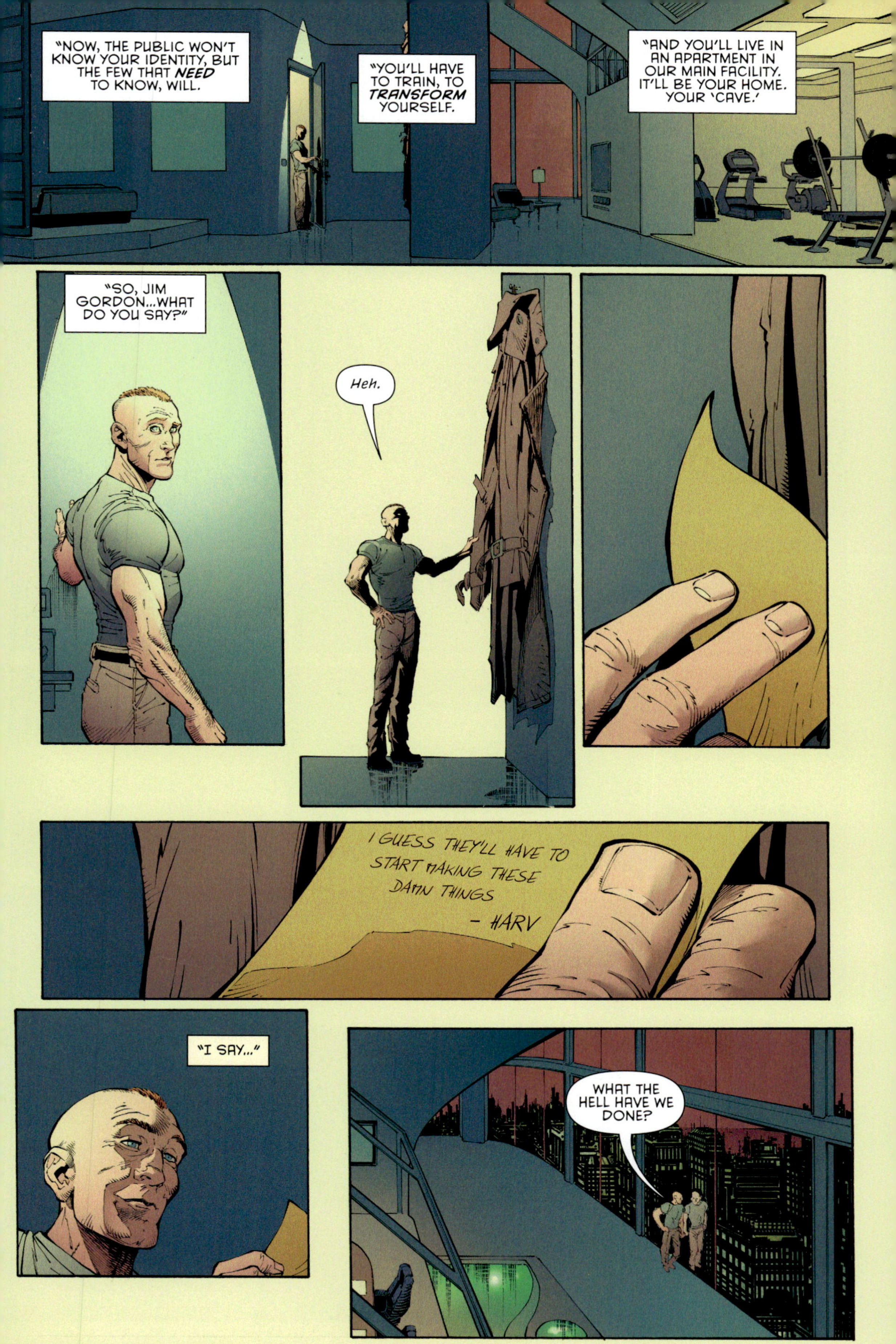
"NOW, THE PUBLIC WON'T KNOW YOUR IDENTITY, BUT THE FEW THAT *NEED* TO KNOW, WILL.
"YOU'LL HAVE TO TRAIN, TO *TRANSFORM* YOURSELF.
"AND YOU'LL LIVE IN AN APARTMENT IN OUR MAIN FACILITY. IT'LL BE YOUR HOME. YOUR 'CAVE.'
"SO, JIM GORDON...WHAT DO YOU SAY?"
Heh.
I GUESS THEY'LL HAVE TO START MAKING THESE DAMN THINGS
- HARV
"I SAY..."
WHAT THE HELL HAVE WE DONE?

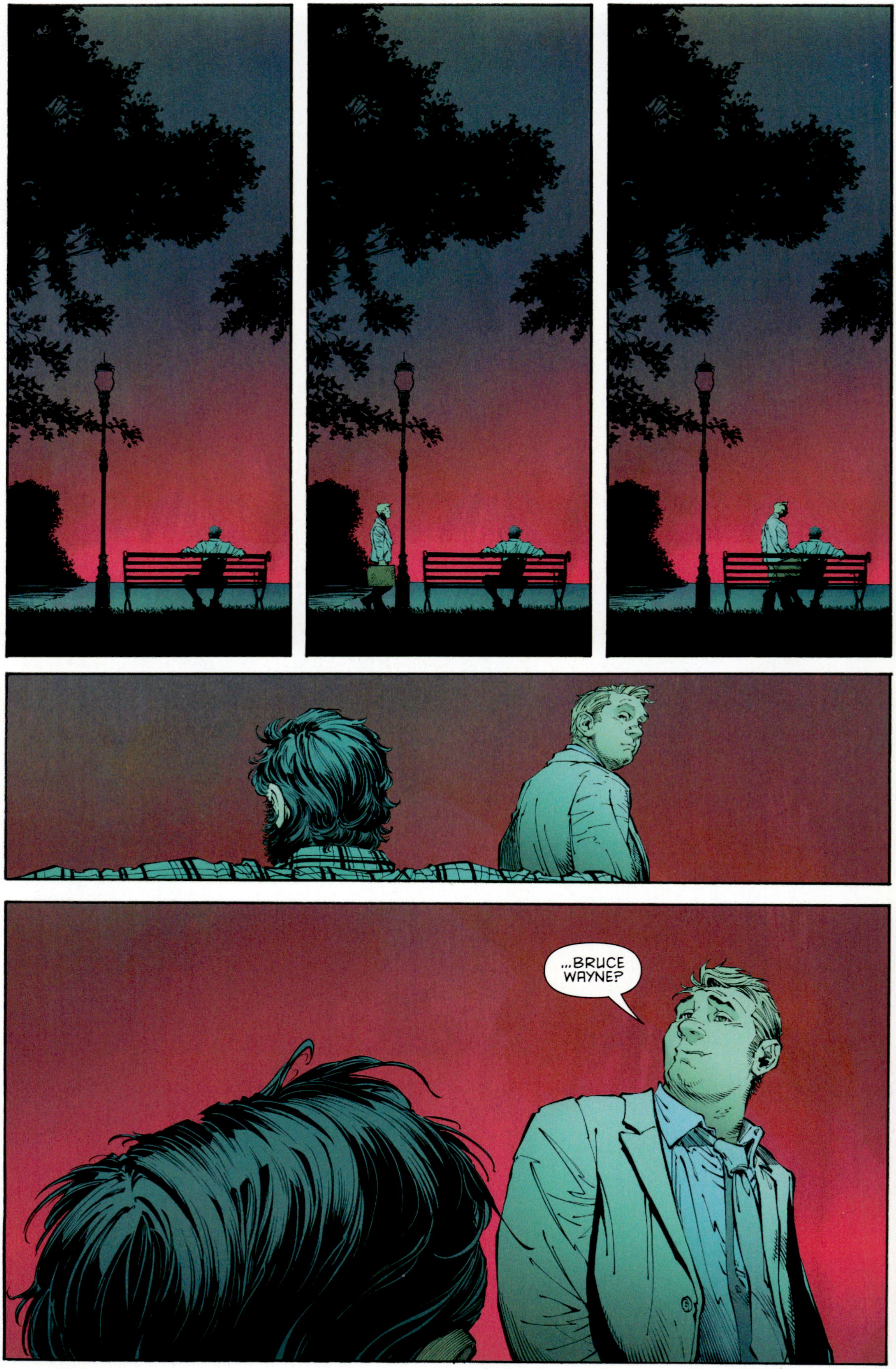
...BRUCE WAYNE?

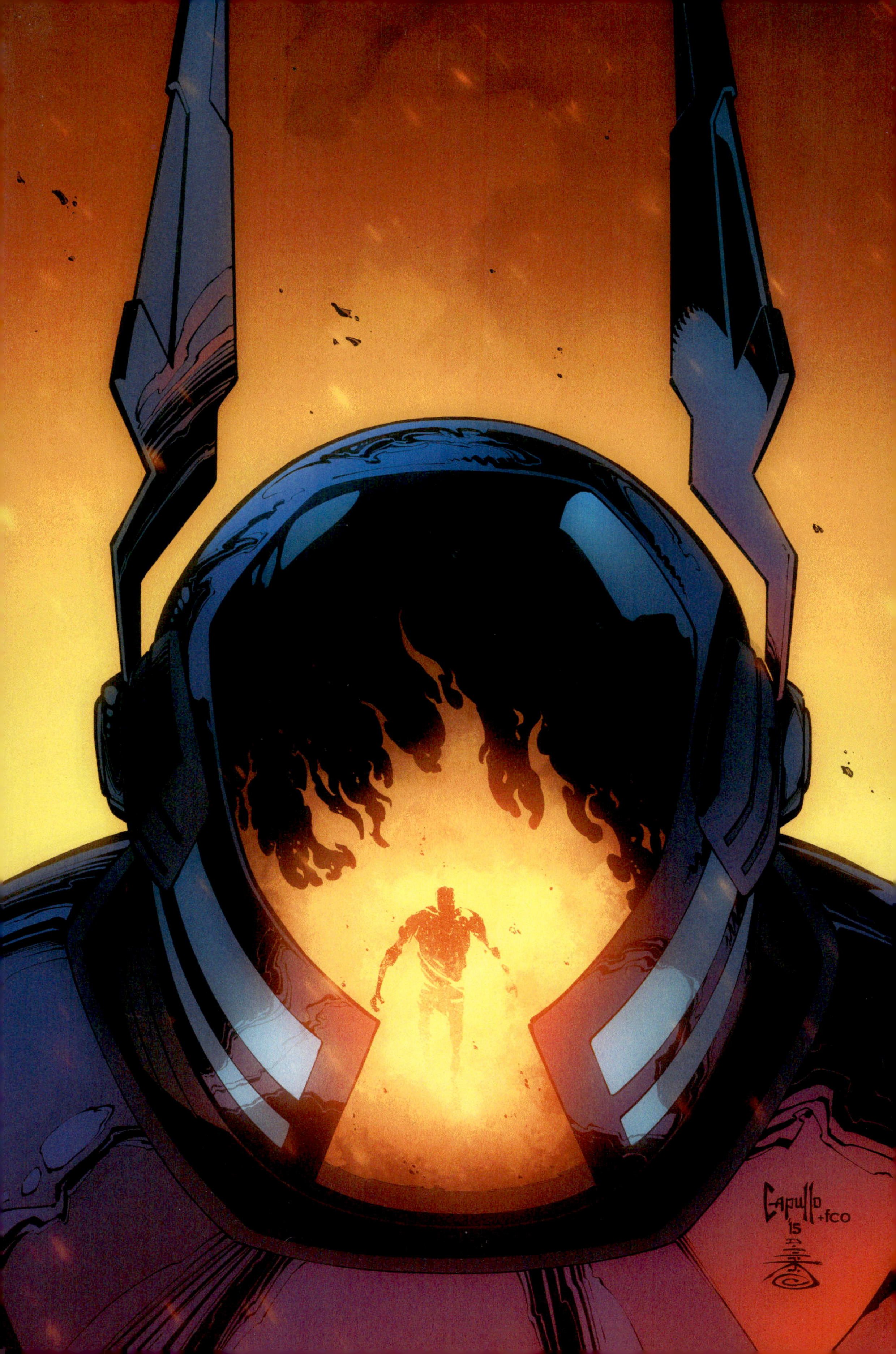
Capullo '15 +fco

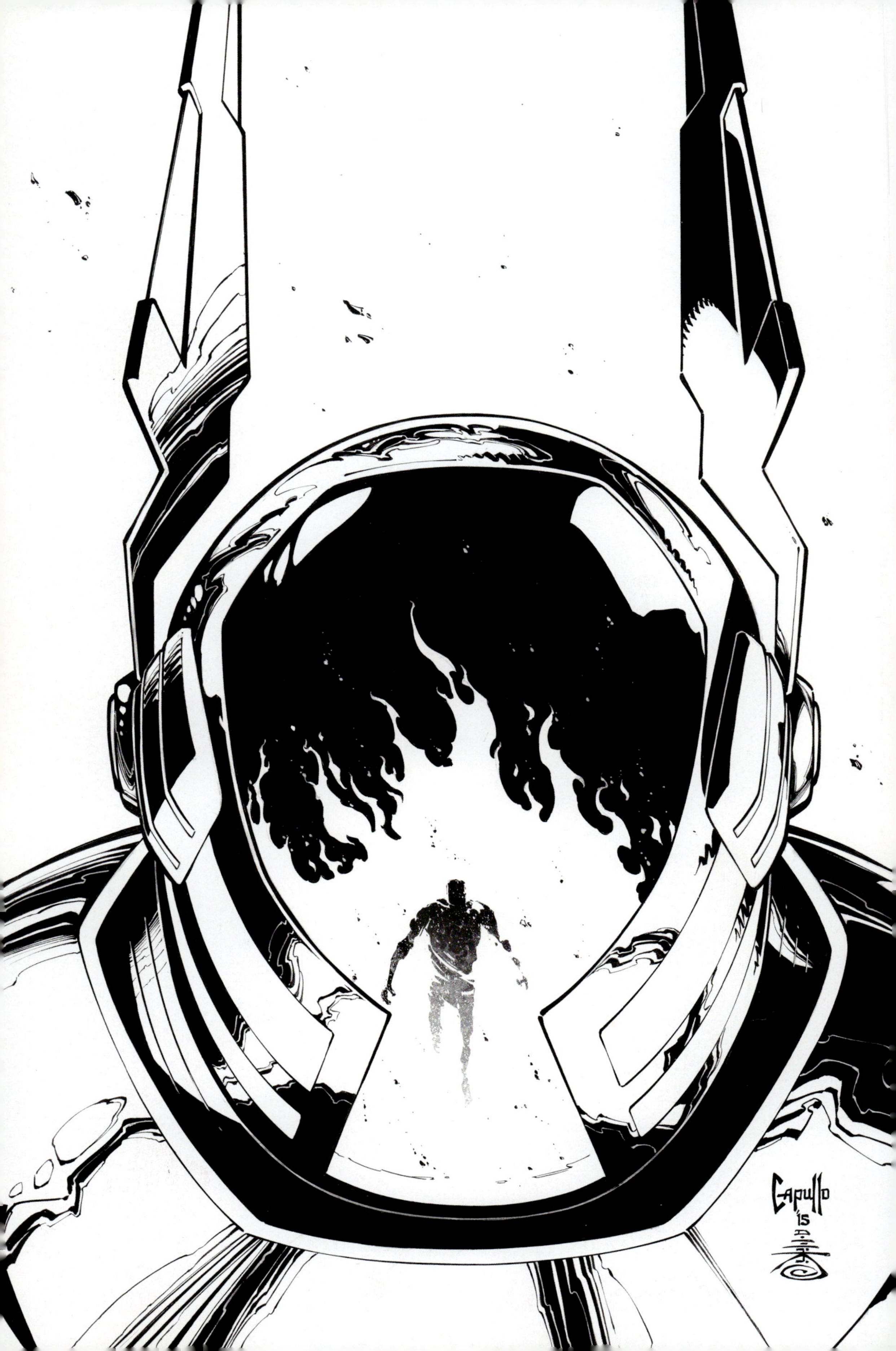
CAPULLO
'15

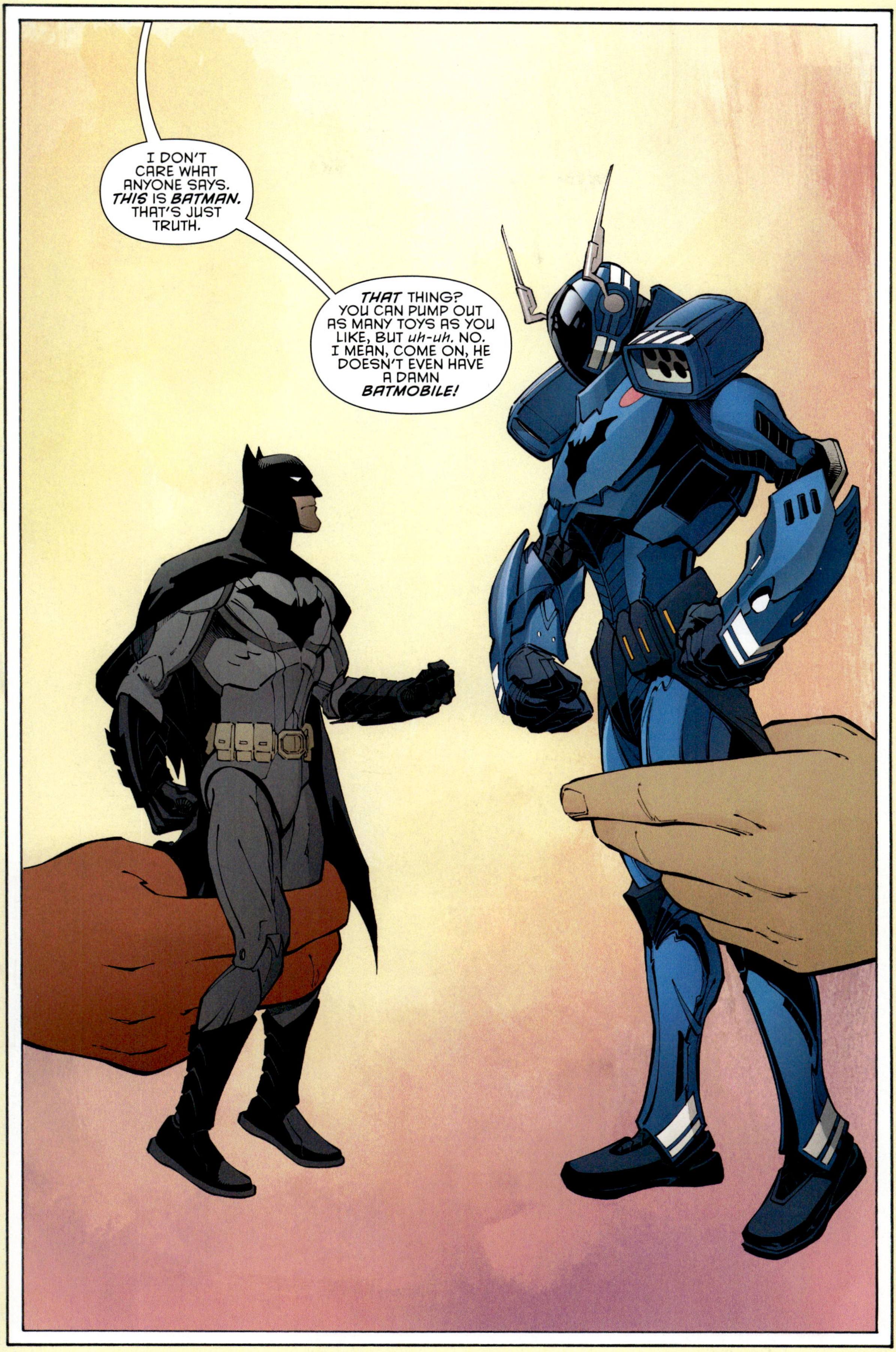
I DON'T CARE WHAT ANYONE SAYS. *THIS* IS *BATMAN.* THAT'S JUST TRUTH.
THAT THING? YOU CAN PUMP OUT AS MANY TOYS AS YOU LIKE, BUT *uh-uh.* NO. I MEAN, COME ON, HE DOESN'T EVEN HAVE A DAMN *BATMOBILE!*

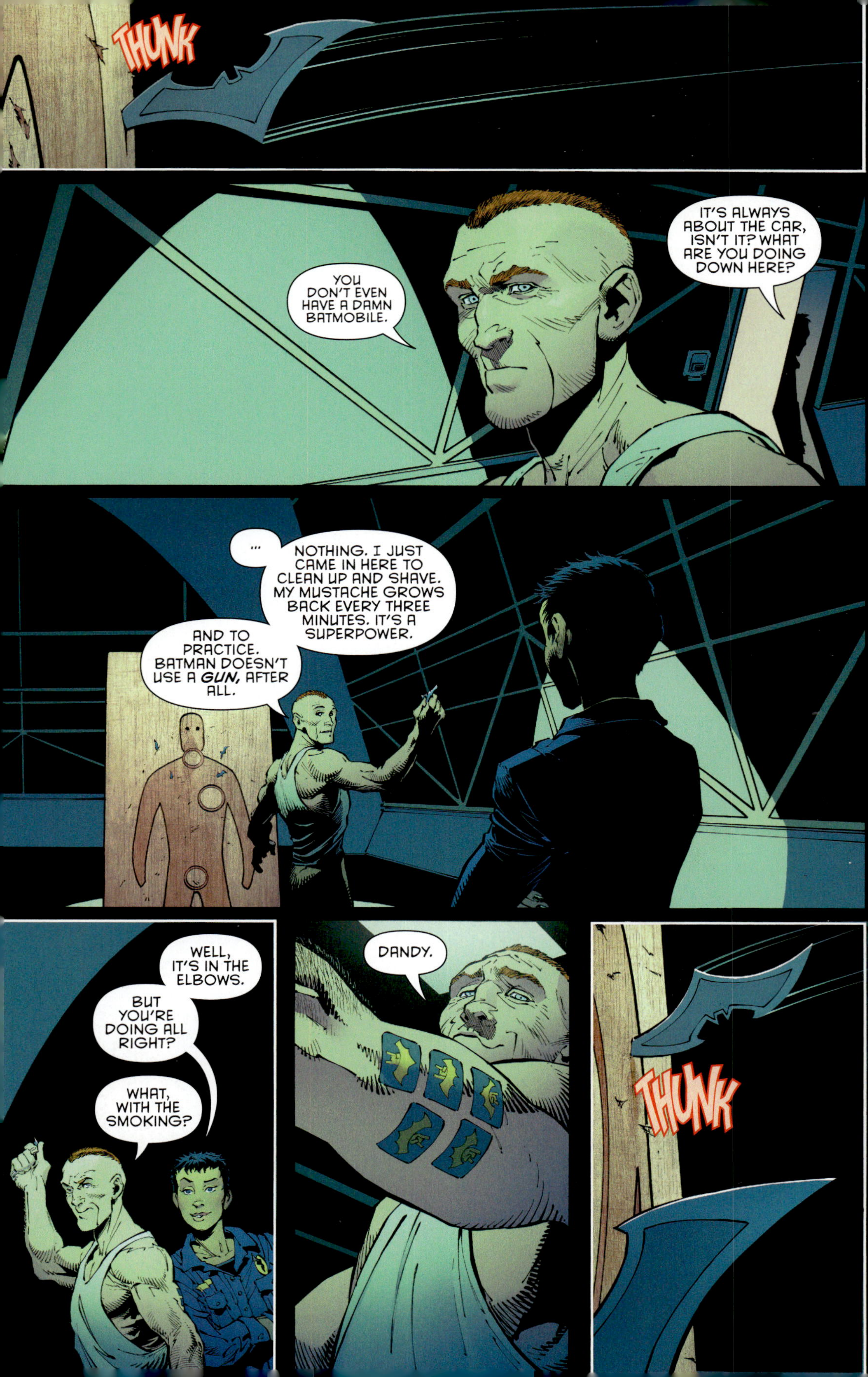
THUNK
YOU DON'T EVEN HAVE A DAMN BATMOBILE.
IT'S ALWAYS ABOUT THE CAR, ISN'T IT? WHAT ARE YOU DOING DOWN HERE?
...
NOTHING. I JUST CAME IN HERE TO CLEAN UP AND SHAVE. MY MUSTACHE GROWS BACK EVERY THREE MINUTES. IT'S A SUPERPOWER.
AND TO PRACTICE. BATMAN DOESN'T USE A GUN, AFTER ALL.
WELL, IT'S IN THE ELBOWS.
BUT YOU'RE DOING ALL RIGHT?
WHAT, WITH THE SMOKING?
DANDY.
THUNK

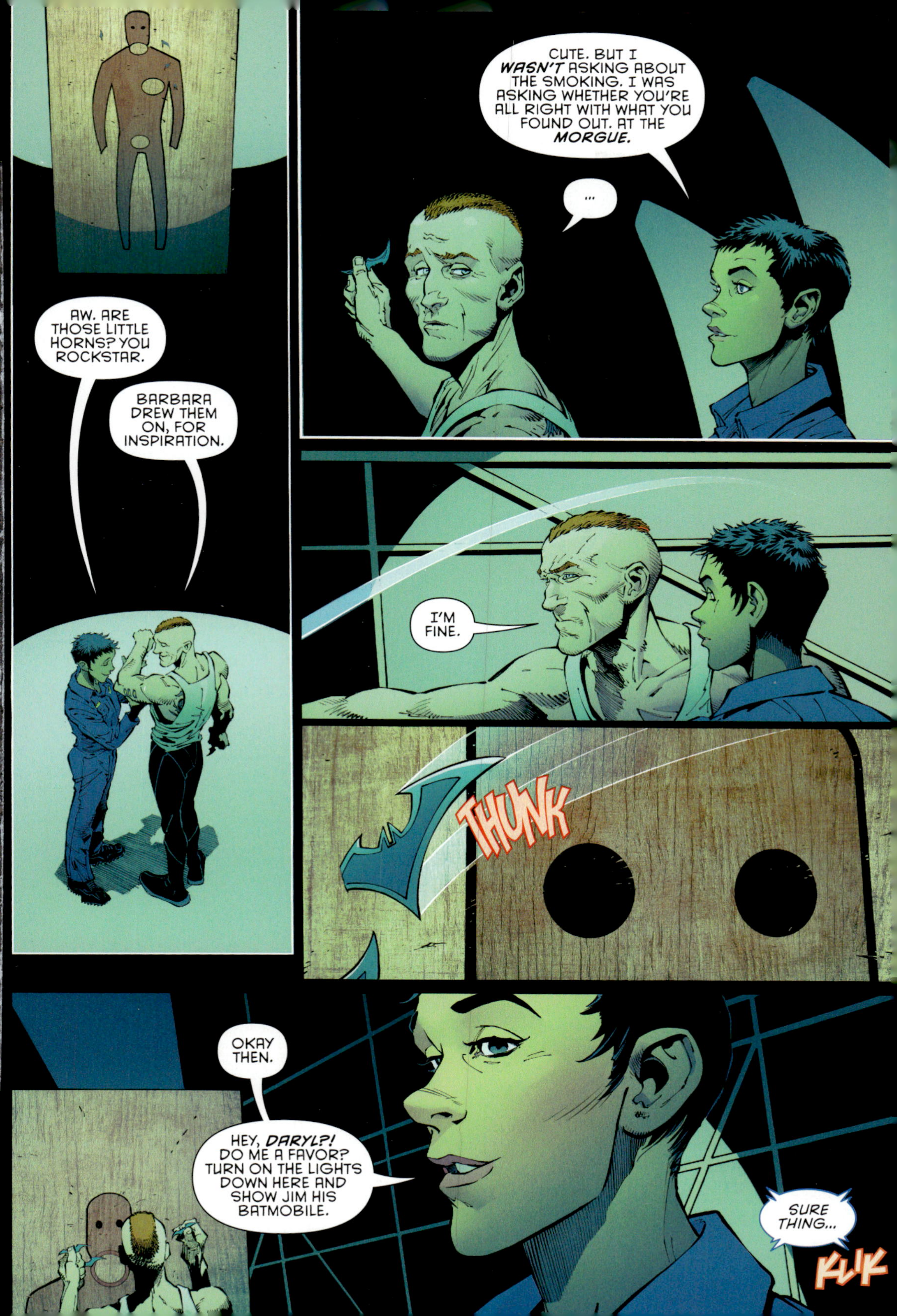

AW. ARE THOSE LITTLE HORNS? YOU ROCKSTAR.
BARBARA DREW THEM ON, FOR INSPIRATION.
CUTE. BUT I WASN'T ASKING ABOUT THE SMOKING. I WAS ASKING WHETHER YOU'RE ALL RIGHT WITH WHAT YOU FOUND OUT. AT THE MORGUE.
...
I'M FINE.
THUNK
OKAY THEN.
HEY, DARYL?! DO ME A FAVOR? TURN ON THE LIGHTS DOWN HERE AND SHOW JIM HIS BATMOBILE.
SURE THING...
KLIK

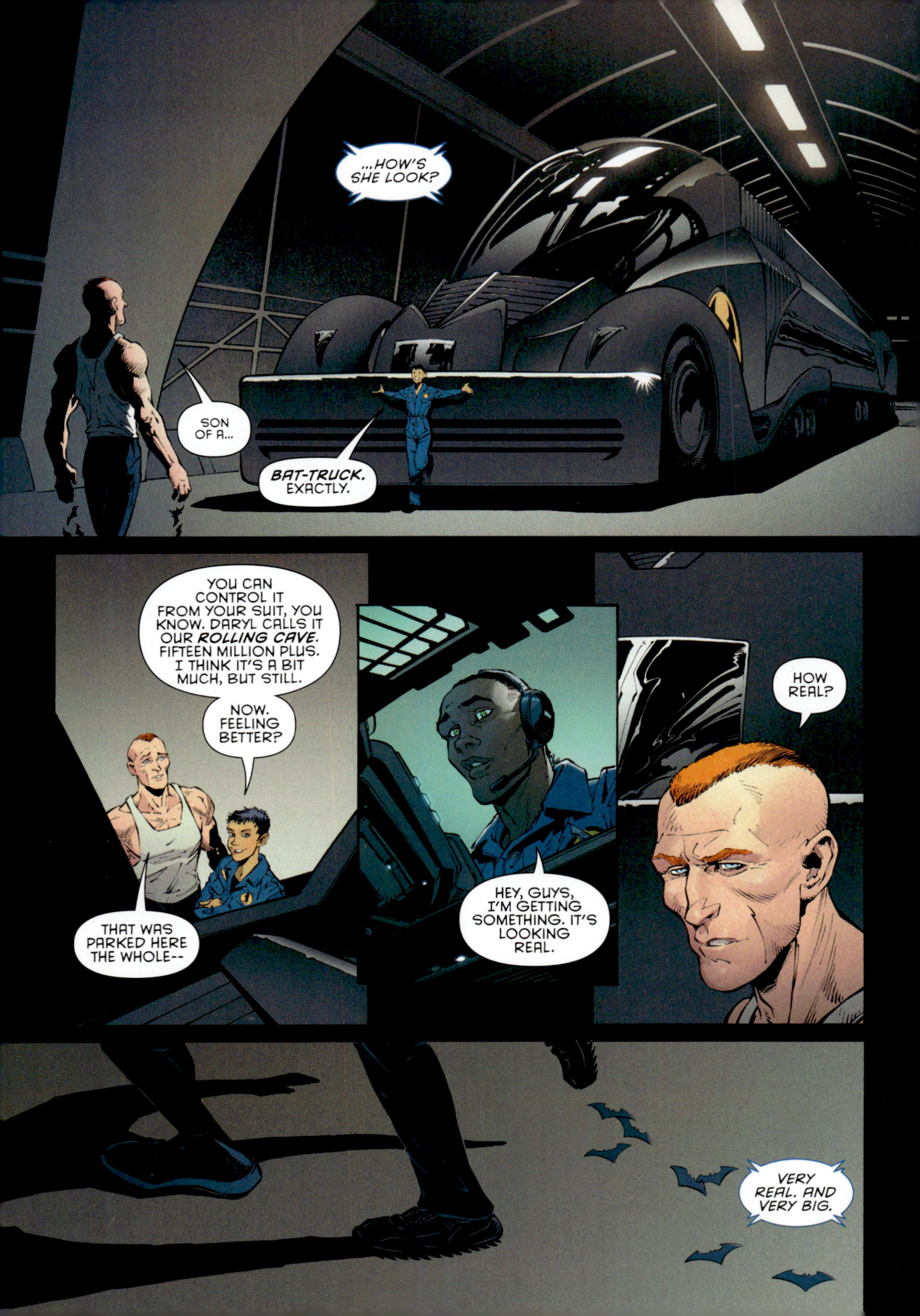
...HOW'S SHE LOOK?
SON OF A...
BAT-TRUCK. EXACTLY.
YOU CAN CONTROL IT FROM YOUR SUIT, YOU KNOW. DARYL CALLS IT OUR ROLLING CAVE. FIFTEEN MILLION PLUS. I THINK IT'S A BIT MUCH, BUT STILL.
NOW. FEELING BETTER?
THAT WAS PARKED HERE THE WHOLE--
HEY, GUYS, I'M GETTING SOMETHING. IT'S LOOKING REAL.
HOW REAL?
VERY REAL. AND VERY BIG.

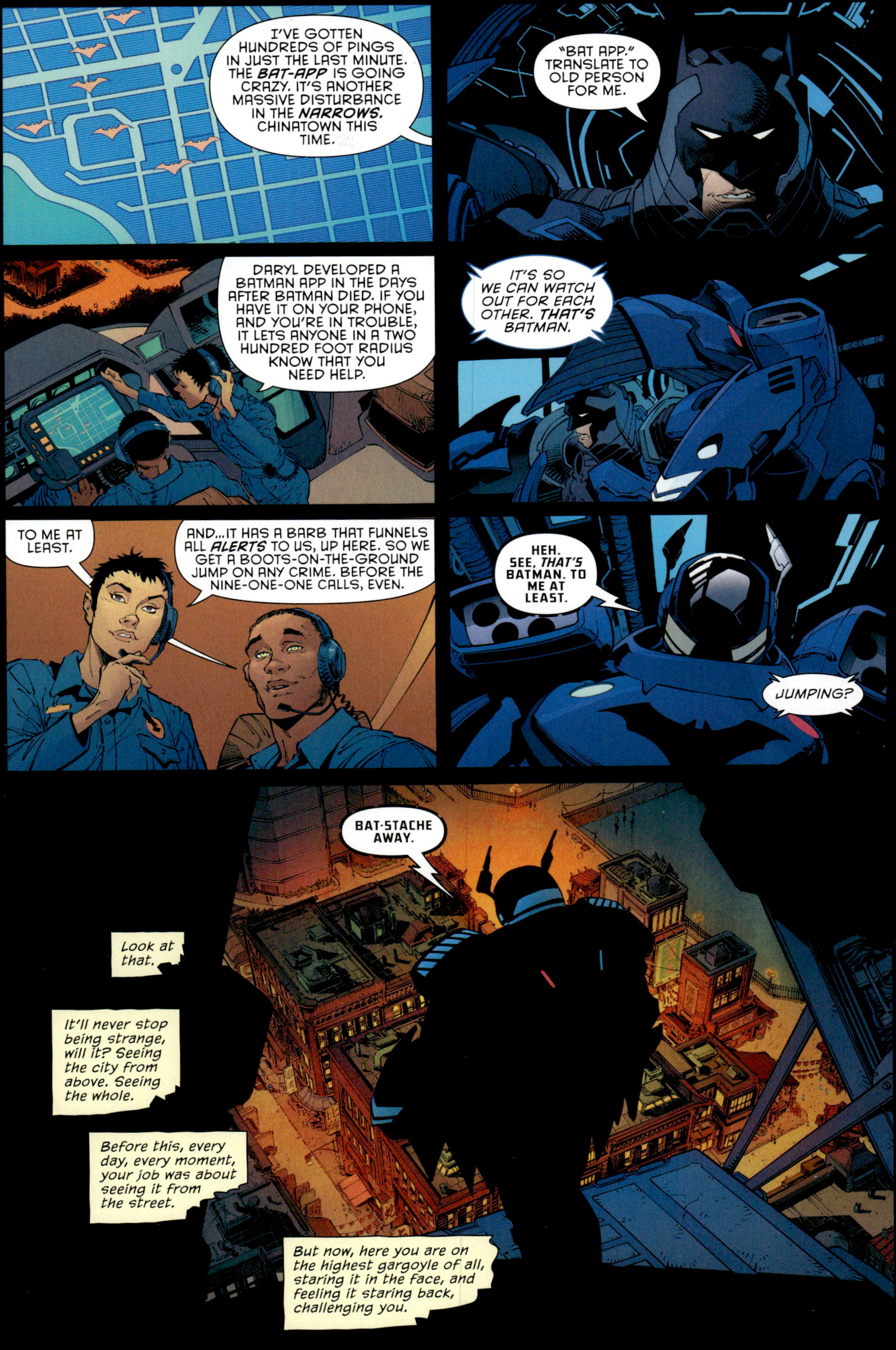
I'VE GOTTEN HUNDREDS OF PINGS IN JUST THE LAST MINUTE. THE BAT-APP IS GOING CRAZY. IT'S ANOTHER MASSIVE DISTURBANCE IN THE NARROWS. CHINATOWN THIS TIME.
"BAT APP." TRANSLATE TO OLD PERSON FOR ME.
DARYL DEVELOPED A BATMAN APP IN THE DAYS AFTER BATMAN DIED. IF YOU HAVE IT ON YOUR PHONE, AND YOU'RE IN TROUBLE, IT LETS ANYONE IN A TWO HUNDRED FOOT RADIUS KNOW THAT YOU NEED HELP.
IT'S SO WE CAN WATCH OUT FOR EACH OTHER. THAT'S BATMAN.
TO ME AT LEAST.
AND...IT HAS A BARB THAT FUNNELS ALL ALERTS TO US, UP HERE. SO WE GET A BOOTS-ON-THE-GROUND JUMP ON ANY CRIME. BEFORE THE NINE-ONE-ONE CALLS, EVEN.
HEH. SEE, THAT'S BATMAN. TO ME AT LEAST.
JUMPING?
BAT-STACHE AWAY.
Look at that.
It'll never stop being strange, will it? Seeing the city from above. Seeing the whole.
Before this, every day, every moment, your job was about seeing it from the street.
But now, here you are on the highest gargoyle of all, staring it in the face, and feeling it staring back, challenging you.

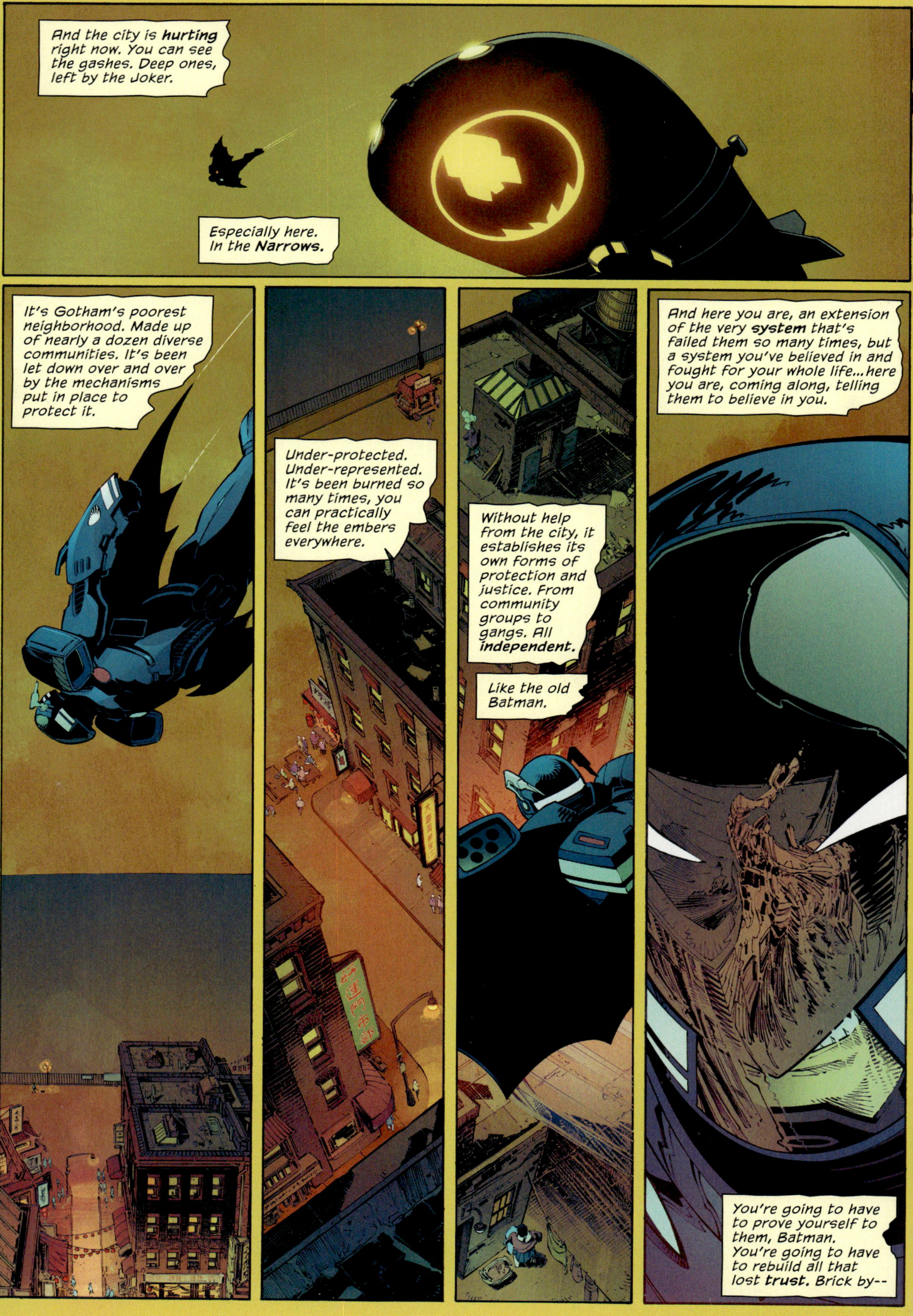
And the city is **hurting** right now. You can see the gashes. Deep ones, left by the Joker.
Especially here. In the **Narrows.**
It's Gotham's poorest neighborhood. Made up of nearly a dozen diverse communities. It's been let down over and over by the mechanisms put in place to protect it.
Under-protected. Under-represented. It's been burned so many times, you can practically feel the embers everywhere.
Without help from the city, it establishes its own forms of protection and justice. From community groups to gangs. All **independent.**
Like the old Batman.
And here you are, an extension of the very **system** that's failed them so many times, but a system you've believed in and fought for your whole life...here you are, coming along, telling them to believe in you.
You're going to have to prove yourself to them, Batman. You're going to have to rebuild all that lost **trust.** Brick by--

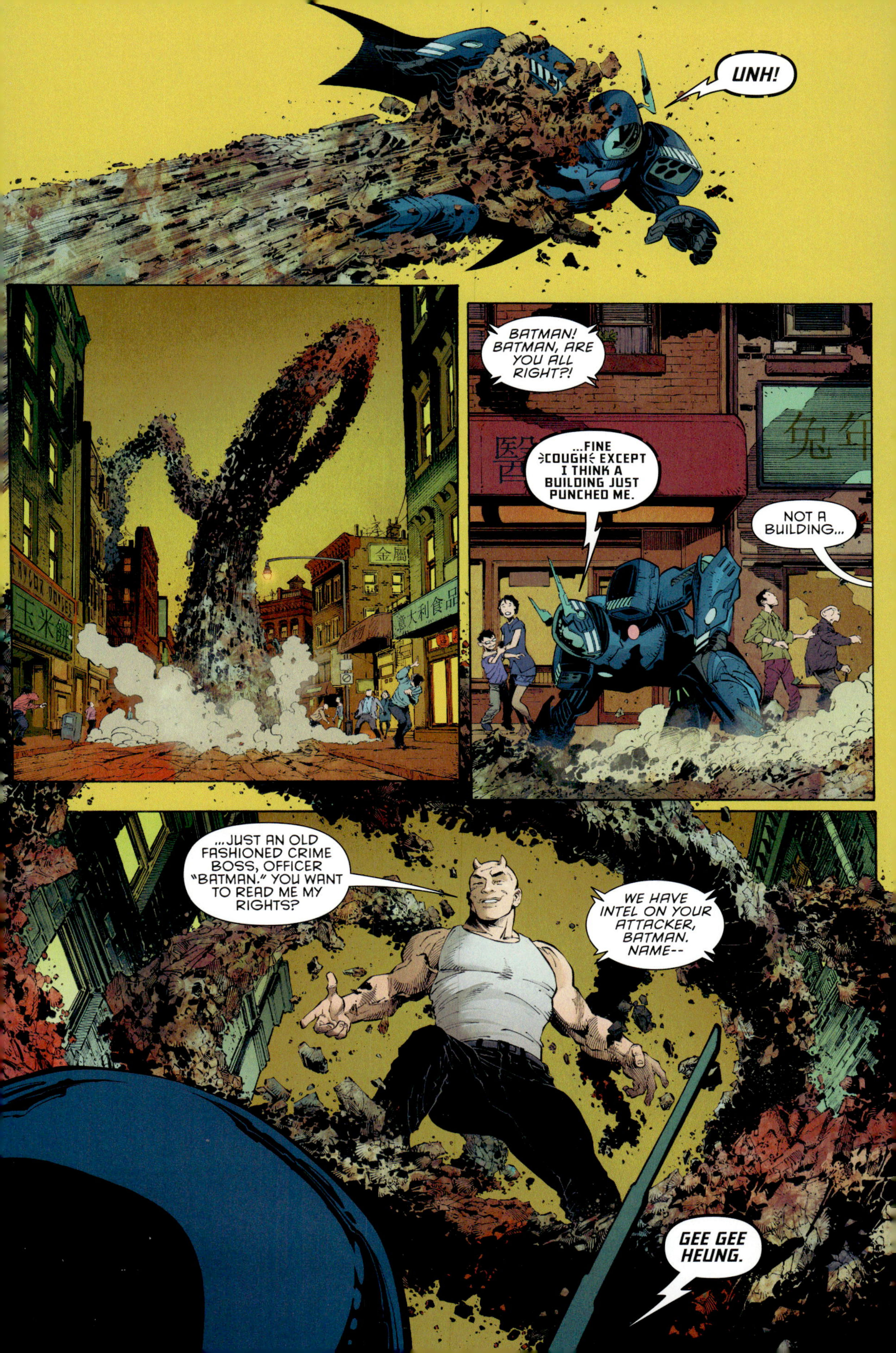
UNH!
BATMAN! BATMAN, ARE YOU ALL RIGHT?!
...FINE *COUGH* EXCEPT I THINK A BUILDING JUST PUNCHED ME.
NOT A BUILDING...
...JUST AN OLD FASHIONED CRIME BOSS, OFFICER "BATMAN." YOU WANT TO READ ME MY RIGHTS?
WE HAVE INTEL ON YOUR ATTACKER, BATMAN. NAME--
GEE GEE HEUNG.

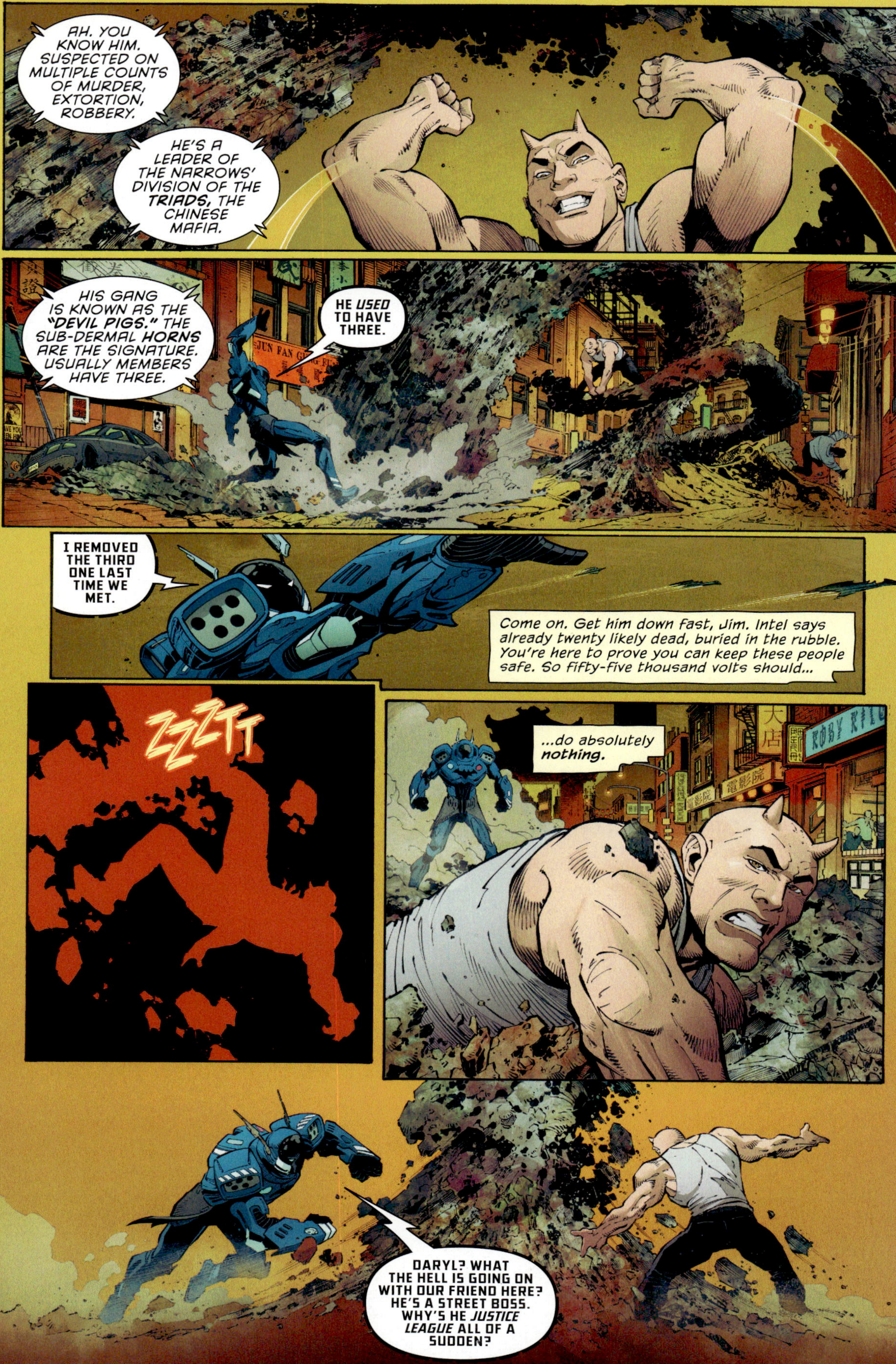
AH. YOU KNOW HIM. SUSPECTED ON MULTIPLE COUNTS OF MURDER, EXTORTION, ROBBERY.
HE'S A LEADER OF THE NARROWS' DIVISION OF THE TRIADS, THE CHINESE MAFIA.
HIS GANG IS KNOWN AS THE "DEVIL PIGS." THE SUB-DERMAL HORNS ARE THE SIGNATURE. USUALLY MEMBERS HAVE THREE.
HE USED TO HAVE THREE.
JUN FAN
I REMOVED THE THIRD ONE LAST TIME WE MET.
Come on. Get him down fast, Jim. Intel says already twenty likely dead, buried in the rubble. You're here to prove you can keep these people safe. So fifty-five thousand volts should...
ZZZTT
...do absolutely nothing.
DARYL? WHAT THE HELL IS GOING ON WITH OUR FRIEND HERE? HE'S A STREET BOSS. WHY'S HE JUSTICE LEAGUE ALL OF A SUDDEN?

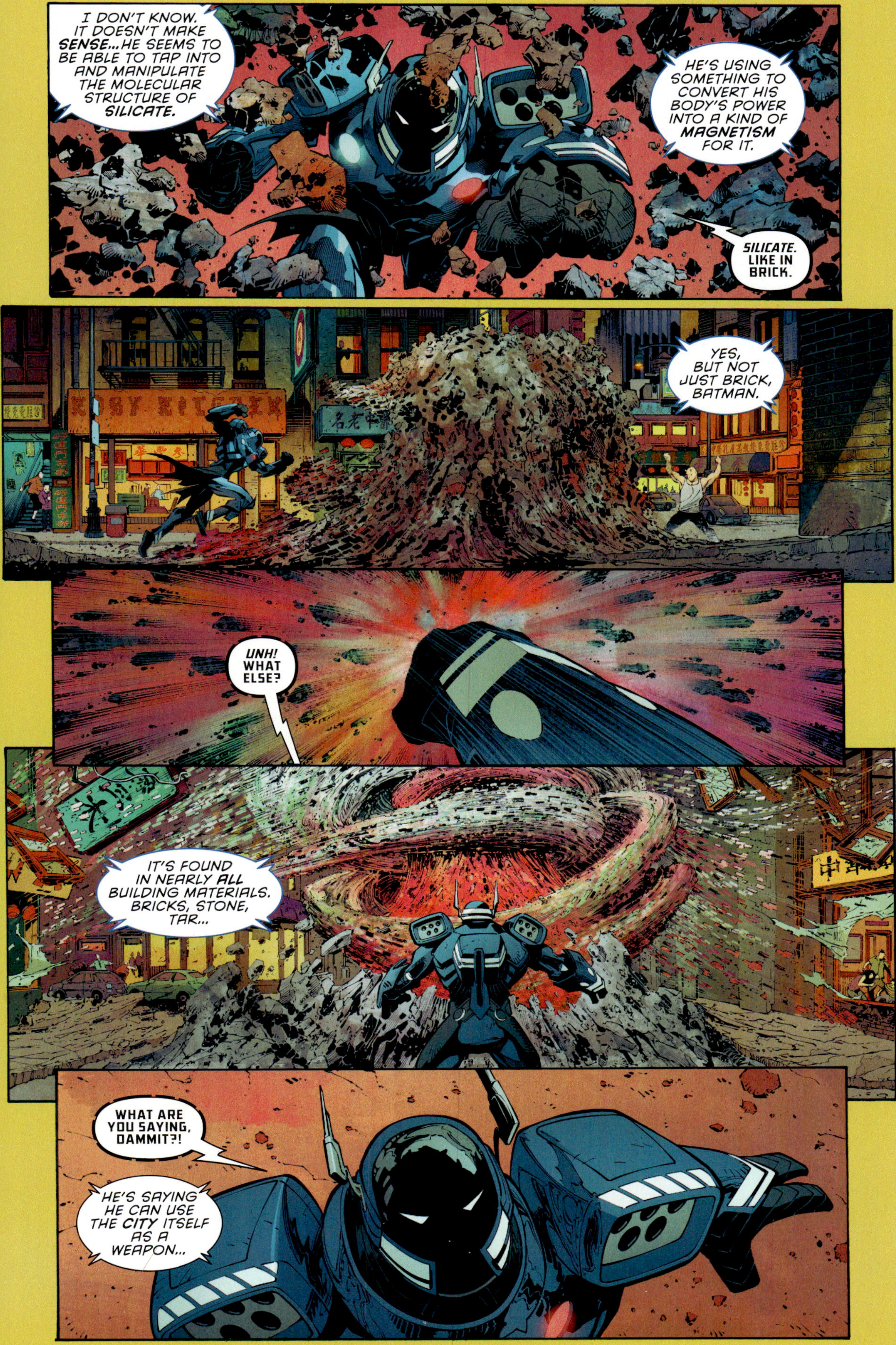
I DON'T KNOW. IT DOESN'T MAKE SENSE... HE SEEMS TO BE ABLE TO TAP INTO AND MANIPULATE THE MOLECULAR STRUCTURE OF SILICATE.
HE'S USING SOMETHING TO CONVERT HIS BODY'S POWER INTO A KIND OF MAGNETISM FOR IT.
SILICATE. LIKE IN BRICK.
YES, BUT NOT JUST BRICK, BATMAN.
UNH! WHAT ELSE?
IT'S FOUND IN NEARLY ALL BUILDING MATERIALS. BRICKS, STONE, TAR...
WHAT ARE YOU SAYING, DAMMIT?!
HE'S SAYING HE CAN USE THE CITY ITSELF AS A WEAPON...

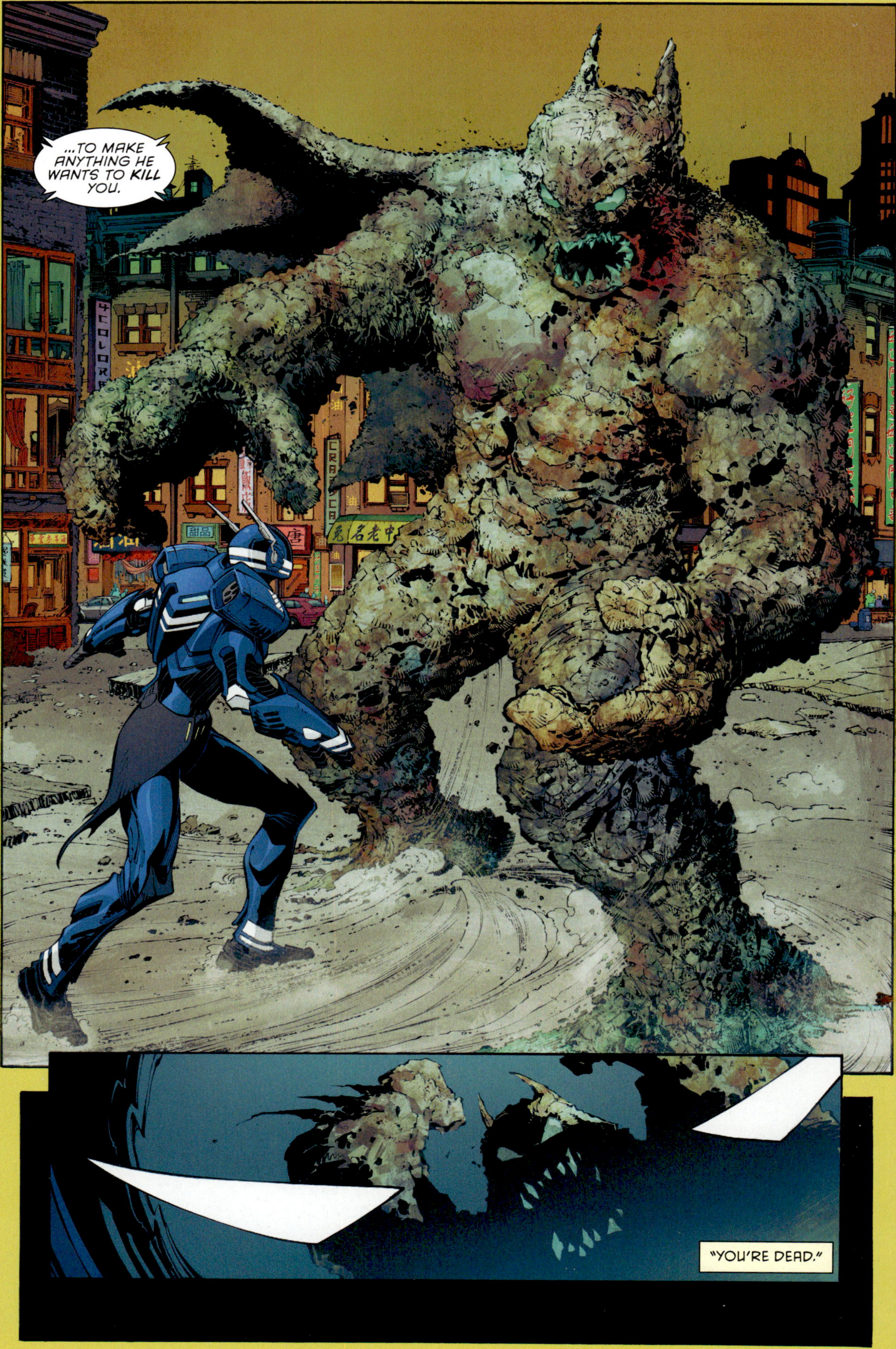
...TO MAKE ANYTHING HE WANTS TO **KILL** YOU.
"YOU'RE DEAD."

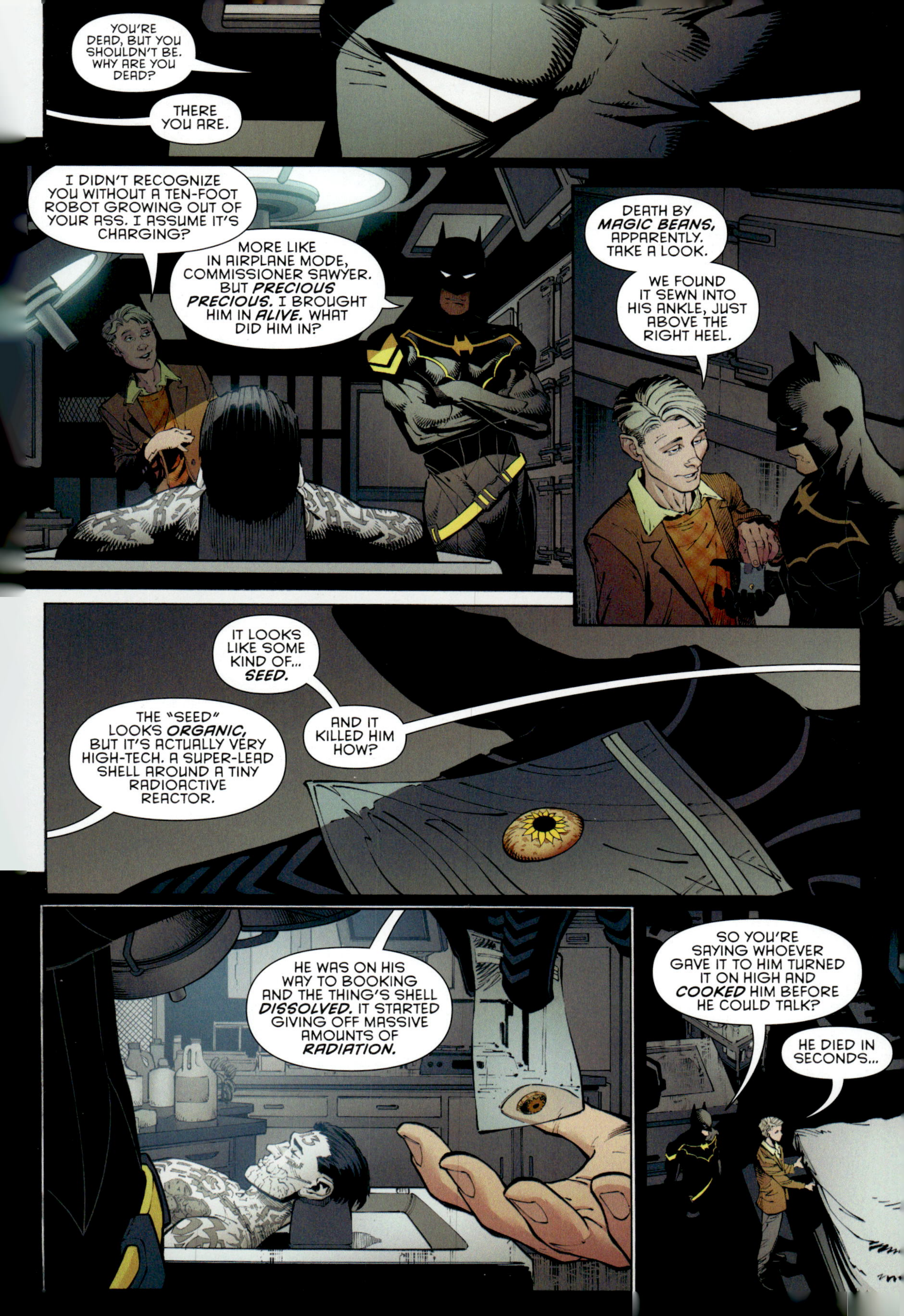

YOU'RE DEAD, BUT YOU SHOULDN'T BE. WHY ARE YOU DEAD?
THERE YOU ARE.
I DIDN'T RECOGNIZE YOU WITHOUT A TEN-FOOT ROBOT GROWING OUT OF YOUR ASS. I ASSUME IT'S CHARGING?
MORE LIKE IN AIRPLANE MODE, COMMISSIONER SAWYER. BUT *PRECIOUS PRECIOUS.* I BROUGHT HIM IN *ALIVE.* WHAT DID HIM IN?
DEATH BY *MAGIC BEANS,* APPARENTLY. TAKE A LOOK.
WE FOUND IT SEWN INTO HIS ANKLE, JUST ABOVE THE RIGHT HEEL.
IT LOOKS LIKE SOME KIND OF... *SEED.*
AND IT KILLED HIM HOW?
THE "SEED" LOOKS *ORGANIC,* BUT IT'S ACTUALLY VERY HIGH-TECH. A SUPER-LEAD SHELL AROUND A TINY RADIOACTIVE REACTOR.
HE WAS ON HIS WAY TO BOOKING AND THE THING'S SHELL *DISSOLVED.* IT STARTED GIVING OFF MASSIVE AMOUNTS OF *RADIATION.*
SO YOU'RE SAYING WHOEVER GAVE IT TO HIM TURNED IT ON HIGH AND *COOKED* HIM BEFORE HE COULD TALK?
HE DIED IN SECONDS...

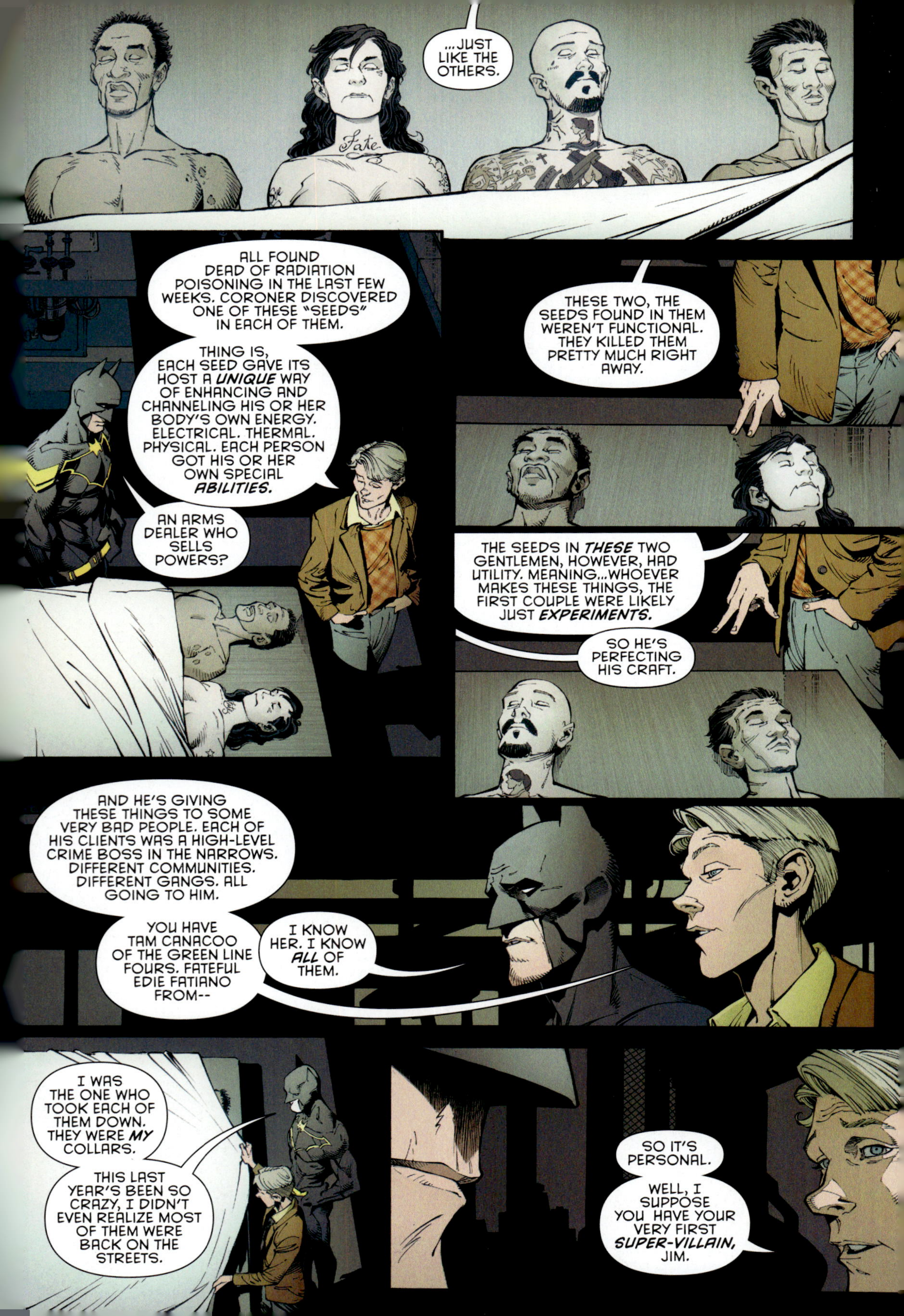
...JUST LIKE THE OTHERS.
ALL FOUND DEAD OF RADIATION POISONING IN THE LAST FEW WEEKS. CORONER DISCOVERED ONE OF THESE "SEEDS" IN EACH OF THEM.
THING IS, EACH SEED GAVE ITS HOST A *UNIQUE* WAY OF ENHANCING AND CHANNELING HIS OR HER BODY'S OWN ENERGY. ELECTRICAL. THERMAL. PHYSICAL. EACH PERSON GOT HIS OR HER OWN SPECIAL *ABILITIES.*
AN ARMS DEALER WHO SELLS POWERS?
THESE TWO, THE SEEDS FOUND IN THEM WEREN'T FUNCTIONAL. THEY KILLED THEM PRETTY MUCH RIGHT AWAY.
THE SEEDS IN *THESE* TWO GENTLEMEN, HOWEVER, HAD UTILITY. MEANING...WHOEVER MAKES THESE THINGS, THE FIRST COUPLE WERE LIKELY JUST *EXPERIMENTS.*
SO HE'S PERFECTING HIS CRAFT.
AND HE'S GIVING THESE THINGS TO SOME VERY BAD PEOPLE. EACH OF HIS CLIENTS WAS A HIGH-LEVEL CRIME BOSS IN THE NARROWS. DIFFERENT COMMUNITIES. DIFFERENT GANGS. ALL GOING TO HIM.
YOU HAVE TAM CANACOO OF THE GREEN LINE FOURS. FATEFUL EDIE FATIANO FROM--
I KNOW HER. I KNOW *ALL* OF THEM.
I WAS THE ONE WHO TOOK EACH OF THEM DOWN. THEY WERE *MY* COLLARS.
THIS LAST YEAR'S BEEN SO CRAZY, I DIDN'T EVEN REALIZE MOST OF THEM WERE BACK ON THE STREETS.
SO IT'S PERSONAL.
WELL, I SUPPOSE YOU HAVE YOUR VERY FIRST *SUPER-VILLAIN,* JIM.

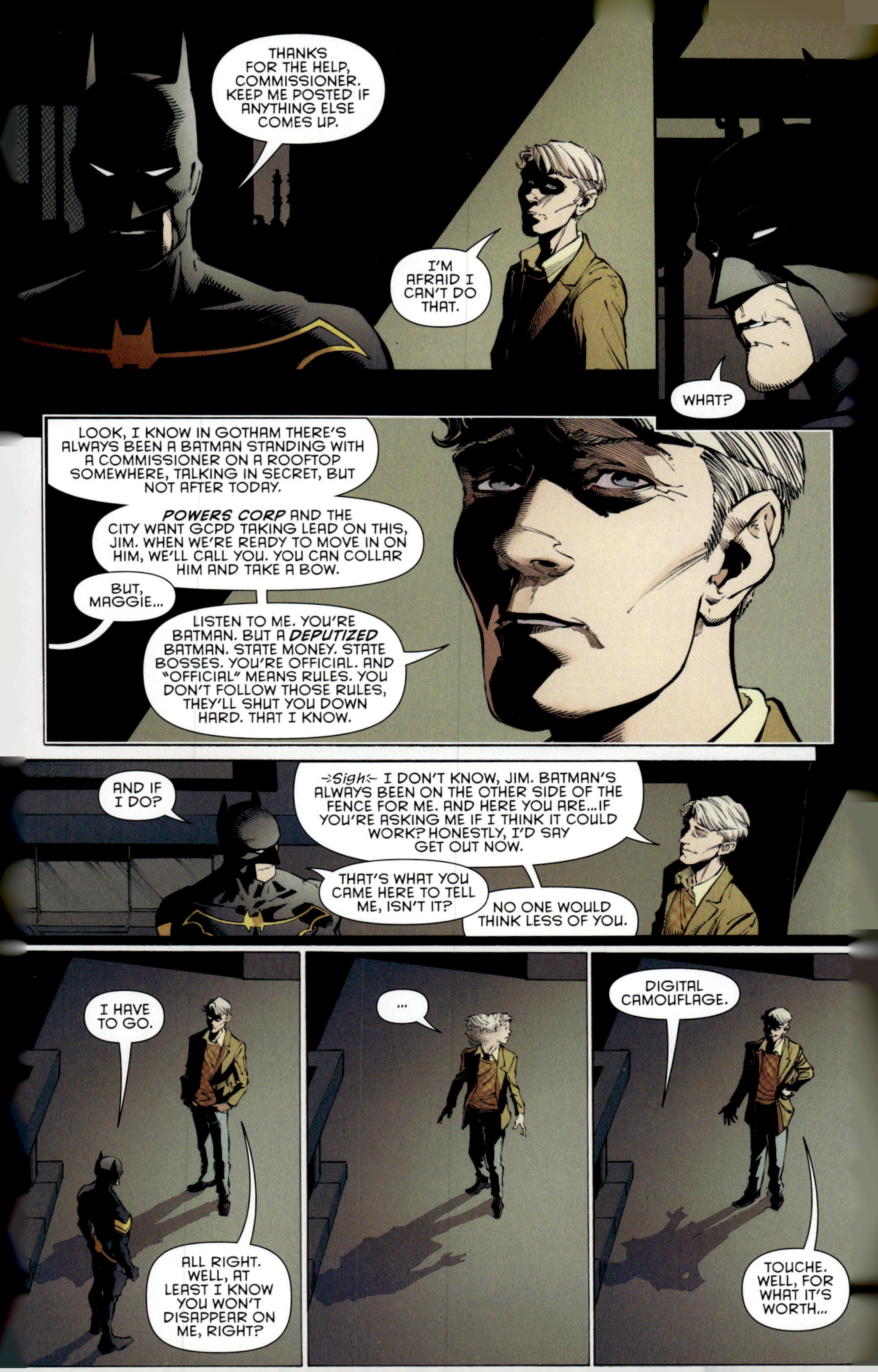
THANKS FOR THE HELP, COMMISSIONER. KEEP ME POSTED IF ANYTHING ELSE COMES UP.
I'M AFRAID I CAN'T DO THAT.
WHAT?
LOOK, I KNOW IN GOTHAM THERE'S ALWAYS BEEN A BATMAN STANDING WITH A COMMISSIONER ON A ROOFTOP SOMEWHERE, TALKING IN SECRET, BUT NOT AFTER TODAY.
POWERS CORP AND THE CITY WANT GCPD TAKING LEAD ON THIS, JIM. WHEN WE'RE READY TO MOVE IN ON HIM, WE'LL CALL YOU. YOU CAN COLLAR HIM AND TAKE A BOW.
BUT, MAGGIE...
LISTEN TO ME. YOU'RE BATMAN. BUT A DEPUTIZED BATMAN. STATE MONEY. STATE BOSSES. YOU'RE OFFICIAL. AND "OFFICIAL" MEANS RULES. YOU DON'T FOLLOW THOSE RULES, THEY'LL SHUT YOU DOWN HARD. THAT I KNOW.
AND IF I DO?
-Sigh- I DON'T KNOW, JIM. BATMAN'S ALWAYS BEEN ON THE OTHER SIDE OF THE FENCE FOR ME. AND HERE YOU ARE...IF YOU'RE ASKING ME IF I THINK IT COULD WORK? HONESTLY, I'D SAY GET OUT NOW.
NO ONE WOULD THINK LESS OF YOU.
THAT'S WHAT YOU CAME HERE TO TELL ME, ISN'T IT?
I HAVE TO GO.
ALL RIGHT. WELL, AT LEAST I KNOW YOU WON'T DISAPPEAR ON ME, RIGHT?
...
DIGITAL CAMOUFLAGE.
TOUCHE. WELL, FOR WHAT IT'S WORTH...

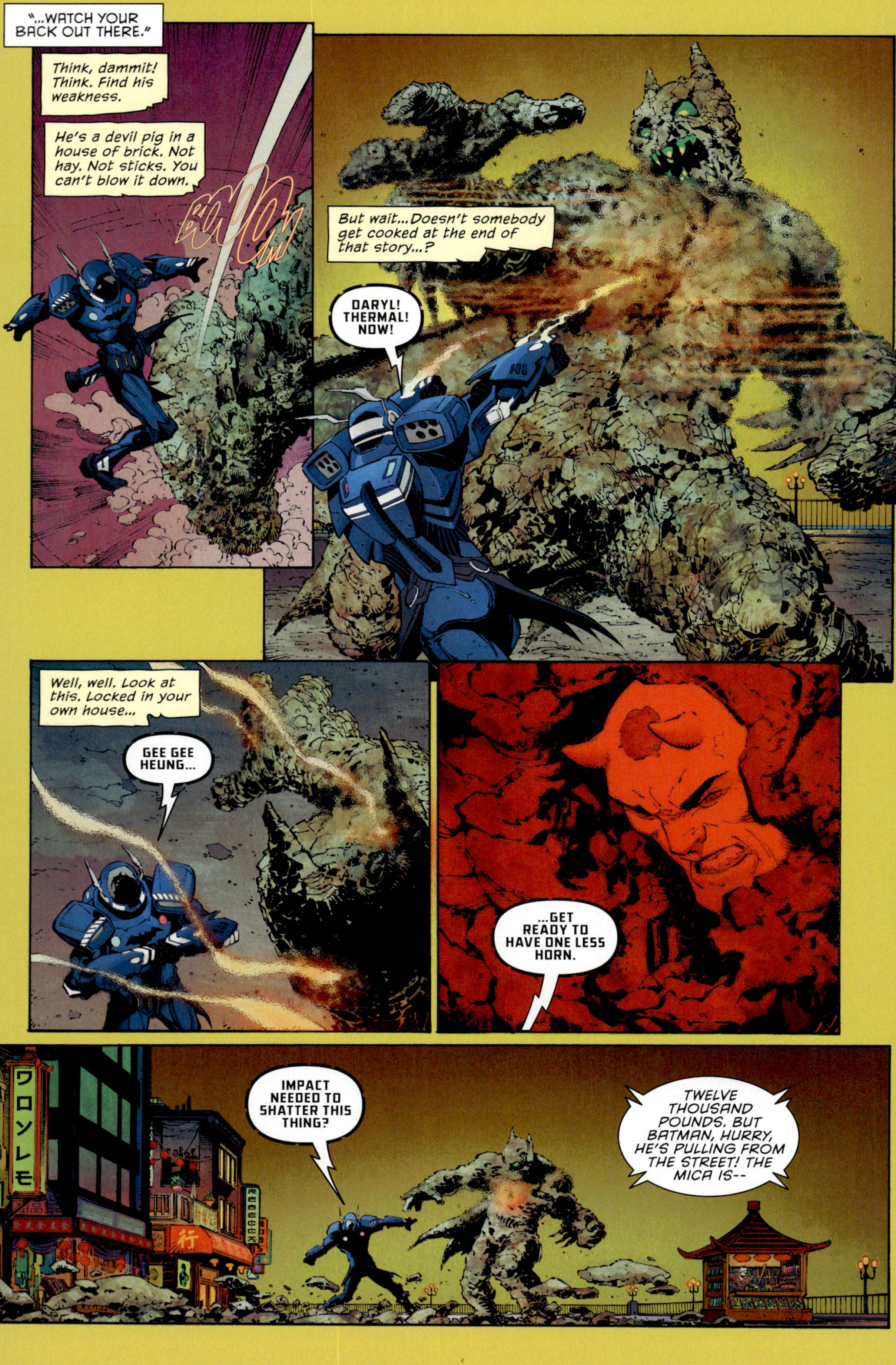
"...WATCH YOUR BACK OUT THERE."
Think, dammit! Think. Find his weakness.
He's a devil pig in a house of brick. Not hay. Not sticks. You can't blow it down.
But wait...Doesn't somebody get cooked at the end of that story...?
DARYL! THERMAL! NOW!
Well, well. Look at this. Locked in your own house...
GEE GEE HEUNG...
...GET READY TO HAVE ONE LESS HORN.
IMPACT NEEDED TO SHATTER THIS THING?
TWELVE THOUSAND POUNDS. BUT BATMAN, HURRY, HE'S PULLING FROM THE STREET! THE MICA IS--

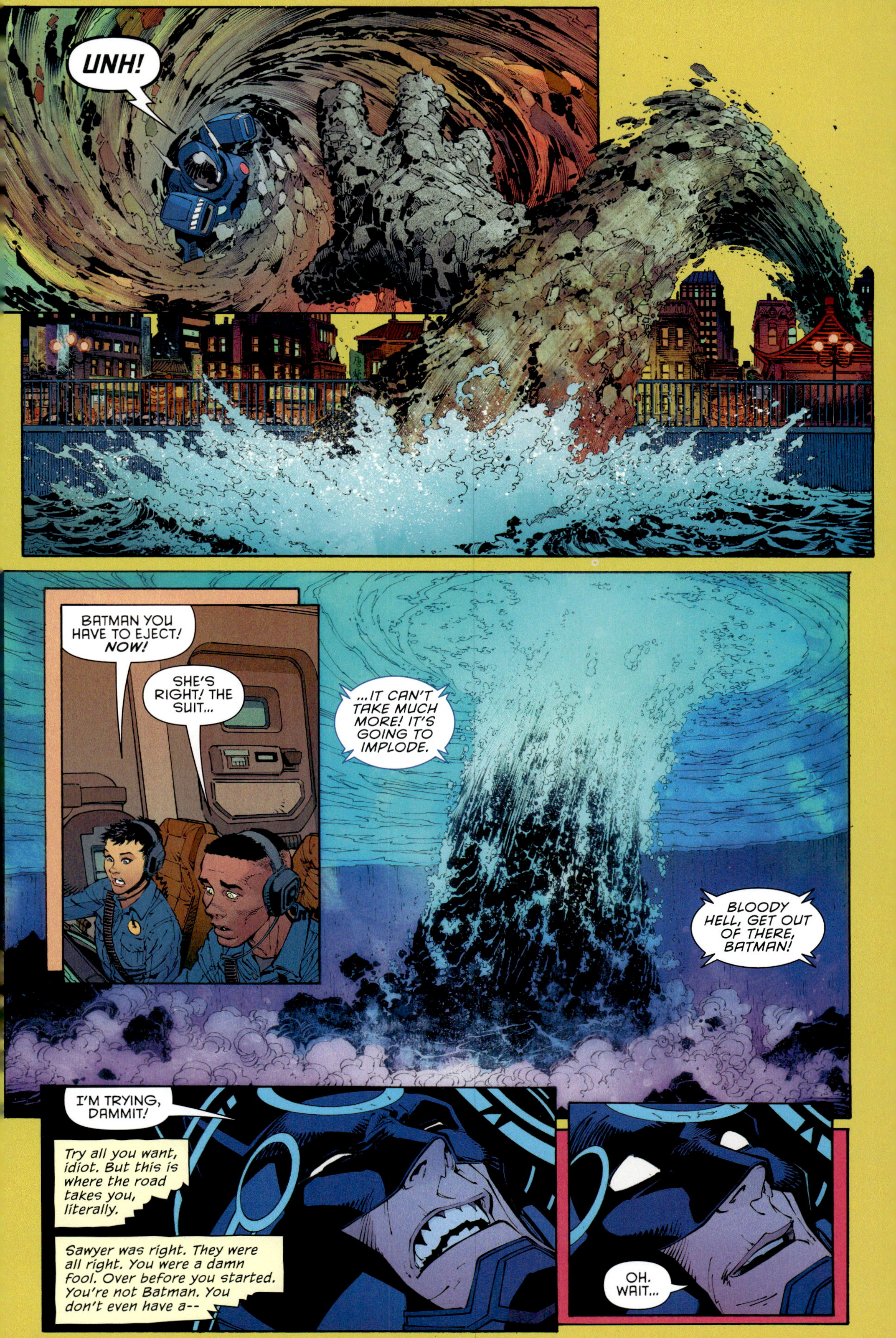
UNH!
BATMAN YOU HAVE TO EJECT! NOW!
SHE'S RIGHT! THE SUIT...
...IT CAN'T TAKE MUCH MORE! IT'S GOING TO IMPLODE.
BLOODY HELL, GET OUT OF THERE, BATMAN!
I'M TRYING, DAMMIT!
Try all you want, idiot. But this is where the road takes you, literally.
Sawyer was right. They were all right. You were a damn fool. Over before you started. You're not Batman. You don't even have a--
OH. WAIT...

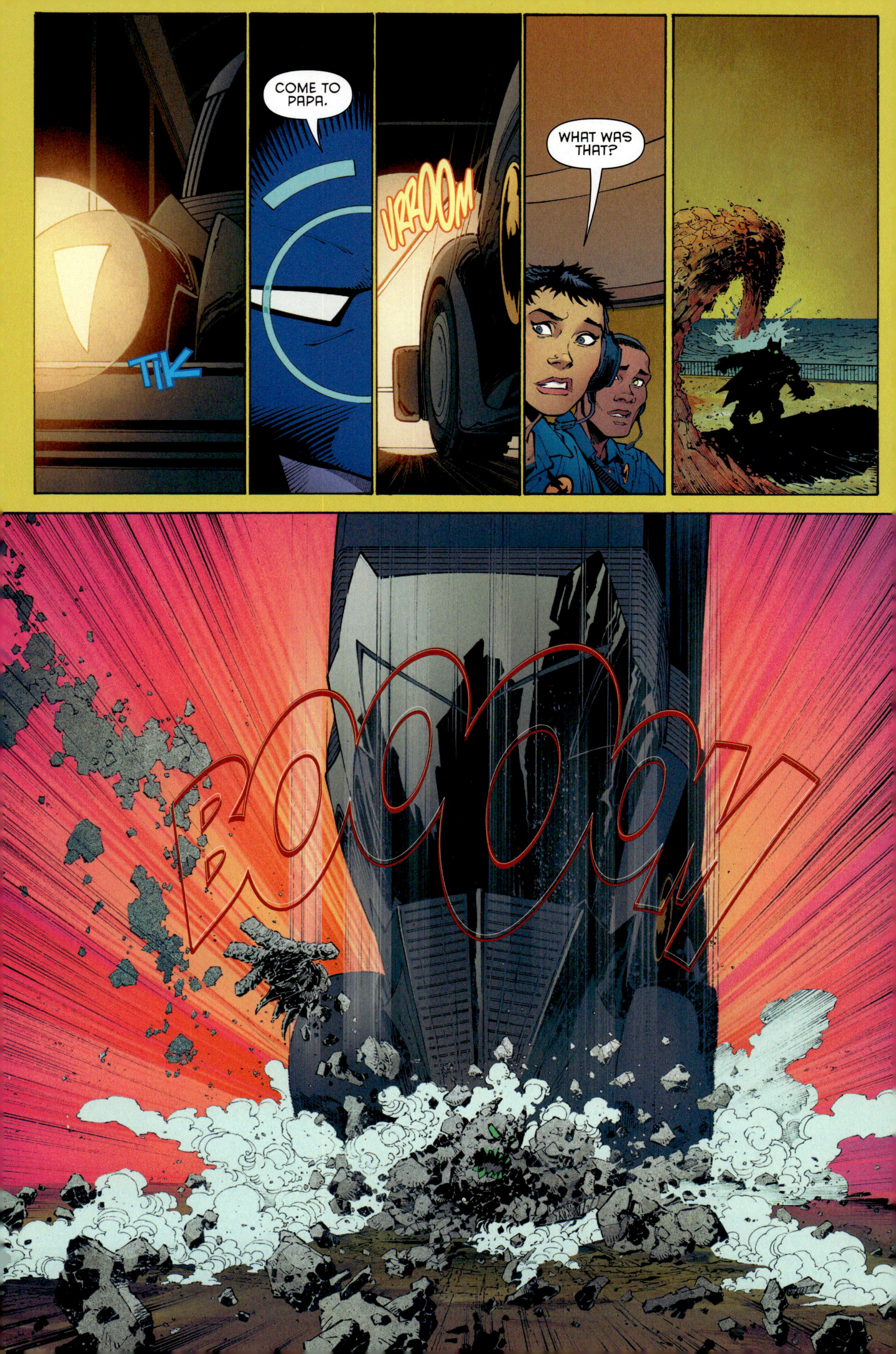
TIK
COME TO PAPA.
VRROOM
WHAT WAS THAT?
BOOOOM

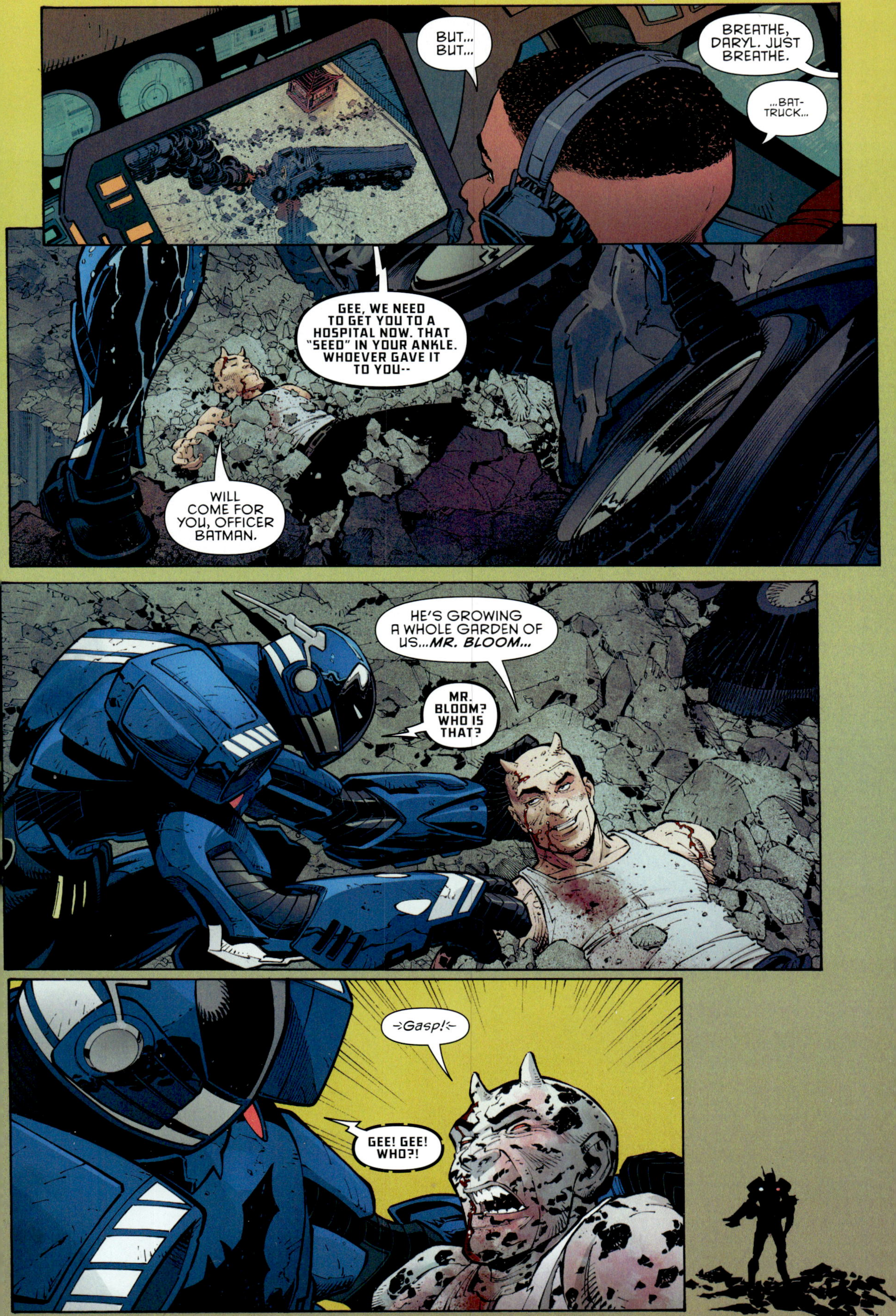
BUT... BUT...
BREATHE, DARYL. JUST BREATHE.
...BAT-TRUCK...
GEE, WE NEED TO GET YOU TO A HOSPITAL NOW. THAT "SEED" IN YOUR ANKLE. WHOEVER GAVE IT TO YOU--
WILL COME FOR YOU, OFFICER BATMAN.
HE'S GROWING A WHOLE GARDEN OF US...MR. BLOOM...
MR. BLOOM? WHO IS THAT?
-Gasp!-
GEE! GEE! WHO?!

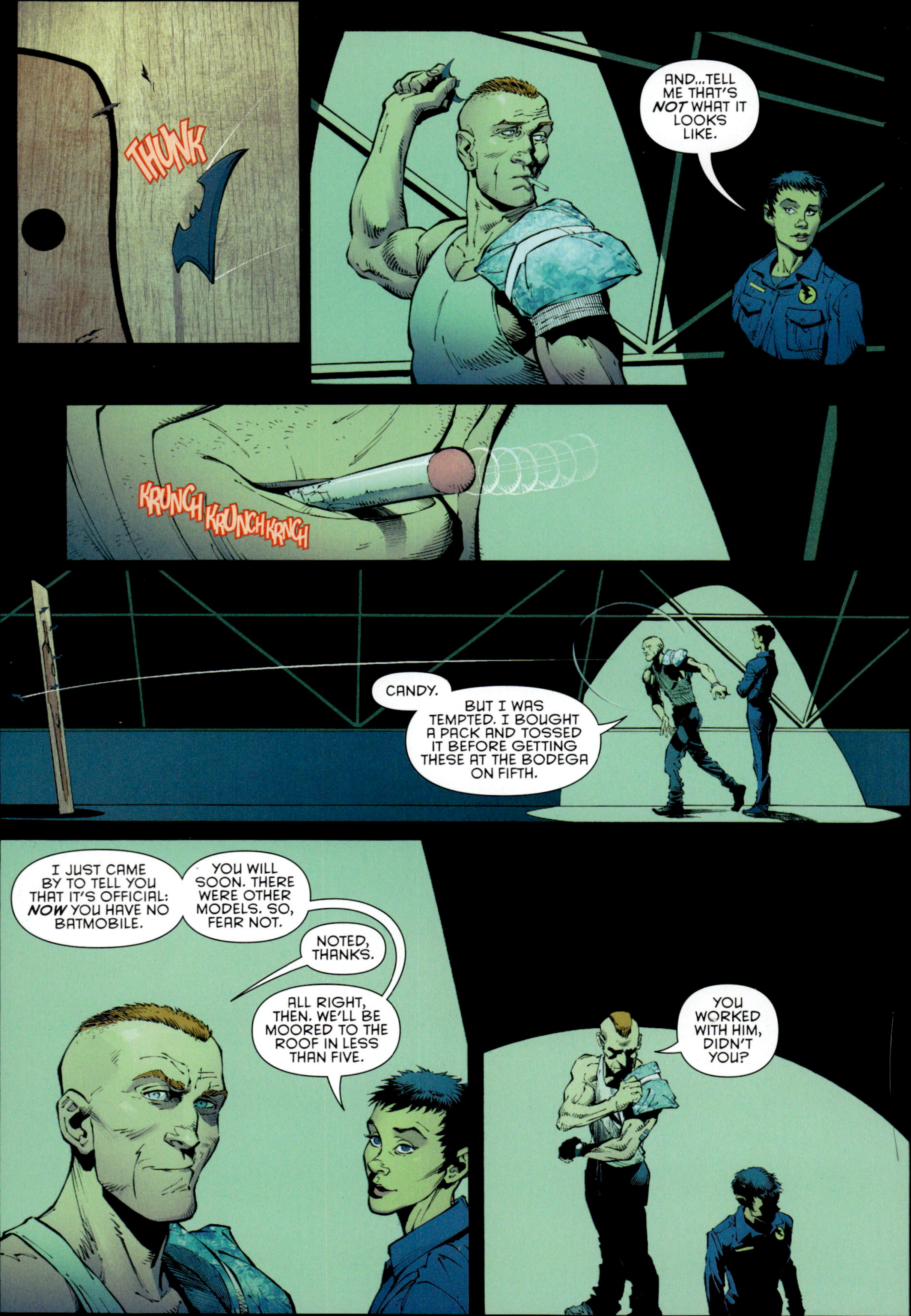
THUNK
AND...TELL ME THAT'S NOT WHAT IT LOOKS LIKE.
KRUNCH KRUNCH KRNCH
CANDY.
BUT I WAS TEMPTED. I BOUGHT A PACK AND TOSSED IT BEFORE GETTING THESE AT THE BODEGA ON FIFTH.
I JUST CAME BY TO TELL YOU THAT IT'S OFFICIAL: NOW YOU HAVE NO BATMOBILE.
YOU WILL SOON. THERE WERE OTHER MODELS. SO, FEAR NOT.
NOTED, THANKS.
ALL RIGHT, THEN. WE'LL BE MOORED TO THE ROOF IN LESS THAN FIVE.
YOU WORKED WITH HIM, DIDN'T YOU?

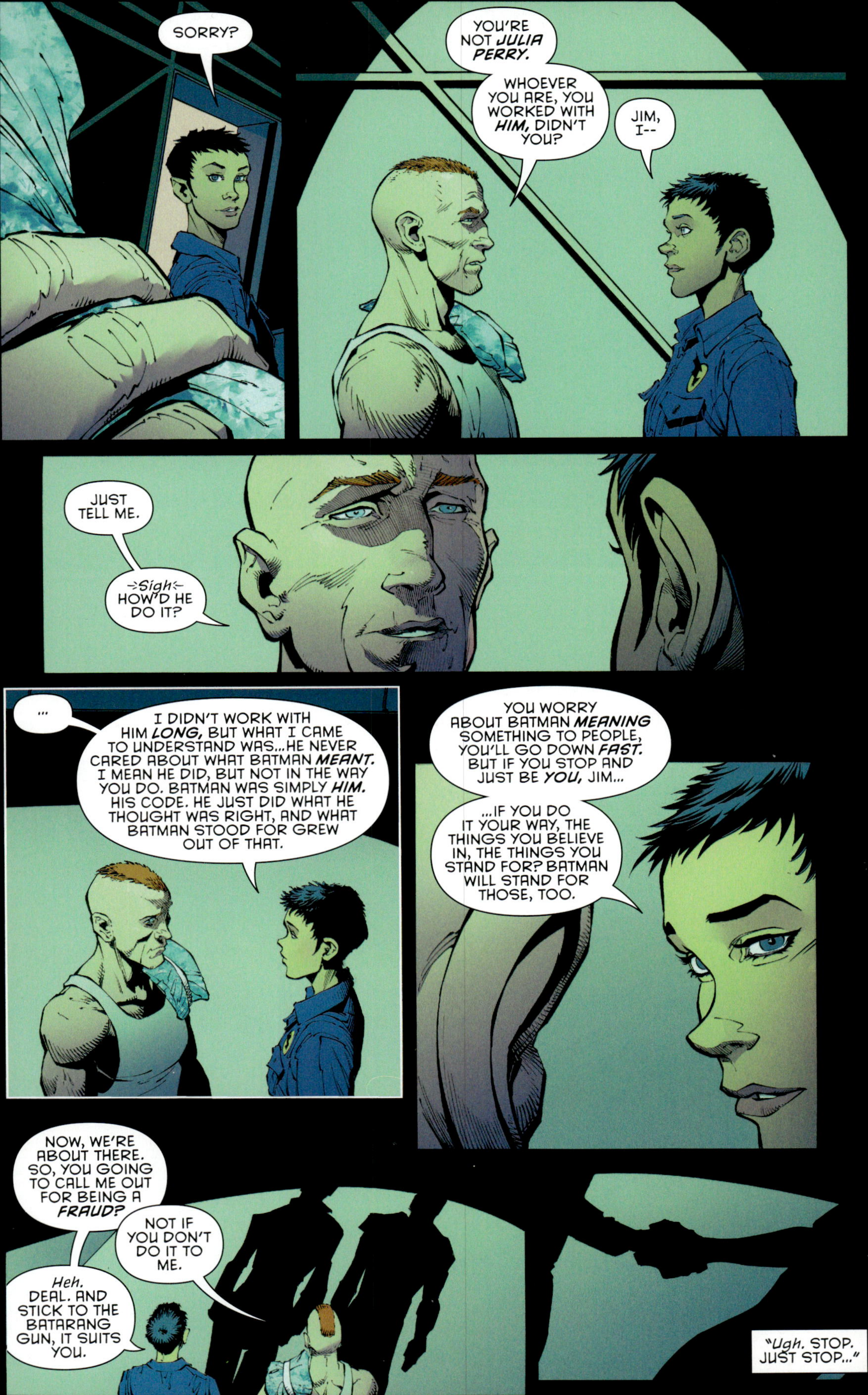
SORRY?
YOU'RE NOT JULIA PERRY.
WHOEVER YOU ARE, YOU WORKED WITH HIM, DIDN'T YOU?
JIM, I--
JUST TELL ME.
>Sigh< HOW'D HE DO IT?
...
I DIDN'T WORK WITH HIM LONG, BUT WHAT I CAME TO UNDERSTAND WAS...HE NEVER CARED ABOUT WHAT BATMAN MEANT. I MEAN HE DID, BUT NOT IN THE WAY YOU DO. BATMAN WAS SIMPLY HIM. HIS CODE. HE JUST DID WHAT HE THOUGHT WAS RIGHT, AND WHAT BATMAN STOOD FOR GREW OUT OF THAT.
YOU WORRY ABOUT BATMAN MEANING SOMETHING TO PEOPLE, YOU'LL GO DOWN FAST. BUT IF YOU STOP AND JUST BE YOU, JIM...
...IF YOU DO IT YOUR WAY, THE THINGS YOU BELIEVE IN, THE THINGS YOU STAND FOR? BATMAN WILL STAND FOR THOSE, TOO.
NOW, WE'RE ABOUT THERE. SO, YOU GOING TO CALL ME OUT FOR BEING A FRAUD?
NOT IF YOU DON'T DO IT TO ME.
Heh. DEAL. AND STICK TO THE BATARANG GUN, IT SUITS YOU.
"Ugh. STOP. JUST STOP..."

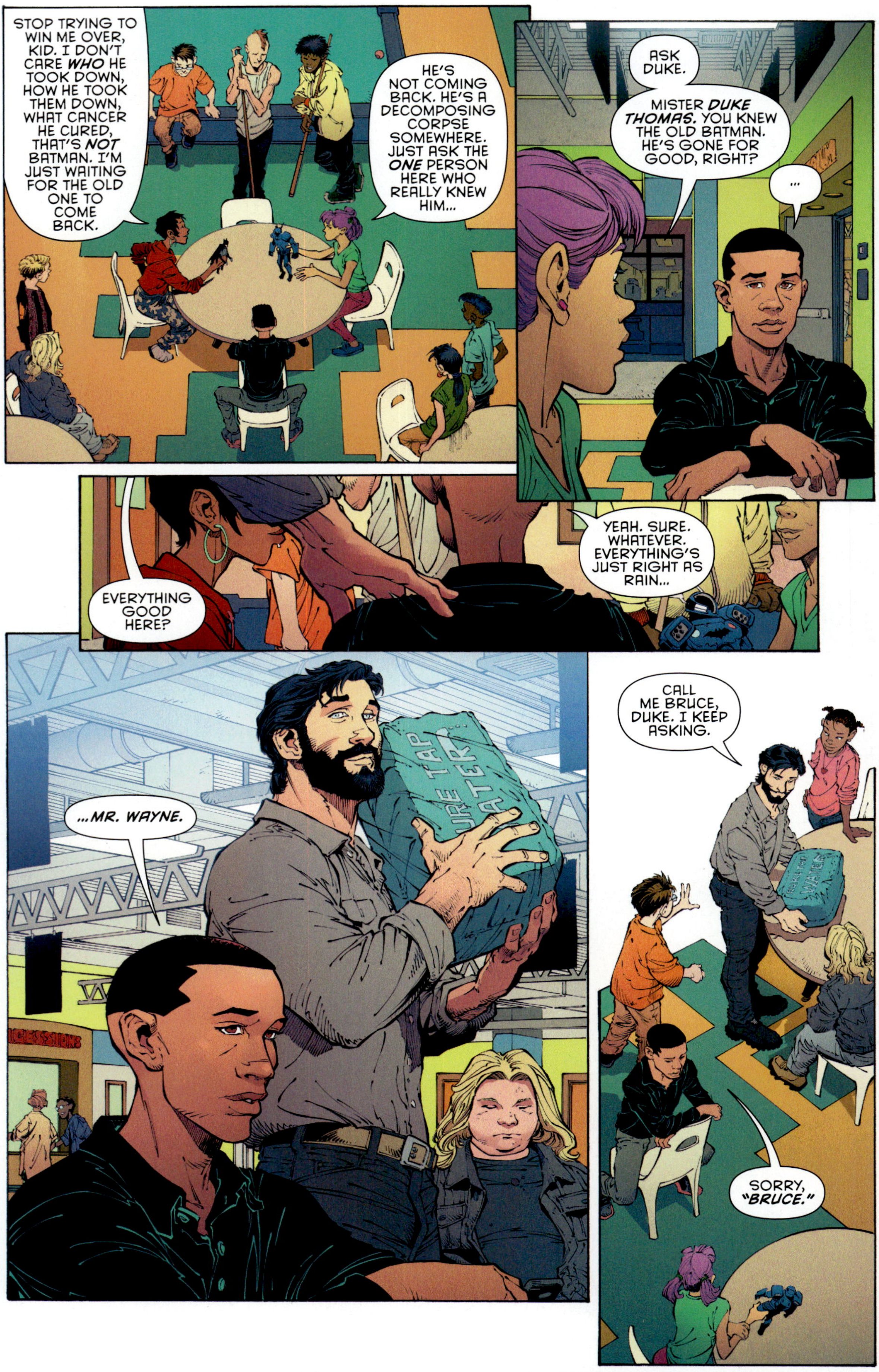
STOP TRYING TO WIN ME OVER, KID. I DON'T CARE *WHO* HE TOOK DOWN, HOW HE TOOK THEM DOWN, WHAT CANCER HE CURED, THAT'S *NOT* BATMAN. I'M JUST WAITING FOR THE OLD ONE TO COME BACK.
HE'S NOT COMING BACK. HE'S A DECOMPOSING CORPSE SOMEWHERE. JUST ASK THE *ONE* PERSON HERE WHO REALLY KNEW HIM...
ASK DUKE.
MISTER *DUKE THOMAS.* YOU KNEW THE OLD BATMAN. HE'S GONE FOR GOOD, RIGHT?
...
EVERYTHING GOOD HERE?
YEAH. SURE. WHATEVER. EVERYTHING'S JUST RIGHT AS RAIN...
...MR. WAYNE.
CALL ME BRUCE, DUKE. I KEEP ASKING.
SORRY, *"BRUCE."*

FACT IS... I DON'T KNOW *WHAT* THE HELL TO THINK ANYMORE.

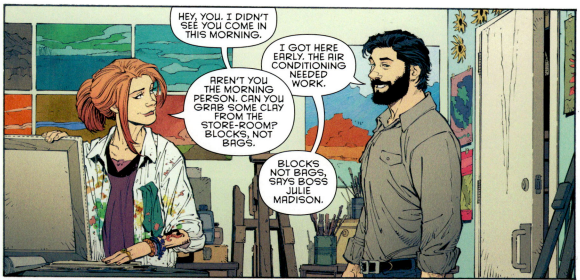

HEY, YOU. I DIDN'T SEE YOU COME IN THIS MORNING.

I GOT HERE EARLY. THE AIR CONDITIONING NEEDED WORK.

AREN'T YOU THE MORNING PERSON. CAN YOU GRAB SOME CLAY FROM THE STORE-ROOM? BLOCKS, NOT BAGS.

BLOCKS NOT BAGS, SAYS BOSS JULIE MADISON.

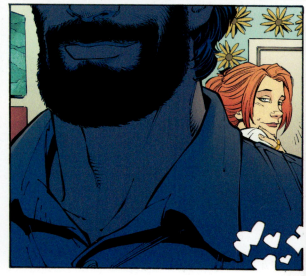

HELLO, BRUCE.

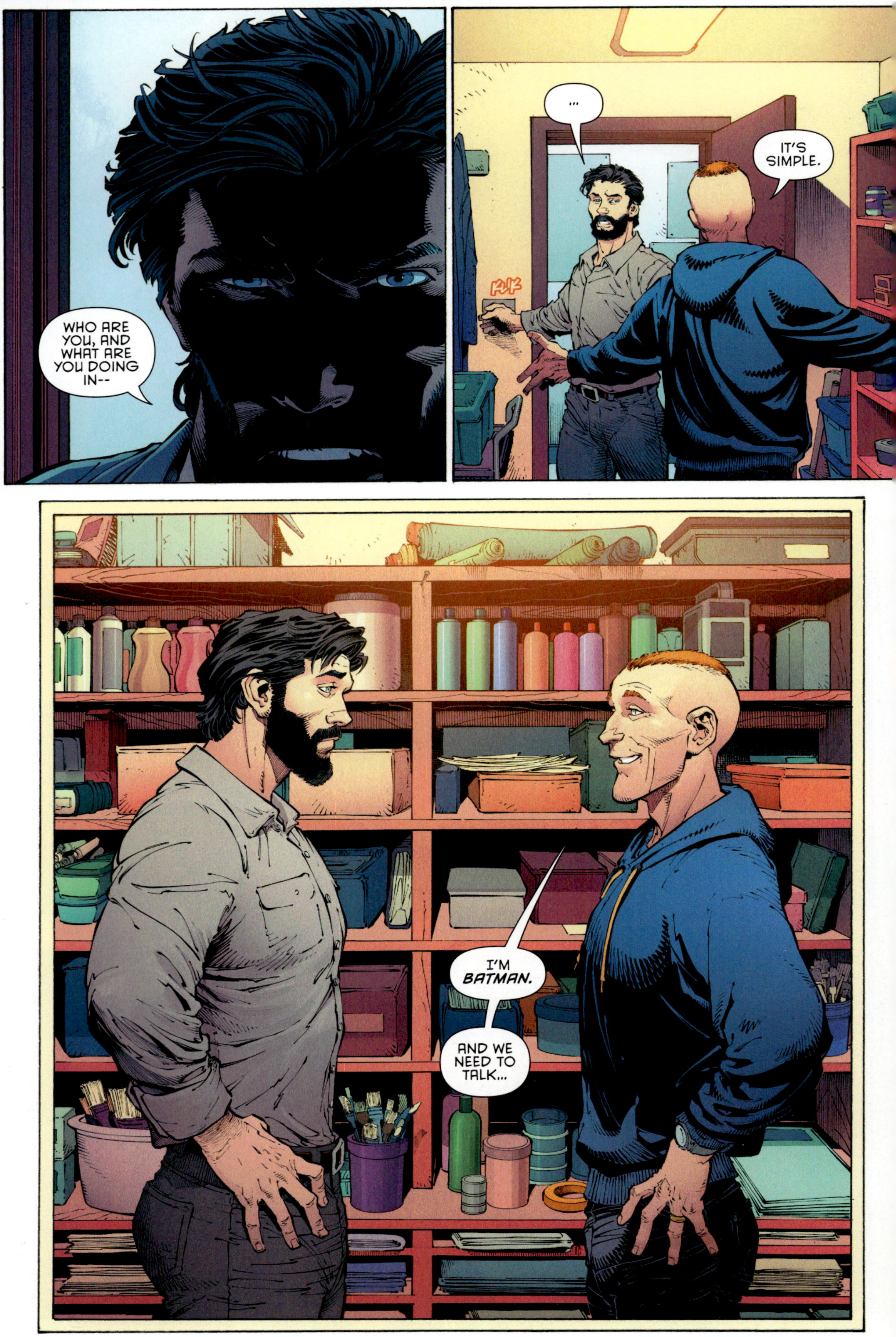
WHO ARE YOU, AND WHAT ARE YOU DOING IN--
...
IT'S SIMPLE.
KLIK
I'M *BATMAN.*
AND WE NEED TO TALK...

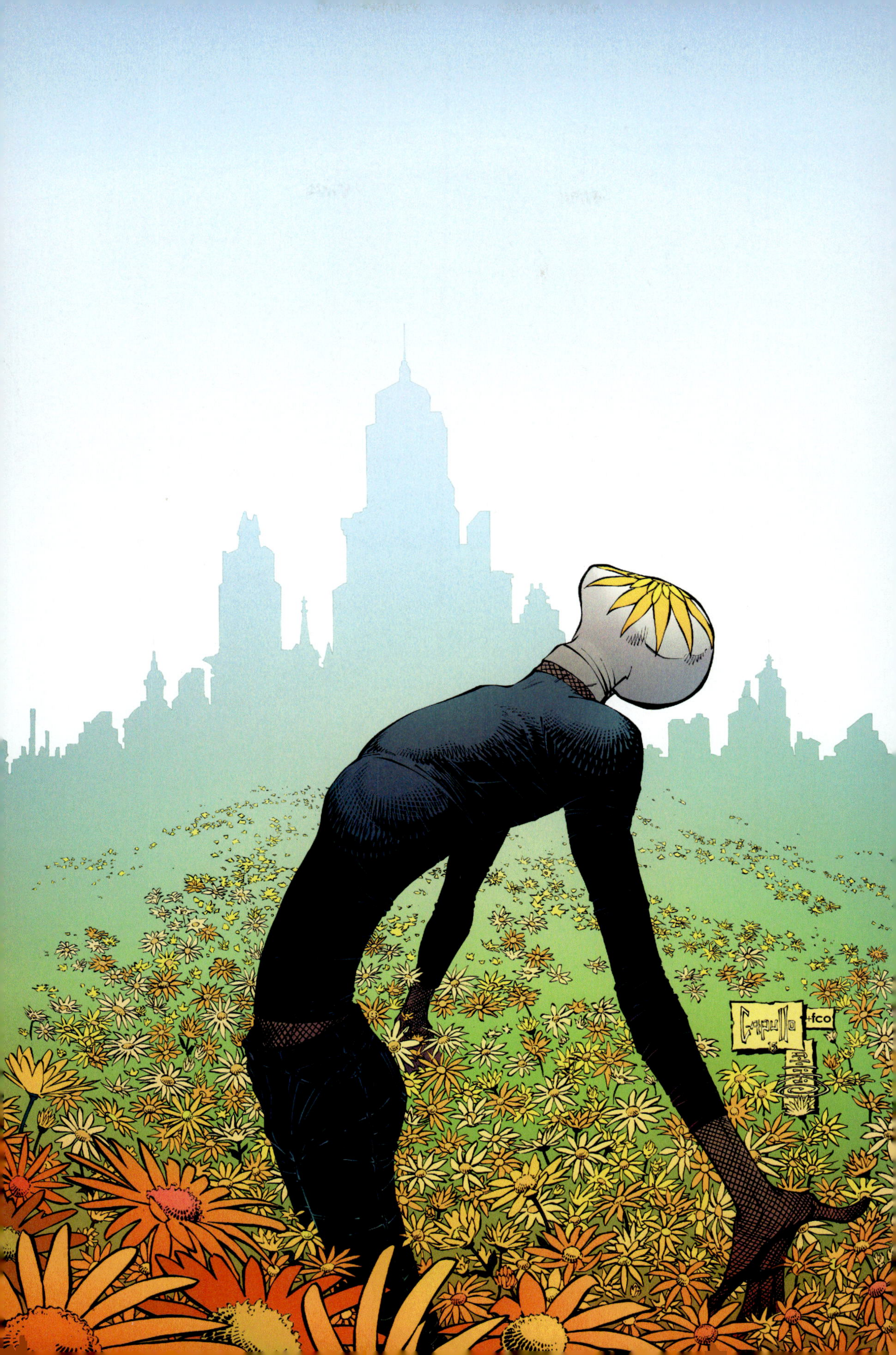
Capullo
+fco

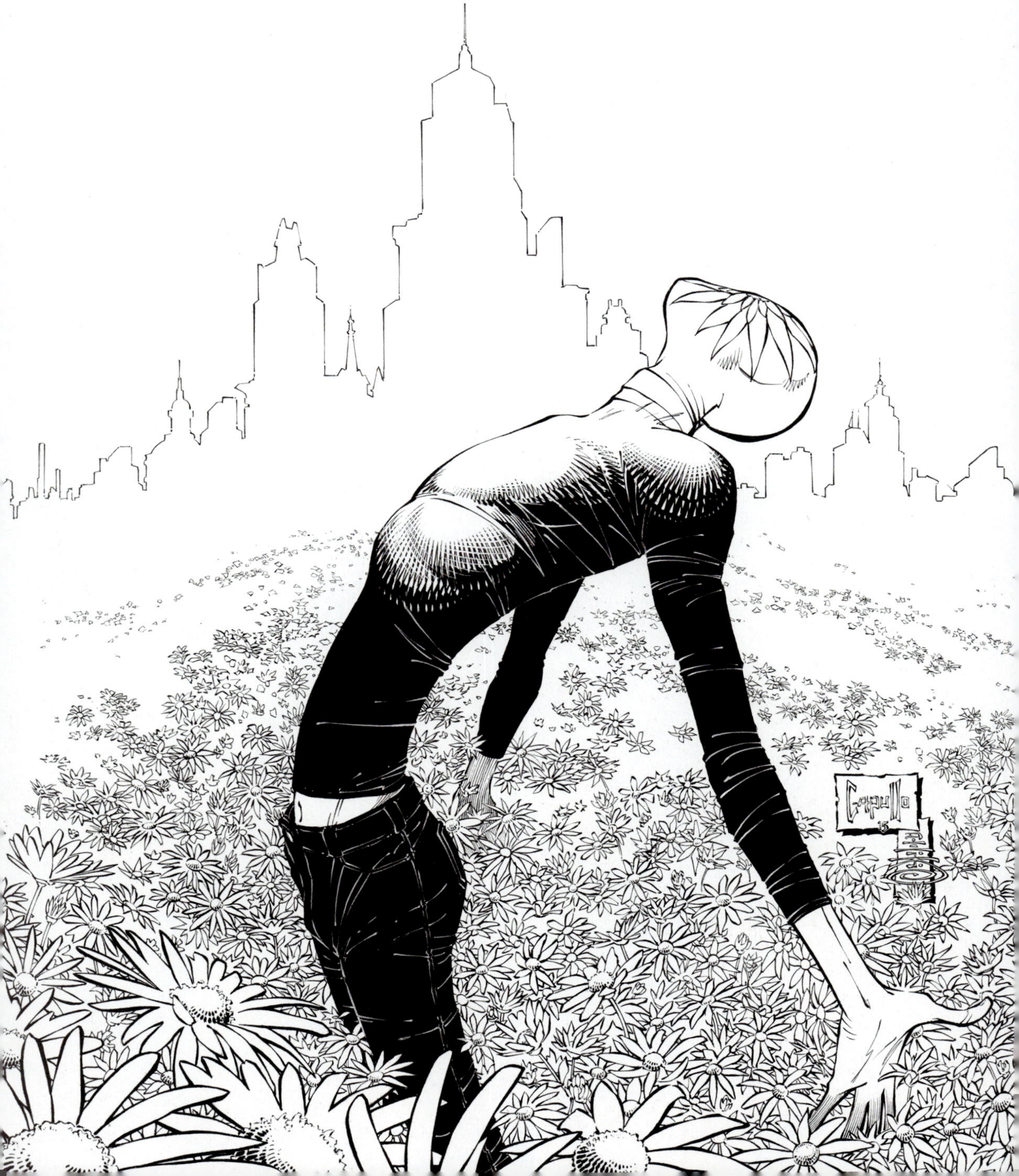

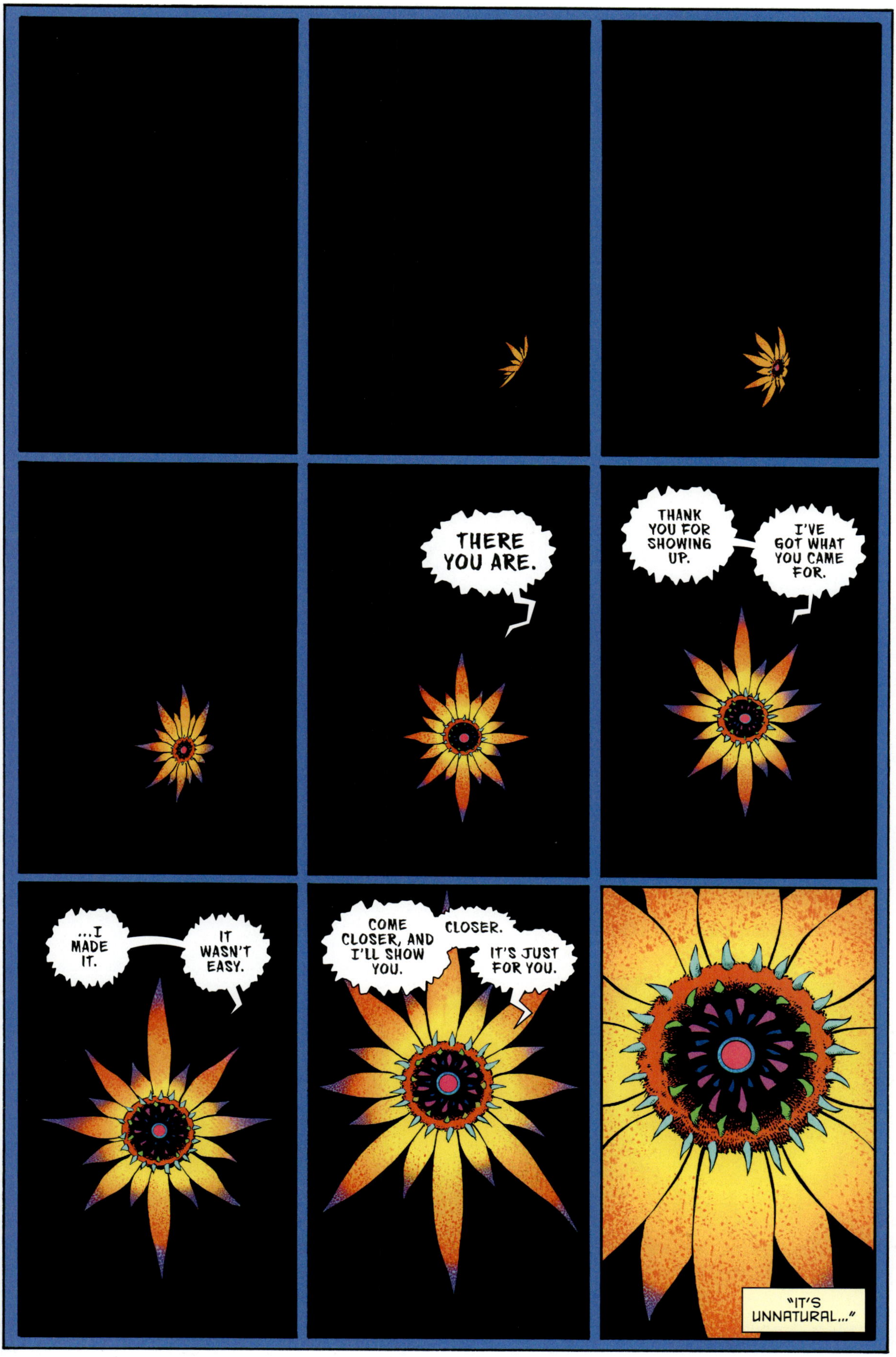
THERE YOU ARE.
THANK YOU FOR SHOWING UP.
I'VE GOT WHAT YOU CAME FOR.
...I MADE IT.
IT WASN'T EASY.
COME CLOSER, AND I'LL SHOW YOU.
CLOSER.
IT'S JUST FOR YOU.
"IT'S UNNATURAL..."

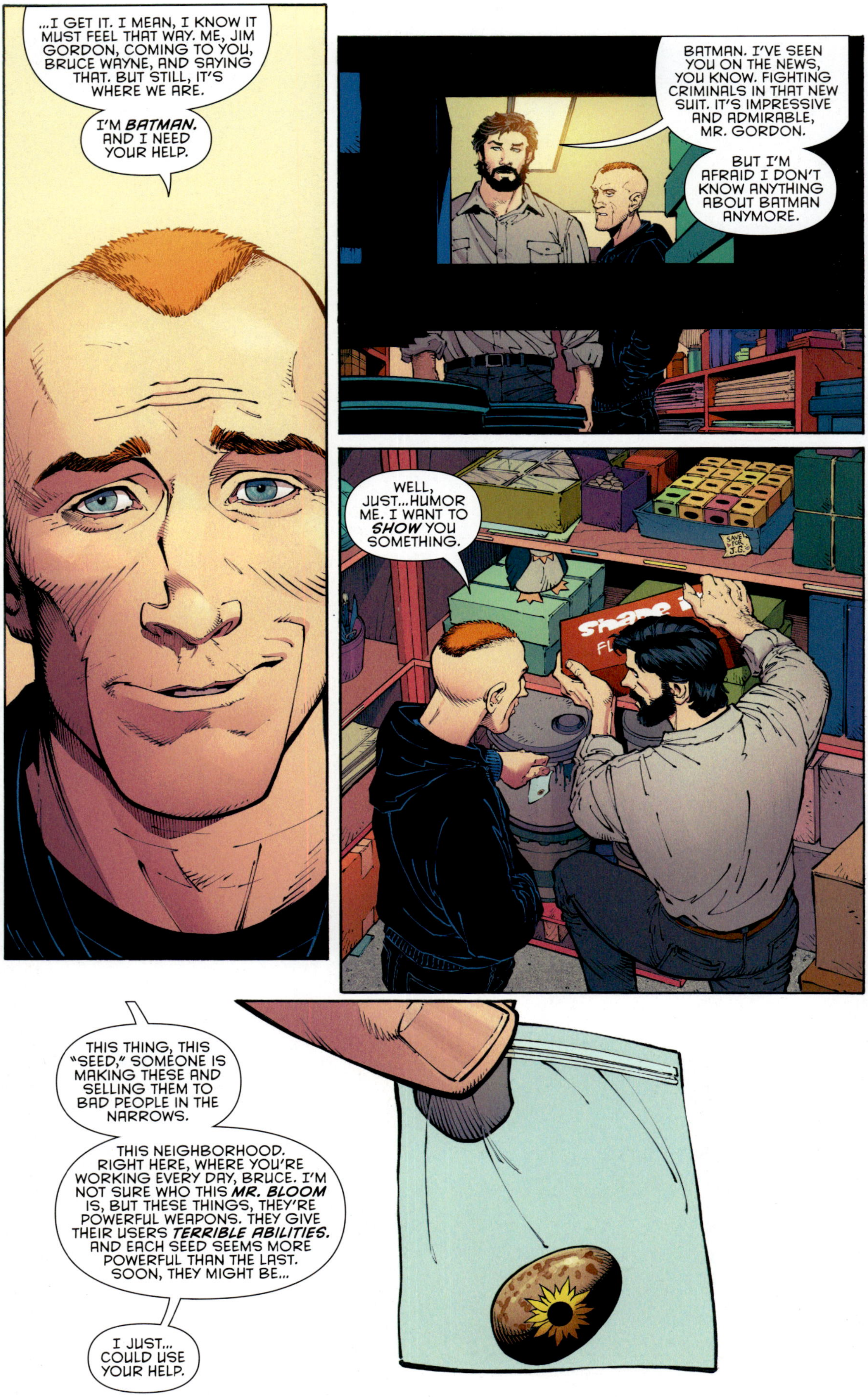
...I GET IT. I MEAN, I KNOW IT MUST FEEL THAT WAY. ME, JIM GORDON, COMING TO YOU, BRUCE WAYNE, AND SAYING THAT. BUT STILL, IT'S WHERE WE ARE.
I'M *BATMAN.* AND I NEED YOUR HELP.
BATMAN. I'VE SEEN YOU ON THE NEWS, YOU KNOW. FIGHTING CRIMINALS IN THAT NEW SUIT. IT'S IMPRESSIVE AND ADMIRABLE, MR. GORDON.
BUT I'M AFRAID I DON'T KNOW ANYTHING ABOUT BATMAN ANYMORE.
WELL, JUST...HUMOR ME. I WANT TO *SHOW* YOU SOMETHING.
SAVE FOR J.G.
THIS THING, THIS "SEED," SOMEONE IS MAKING THESE AND SELLING THEM TO BAD PEOPLE IN THE NARROWS.
THIS NEIGHBORHOOD. RIGHT HERE, WHERE YOU'RE WORKING EVERY DAY, BRUCE. I'M NOT SURE WHO THIS *MR. BLOOM* IS, BUT THESE THINGS, THEY'RE POWERFUL WEAPONS. THEY GIVE THEIR USERS *TERRIBLE ABILITIES.* AND EACH SEED SEEMS MORE POWERFUL THAN THE LAST. SOON, THEY MIGHT BE...
I JUST... COULD USE YOUR HELP.

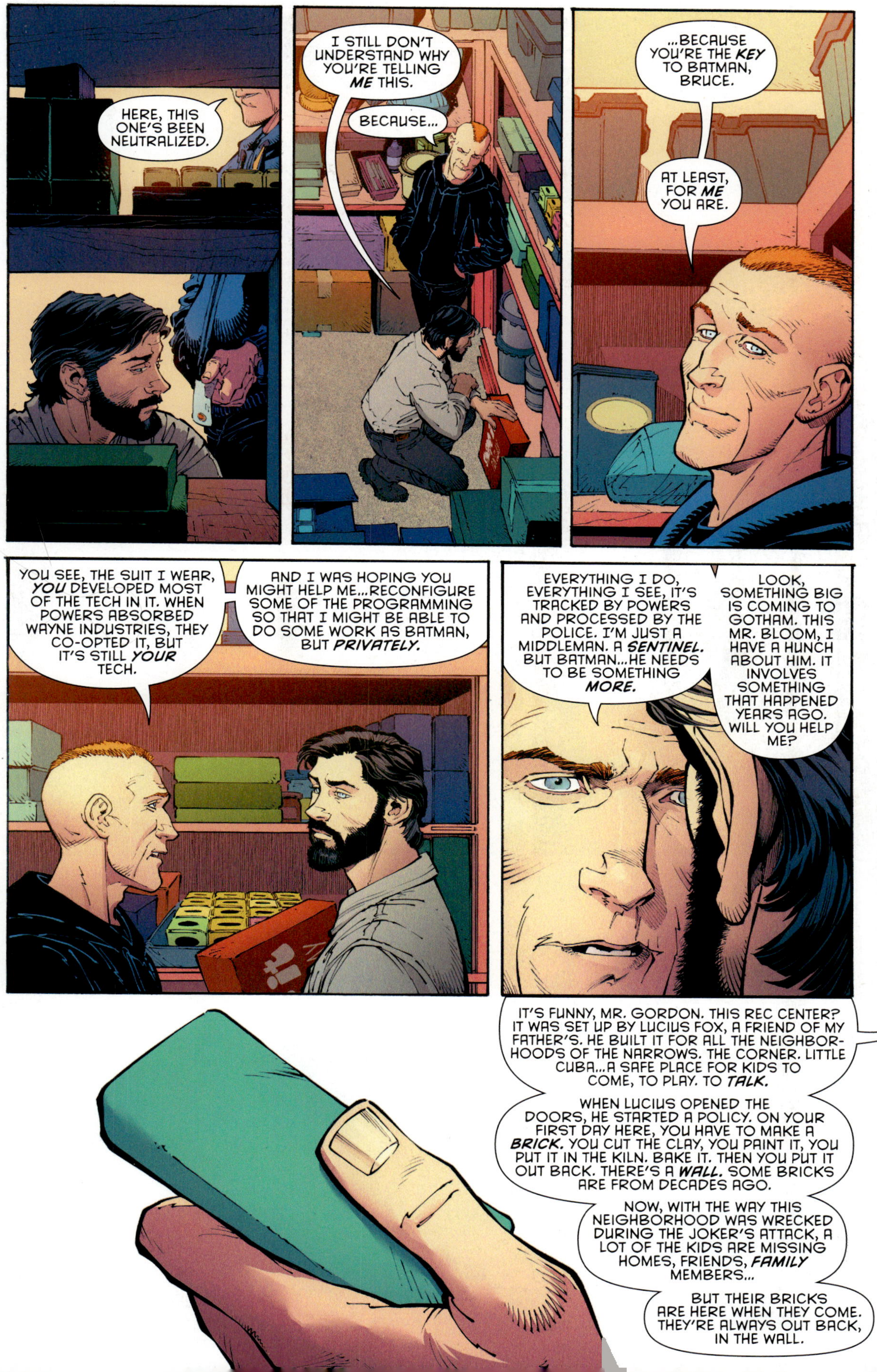
HERE, THIS ONE'S BEEN NEUTRALIZED.
I STILL DON'T UNDERSTAND WHY YOU'RE TELLING ME THIS.
BECAUSE...
...BECAUSE YOU'RE THE KEY TO BATMAN, BRUCE.
AT LEAST, FOR ME YOU ARE.
YOU SEE, THE SUIT I WEAR, YOU DEVELOPED MOST OF THE TECH IN IT. WHEN POWERS ABSORBED WAYNE INDUSTRIES, THEY CO-OPTED IT, BUT IT'S STILL YOUR TECH.
AND I WAS HOPING YOU MIGHT HELP ME...RECONFIGURE SOME OF THE PROGRAMMING SO THAT I MIGHT BE ABLE TO DO SOME WORK AS BATMAN, BUT PRIVATELY.
EVERYTHING I DO, EVERYTHING I SEE, IT'S TRACKED BY POWERS AND PROCESSED BY THE POLICE. I'M JUST A MIDDLEMAN. A SENTINEL. BUT BATMAN...HE NEEDS TO BE SOMETHING MORE.
LOOK, SOMETHING BIG IS COMING TO GOTHAM. THIS MR. BLOOM, I HAVE A HUNCH ABOUT HIM. IT INVOLVES SOMETHING THAT HAPPENED YEARS AGO. WILL YOU HELP ME?
IT'S FUNNY, MR. GORDON. THIS REC CENTER? IT WAS SET UP BY LUCIUS FOX, A FRIEND OF MY FATHER'S. HE BUILT IT FOR ALL THE NEIGHBORHOODS OF THE NARROWS. THE CORNER. LITTLE CUBA...A SAFE PLACE FOR KIDS TO COME, TO PLAY. TO TALK.
WHEN LUCIUS OPENED THE DOORS, HE STARTED A POLICY. ON YOUR FIRST DAY HERE, YOU HAVE TO MAKE A BRICK. YOU CUT THE CLAY, YOU PAINT IT, YOU PUT IT IN THE KILN. BAKE IT. THEN YOU PUT IT OUT BACK. THERE'S A WALL. SOME BRICKS ARE FROM DECADES AGO.
NOW, WITH THE WAY THIS NEIGHBORHOOD WAS WRECKED DURING THE JOKER'S ATTACK, A LOT OF THE KIDS ARE MISSING HOMES, FRIENDS, FAMILY MEMBERS...
BUT THEIR BRICKS ARE HERE WHEN THEY COME. THEY'RE ALWAYS OUT BACK, IN THE WALL.

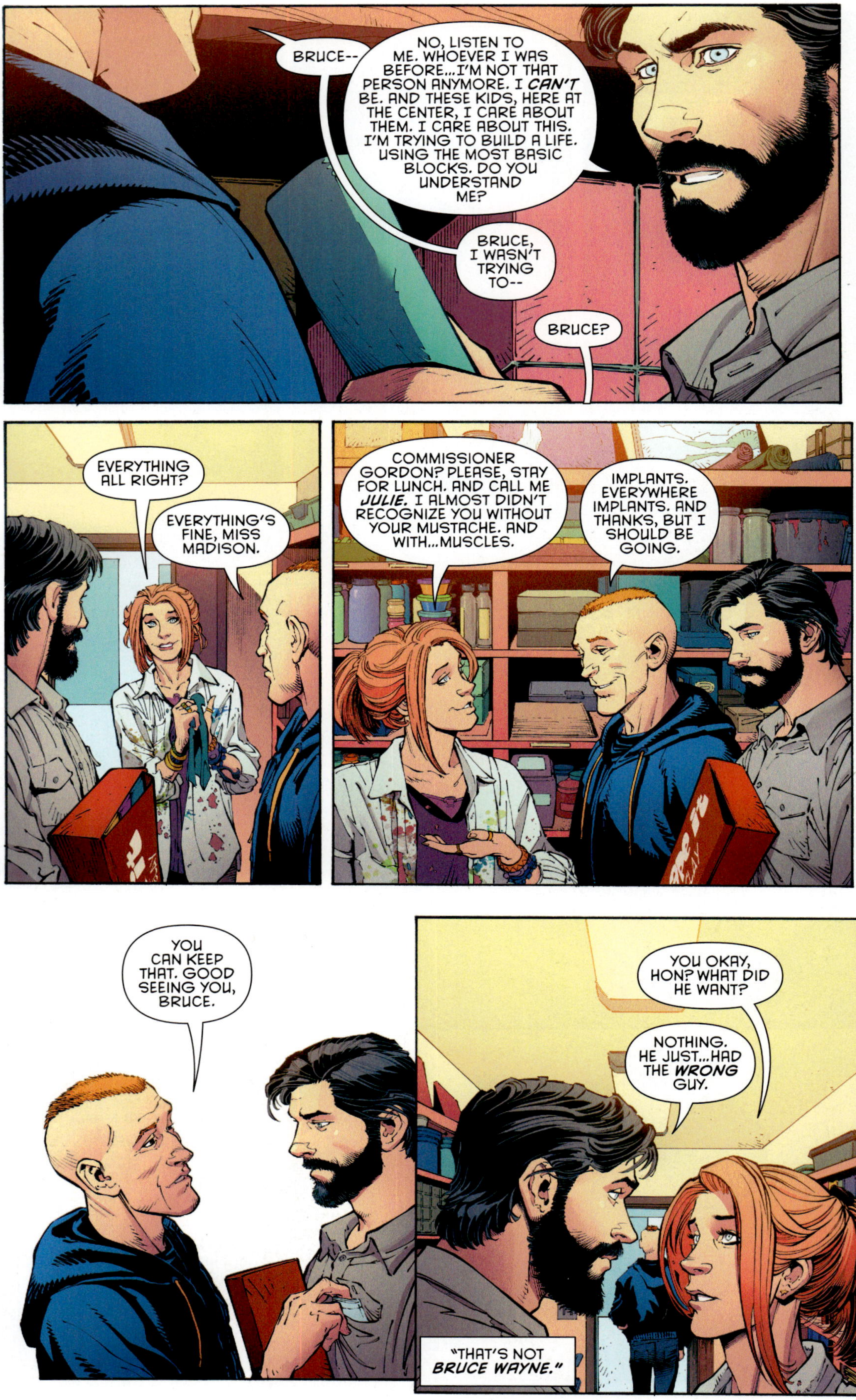
BRUCE--
NO, LISTEN TO ME. WHOEVER I WAS BEFORE...I'M NOT THAT PERSON ANYMORE. I CAN'T BE. AND THESE KIDS, HERE AT THE CENTER, I CARE ABOUT THEM. I CARE ABOUT THIS. I'M TRYING TO BUILD A LIFE. USING THE MOST BASIC BLOCKS. DO YOU UNDERSTAND ME?
BRUCE, I WASN'T TRYING TO--
BRUCE?
EVERYTHING ALL RIGHT?
EVERYTHING'S FINE, MISS MADISON.
COMMISSIONER GORDON? PLEASE, STAY FOR LUNCH. AND CALL ME JULIE. I ALMOST DIDN'T RECOGNIZE YOU WITHOUT YOUR MUSTACHE. AND WITH...MUSCLES.
IMPLANTS. EVERYWHERE IMPLANTS. AND THANKS, BUT I SHOULD BE GOING.
YOU CAN KEEP THAT. GOOD SEEING YOU, BRUCE.
YOU OKAY, HON? WHAT DID HE WANT?
NOTHING. HE JUST...HAD THE WRONG GUY.
"THAT'S NOT BRUCE WAYNE."

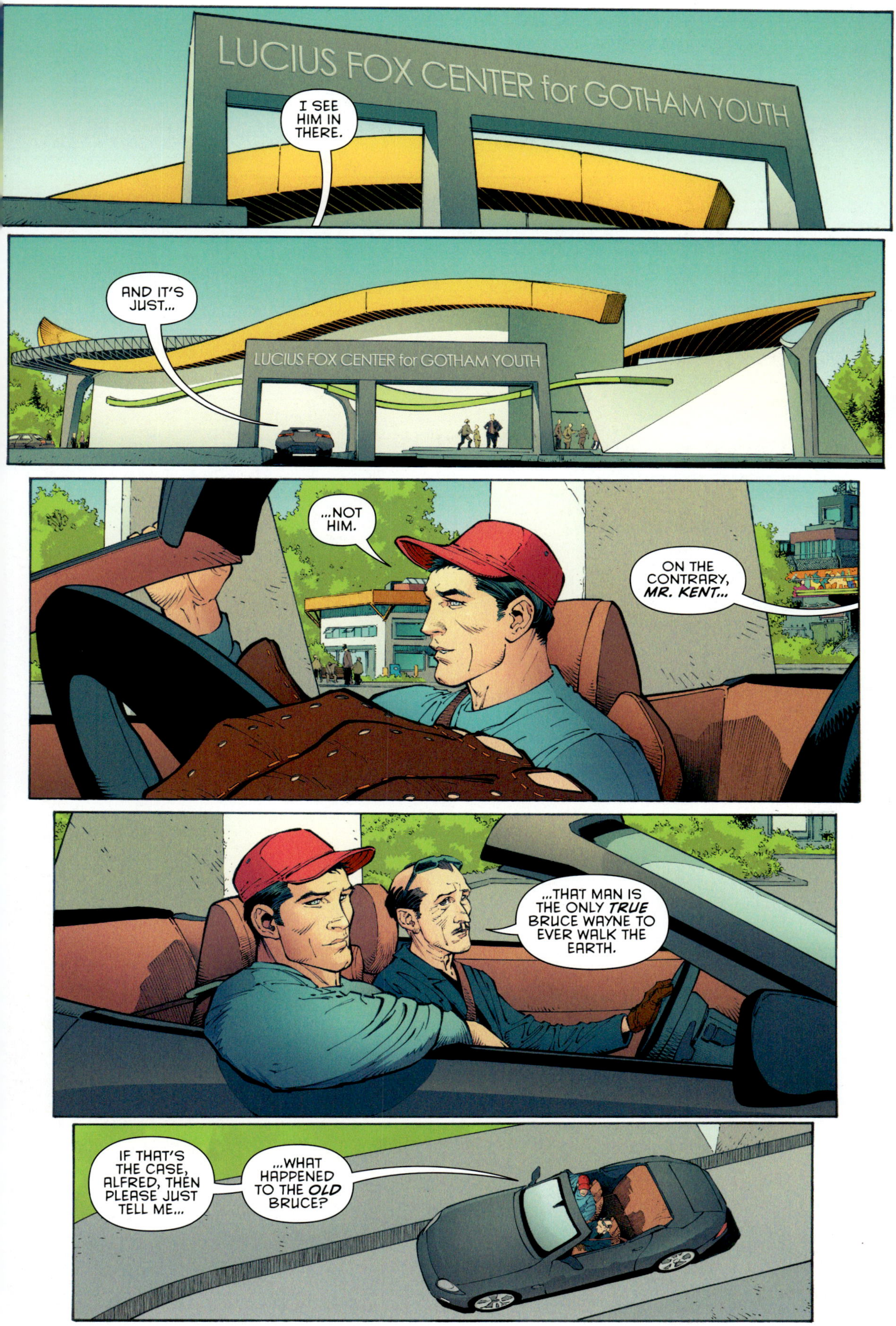
LUCIUS FOX CENTER for GOTHAM YOUTH
I SEE HIM IN THERE.
AND IT'S JUST...
LUCIUS FOX CENTER for GOTHAM YOUTH
...NOT HIM.
ON THE CONTRARY, MR. KENT...
...THAT MAN IS THE ONLY TRUE BRUCE WAYNE TO EVER WALK THE EARTH.
IF THAT'S THE CASE, ALFRED, THEN PLEASE JUST TELL ME...
...WHAT HAPPENED TO THE OLD BRUCE?

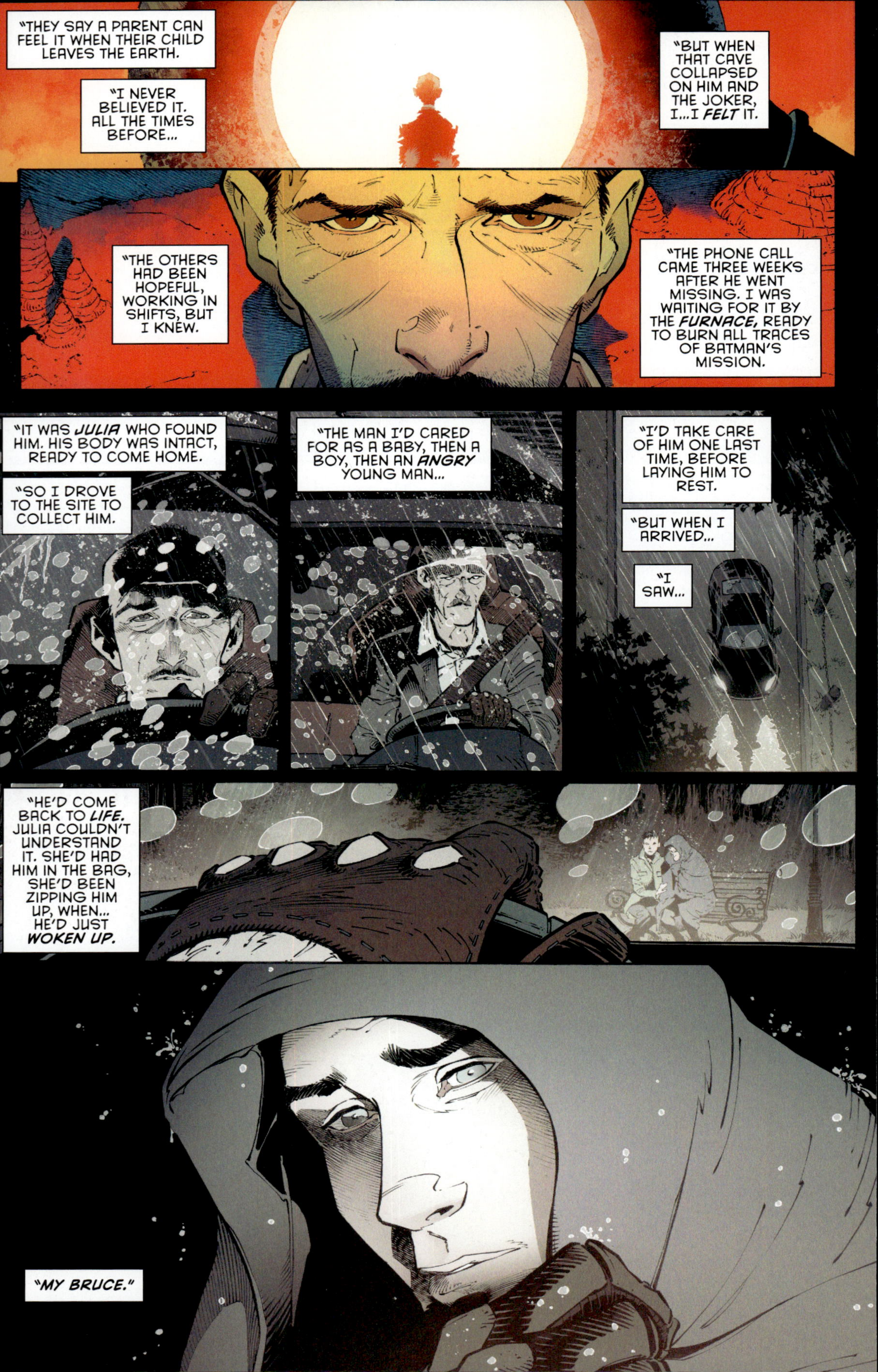
"THEY SAY A PARENT CAN FEEL IT WHEN THEIR CHILD LEAVES THE EARTH.
"I NEVER BELIEVED IT. ALL THE TIMES BEFORE...
"BUT WHEN THAT CAVE COLLAPSED ON HIM AND THE JOKER, I...I FELT IT.
"THE OTHERS HAD BEEN HOPEFUL, WORKING IN SHIFTS, BUT I KNEW.
"THE PHONE CALL CAME THREE WEEKS AFTER HE WENT MISSING. I WAS WAITING FOR IT BY THE FURNACE, READY TO BURN ALL TRACES OF BATMAN'S MISSION.
"IT WAS JULIA WHO FOUND HIM. HIS BODY WAS INTACT, READY TO COME HOME.
"SO I DROVE TO THE SITE TO COLLECT HIM.
"THE MAN I'D CARED FOR AS A BABY, THEN A BOY, THEN AN ANGRY YOUNG MAN...
"I'D TAKE CARE OF HIM ONE LAST TIME, BEFORE LAYING HIM TO REST.
"BUT WHEN I ARRIVED...
"I SAW...
"HE'D COME BACK TO LIFE. JULIA COULDN'T UNDERSTAND IT. SHE'D HAD HIM IN THE BAG, SHE'D BEEN ZIPPING HIM UP, WHEN... HE'D JUST WOKEN UP.
"MY BRUCE."

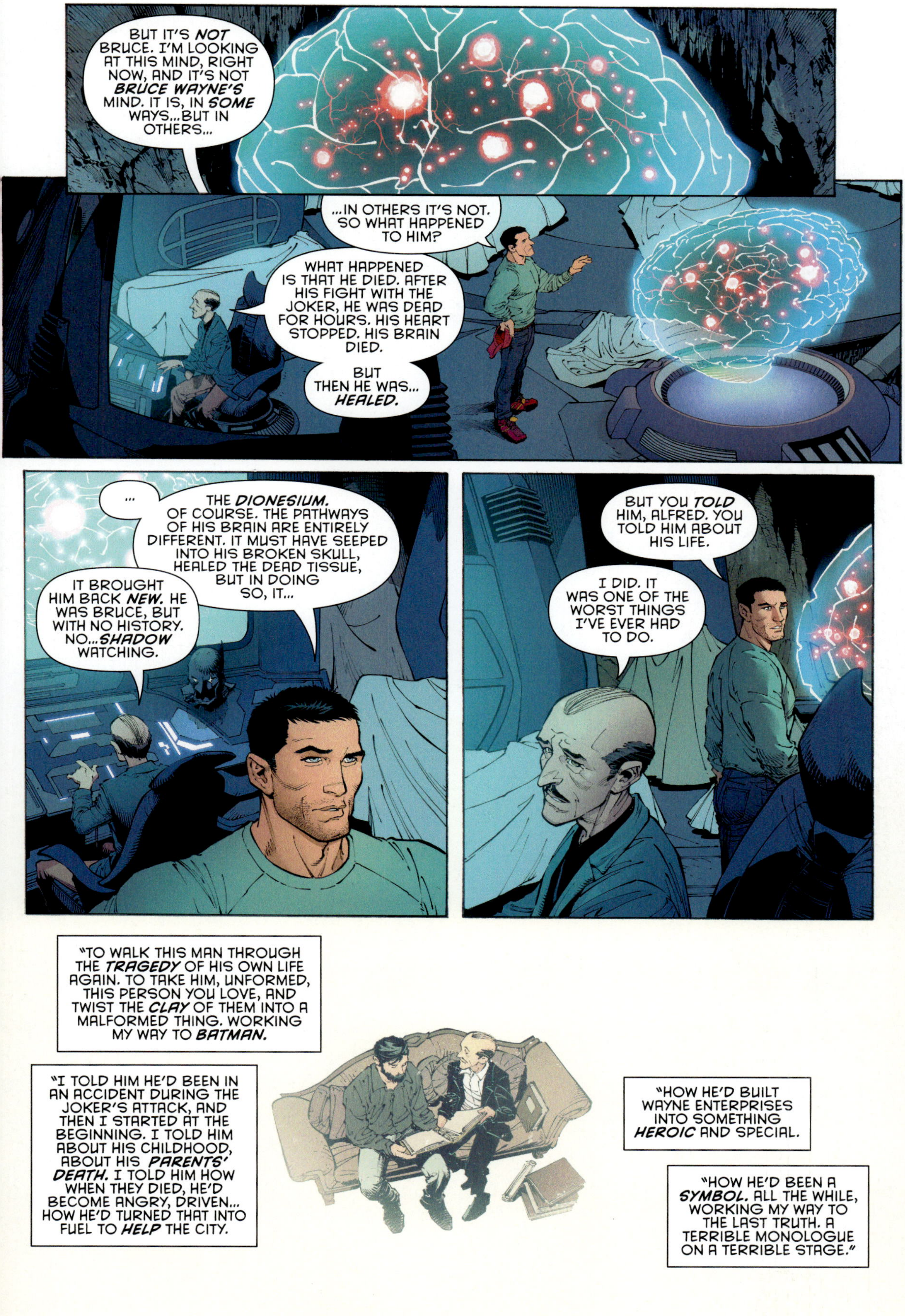
BUT IT'S NOT BRUCE. I'M LOOKING AT THIS MIND, RIGHT NOW, AND IT'S NOT BRUCE WAYNE'S MIND. IT IS, IN SOME WAYS...BUT IN OTHERS...
...IN OTHERS IT'S NOT. SO WHAT HAPPENED TO HIM?
WHAT HAPPENED IS THAT HE DIED. AFTER HIS FIGHT WITH THE JOKER, HE WAS DEAD FOR HOURS. HIS HEART STOPPED. HIS BRAIN DIED.
BUT THEN HE WAS... HEALED.
...
THE DIONESIUM. OF COURSE. THE PATHWAYS OF HIS BRAIN ARE ENTIRELY DIFFERENT. IT MUST HAVE SEEPED INTO HIS BROKEN SKULL, HEALED THE DEAD TISSUE, BUT IN DOING SO, IT...
IT BROUGHT HIM BACK NEW. HE WAS BRUCE, BUT WITH NO HISTORY. NO...SHADOW WATCHING.
BUT YOU TOLD HIM, ALFRED. YOU TOLD HIM ABOUT HIS LIFE.
I DID. IT WAS ONE OF THE WORST THINGS I'VE EVER HAD TO DO.
"TO WALK THIS MAN THROUGH THE TRAGEDY OF HIS OWN LIFE AGAIN. TO TAKE HIM, UNFORMED, THIS PERSON YOU LOVE, AND TWIST THE CLAY OF THEM INTO A MALFORMED THING. WORKING MY WAY TO BATMAN.
"I TOLD HIM HE'D BEEN IN AN ACCIDENT DURING THE JOKER'S ATTACK, AND THEN I STARTED AT THE BEGINNING. I TOLD HIM ABOUT HIS CHILDHOOD, ABOUT HIS PARENTS' DEATH. I TOLD HIM HOW WHEN THEY DIED, HE'D BECOME ANGRY, DRIVEN... HOW HE'D TURNED THAT INTO FUEL TO HELP THE CITY.
"HOW HE'D BUILT WAYNE ENTERPRISES INTO SOMETHING HEROIC AND SPECIAL.
"HOW HE'D BEEN A SYMBOL. ALL THE WHILE, WORKING MY WAY TO THE LAST TRUTH. A TERRIBLE MONOLOGUE ON A TERRIBLE STAGE."

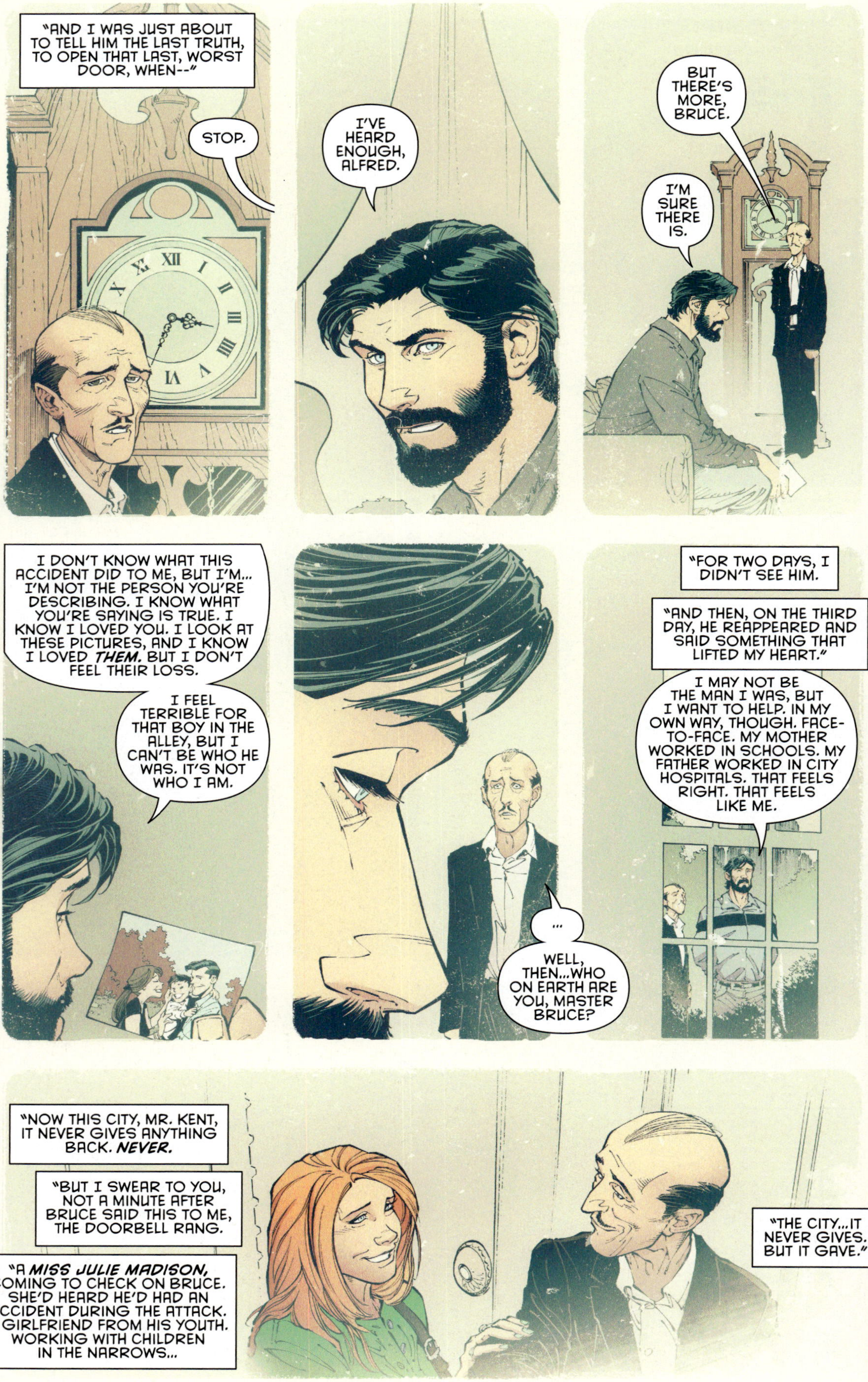
"AND I WAS JUST ABOUT TO TELL HIM THE LAST TRUTH, TO OPEN THAT LAST, WORST DOOR, WHEN--"
STOP.
I'VE HEARD ENOUGH, ALFRED.
BUT THERE'S MORE, BRUCE.
I'M SURE THERE IS.
I DON'T KNOW WHAT THIS ACCIDENT DID TO ME, BUT I'M... I'M NOT THE PERSON YOU'RE DESCRIBING. I KNOW WHAT YOU'RE SAYING IS TRUE. I KNOW I LOVED YOU. I LOOK AT THESE PICTURES, AND I KNOW I LOVED *THEM.* BUT I DON'T FEEL THEIR LOSS.
I FEEL TERRIBLE FOR THAT BOY IN THE ALLEY, BUT I CAN'T BE WHO HE WAS. IT'S NOT WHO I AM.
...
WELL, THEN...WHO ON EARTH ARE YOU, MASTER BRUCE?
"FOR TWO DAYS, I DIDN'T SEE HIM.
"AND THEN, ON THE THIRD DAY, HE REAPPEARED AND SAID SOMETHING THAT LIFTED MY HEART."
I MAY NOT BE THE MAN I WAS, BUT I WANT TO HELP. IN MY OWN WAY, THOUGH. FACE-TO-FACE. MY MOTHER WORKED IN SCHOOLS. MY FATHER WORKED IN CITY HOSPITALS. THAT FEELS RIGHT. THAT FEELS LIKE ME.
"NOW THIS CITY, MR. KENT, IT NEVER GIVES ANYTHING BACK. ***NEVER.***
"BUT I SWEAR TO YOU, NOT A MINUTE AFTER BRUCE SAID THIS TO ME, THE DOORBELL RANG.
"A ***MISS JULIE MADISON,*** COMING TO CHECK ON BRUCE. SHE'D HEARD HE'D HAD AN ACCIDENT DURING THE ATTACK. A GIRLFRIEND FROM HIS YOUTH. WORKING WITH CHILDREN IN THE NARROWS...
"THE CITY...IT NEVER GIVES. BUT IT GAVE."

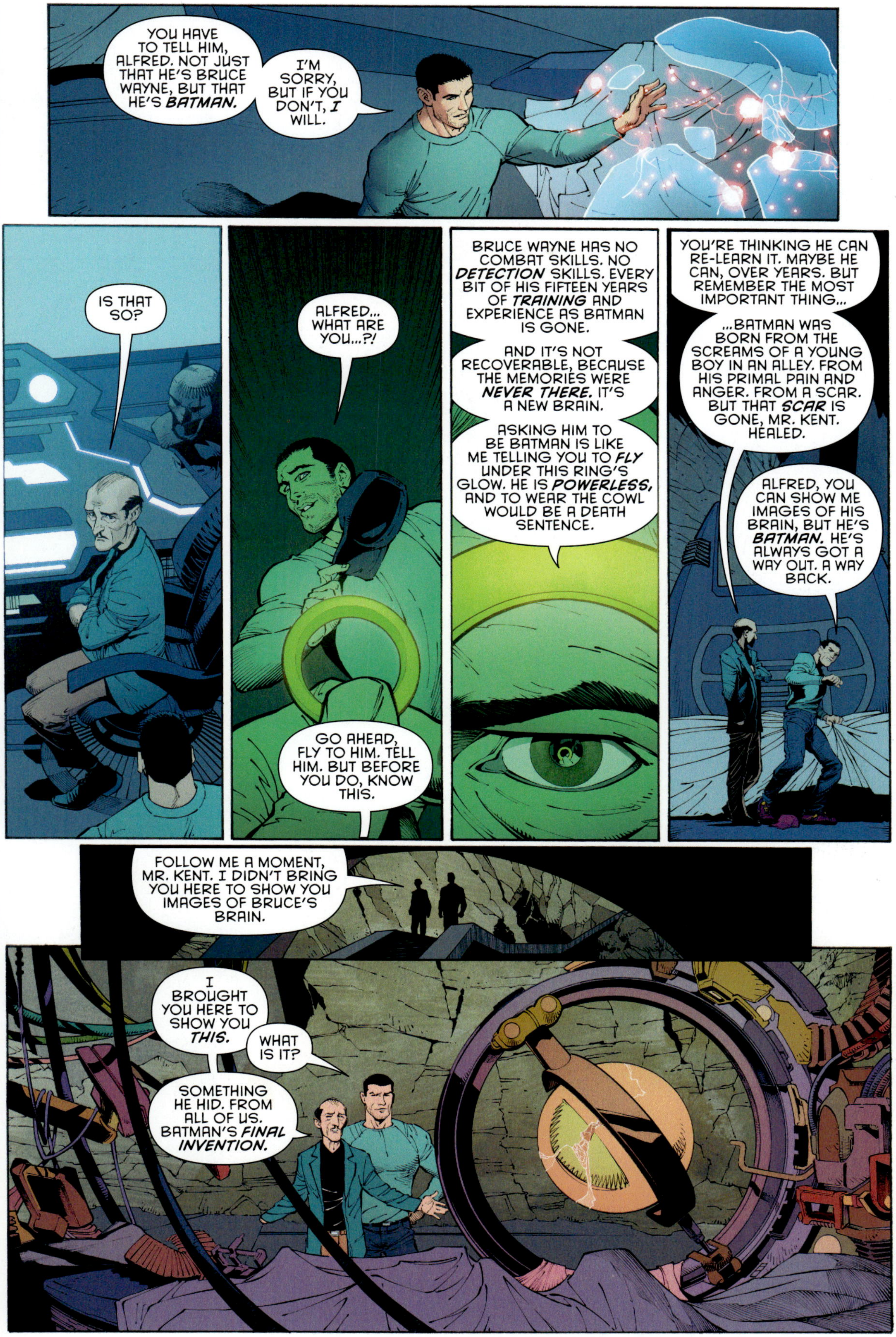
YOU HAVE TO TELL HIM, ALFRED. NOT JUST THAT HE'S BRUCE WAYNE, BUT THAT HE'S BATMAN.
I'M SORRY, BUT IF YOU DON'T, I WILL.
IS THAT SO?
ALFRED... WHAT ARE YOU...?!
GO AHEAD, FLY TO HIM. TELL HIM. BUT BEFORE YOU DO, KNOW THIS.
BRUCE WAYNE HAS NO COMBAT SKILLS. NO DETECTION SKILLS. EVERY BIT OF HIS FIFTEEN YEARS OF TRAINING AND EXPERIENCE AS BATMAN IS GONE.
AND IT'S NOT RECOVERABLE, BECAUSE THE MEMORIES WERE NEVER THERE. IT'S A NEW BRAIN.
ASKING HIM TO BE BATMAN IS LIKE ME TELLING YOU TO FLY UNDER THIS RING'S GLOW. HE IS POWERLESS, AND TO WEAR THE COWL WOULD BE A DEATH SENTENCE.
YOU'RE THINKING HE CAN RE-LEARN IT. MAYBE HE CAN, OVER YEARS. BUT REMEMBER THE MOST IMPORTANT THING...
...BATMAN WAS BORN FROM THE SCREAMS OF A YOUNG BOY IN AN ALLEY. FROM HIS PRIMAL PAIN AND ANGER. FROM A SCAR. BUT THAT SCAR IS GONE, MR. KENT. HEALED.
ALFRED, YOU CAN SHOW ME IMAGES OF HIS BRAIN, BUT HE'S BATMAN. HE'S ALWAYS GOT A WAY OUT. A WAY BACK.
FOLLOW ME A MOMENT, MR. KENT. I DIDN'T BRING YOU HERE TO SHOW YOU IMAGES OF BRUCE'S BRAIN.
I BROUGHT YOU HERE TO SHOW YOU THIS.
WHAT IS IT?
SOMETHING HE HID. FROM ALL OF US. BATMAN'S FINAL INVENTION.

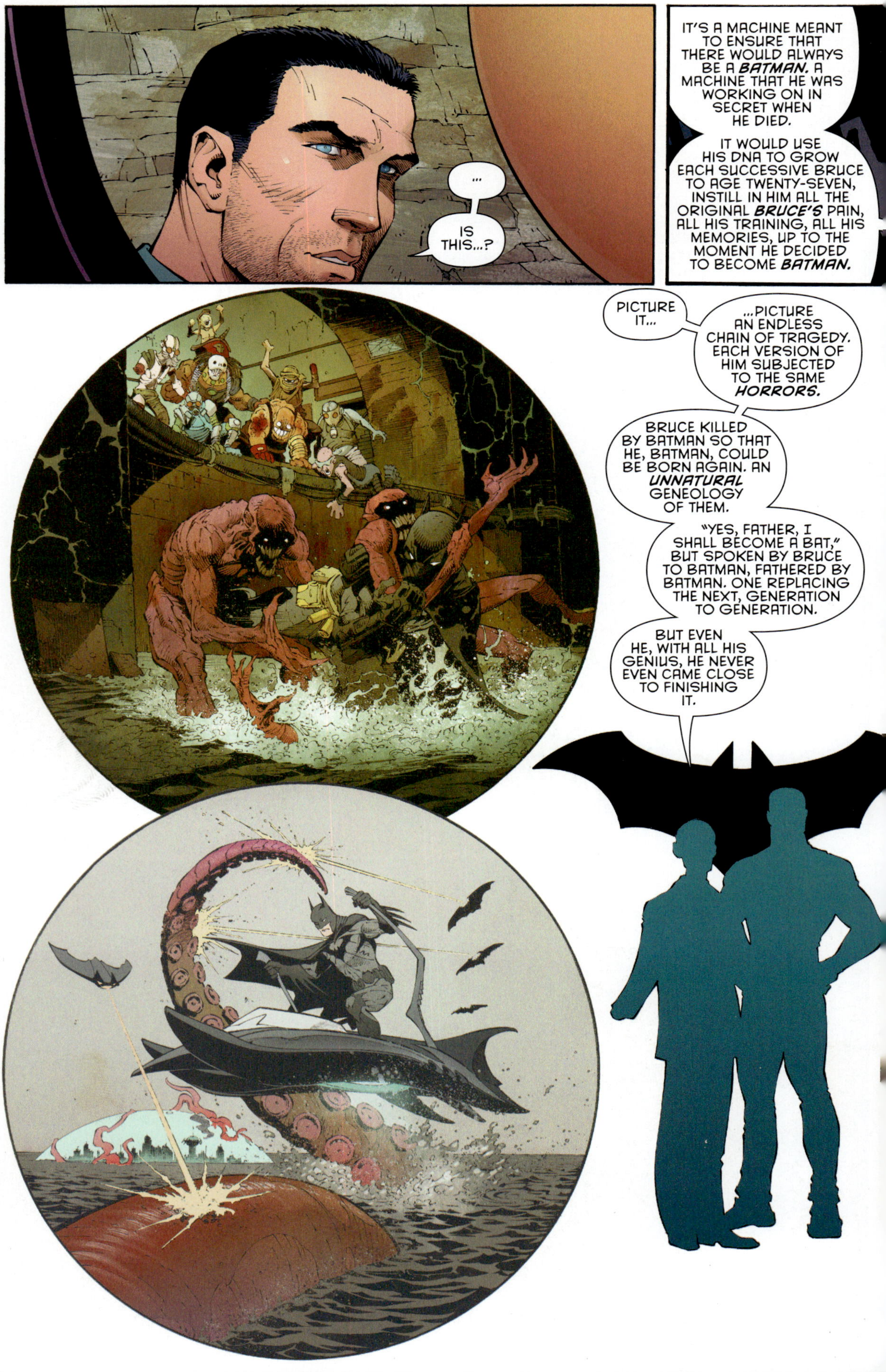
...
IS THIS...?
IT'S A MACHINE MEANT TO ENSURE THAT THERE WOULD ALWAYS BE A BATMAN. A MACHINE THAT HE WAS WORKING ON IN SECRET WHEN HE DIED.
IT WOULD USE HIS DNA TO GROW EACH SUCCESSIVE BRUCE TO AGE TWENTY-SEVEN, INSTILL IN HIM ALL THE ORIGINAL BRUCE'S PAIN, ALL HIS TRAINING, ALL HIS MEMORIES, UP TO THE MOMENT HE DECIDED TO BECOME BATMAN.
PICTURE IT...
...PICTURE AN ENDLESS CHAIN OF TRAGEDY. EACH VERSION OF HIM SUBJECTED TO THE SAME HORRORS.
BRUCE KILLED BY BATMAN SO THAT HE, BATMAN, COULD BE BORN AGAIN. AN UNNATURAL GENEOLOGY OF THEM.
"YES, FATHER, I SHALL BECOME A BAT," BUT SPOKEN BY BRUCE TO BATMAN, FATHERED BY BATMAN. ONE REPLACING THE NEXT, GENERATION TO GENERATION.
BUT EVEN HE, WITH ALL HIS GENIUS, HE NEVER EVEN CAME CLOSE TO FINISHING IT.

BECAUSE HE WASN'T *MEANT* TO LIVE FOREVER.

THE CIRCLE WAS MEANT TO BE BROKEN, AND NOW IT HAS BEEN.

DON'T YOU SEE, CLARK? *BATMAN DIED. AND BRUCE WAYNE CAME BACK.*

ALFRED...

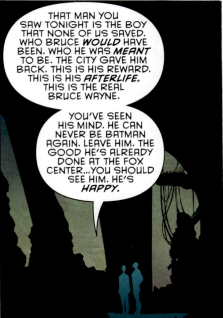

THAT MAN YOU SAW TONIGHT IS THE BOY THAT NONE OF US SAVED. WHO BRUCE *WOULD* HAVE BEEN. WHO HE WAS *MEANT* TO BE. THE CITY GAVE HIM BACK. THIS IS HIS REWARD. THIS IS HIS *AFTERLIFE.* THIS IS THE REAL BRUCE WAYNE.

YOU'VE SEEN HIS MIND. HE CAN NEVER BE BATMAN AGAIN. LEAVE HIM. THE GOOD HE'S ALREADY DONE AT THE FOX CENTER...YOU SHOULD SEE HIM. HE'S *HAPPY.*

LET HIM LIVE, MR. KENT. CONSIGN THE REST TO THE *FURNACE.* PLEASE...

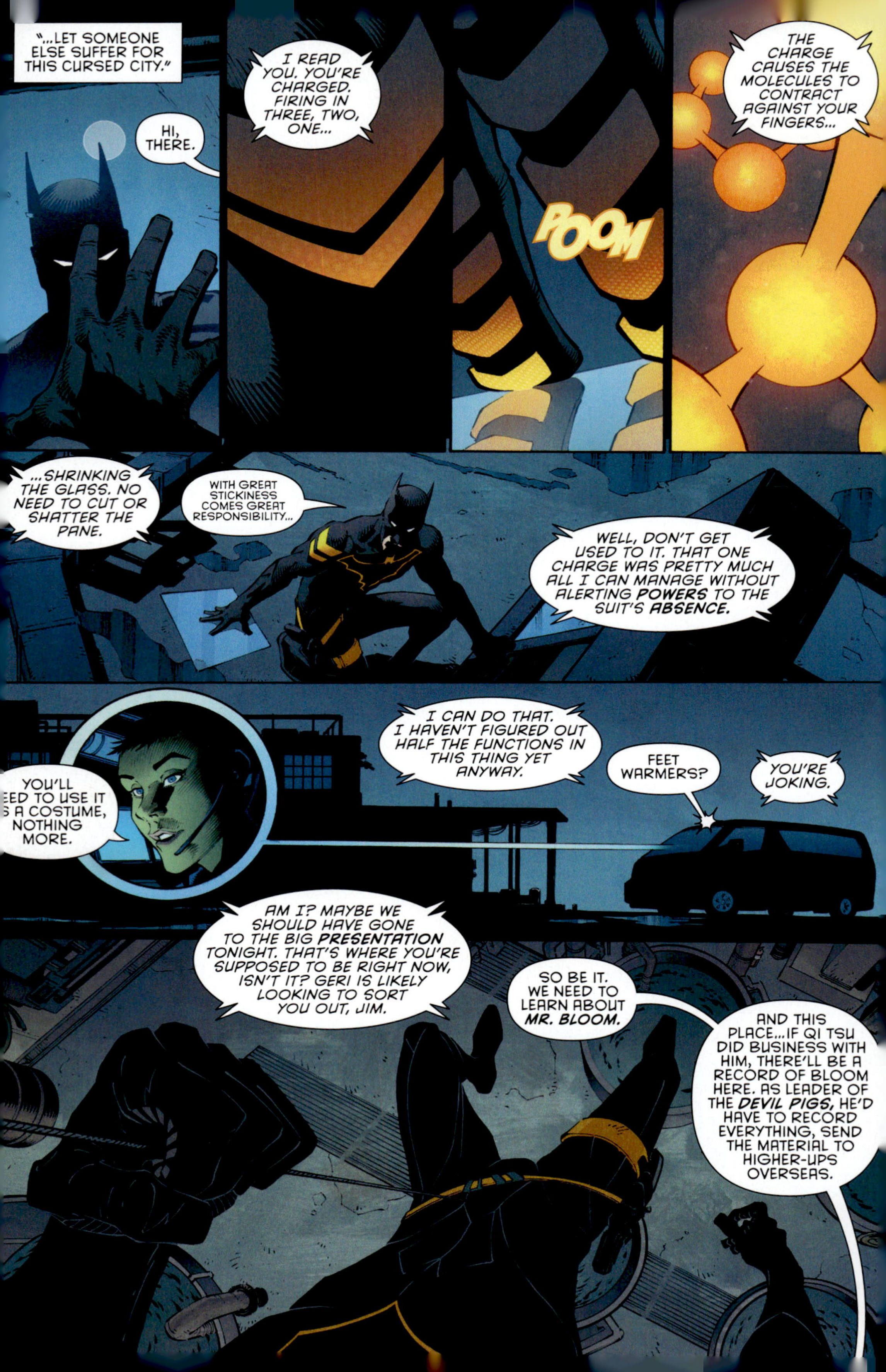
"...LET SOMEONE ELSE SUFFER FOR THIS CURSED CITY."
HI, THERE.
I READ YOU. YOU'RE CHARGED. FIRING IN THREE, TWO, ONE...
POOM
THE CHARGE CAUSES THE MOLECULES TO CONTRACT AGAINST YOUR FINGERS...
...SHRINKING THE GLASS. NO NEED TO CUT OR SHATTER THE PANE.
WITH GREAT STICKINESS COMES GREAT RESPONSIBILITY...
WELL, DON'T GET USED TO IT. THAT ONE CHARGE WAS PRETTY MUCH ALL I CAN MANAGE WITHOUT ALERTING POWERS TO THE SUIT'S ABSENCE.
YOU'LL EED TO USE IT S A COSTUME, NOTHING MORE.
I CAN DO THAT. I HAVEN'T FIGURED OUT HALF THE FUNCTIONS IN THIS THING YET ANYWAY.
FEET WARMERS?
YOU'RE JOKING.
AM I? MAYBE WE SHOULD HAVE GONE TO THE BIG PRESENTATION TONIGHT. THAT'S WHERE YOU'RE SUPPOSED TO BE RIGHT NOW, ISN'T IT? GERI IS LIKELY LOOKING TO SORT YOU OUT, JIM.
SO BE IT. WE NEED TO LEARN ABOUT MR. BLOOM.
AND THIS PLACE...IF QI TSU DID BUSINESS WITH HIM, THERE'LL BE A RECORD OF BLOOM HERE. AS LEADER OF THE DEVIL PIGS, HE'D HAVE TO RECORD EVERYTHING, SEND THE MATERIAL TO HIGHER-UPS OVERSEAS.

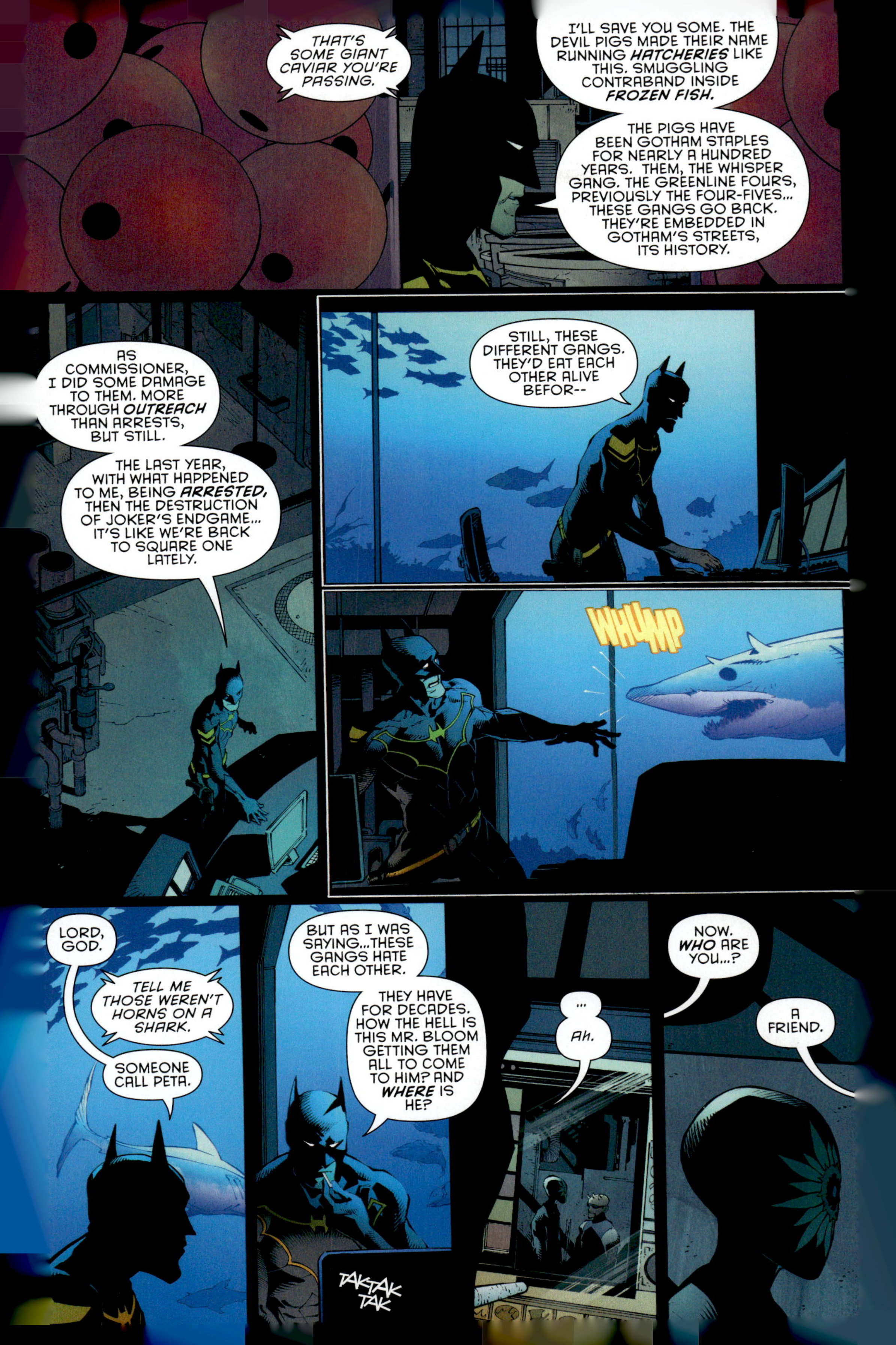
THAT'S SOME GIANT CAVIAR YOU'RE PASSING.
I'LL SAVE YOU SOME. THE DEVIL PIGS MADE THEIR NAME RUNNING HATCHERIES LIKE THIS. SMUGGLING CONTRABAND INSIDE FROZEN FISH.
THE PIGS HAVE BEEN GOTHAM STAPLES FOR NEARLY A HUNDRED YEARS. THEM, THE WHISPER GANG. THE GREENLINE FOURS, PREVIOUSLY THE FOUR-FIVES... THESE GANGS GO BACK. THEY'RE EMBEDDED IN GOTHAM'S STREETS, ITS HISTORY.
AS COMMISSIONER, I DID SOME DAMAGE TO THEM. MORE THROUGH OUTREACH THAN ARRESTS, BUT STILL.
THE LAST YEAR, WITH WHAT HAPPENED TO ME, BEING ARRESTED, THEN THE DESTRUCTION OF JOKER'S ENDGAME... IT'S LIKE WE'RE BACK TO SQUARE ONE LATELY.
STILL, THESE DIFFERENT GANGS. THEY'D EAT EACH OTHER ALIVE BEFOR--
WHUMP
LORD, GOD.
TELL ME THOSE WEREN'T HORNS ON A SHARK.
SOMEONE CALL PETA.
BUT AS I WAS SAYING...THESE GANGS HATE EACH OTHER.
THEY HAVE FOR DECADES. HOW THE HELL IS THIS MR. BLOOM GETTING THEM ALL TO COME TO HIM? AND WHERE IS HE?
TAKTAK TAK
...
Ah.
NOW. WHO ARE YOU...?
A FRIEND.

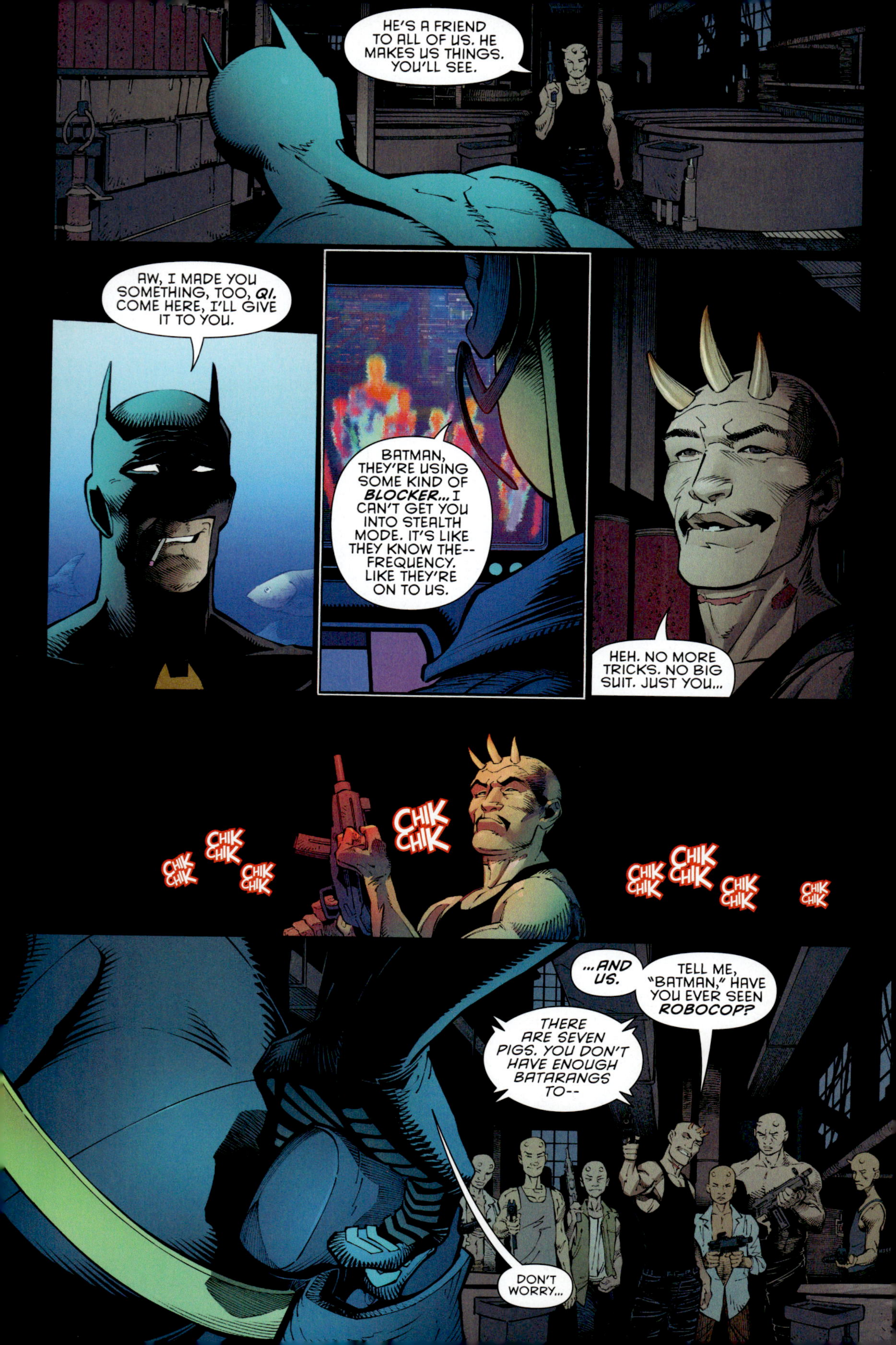

HE'S A FRIEND TO ALL OF US. HE MAKES US THINGS. YOU'LL SEE.
AW, I MADE YOU SOMETHING, TOO, QI. COME HERE, I'LL GIVE IT TO YOU.
BATMAN, THEY'RE USING SOME KIND OF BLOCKER... I CAN'T GET YOU INTO STEALTH MODE. IT'S LIKE THEY KNOW THE--FREQUENCY. LIKE THEY'RE ON TO US.
HEH. NO MORE TRICKS. NO BIG SUIT. JUST YOU...
CHIK CHIK
CHIK CHIK
CHIK CHIK
CHIK CHIK
CHIK CHIK
CHIK CHIK
CHIK CHIK
CHIK CHIK
...AND US.
TELL ME, "BATMAN," HAVE YOU EVER SEEN ROBOCOP?
THERE ARE SEVEN PIGS. YOU DON'T HAVE ENOUGH BATARANGS TO--
DON'T WORRY...

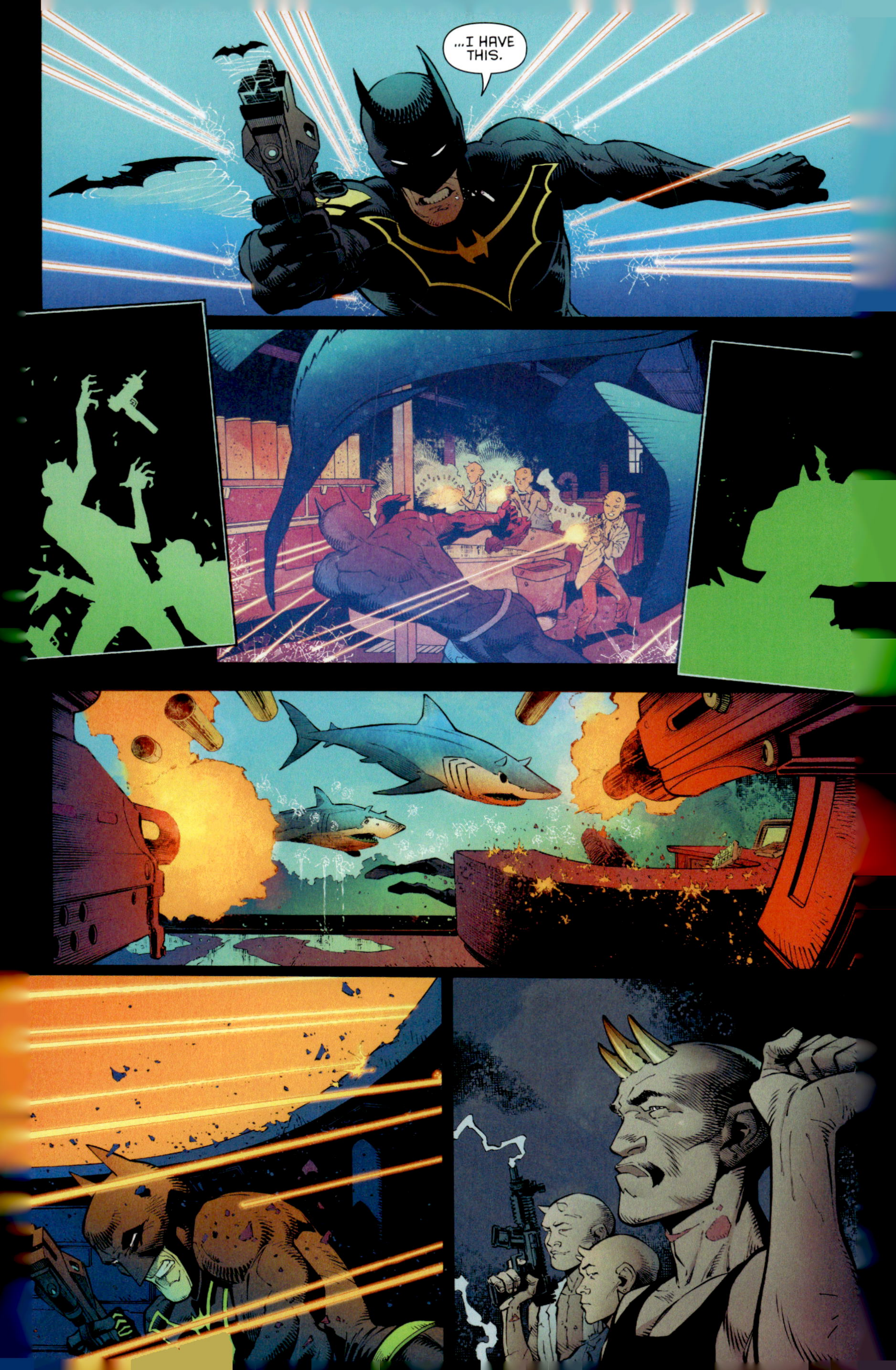
...I HAVE THIS.

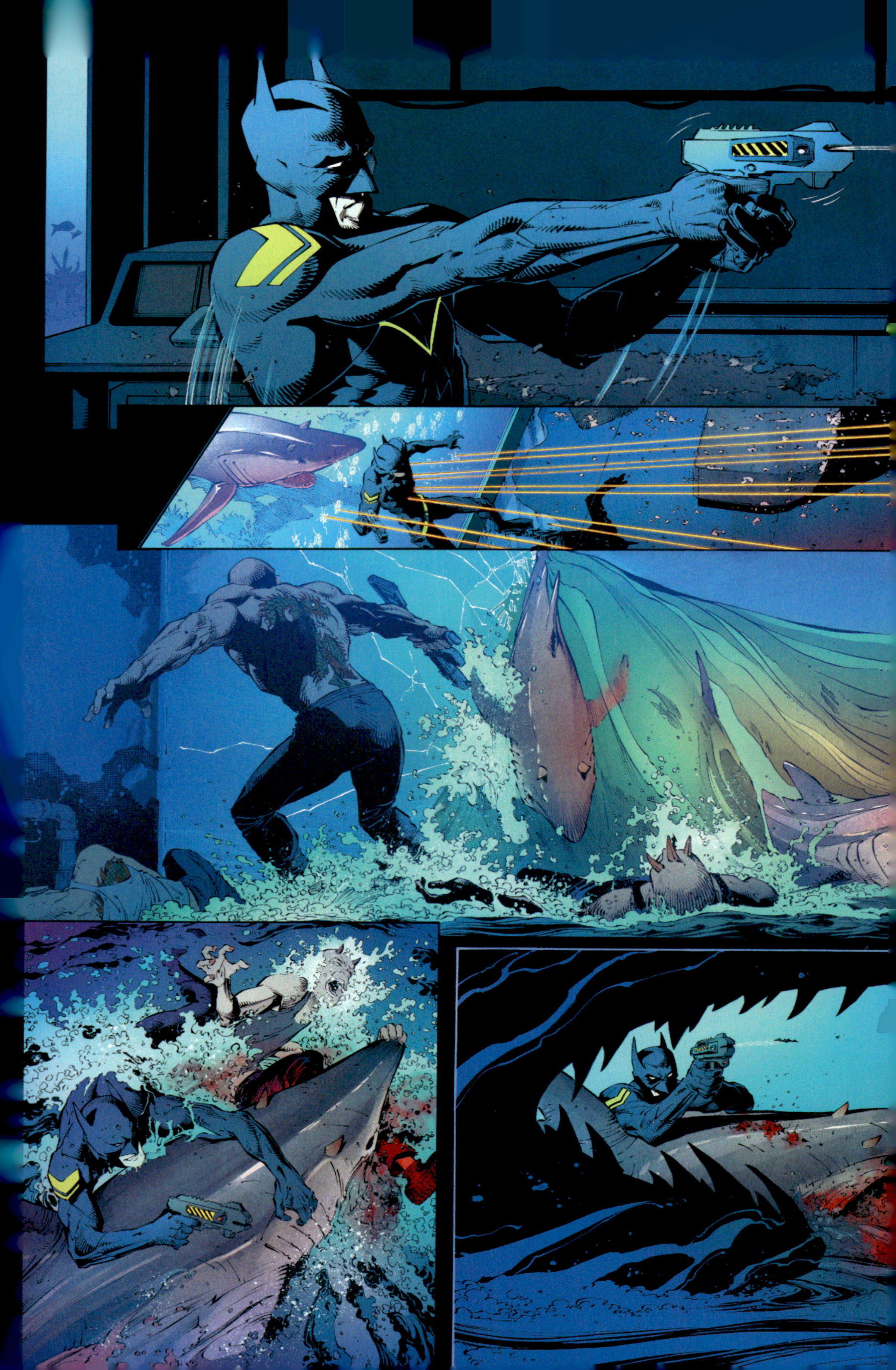

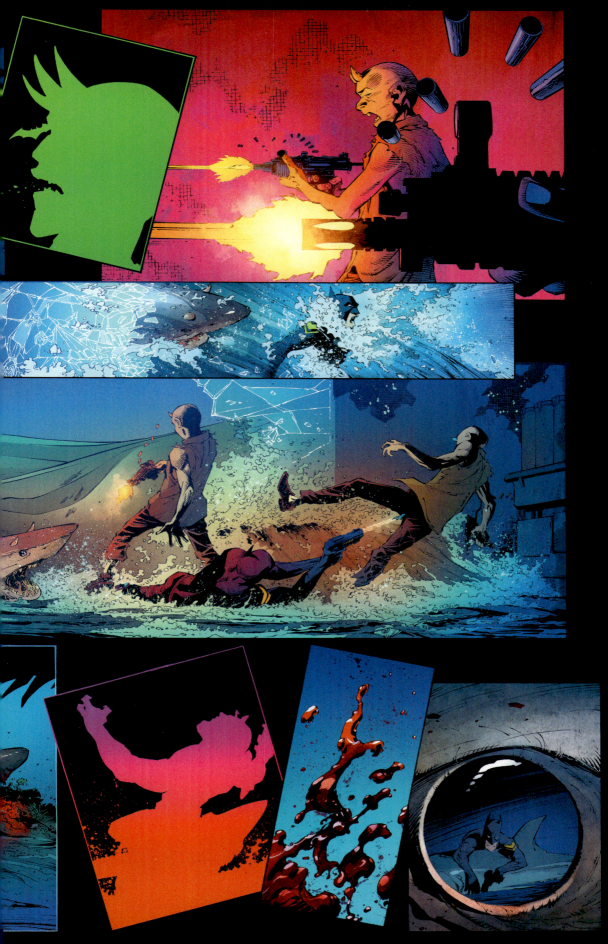

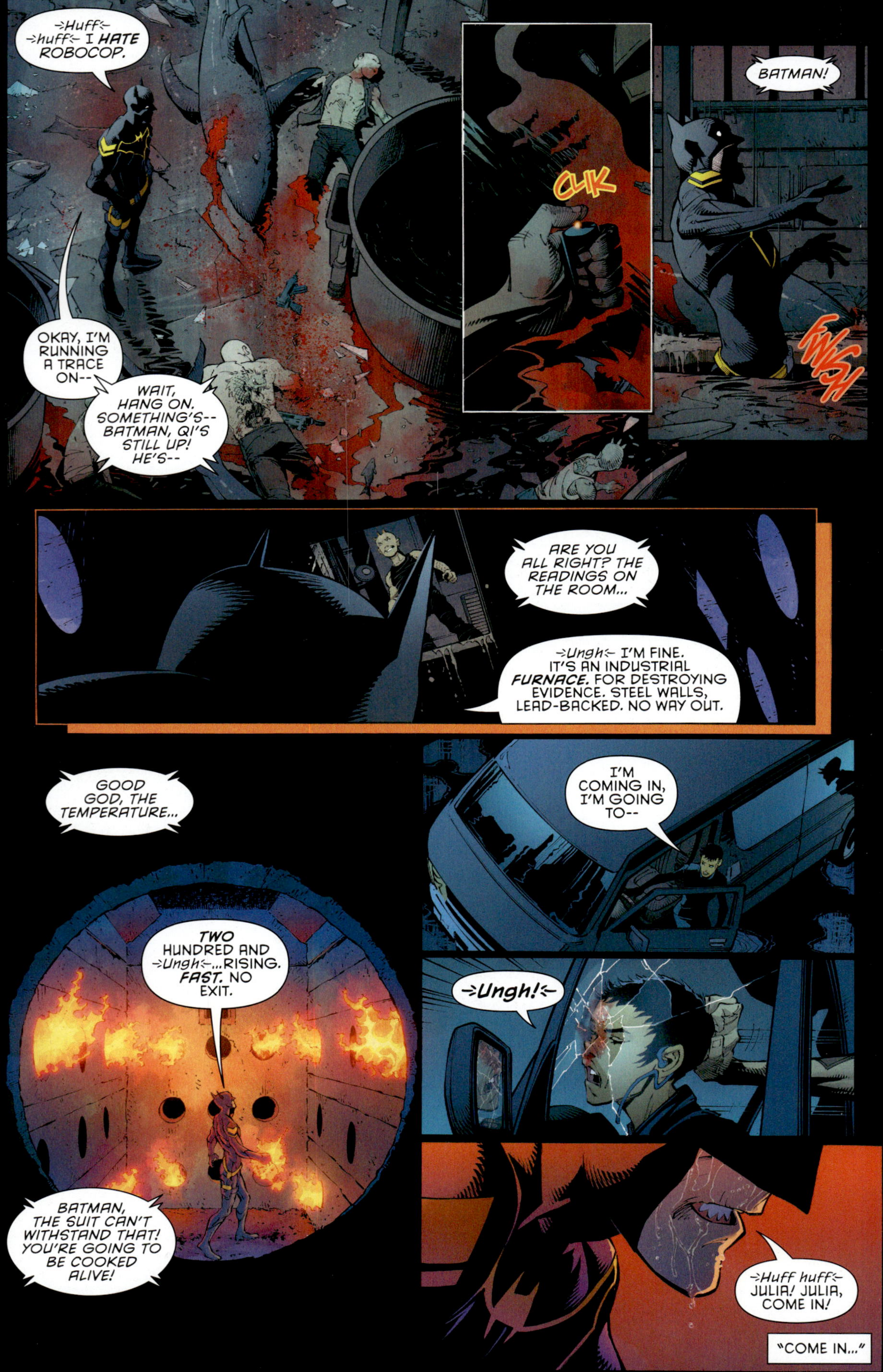

–Huff– –huff– I HATE ROBOCOP.
OKAY, I'M RUNNING A TRACE ON--
WAIT, HANG ON. SOMETHING'S-- BATMAN, QI'S STILL UP! HE'S--
CLIK
BATMAN!
FWSH
ARE YOU ALL RIGHT? THE READINGS ON THE ROOM...
–Ungh– I'M FINE. IT'S AN INDUSTRIAL FURNACE. FOR DESTROYING EVIDENCE. STEEL WALLS, LEAD-BACKED. NO WAY OUT.
GOOD GOD, THE TEMPERATURE...
TWO HUNDRED AND –Ungh–...RISING. FAST. NO EXIT.
BATMAN, THE SUIT CAN'T WITHSTAND THAT! YOU'RE GOING TO BE COOKED ALIVE!
I'M COMING IN, I'M GOING TO--
–Ungh!–
–Huff huff– JULIA! JULIA, COME IN!
"COME IN..."

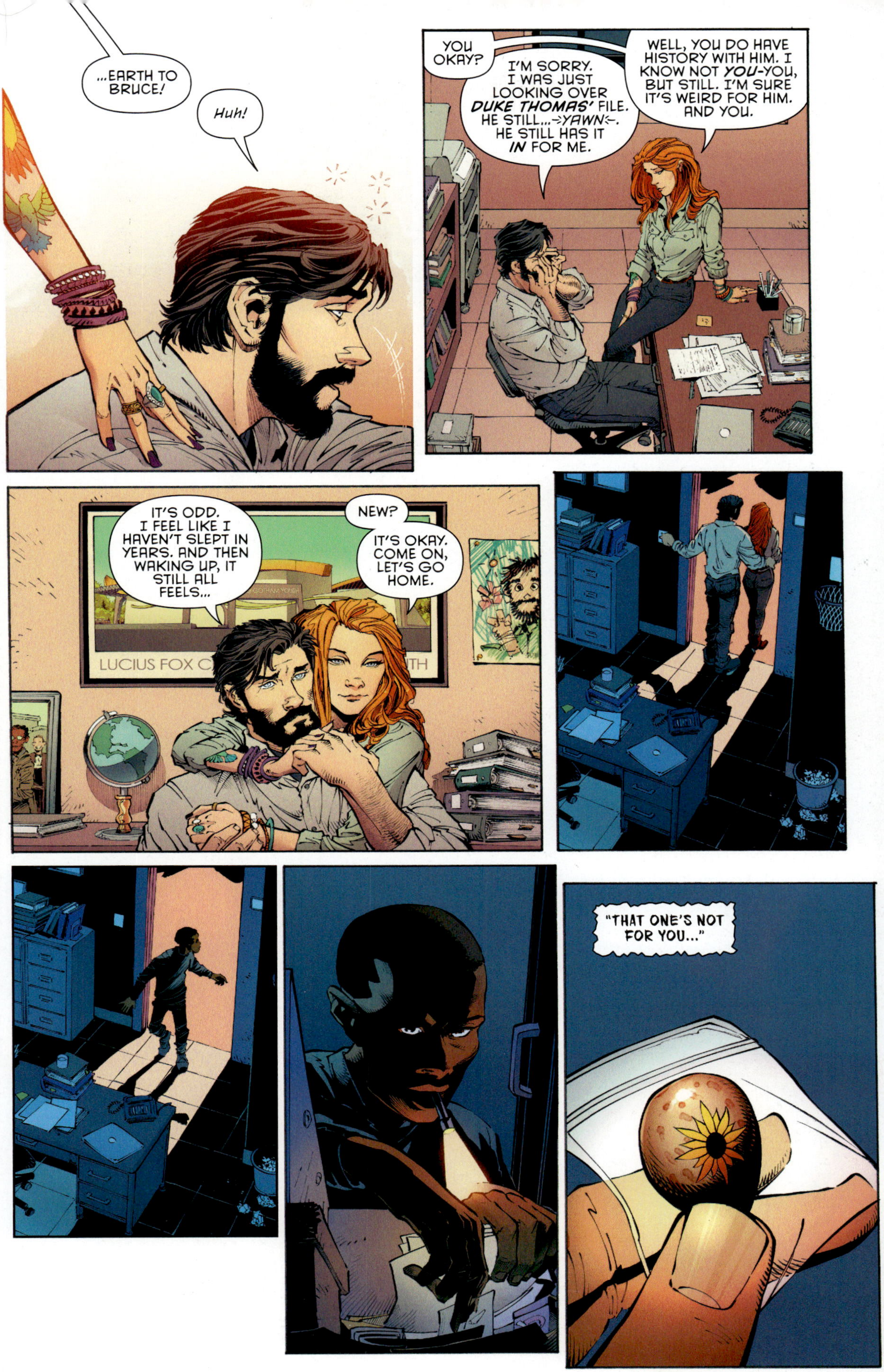
...EARTH TO BRUCE!
Huh!
YOU OKAY?
I'M SORRY. I WAS JUST LOOKING OVER DUKE THOMAS' FILE. HE STILL... ⇒YAWN⇐. HE STILL HAS IT IN FOR ME.
WELL, YOU DO HAVE HISTORY WITH HIM. I KNOW NOT YOU-YOU, BUT STILL. I'M SURE IT'S WEIRD FOR HIM. AND YOU.
IT'S ODD. I FEEL LIKE I HAVEN'T SLEPT IN YEARS. AND THEN WAKING UP, IT STILL ALL FEELS...
NEW?
IT'S OKAY. COME ON, LET'S GO HOME.
LUCIUS FOX C
TH
"THAT ONE'S NOT FOR YOU..."

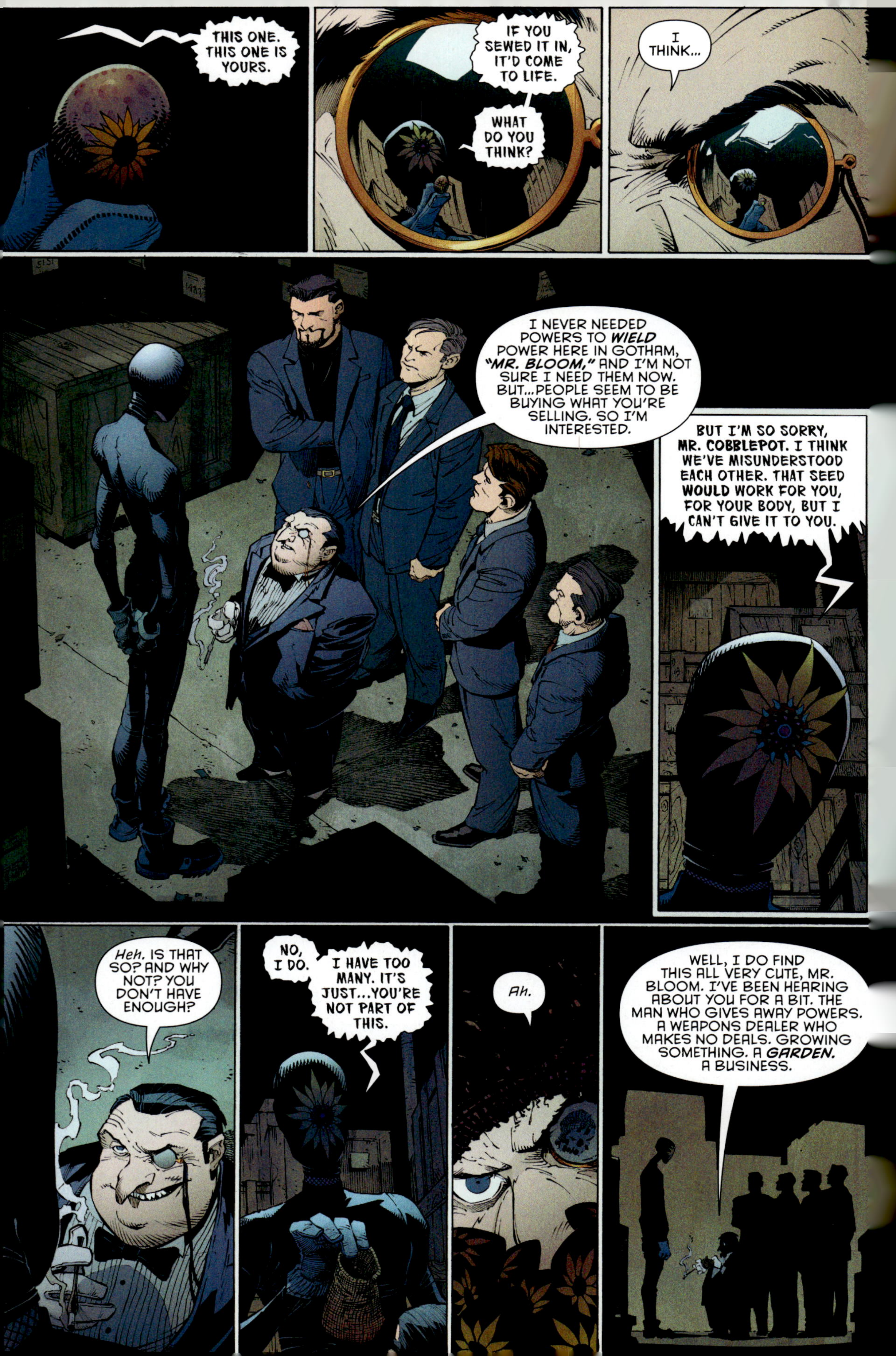
THIS ONE. THIS ONE IS YOURS.
IF YOU SEWED IT IN, IT'D COME TO LIFE.
WHAT DO YOU THINK?
I THINK...
I NEVER NEEDED POWERS TO *WIELD* POWER HERE IN GOTHAM, *"MR. BLOOM,"* AND I'M NOT SURE I NEED THEM NOW. BUT...PEOPLE SEEM TO BE BUYING WHAT YOU'RE SELLING. SO I'M INTERESTED.
BUT I'M SO SORRY, MR. COBBLEPOT. I THINK WE'VE MISUNDERSTOOD EACH OTHER. THAT SEED WOULD WORK FOR YOU, FOR YOUR BODY, BUT I CAN'T GIVE IT TO YOU.
Heh. IS THAT SO? AND WHY NOT? YOU DON'T HAVE ENOUGH?
NO, I DO.
I HAVE TOO MANY. IT'S JUST...YOU'RE NOT PART OF THIS.
Ah.
WELL, I DO FIND THIS ALL VERY CUTE, MR. BLOOM. I'VE BEEN HEARING ABOUT YOU FOR A BIT. THE MAN WHO GIVES AWAY POWERS. A WEAPONS DEALER WHO MAKES NO DEALS. GROWING SOMETHING. A *GARDEN.* A BUSINESS.

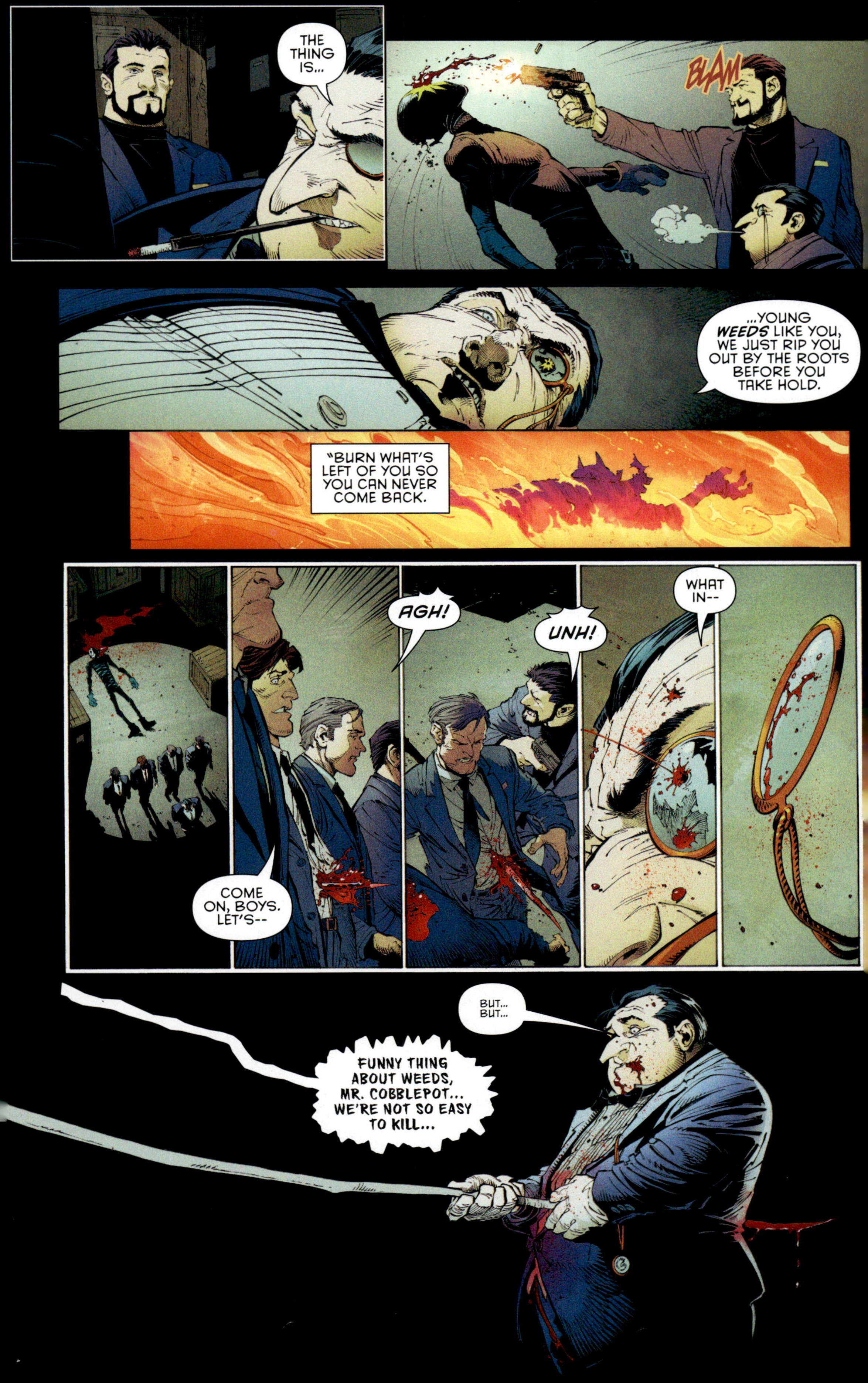
THE THING IS...
BLAM
...YOUNG WEEDS LIKE YOU, WE JUST RIP YOU OUT BY THE ROOTS BEFORE YOU TAKE HOLD.
"BURN WHAT'S LEFT OF YOU SO YOU CAN NEVER COME BACK.
COME ON, BOYS. LET'S--
AGH!
UNH!
WHAT IN--
BUT... BUT...
FUNNY THING ABOUT WEEDS, MR. COBBLEPOT... WE'RE NOT SO EASY TO KILL...

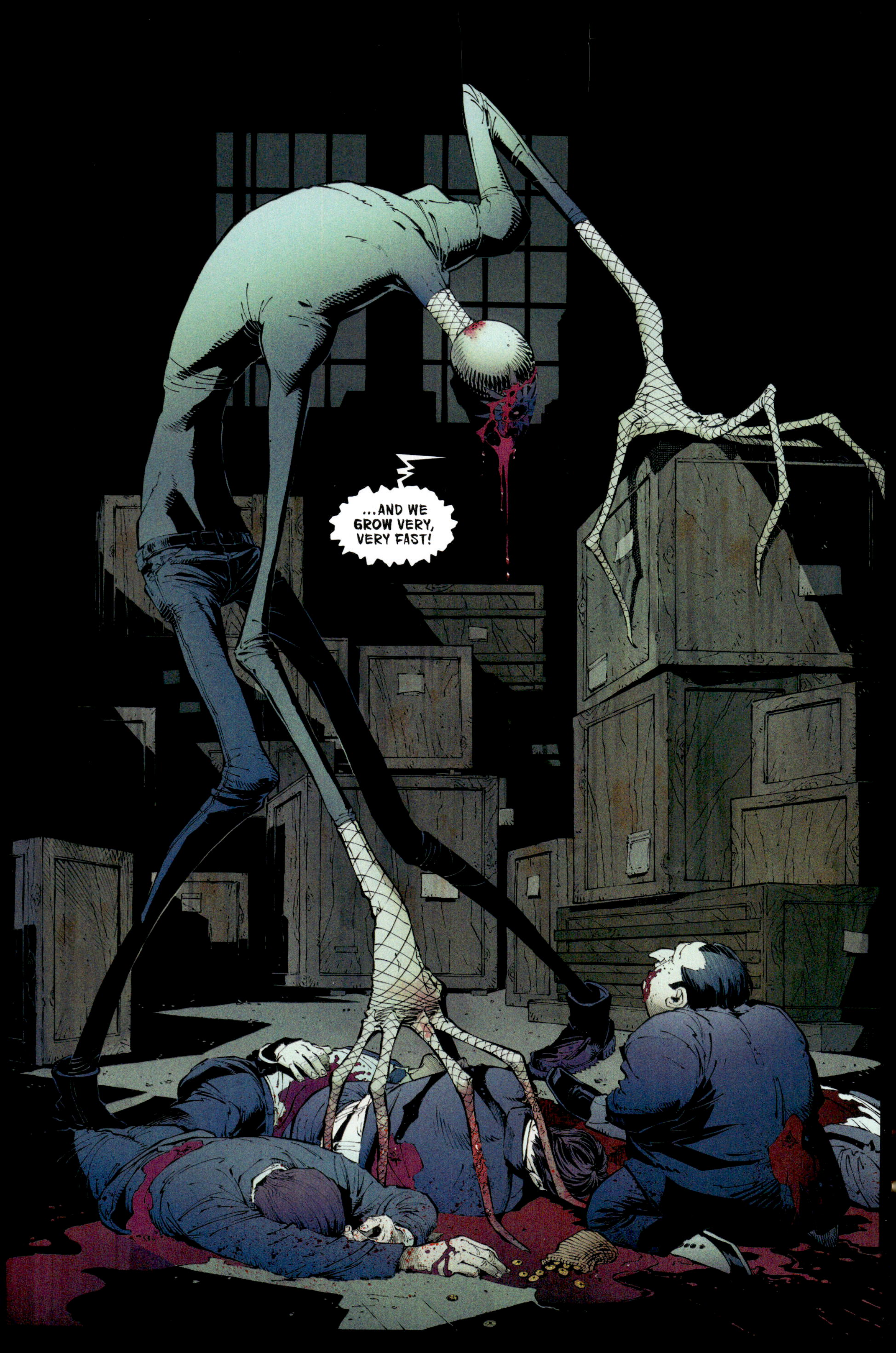
...AND WE GROW VERY, VERY FAST!

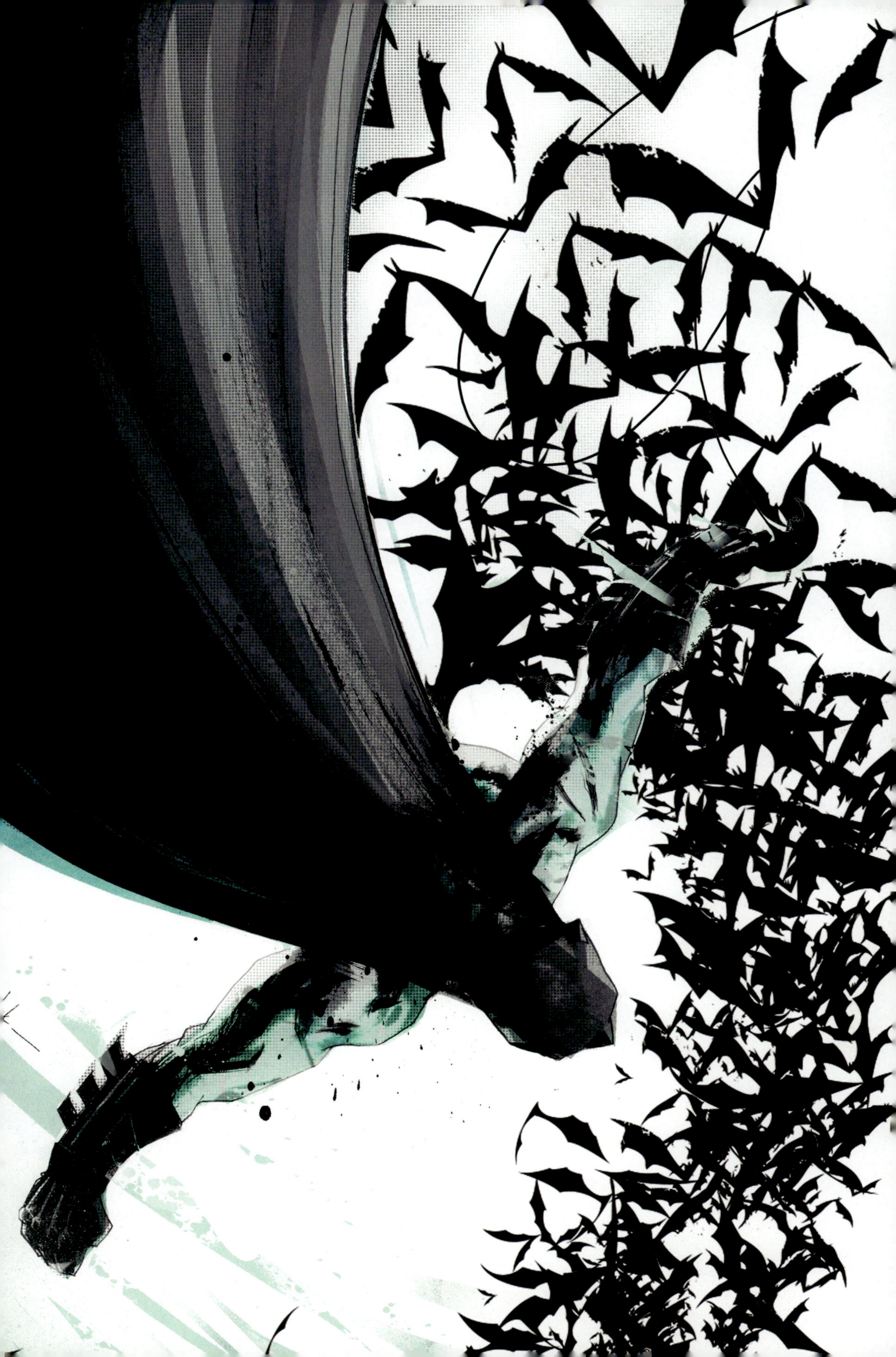

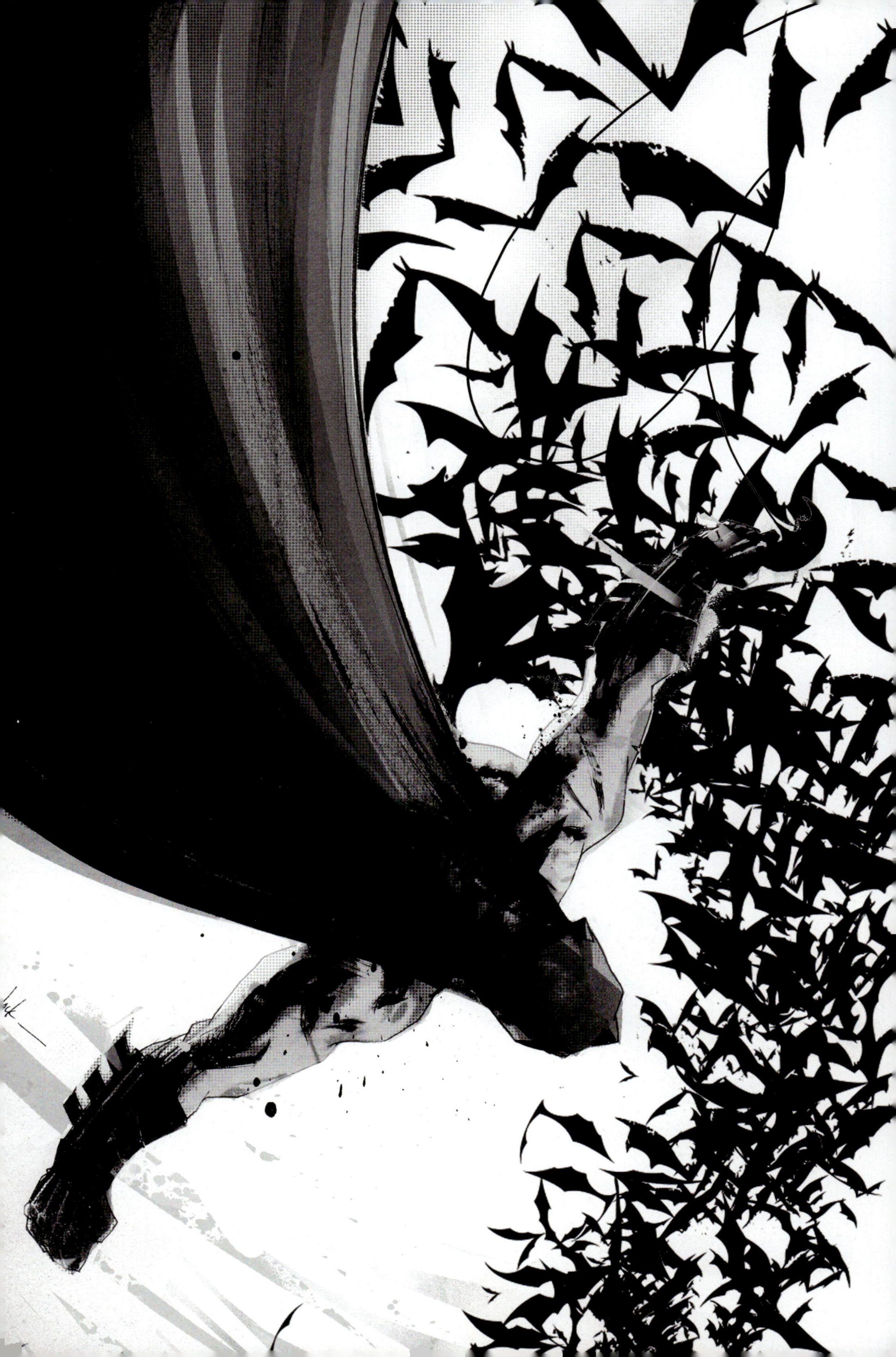

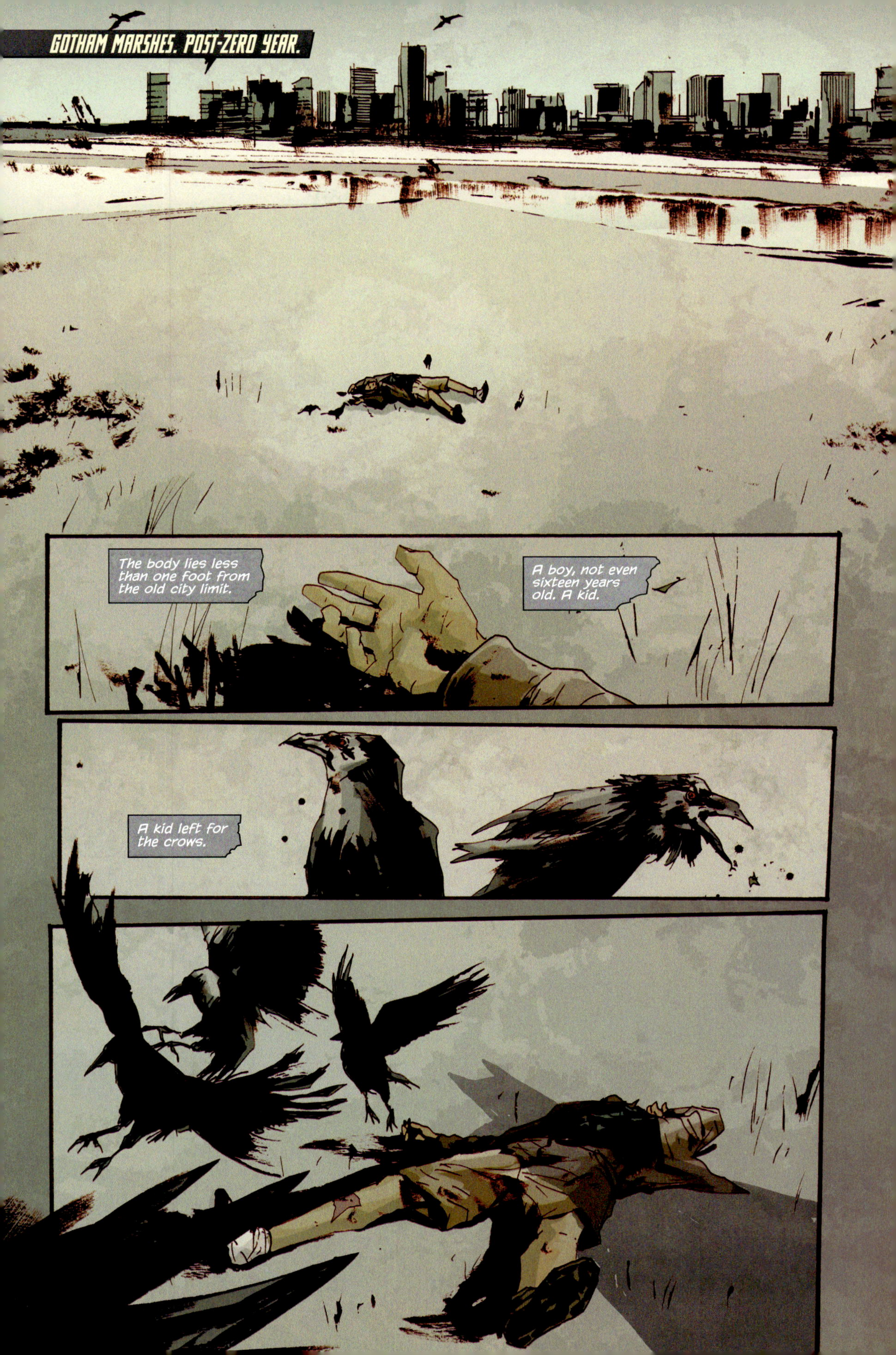
GOTHAM MARSHES. POST-ZERO YEAR.
The body lies less than one foot from the old city limit.
A boy, not even sixteen years old. A kid.
A kid left for the crows.

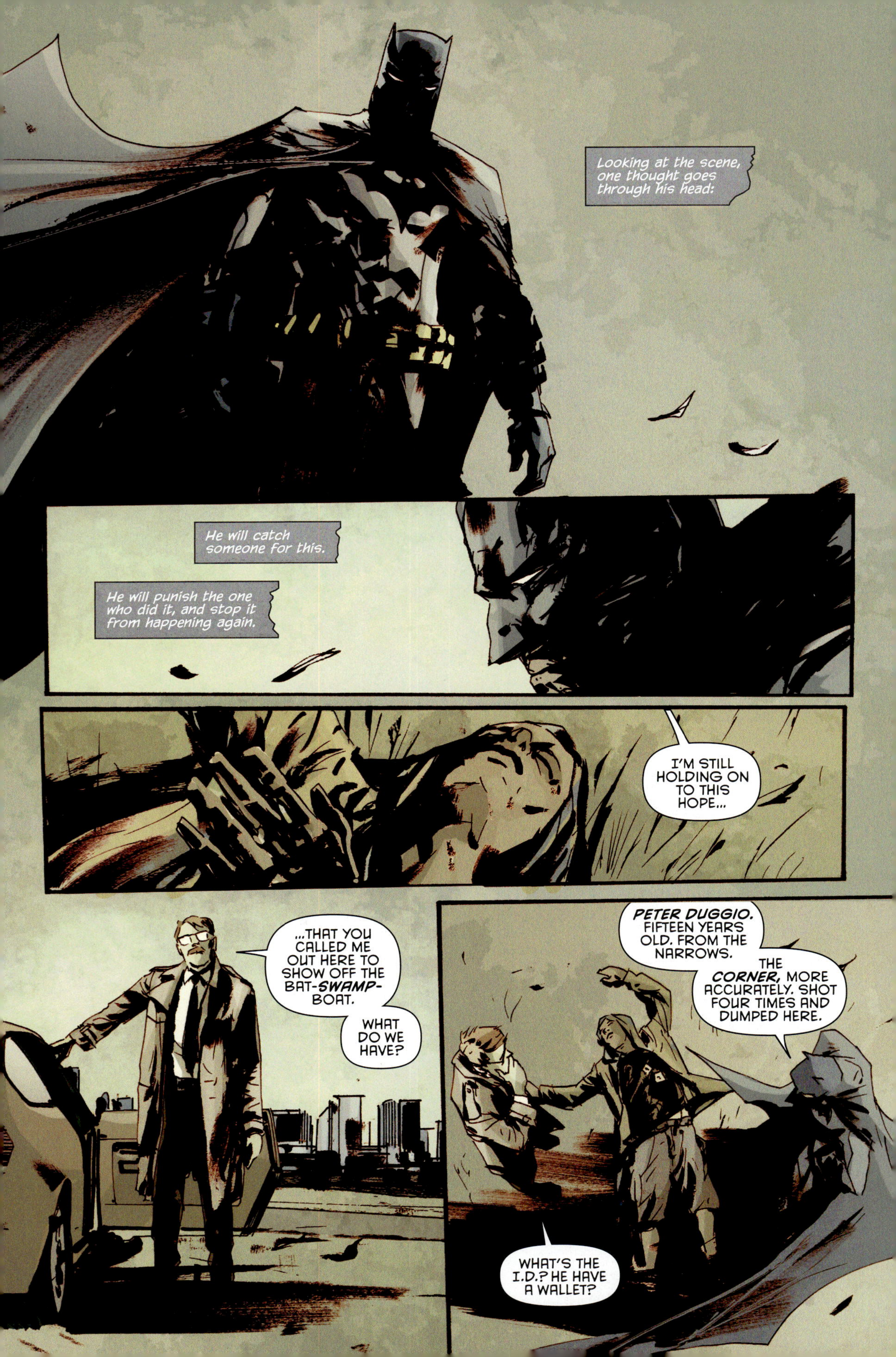
Looking at the scene, one thought goes through his head:
He will catch someone for this.
He will punish the one who did it, and stop it from happening again.
I'M STILL HOLDING ON TO THIS HOPE...
...THAT YOU CALLED ME OUT HERE TO SHOW OFF THE BAT-SWAMP-BOAT.
WHAT DO WE HAVE?
WHAT'S THE I.D.? HE HAVE A WALLET?
PETER DUGGIO. FIFTEEN YEARS OLD. FROM THE NARROWS.
THE CORNER, MORE ACCURATELY. SHOT FOUR TIMES AND DUMPED HERE.

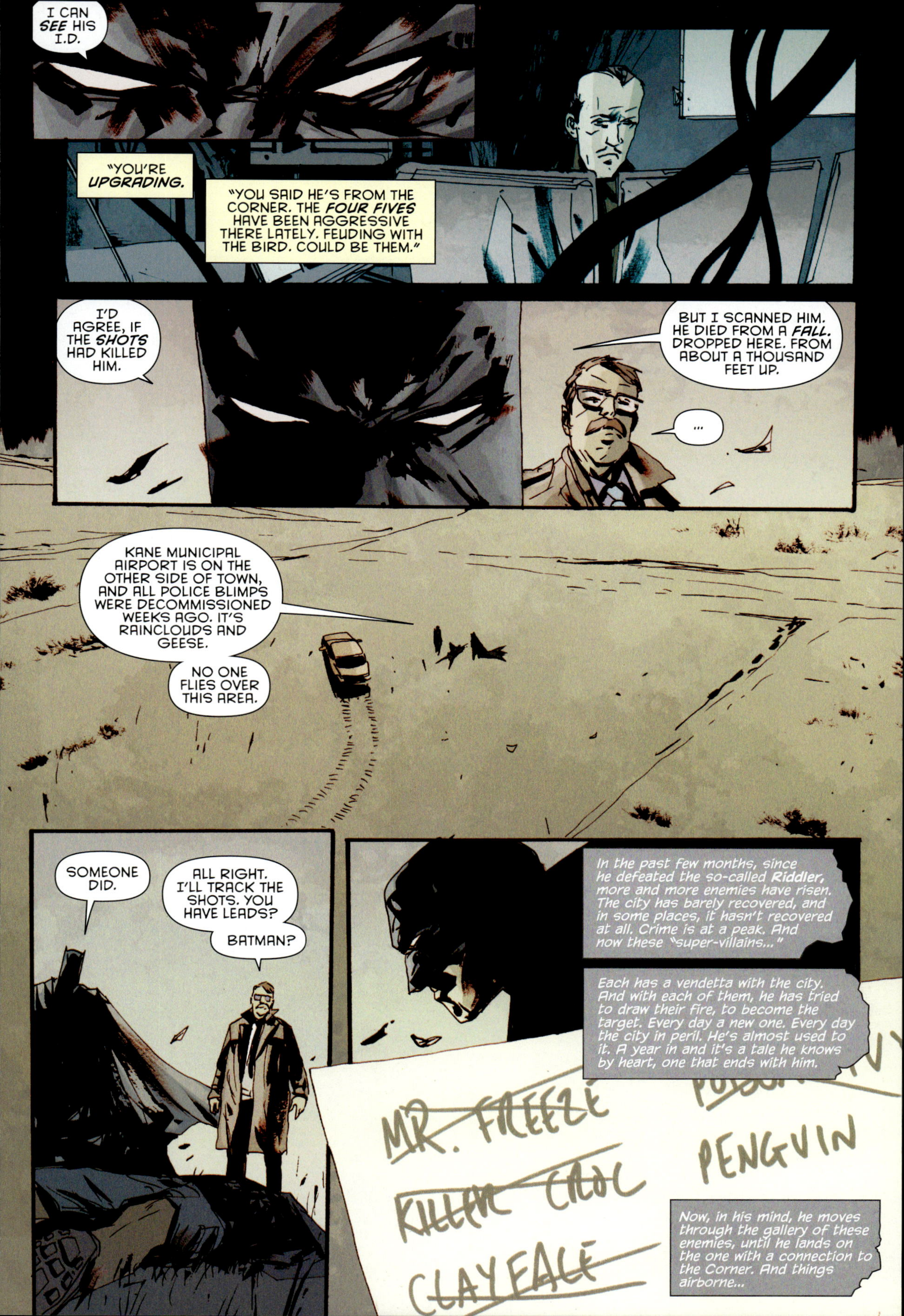

I CAN SEE HIS I.D.
"YOU'RE UPGRADING.
"YOU SAID HE'S FROM THE CORNER. THE FOUR FIVES HAVE BEEN AGGRESSIVE THERE LATELY. FEUDING WITH THE BIRD. COULD BE THEM."
I'D AGREE, IF THE SHOTS HAD KILLED HIM.
BUT I SCANNED HIM. HE DIED FROM A FALL. DROPPED HERE. FROM ABOUT A THOUSAND FEET UP.
...
KANE MUNICIPAL AIRPORT IS ON THE OTHER SIDE OF TOWN, AND ALL POLICE BLIMPS WERE DECOMMISSIONED WEEKS AGO. IT'S RAINCLOUDS AND GEESE.
NO ONE FLIES OVER THIS AREA.
SOMEONE DID.
ALL RIGHT. I'LL TRACK THE SHOTS. YOU HAVE LEADS?
BATMAN?
In the past few months, since he defeated the so-called Riddler, more and more enemies have risen. The city has barely recovered, and in some places, it hasn't recovered at all. Crime is at a peak. And now these "super-villains..."
Each has a vendetta with the city. And with each of them, he has tried to draw their fire, to become the target. Every day a new one. Every day the city in peril. He's almost used to it. A year in and it's a tale he knows by heart, one that ends with him.
MR. FREEZE
PENGUIN
KILLER CROC
CLAYFACE
Now, in his mind, he moves through the gallery of these enemies, until he lands on the one with a connection to the Corner. And things airborne...

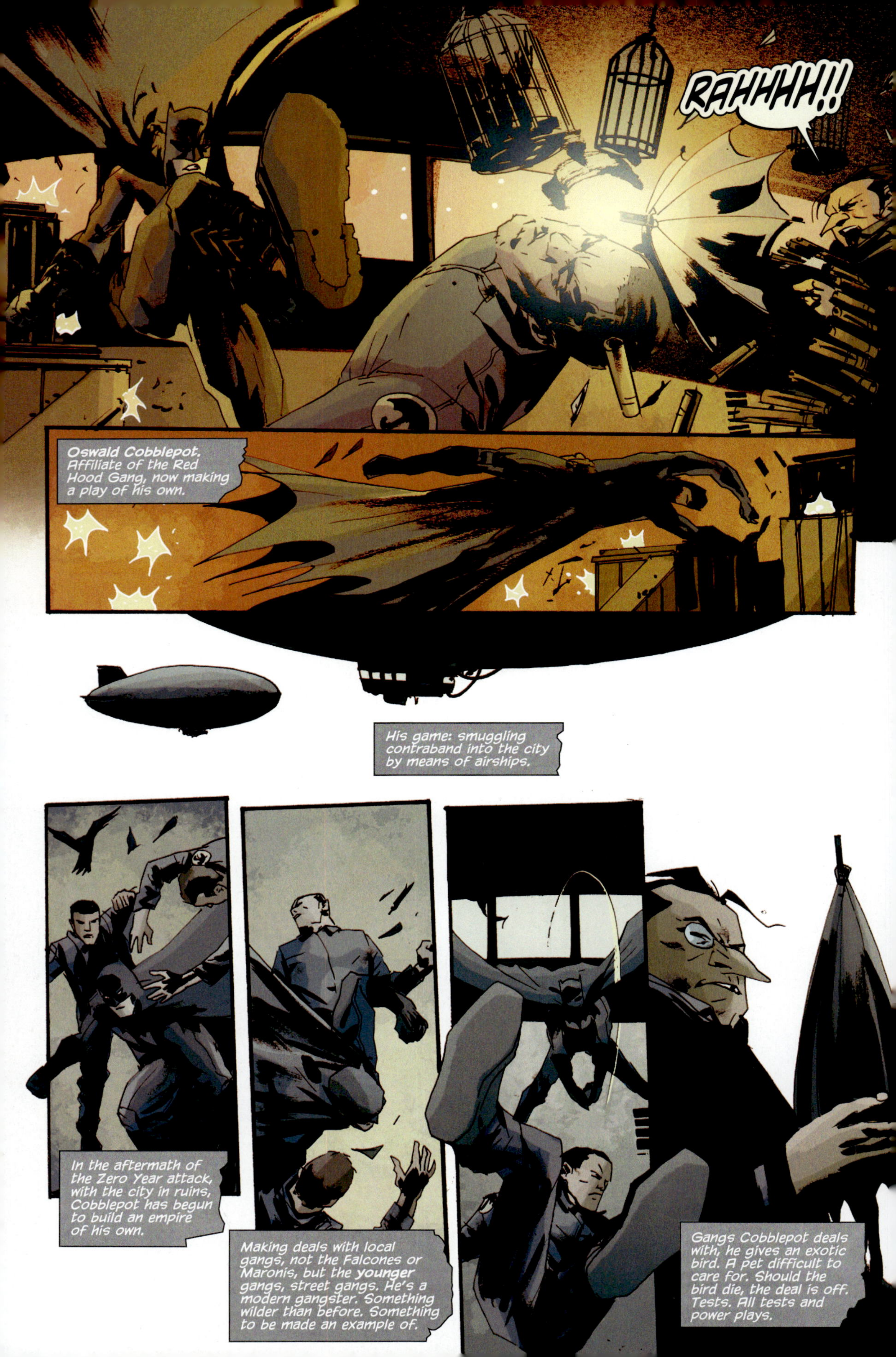
RAHHHH!!
Oswald Cobblepot. Affiliate of the Red Hood Gang, now making a play of his own.
His game: smuggling contraband into the city by means of airships.
In the aftermath of the Zero Year attack, with the city in ruins, Cobblepot has begun to build an empire of his own.
Making deals with local gangs, not the Falcones or Maronis, but the younger gangs, street gangs. He's a modern gangster. Something wilder than before. Something to be made an example of.
Gangs Cobblepot deals with, he gives an exotic bird. A pet difficult to care for. Should the bird die, the deal is off. Tests. All tests and power plays.

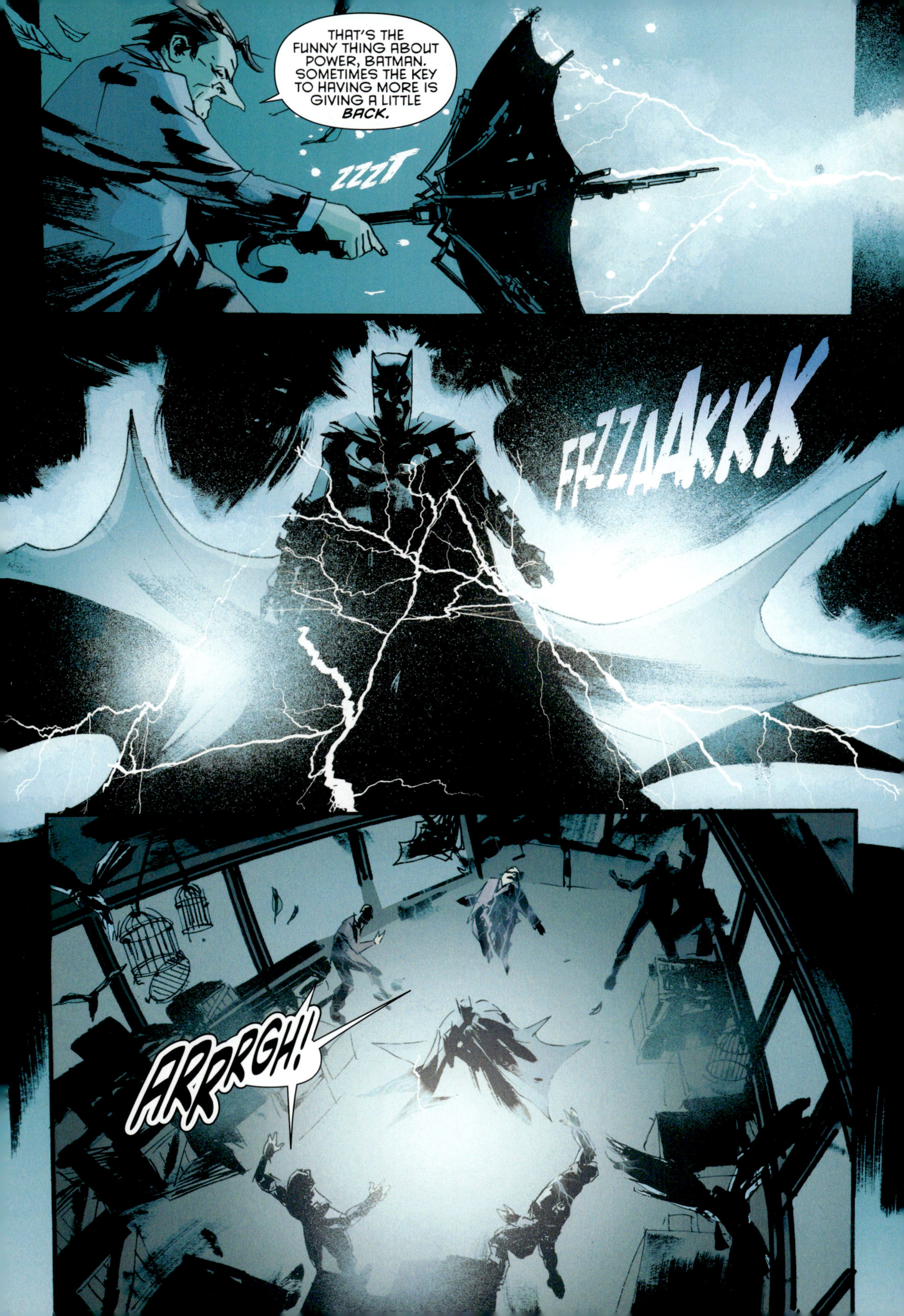
THAT'S THE FUNNY THING ABOUT POWER, BATMAN. SOMETIMES THE KEY TO HAVING MORE IS GIVING A LITTLE *BACK.*
ZZZT
FZZZAAKKK
ARRRGH!

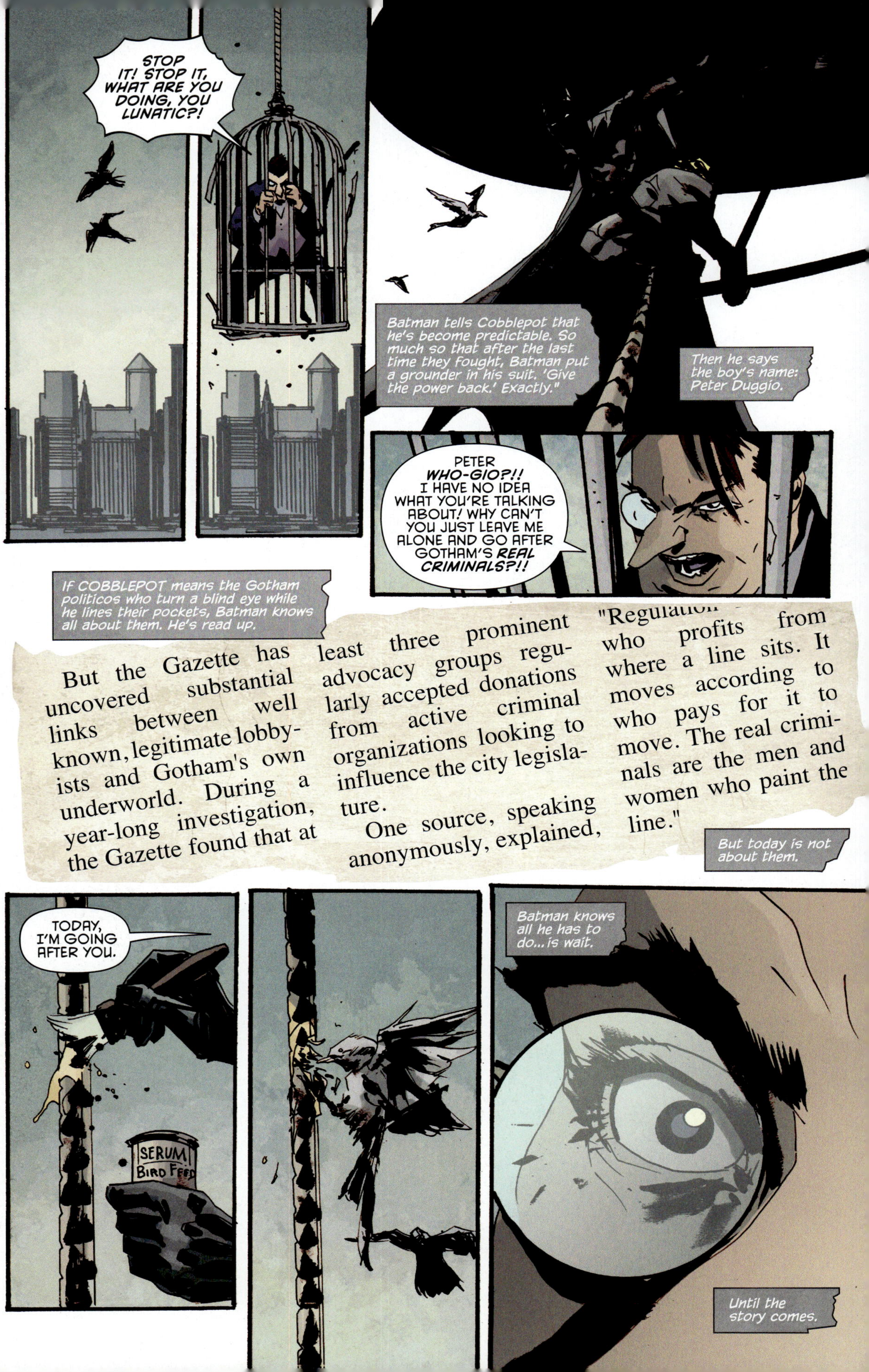
STOP IT! STOP IT, WHAT ARE YOU DOING, YOU LUNATIC?!
Batman tells Cobblepot that he's become predictable. So much so that after the last time they fought, Batman put a grounder in his suit. 'Give the power back.' Exactly."
Then he says the boy's name: Peter Duggio.
PETER WHO-GIO?!! I HAVE NO IDEA WHAT YOU'RE TALKING ABOUT! WHY CAN'T YOU JUST LEAVE ME ALONE AND GO AFTER GOTHAM'S REAL CRIMINALS?!!
If COBBLEPOT means the Gotham politicos who turn a blind eye while he lines their pockets, Batman knows all about them. He's read up.
But the Gazette has uncovered substantial links between well known, legitimate lobbyists and Gotham's own underworld. During a year-long investigation, the Gazette found that at least three prominent advocacy groups regularly accepted donations from active criminal organizations looking to influence the city legislature.
One source, speaking anonymously, explained, "Regulation who profits from where a line sits. It moves according to who pays for it to move. The real criminals are the men and women who paint the line."
But today is not about them.
TODAY, I'M GOING AFTER YOU.
SERUM
BIRD FEED
Batman knows all he has to do... is wait.
Until the story comes.

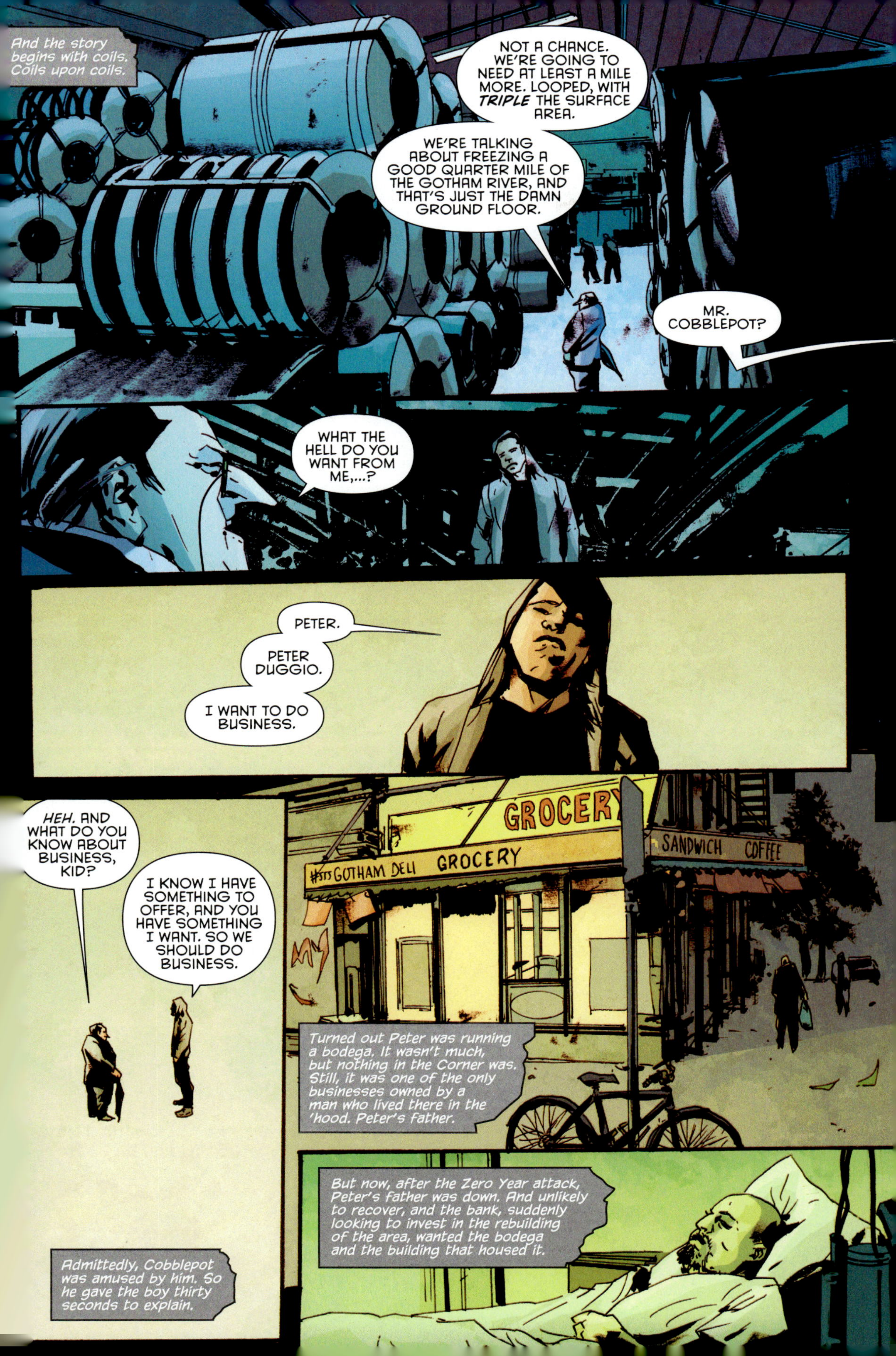
And the story begins with coils. Coils upon coils.
NOT A CHANCE. WE'RE GOING TO NEED AT LEAST A MILE MORE. LOOPED, WITH TRIPLE THE SURFACE AREA.
WE'RE TALKING ABOUT FREEZING A GOOD QUARTER MILE OF THE GOTHAM RIVER, AND THAT'S JUST THE DAMN GROUND FLOOR.
MR. COBBLEPOT?
WHAT THE HELL DO YOU WANT FROM ME,...?
PETER.
PETER DUGGIO.
I WANT TO DO BUSINESS.
HEH. AND WHAT DO YOU KNOW ABOUT BUSINESS, KID?
I KNOW I HAVE SOMETHING TO OFFER, AND YOU HAVE SOMETHING I WANT. SO WE SHOULD DO BUSINESS.
Admittedly, Cobblepot was amused by him. So he gave the boy thirty seconds to explain.
GROCERY
GOTHAM DELI GROCERY
SANDWICH COFFEE
Turned out Peter was running a bodega. It wasn't much, but nothing in the Corner was. Still, it was one of the only businesses owned by a man who lived there in the 'hood. Peter's father.
But now, after the Zero Year attack, Peter's father was down. And unlikely to recover, and the bank, suddenly looking to invest in the rebuilding of the area, wanted the bodega and the building that housed it.

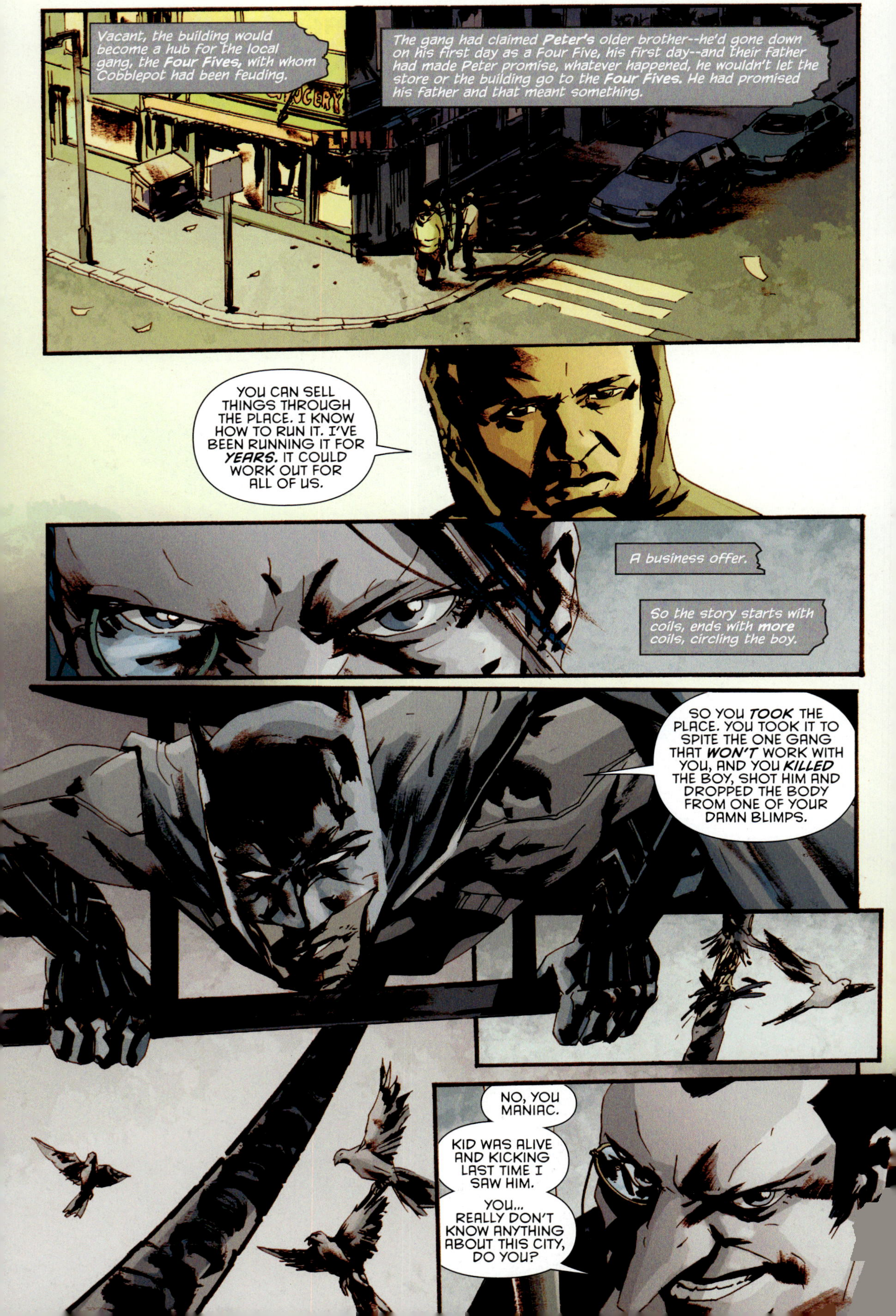
Vacant, the building would become a hub for the local gang, the **Four Fives,** with whom Cobblepot had been feuding.
The gang had claimed **Peter's** older brother--he'd gone down on his first day as a Four Five, his first day--and their father had made Peter promise, whatever happened, he wouldn't let the store or the building go to the **Four Fives.** He had promised his father and that meant something.
YOU CAN SELL THINGS THROUGH THE PLACE. I KNOW HOW TO RUN IT. I'VE BEEN RUNNING IT FOR ***YEARS.*** IT COULD WORK OUT FOR ALL OF US.
A business offer.
So the story starts with coils, ends with **more** coils, circling the boy.
SO YOU ***TOOK*** THE PLACE. YOU TOOK IT TO SPITE THE ONE GANG THAT ***WON'T*** WORK WITH YOU, AND YOU ***KILLED*** THE BOY, SHOT HIM AND DROPPED THE BODY FROM ONE OF YOUR DAMN BLIMPS.
NO, YOU MANIAC.
KID WAS ALIVE AND KICKING LAST TIME I SAW HIM.
YOU... REALLY DON'T KNOW ANYTHING ABOUT THIS CITY, DO YOU?

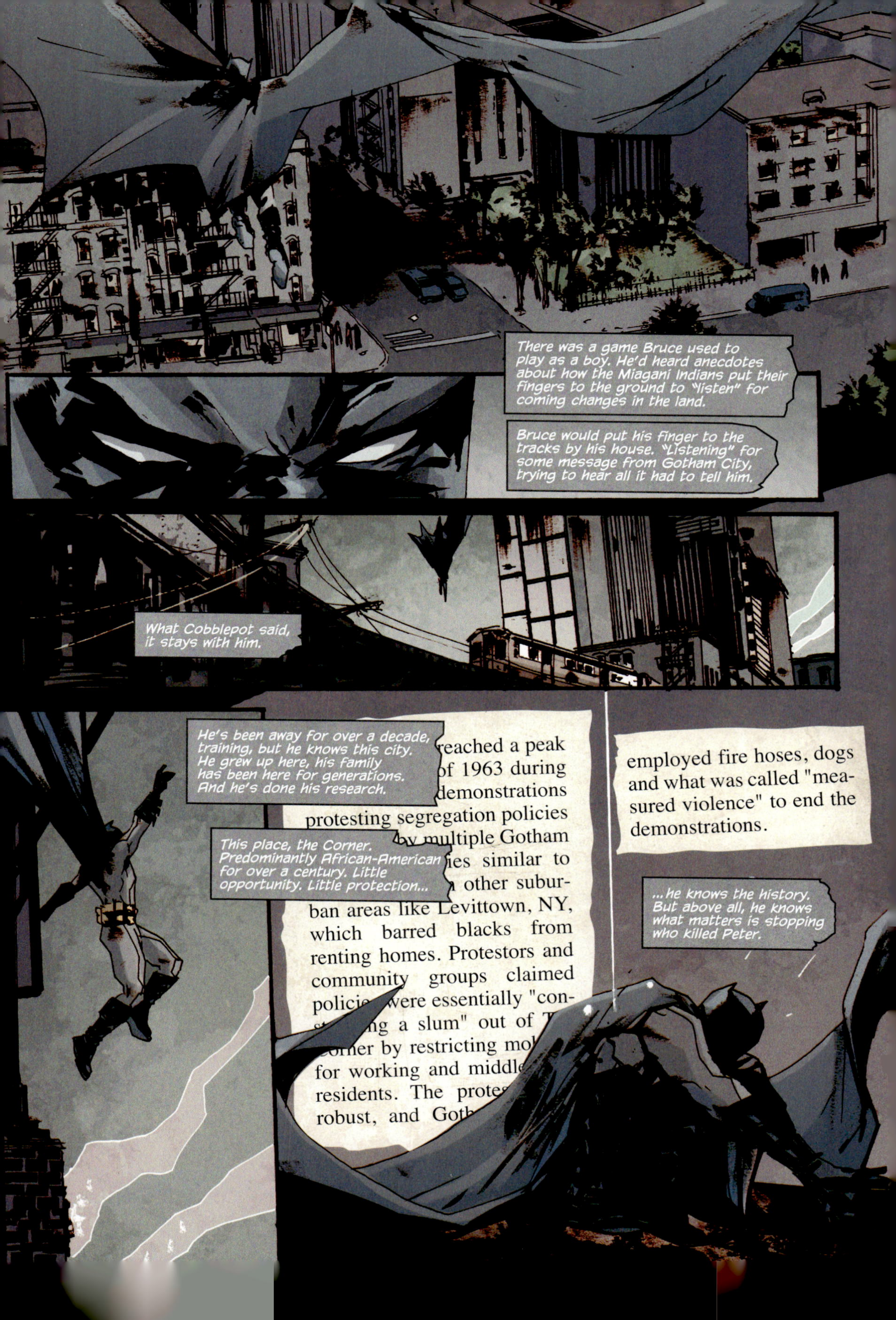
There was a game Bruce used to play as a boy. He'd heard anecdotes about how the Miagani Indians put their fingers to the ground to "listen" for coming changes in the land.
Bruce would put his finger to the tracks by his house. "Listening" for some message from Gotham City, trying to hear all it had to tell him.
What Cobblepot said, it stays with him.
He's been away for over a decade, training, but he knows this city. He grew up here, his family has been here for generations. And he's done his research.
reached a peak of 1963 during demonstrations protesting segregation policies multiple Gotham ies similar to other subur- ban areas like Levittown, NY, which barred blacks from renting homes. Protestors and community groups claimed were essentially "con- a slum" out of corner by restricting for working and middle residents. The robust, and
This place, the Corner. Predominantly African-American for over a century. Little opportunity. Little protection...
employed fire hoses, dogs and what was called "mea- sured violence" to end the demonstrations.
...he knows the history. But above all, he knows what matters is stopping who killed Peter.

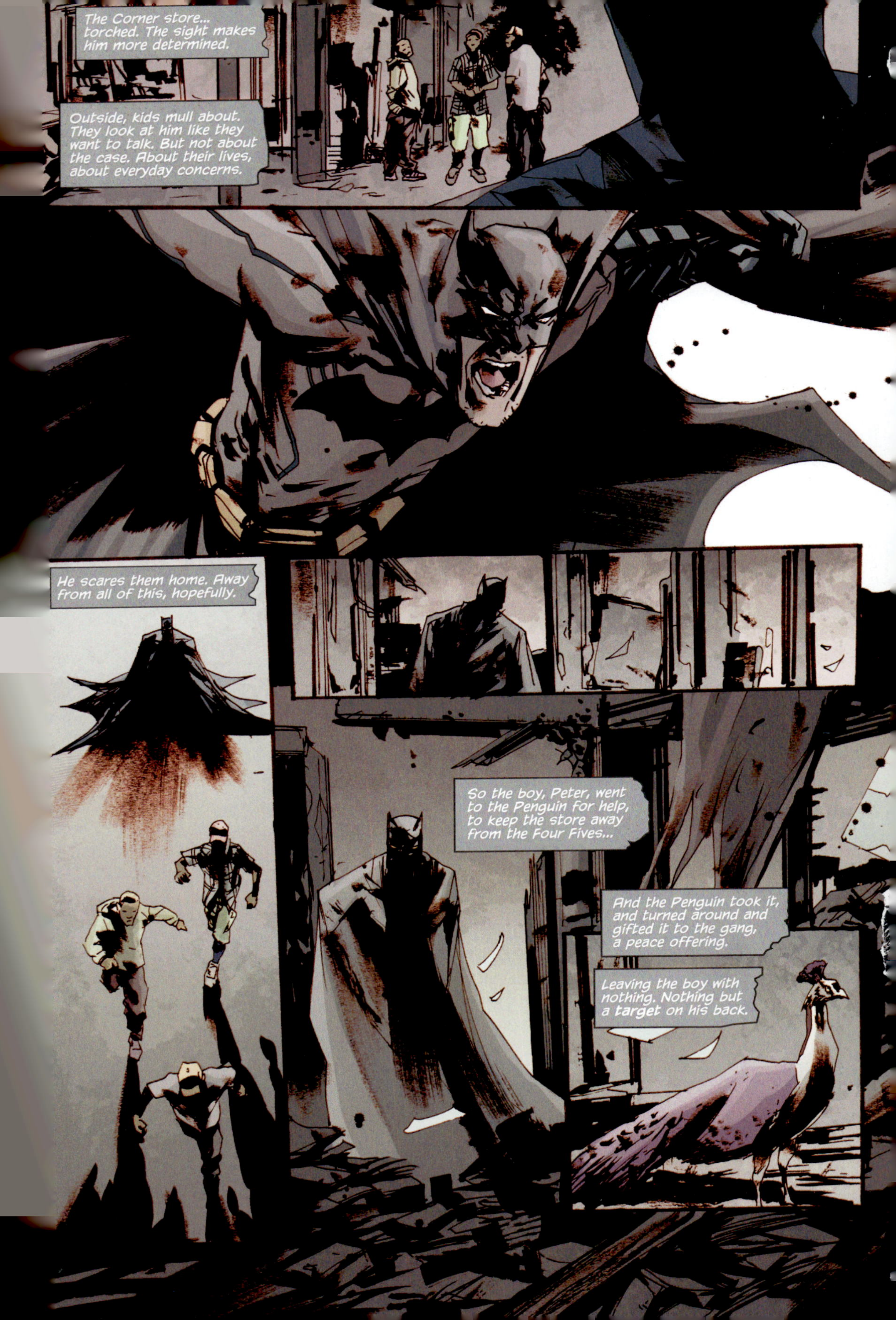

The Corner store... torched. The sight makes him more determined.
Outside, kids mull about. They look at him like they want to talk. But not about the case. About their lives, about everyday concerns.
He scares them home. Away from all of this, hopefully.
So the boy, Peter, went to the Penguin for help, to keep the store away from the Four Fives...
And the Penguin took it, and turned around and gifted it to the gang, a peace offering.
Leaving the boy with nothing. Nothing but a **target** on his back.

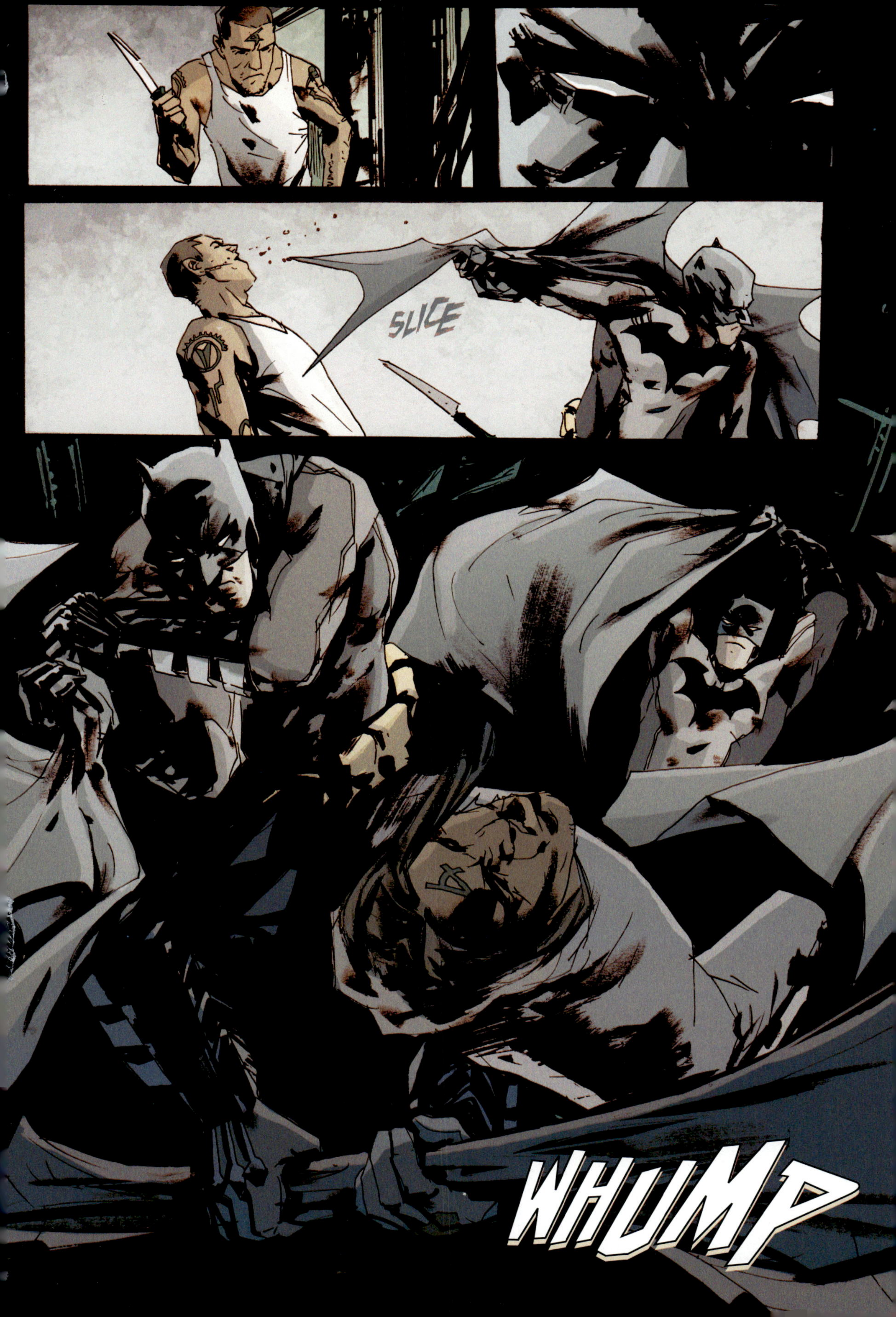
SLICE
WHUMP

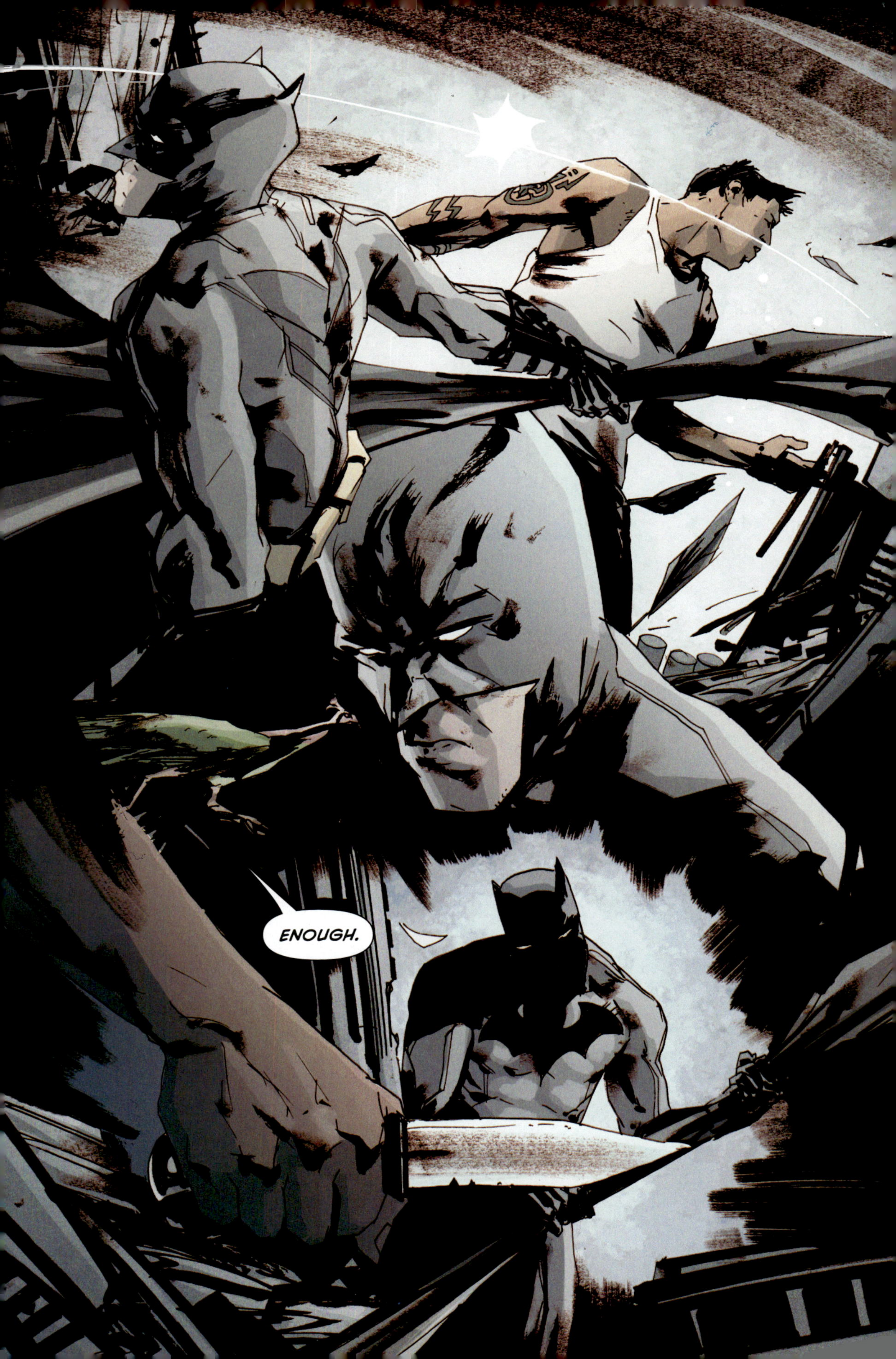
ENOUGH.

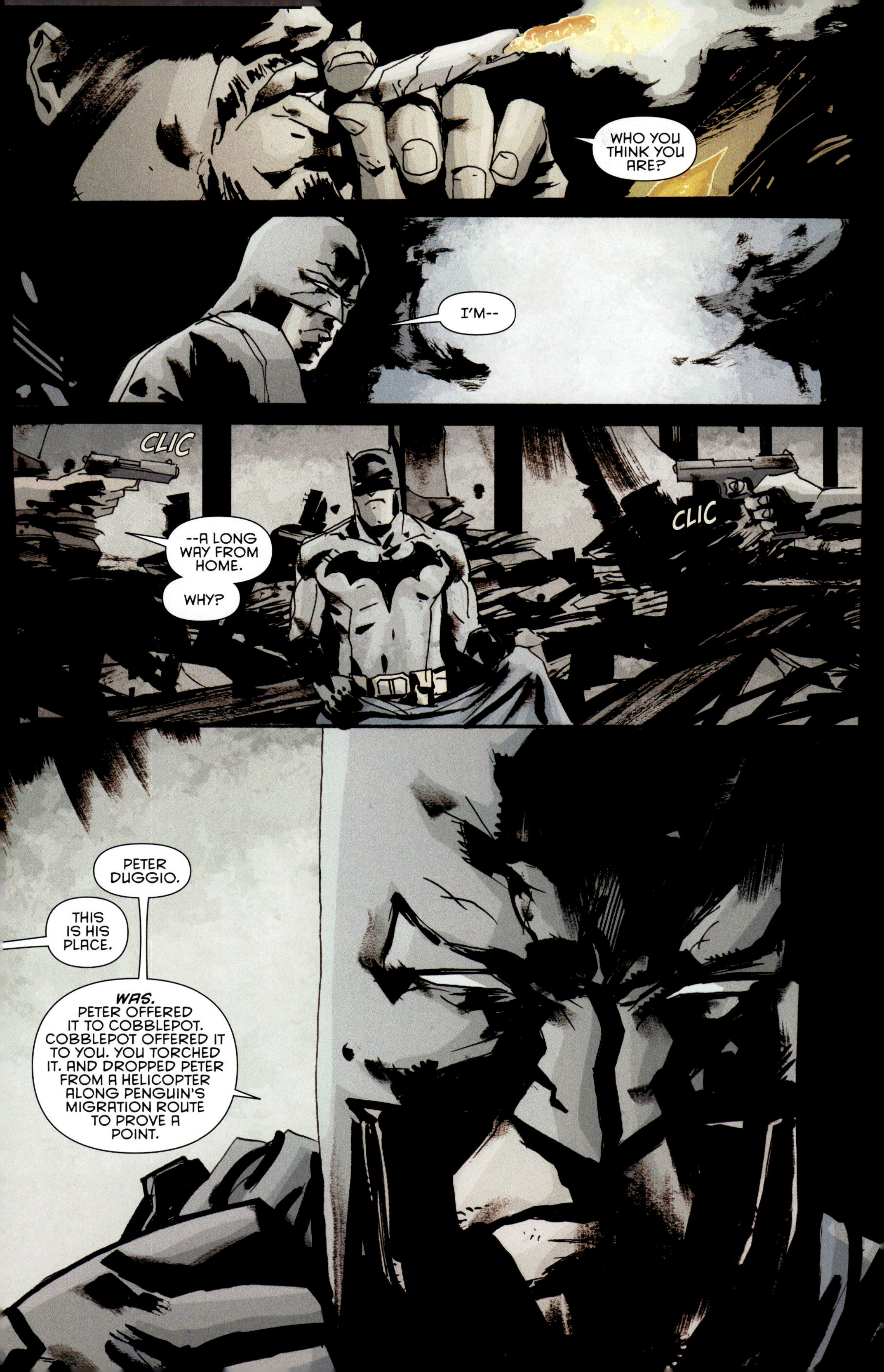
WHO YOU THINK YOU ARE?
I'M--
CLIC
CLIC
--A LONG WAY FROM HOME.
WHY?
PETER DUGGIO.
THIS IS HIS PLACE.
WAS. PETER OFFERED IT TO COBBLEPOT. COBBLEPOT OFFERED IT TO YOU. YOU TORCHED IT. AND DROPPED PETER FROM A HELICOPTER ALONG PENGUIN'S MIGRATION ROUTE TO PROVE A POINT.

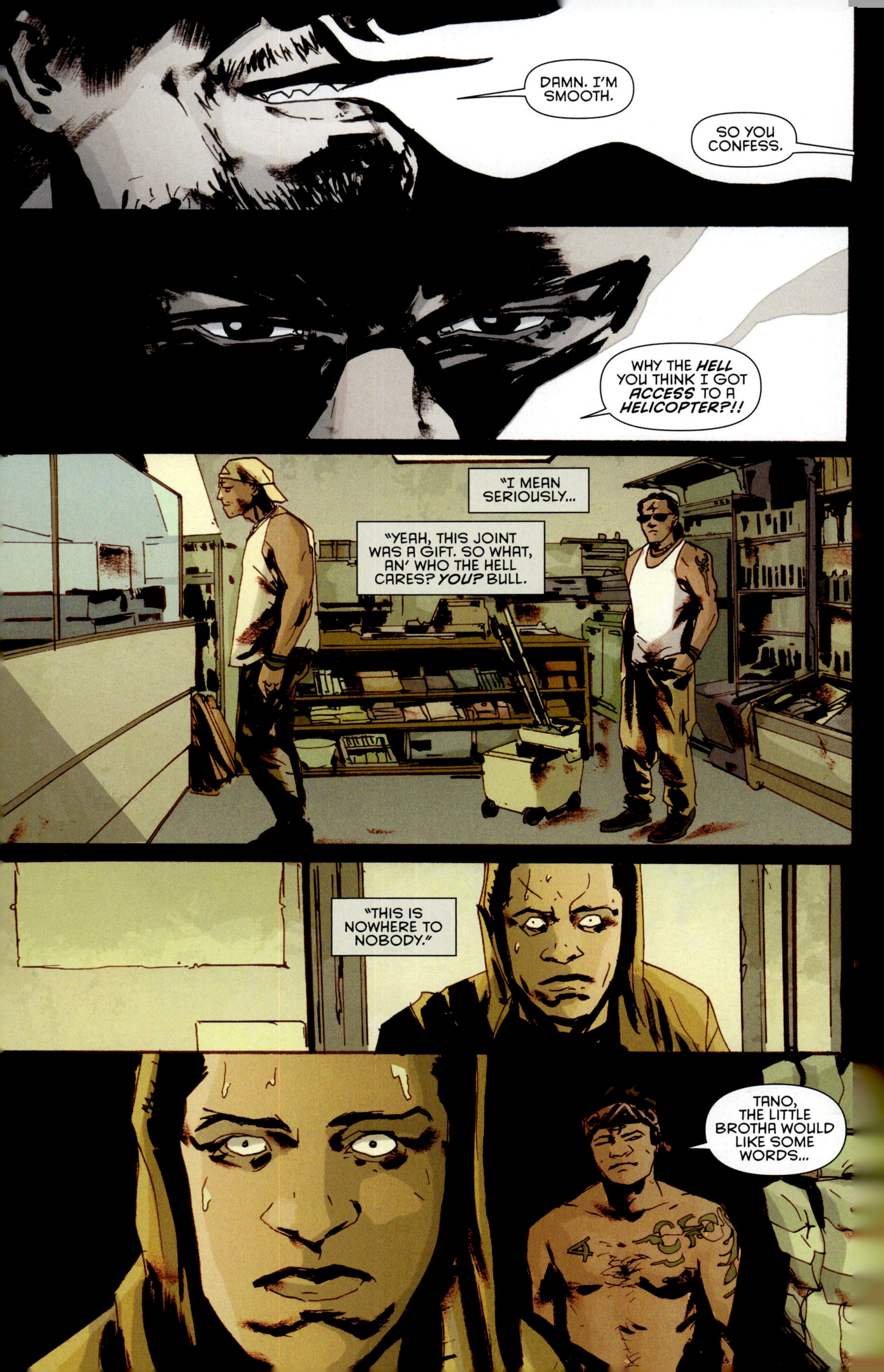
DAMN. I'M SMOOTH.
SO YOU CONFESS.
WHY THE *HELL* YOU THINK I GOT *ACCESS* TO A *HELICOPTER?!!*
"I MEAN SERIOUSLY...
"YEAH, THIS JOINT WAS A GIFT. SO WHAT, AN' WHO THE HELL CARES? *YOU?* BULL.
"THIS IS NOWHERE TO NOBODY."
TANO, THE LITTLE BROTHA WOULD LIKE SOME WORDS...

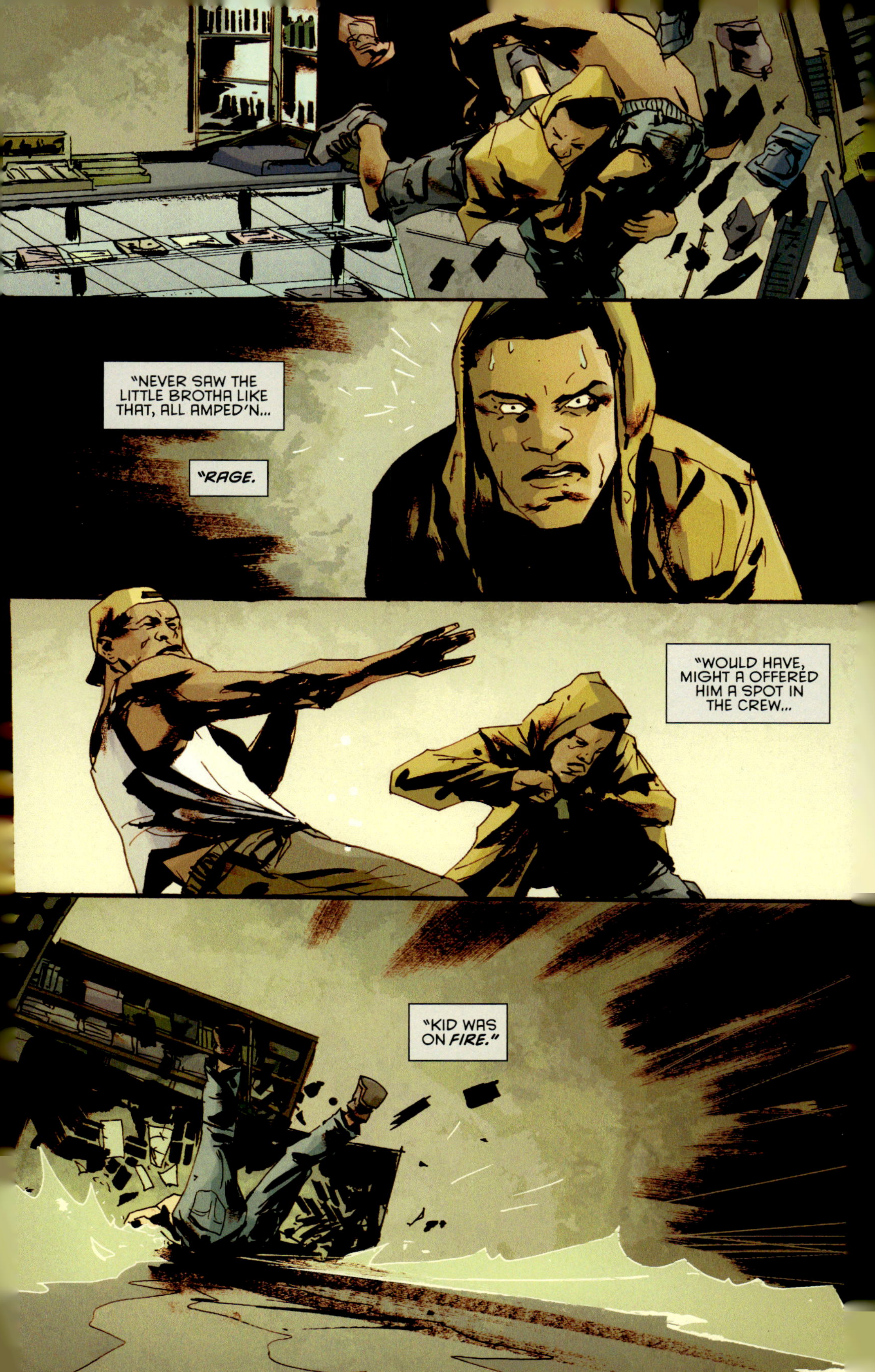
"NEVER SAW THE LITTLE BROTHA LIKE THAT, ALL AMPED'N...
"RAGE.
"WOULD HAVE, MIGHT A OFFERED HIM A SPOT IN THE CREW...
"KID WAS ON FIRE."

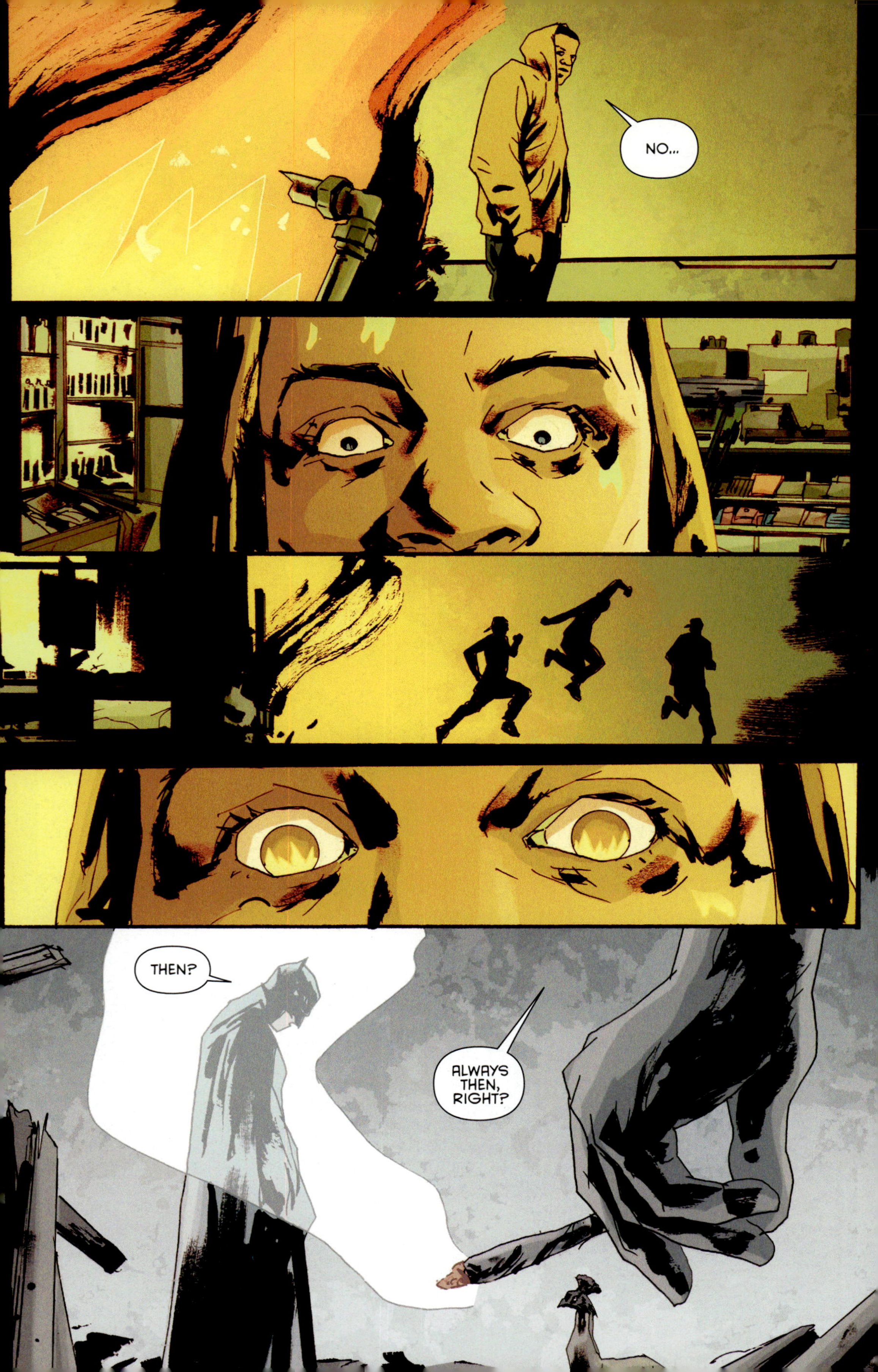
NO...
THEN?
ALWAYS THEN, RIGHT?

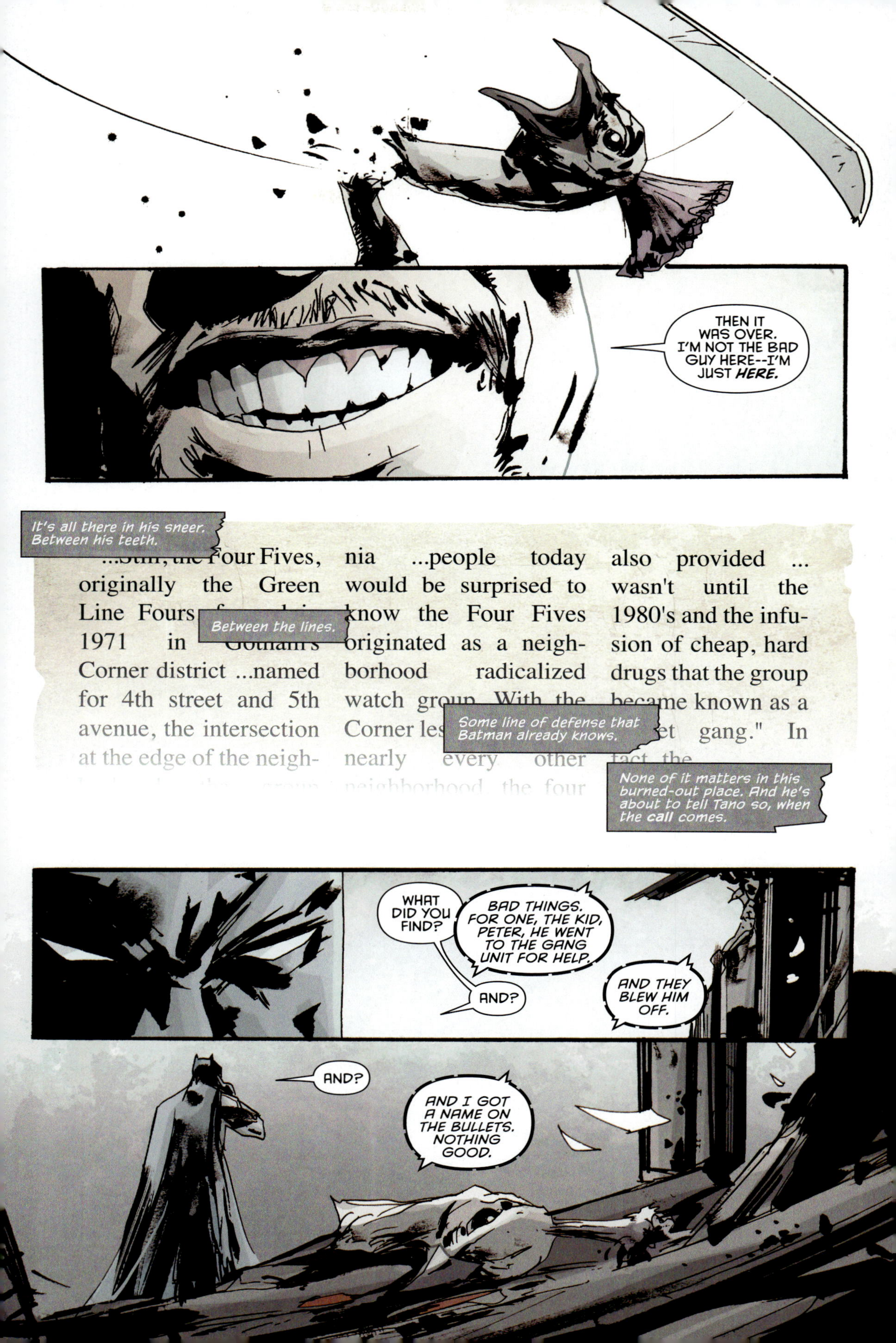

THEN IT WAS OVER. I'M NOT THE BAD GUY HERE--I'M JUST *HERE.*
It's all there in his sneer. Between his teeth.
Four Fives, originally the Green Line Fours
1971 in
Corner district ...named for 4th street and 5th avenue, the intersection at the edge of the neigh-
Between the lines.
nia ...people today would be surprised to know the Four Fives originated as a neighborhood radicalized watch gro
Corner les
nearly every other
also provided ... wasn't until the 1980's and the infusion of cheap, hard drugs that the group became known as a
gang." In
Some line of defense that Batman already knows.
None of it matters in this burned-out place. And he's about to tell Tano so, when the **call** comes.
WHAT DID YOU FIND?
BAD THINGS. FOR ONE, THE KID, PETER, HE WENT TO THE GANG UNIT FOR HELP.
AND?
AND THEY BLEW HIM OFF.
AND?
AND I GOT A NAME ON THE BULLETS. NOTHING GOOD.

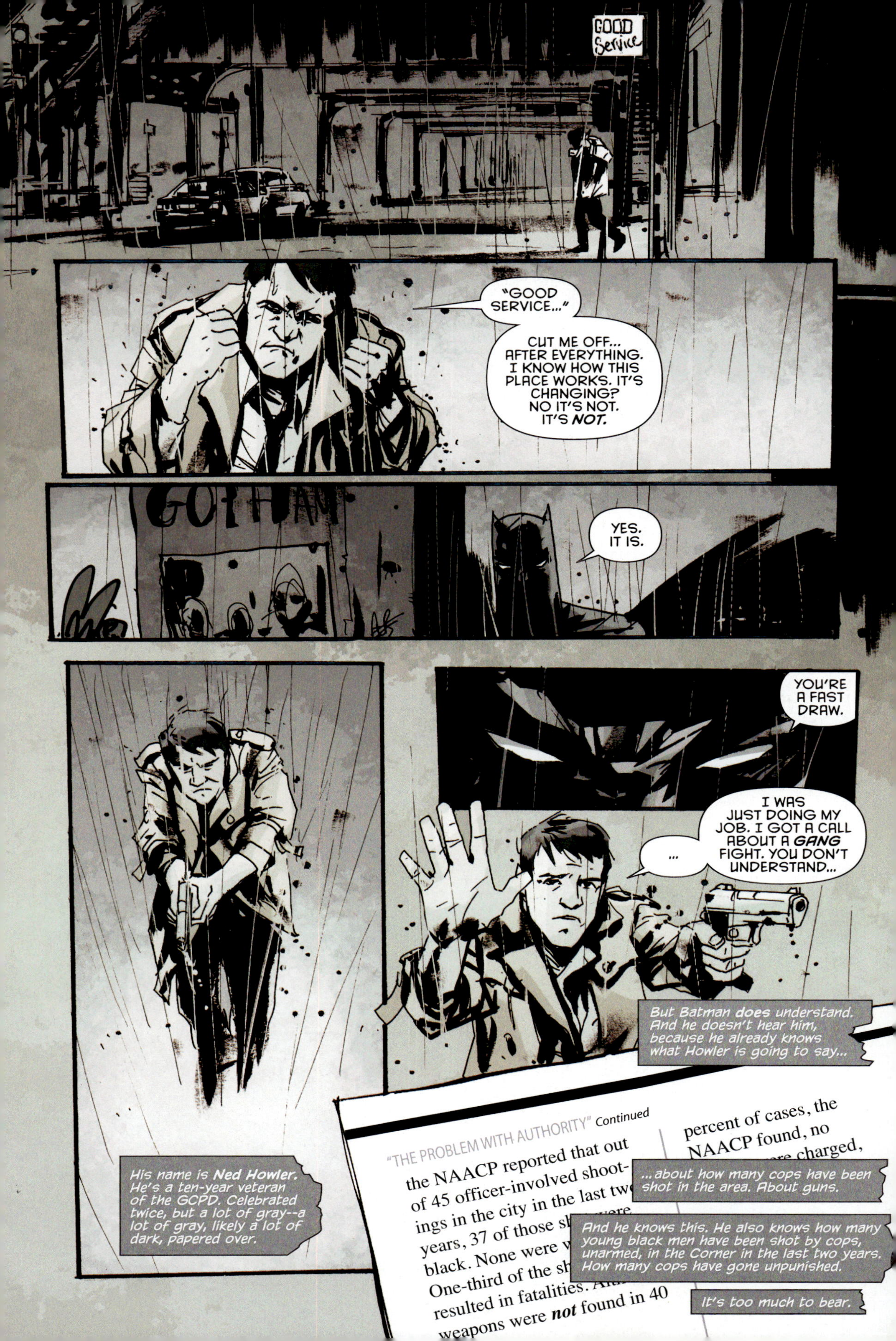

GOOD Service
"GOOD SERVICE..."
CUT ME OFF... AFTER EVERYTHING. I KNOW HOW THIS PLACE WORKS. IT'S CHANGING? NO IT'S NOT. IT'S ***NOT.***
GOTHAM
YES. IT IS.
YOU'RE A FAST DRAW.
...
I WAS JUST DOING MY JOB. I GOT A CALL ABOUT A ***GANG*** FIGHT. YOU DON'T UNDERSTAND...
*But Batman **does** understand. And he doesn't hear him, because he already knows what Howler is going to say...*
*His name is **Ned Howler.** He's a ten-year veteran of the GCPD. Celebrated twice, but a lot of gray--a lot of gray, likely a lot of dark, papered over.*
"THE PROBLEM WITH AUTHORITY" Continued
the NAACP reported that out of 45 officer-involved shootings in the city in the last two years, 37 of those shot were black. None were
One-third of the sh
resulted in fatalities.
weapons were ***not*** found in 40
percent of cases, the NAACP found, no
charged,
...about how many cops have been shot in the area. About guns.
And he knows this. He also knows how many young black men have been shot by cops, unarmed, in the Corner in the last two years. How many cops have gone unpunished.
It's too much to bear.

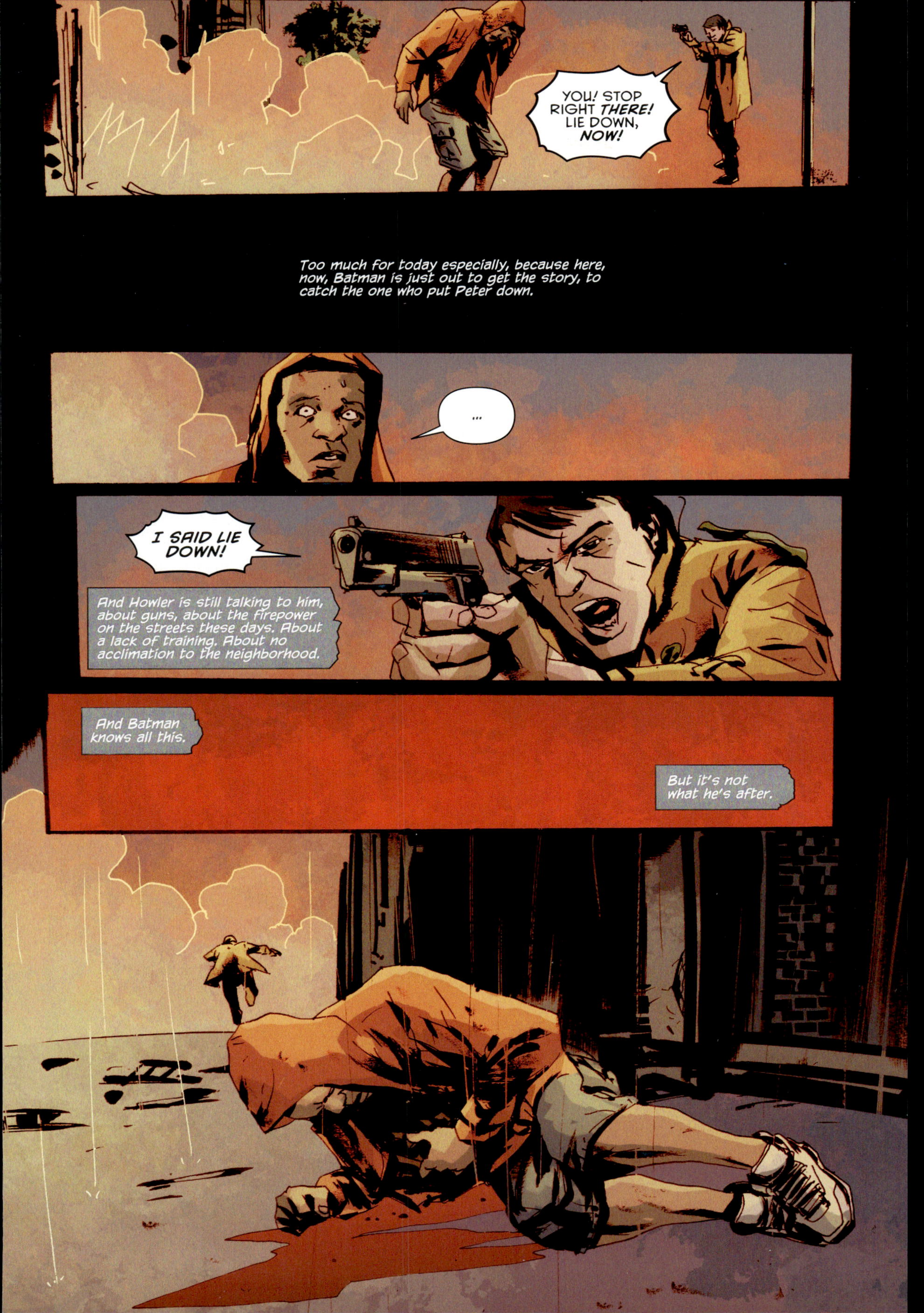
YOU! STOP RIGHT THERE! LIE DOWN, NOW!
Too much for today especially, because here, now, Batman is just out to get the story, to catch the one who put Peter down.
...
I SAID LIE DOWN!
And Howler is still talking to him, about guns, about the firepower on the streets these days. About a lack of training. About no acclimation to the neighborhood.
And Batman knows all this.
But it's not what he's after.

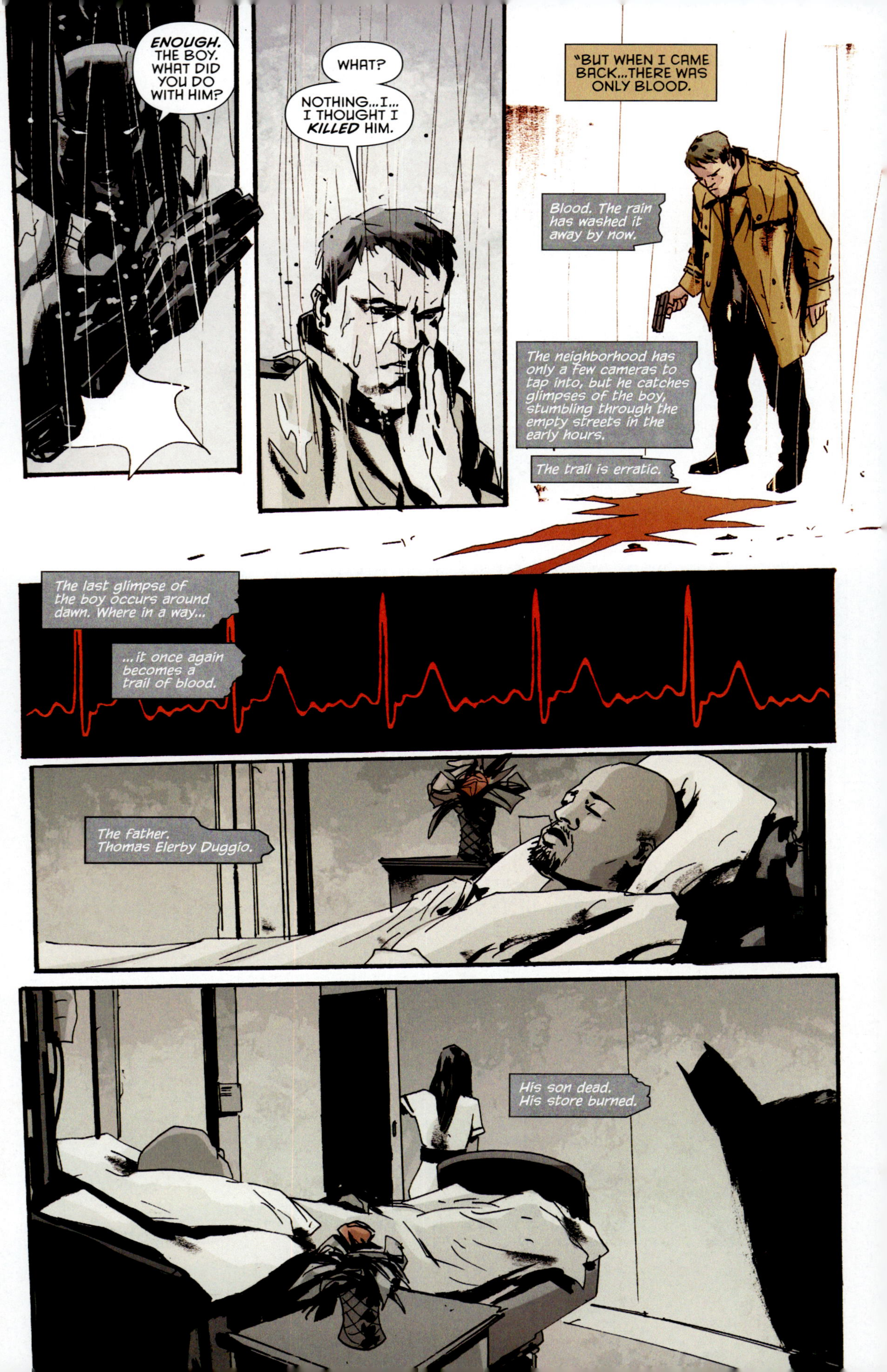

ENOUGH. THE BOY. WHAT DID YOU DO WITH HIM?
WHAT?
NOTHING...I... I THOUGHT I KILLED HIM.
"BUT WHEN I CAME BACK...THERE WAS ONLY BLOOD.
Blood. The rain has washed it away by now.
The neighborhood has only a few cameras to tap into, but he catches glimpses of the boy, stumbling through the empty streets in the early hours.
The trail is erratic.
The last glimpse of the boy occurs around dawn. Where in a way...
...it once again becomes a trail of blood.
The father. Thomas Elerby Duggio.
His son dead. His store burned.

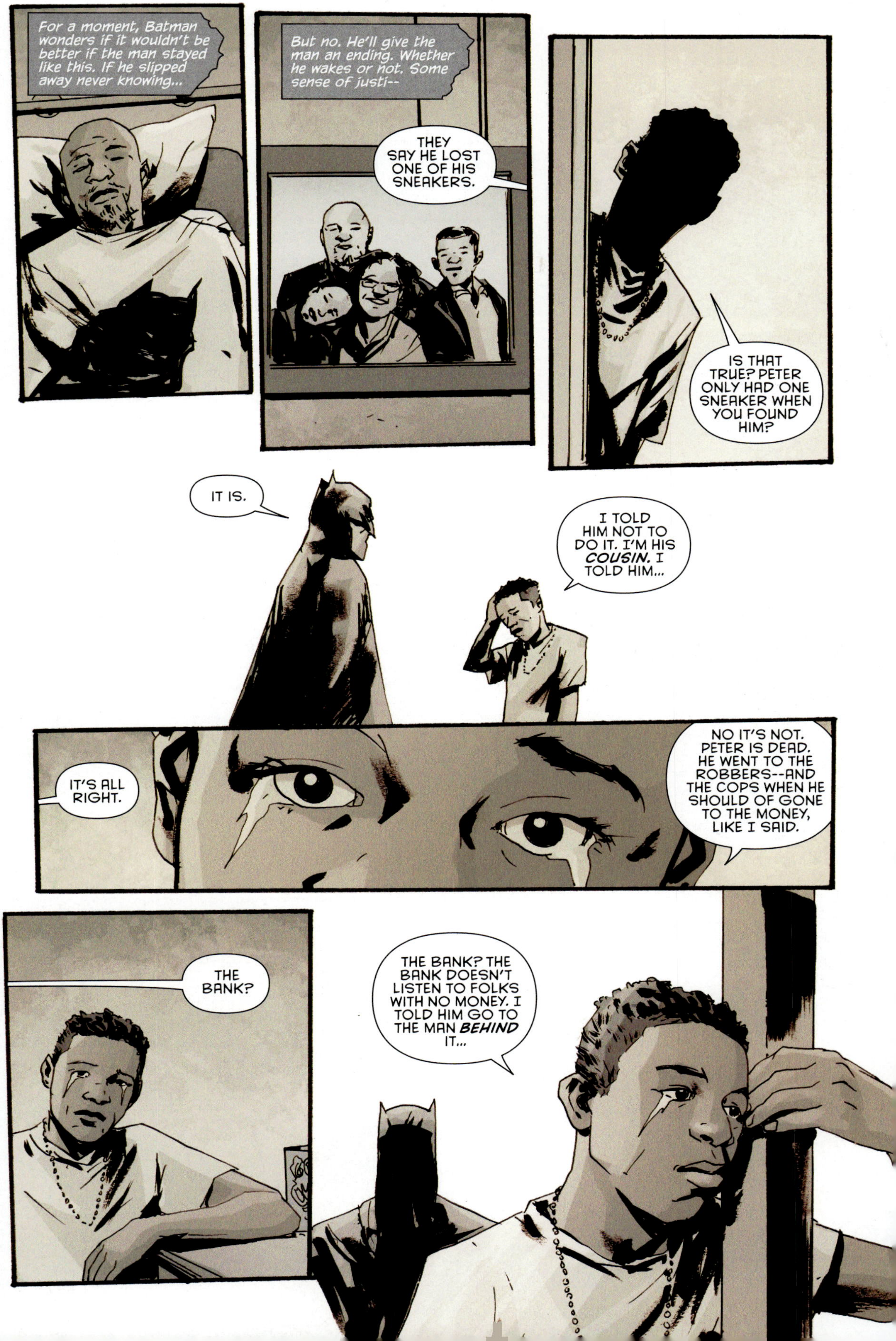

For a moment, Batman wonders if it wouldn't be better if the man stayed like this. If he slipped away never knowing...
But no. He'll give the man an ending. Whether he wakes or not. Some sense of justi--
THEY SAY HE LOST ONE OF HIS SNEAKERS.
IS THAT TRUE? PETER ONLY HAD ONE SNEAKER WHEN YOU FOUND HIM?
IT IS.
I TOLD HIM NOT TO DO IT. I'M HIS COUSIN. I TOLD HIM...
IT'S ALL RIGHT.
NO IT'S NOT. PETER IS DEAD. HE WENT TO THE ROBBERS--AND THE COPS WHEN HE SHOULD OF GONE TO THE MONEY, LIKE I SAID.
THE BANK?
THE BANK? THE BANK DOESN'T LISTEN TO FOLKS WITH NO MONEY. I TOLD HIM GO TO THE MAN BEHIND IT...

"...I TOLD HIM TO GO TO *BRUCE WAYNE*."

MR. WAYNE! BRUCE WAYNE! HEY!

"PETER'S STORE WAS ONLY WORTH SOMETHING ONCE BRUCE WAYNE ANNOUNCED HE WAS GONNA DEVELOP THE NEIGHBORHOOD. I SAID TO PETER, I SAID, 'YOU SHOULD TRY TALKING TO THE MAN.' ASKING HIM TO HELP, OR NOT TO BUILD. I DON'T KNOW..."

While some think an infusion of capital is needed, others question whether private developments -- even ones like Wayne Apartments, designed to provide upscale living conditions for lower-middle class families in the Corner -- might drive up property values and force out longtime residents. The debate... roponents on both sides, but in

"BUT IT DIDN'T WORK.

"AND THAT WAS IT. NO MORE OPTIONS. THAT'S WHEN HE STARTED TALKING ABOUT *IT*."

ABOUT WHAT?

ABOUT YOU. HE WANTED TO STAND UP FOR HIMSELF. TO PUSH BACK.

LIKE *YOU* DO.

...

HOW?

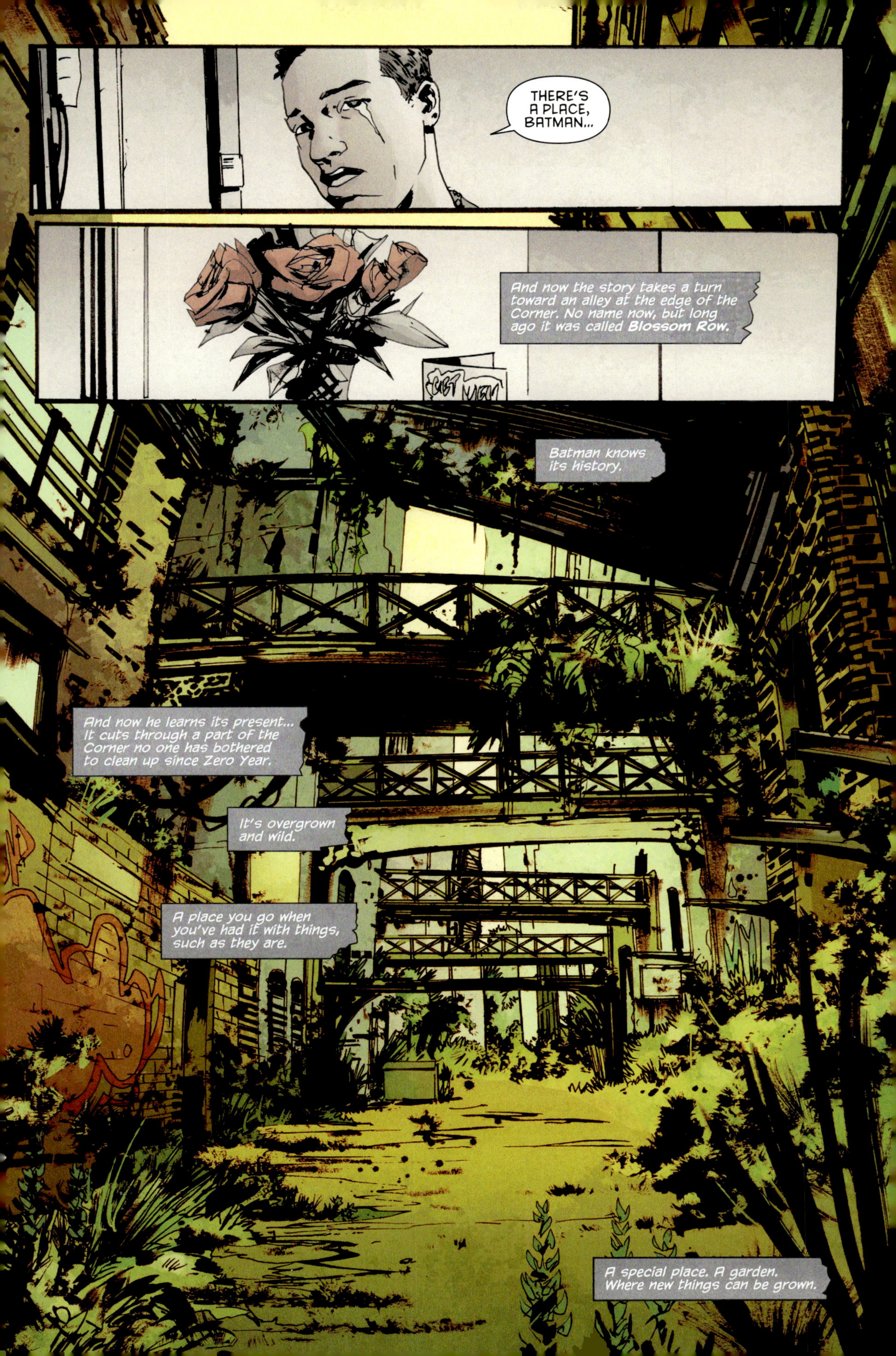

THERE'S A PLACE, BATMAN...
And now the story takes a turn toward an alley at the edge of the Corner. No name now, but long ago it was called **Blossom Row.**
Batman knows its history.
And now he learns its present... It cuts through a part of the Corner no one has bothered to clean up since Zero Year.
It's overgrown and wild.
A place you go when you've had it with things, such as they are.
A special place. A garden. Where new things can be grown.

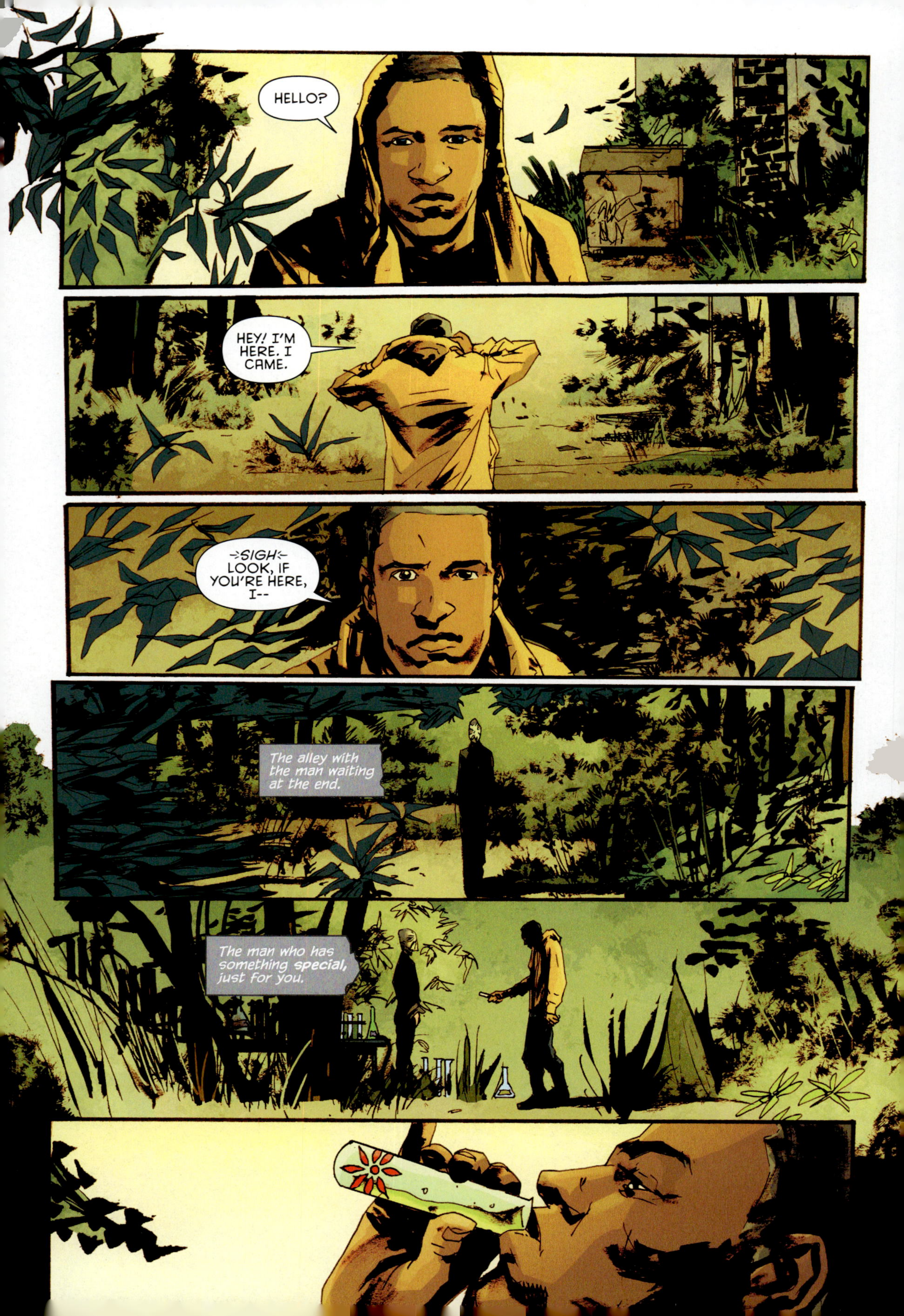

HELLO?
HEY! I'M HERE. I CAME.
-SIGH- LOOK, IF YOU'RE HERE, I--
The alley with the man waiting at the end.
The man who has something **special**, just for you.

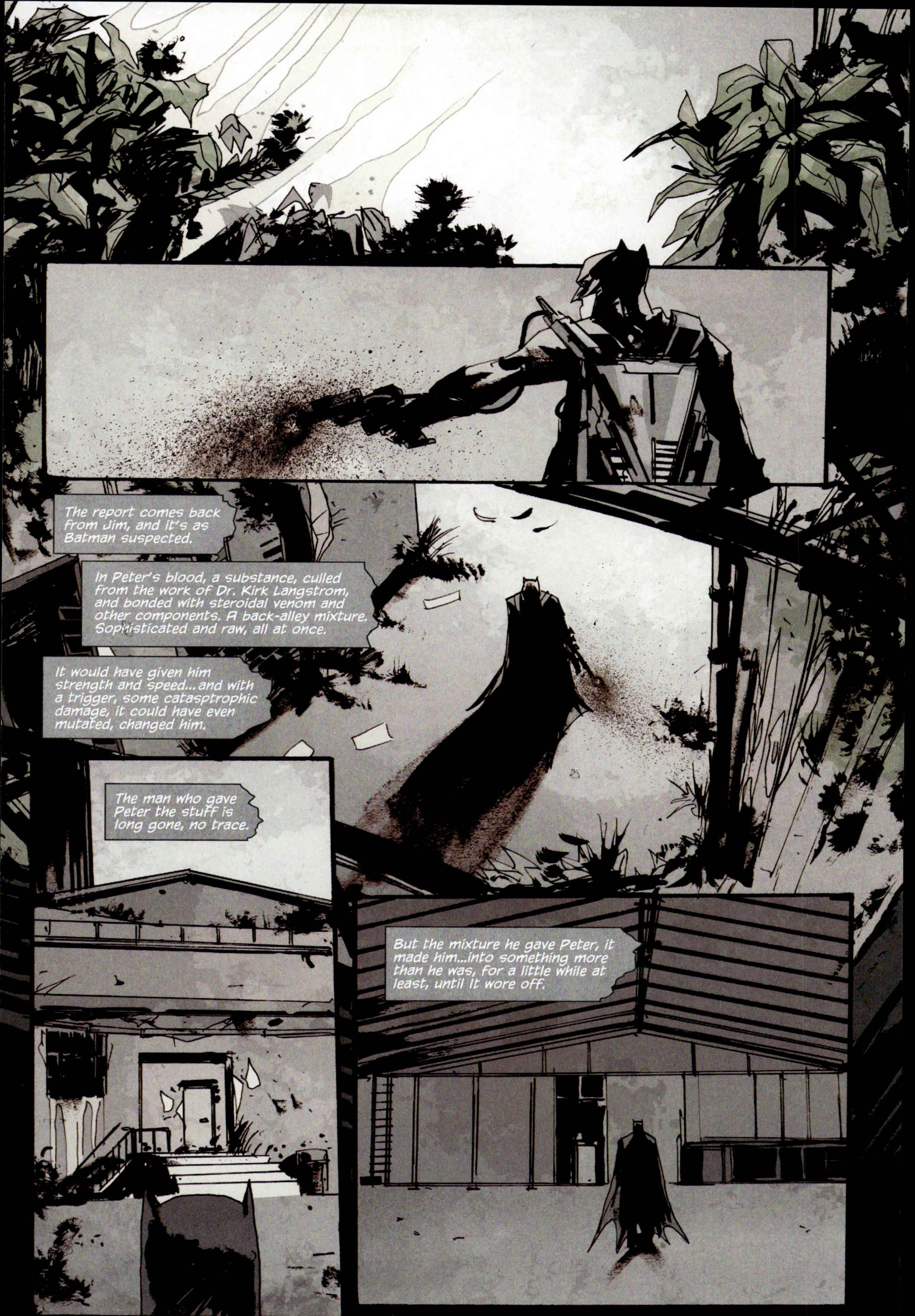
The report comes back from Jim, and it's as Batman suspected.
In Peter's blood, a substance, culled from the work of Dr. Kirk Langstrom, and bonded with steroidal venom and other components. A back-alley mixture. Sophisticated and raw, all at once.
It would have given him strength and speed...and with a trigger, some catasptrophic damage, it could have even mutated, changed him.
The man who gave Peter the stuff is long gone, no trace.
But the mixture he gave Peter, it made him...into something more than he was, for a little while at least, until it wore off.

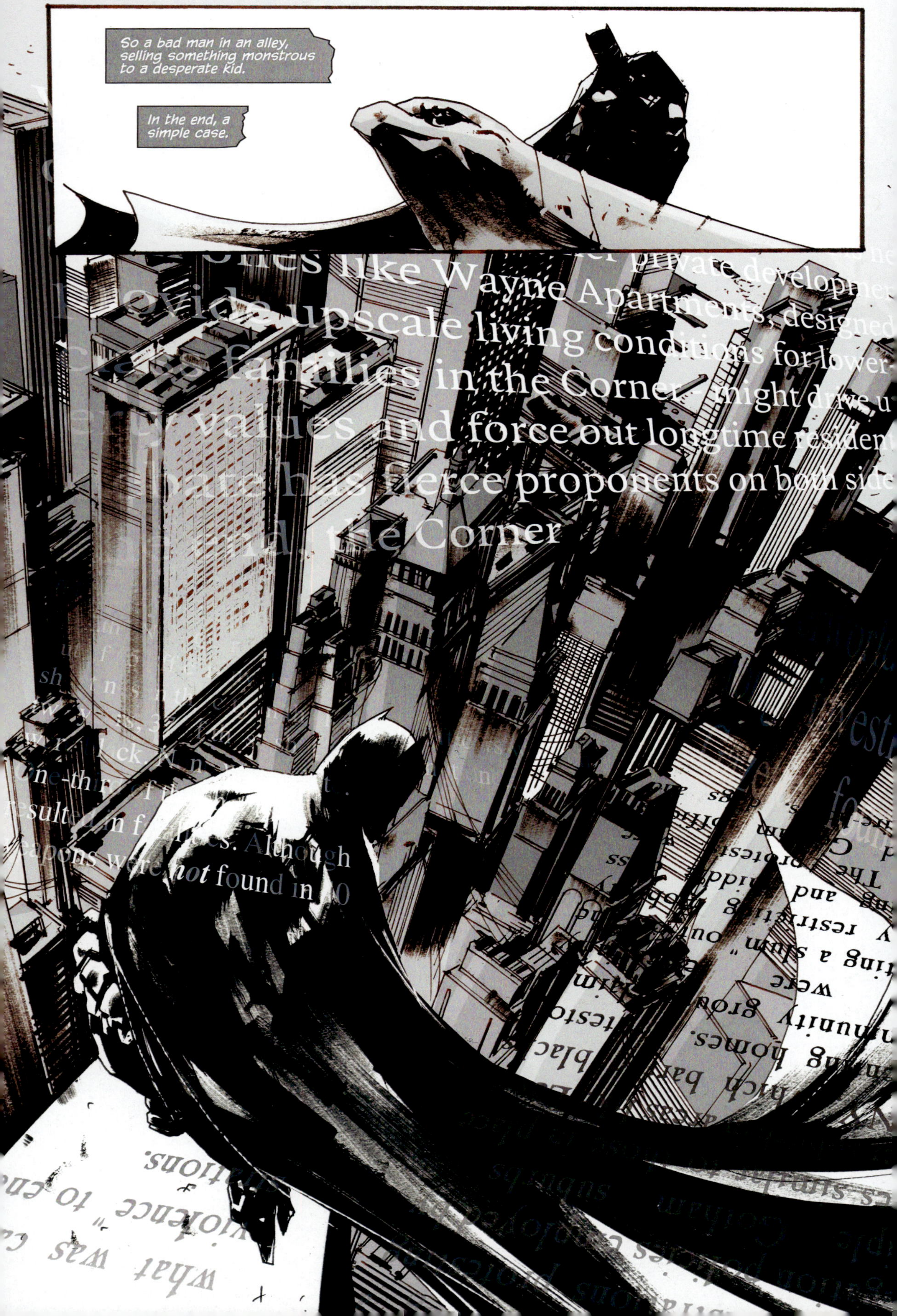
So a bad man in an alley, selling something monstrous to a desperate kid.
In the end, a simple case.

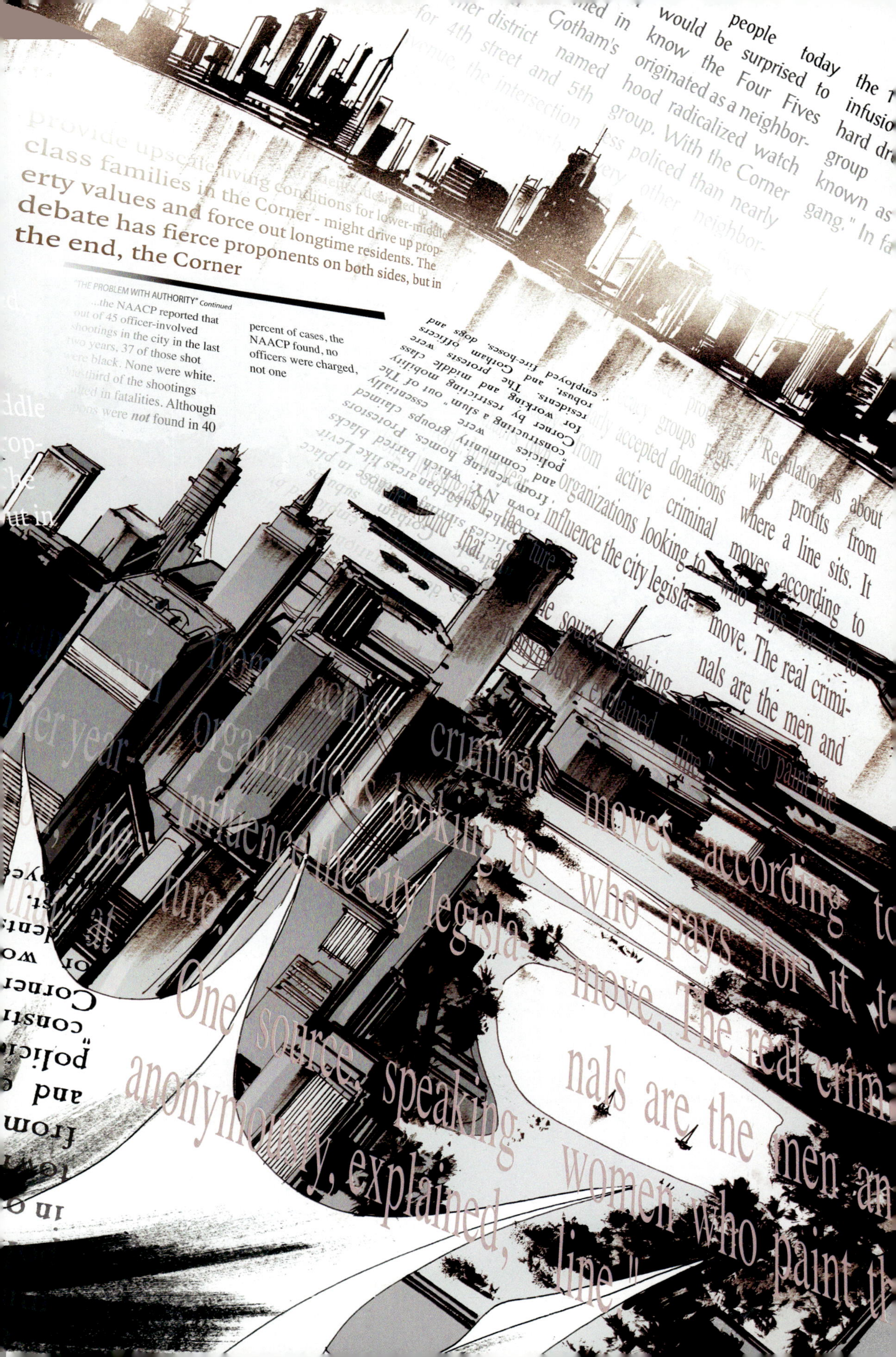

Gotham's
would be surprised to
people today the
know the Four Fives
originated as a neighbor-
hood radicalized watch group
group. With the Corner
known as
less policed than nearly
gang." In fa
class families in the Corner - might drive up property values and force out longtime residents. The
debate has fierce proponents on both sides, but in
the end, the Corner
"THE PROBLEM WITH AUTHORITY" Continued
...the NAACP reported that out of 45 officer-involved shootings in the city in the last two years, 37 of those shot were black. None were white. One-third of the shootings resulted in fatalities. Although
were *not* found in 40
percent of cases, the NAACP found, no officers were charged, not one
"Regulation is about who profits from where a line sits. It moves according to who pays for it to move. The real criminals are the men and women who paint the line."
organizations looking to influence the city legisla-
active criminal
One source, speaking anonymously, explained,

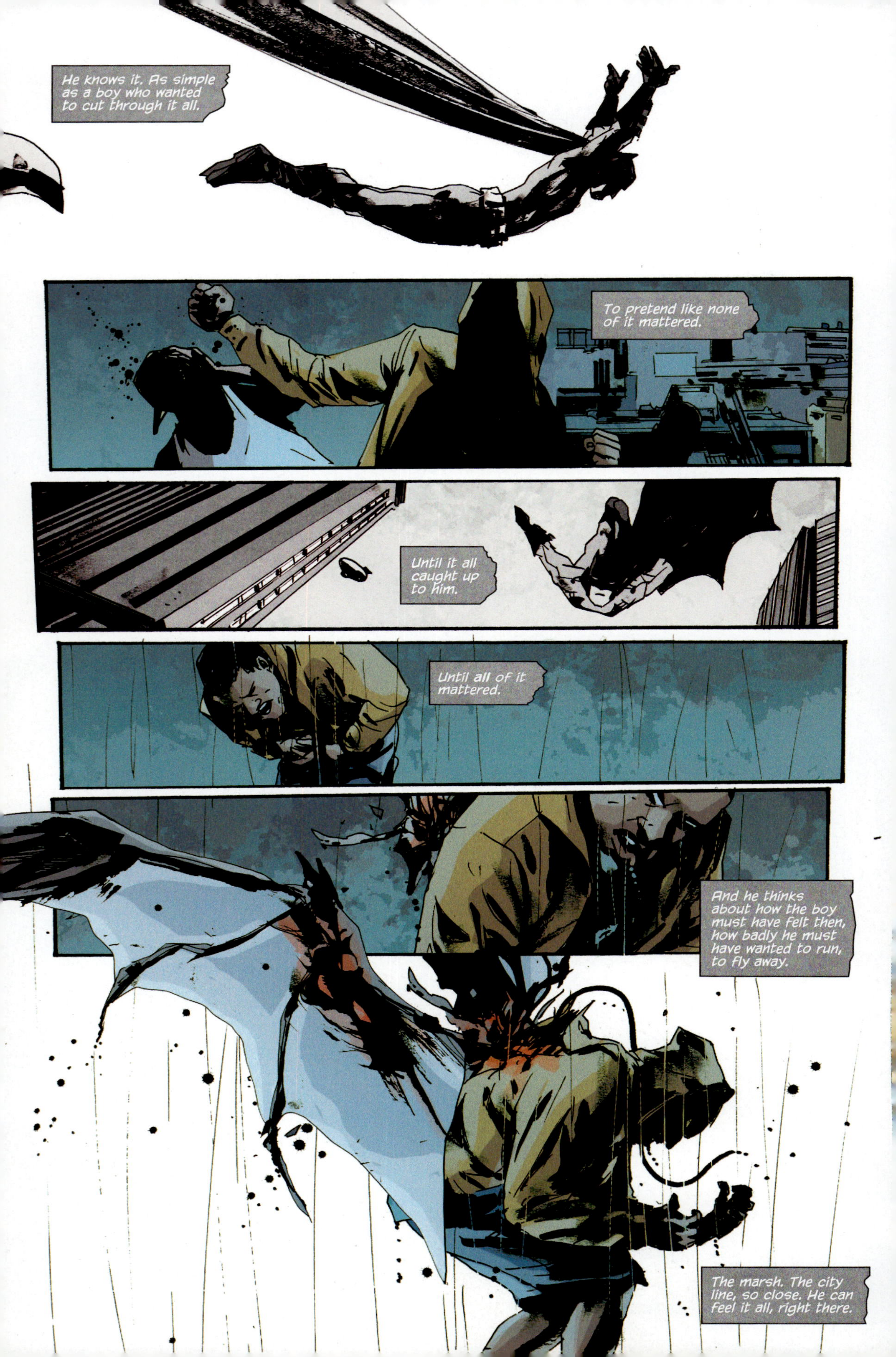
He knows it. As simple as a boy who wanted to cut through it all.
To pretend like none of it mattered.
Until it all caught up to him.
Until all of it mattered.
And he thinks about how the boy must have felt then, how badly he must have wanted to run, to fly away.
The marsh. The city line, so close. He can feel it all, right there.

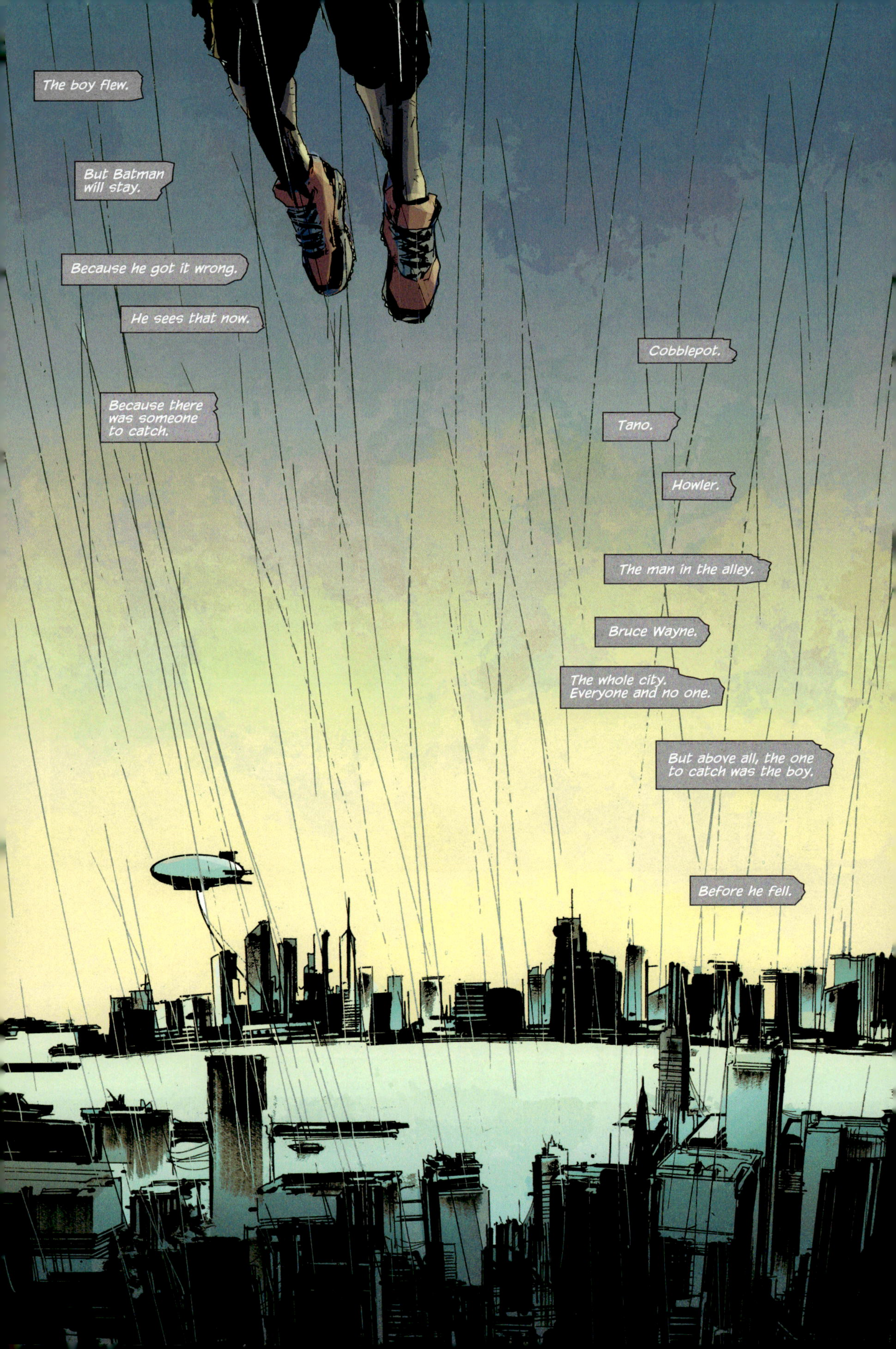

The boy flew.
But Batman will stay.
Because he got it wrong.
He sees that now.
Because there was someone to catch.
Cobblepot.
Tano.
Howler.
The man in the alley.
Bruce Wayne.
The whole city. Everyone and no one.
But above all, the one to catch was the boy.
Before he fell.

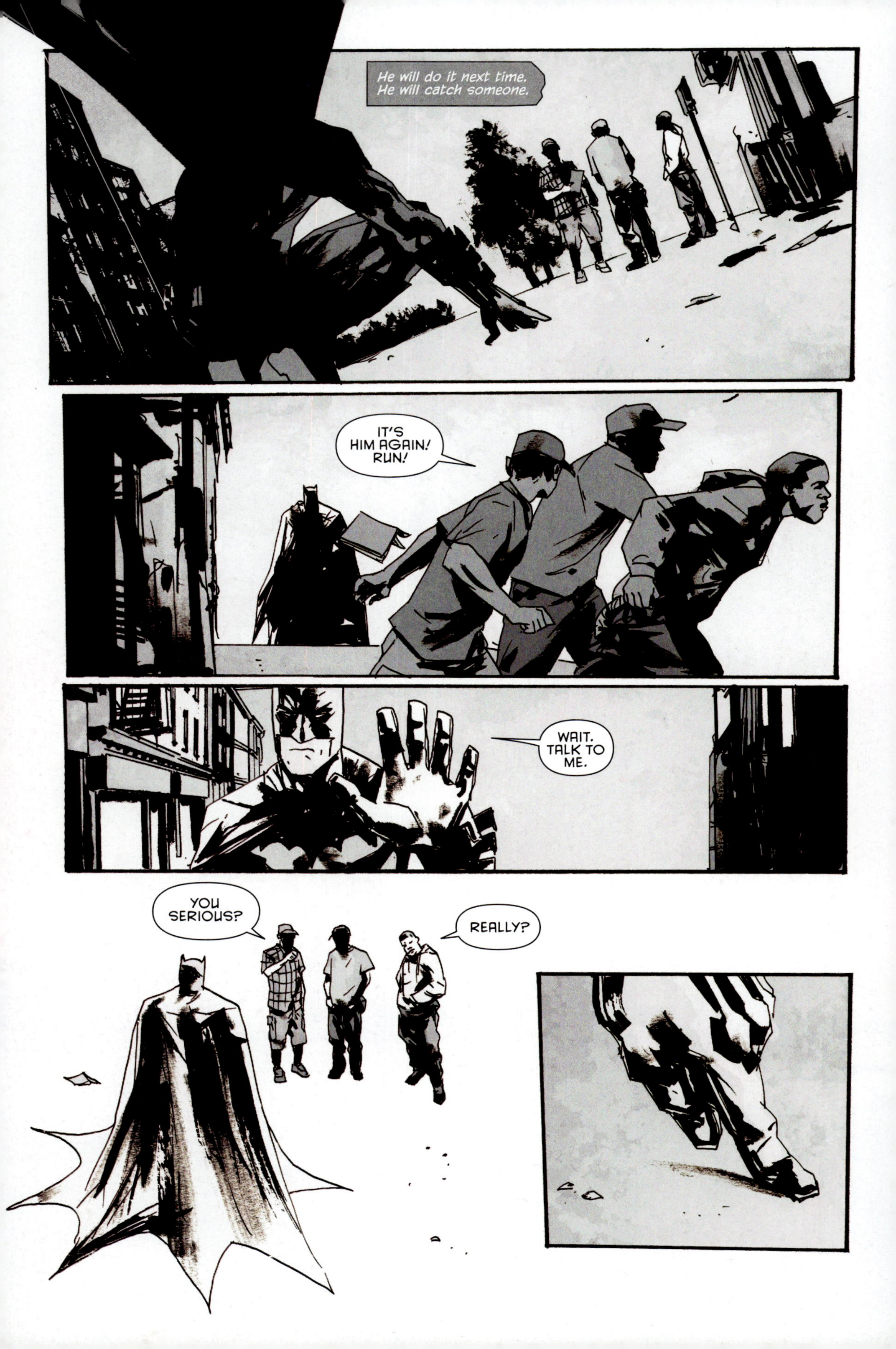
He will do it next time. He will catch someone.
IT'S HIM AGAIN! RUN!
WAIT. TALK TO ME.
YOU SERIOUS?
REALLY?

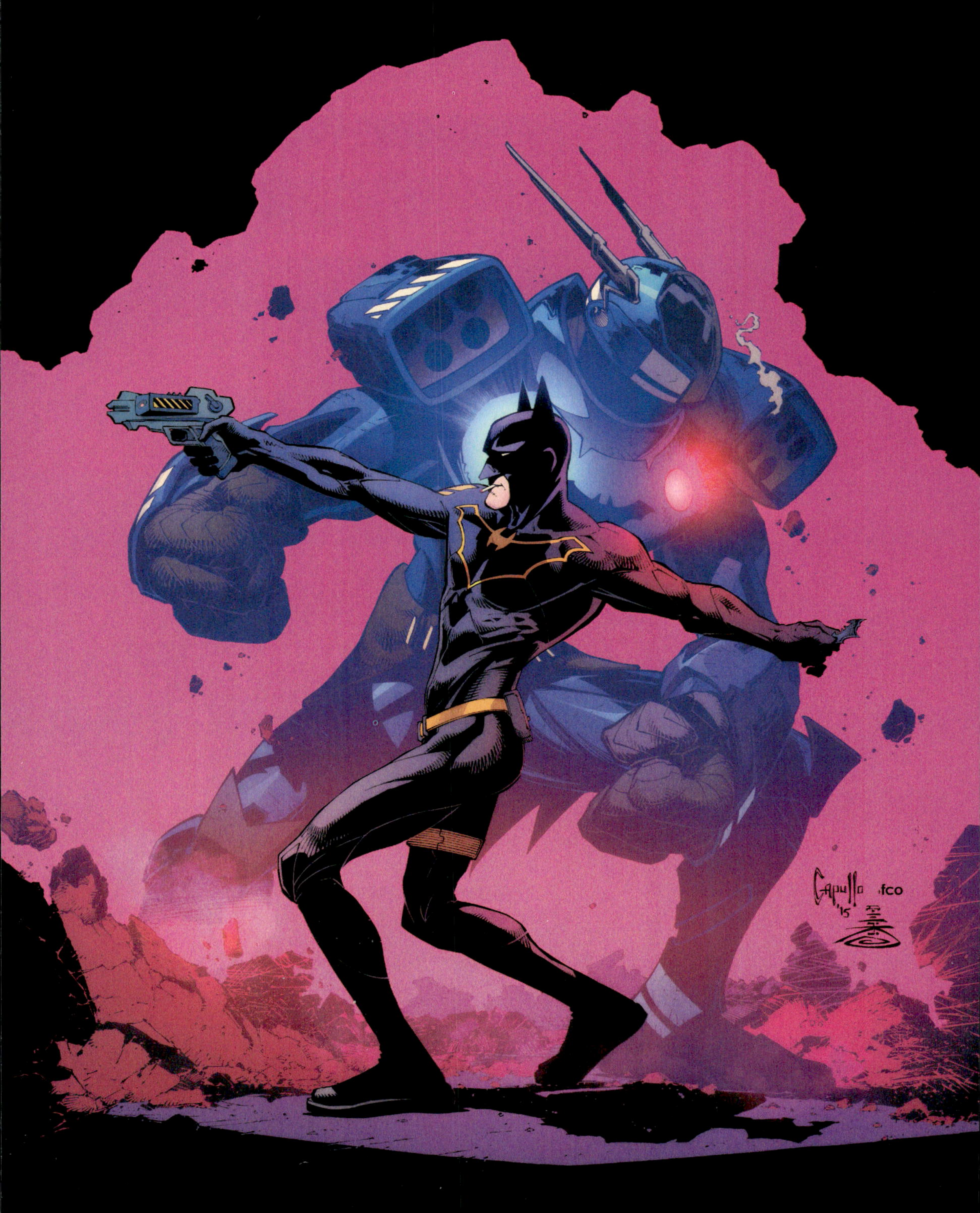

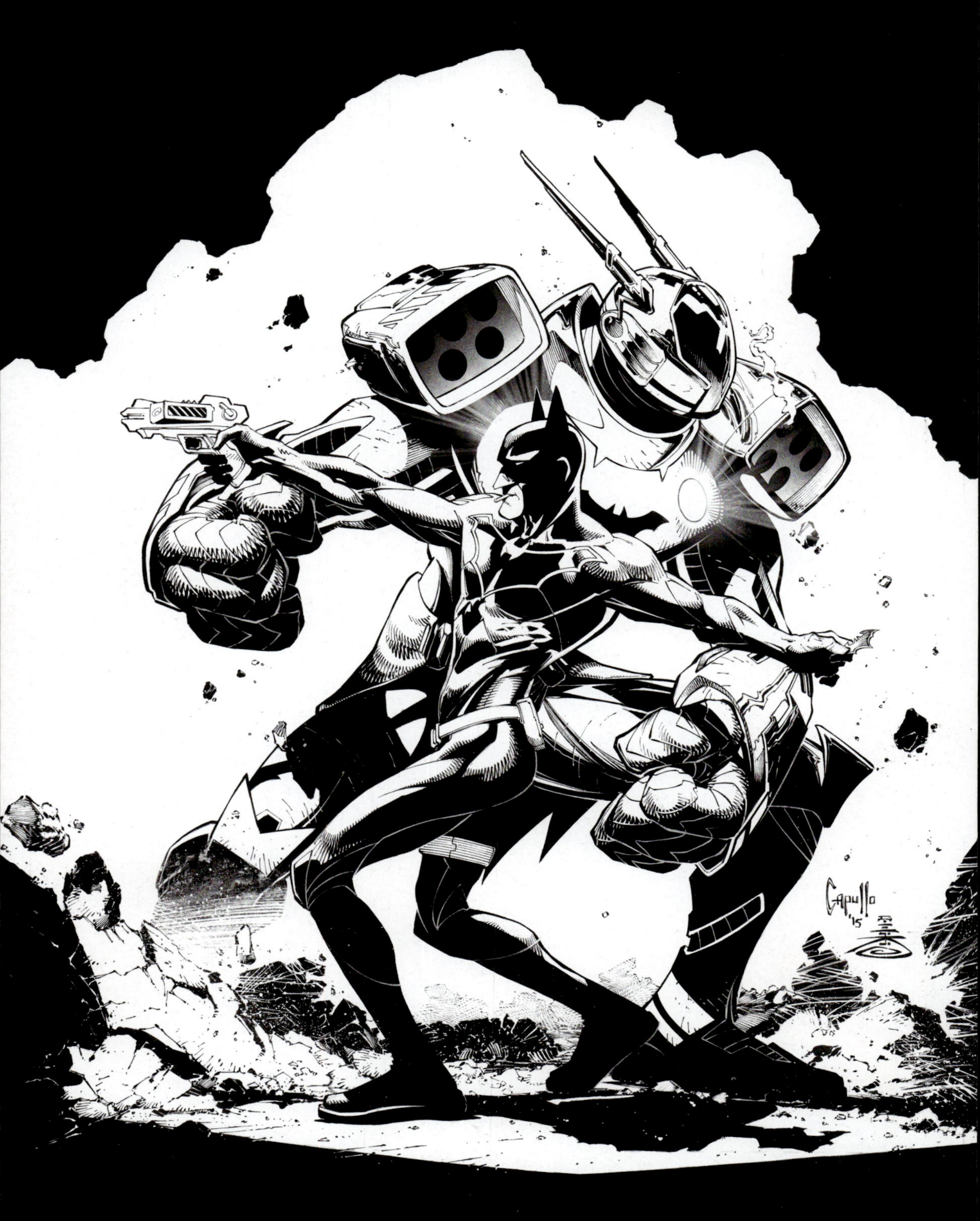
Capullo '15

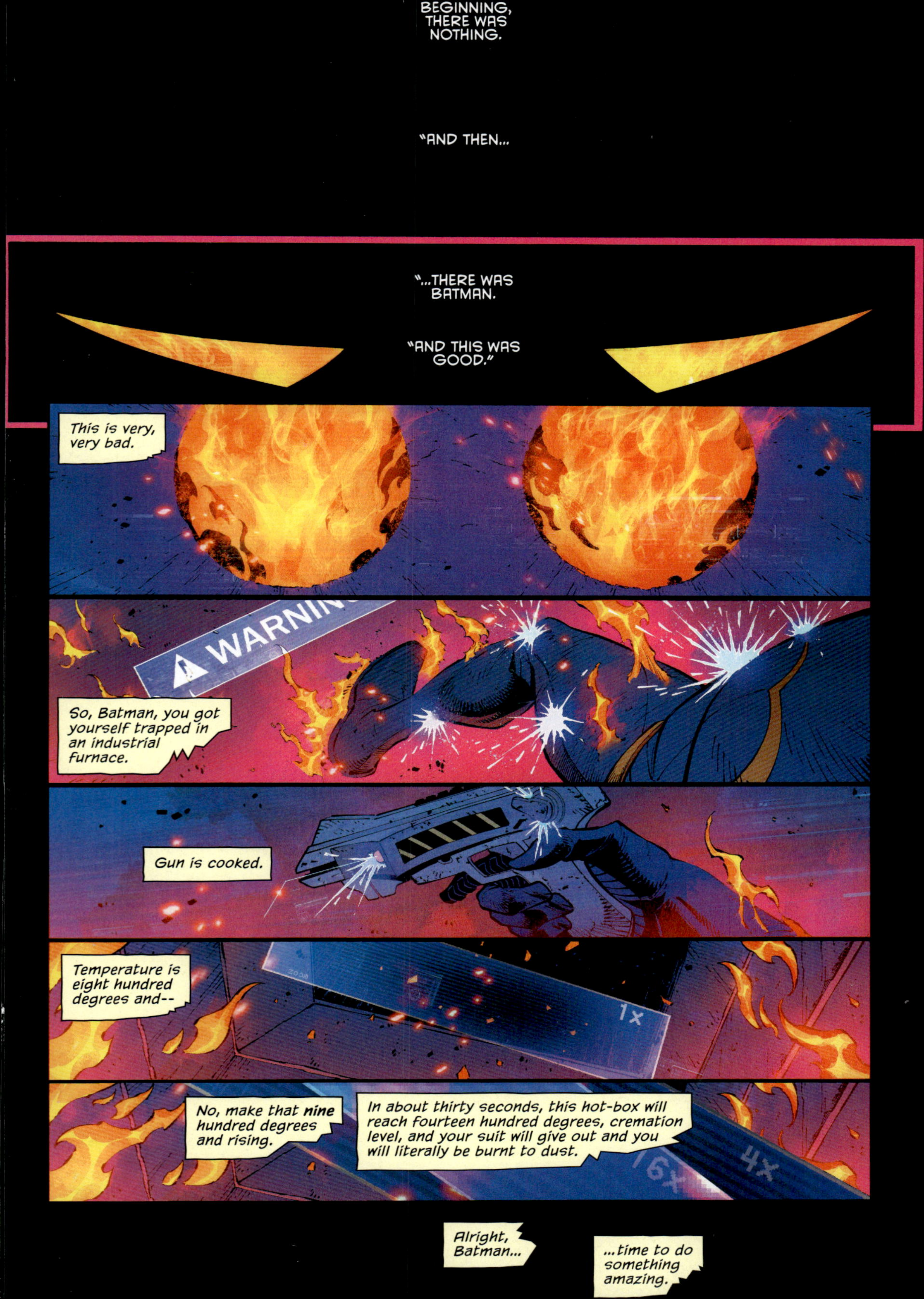
BEGINNING, THERE WAS NOTHING.
"AND THEN...
"...THERE WAS BATMAN.
"AND THIS WAS GOOD."
This is very, very bad.
WARNIN
So, Batman, you got yourself trapped in an industrial furnace.
Gun is cooked.
Temperature is eight hundred degrees and--
1x
No, make that **nine** hundred degrees and rising.
In about thirty seconds, this hot-box will reach fourteen hundred degrees, cremation level, and your suit will give out and you will literally be burnt to dust.
16x
4x
Alright, Batman...
...time to do something amazing.

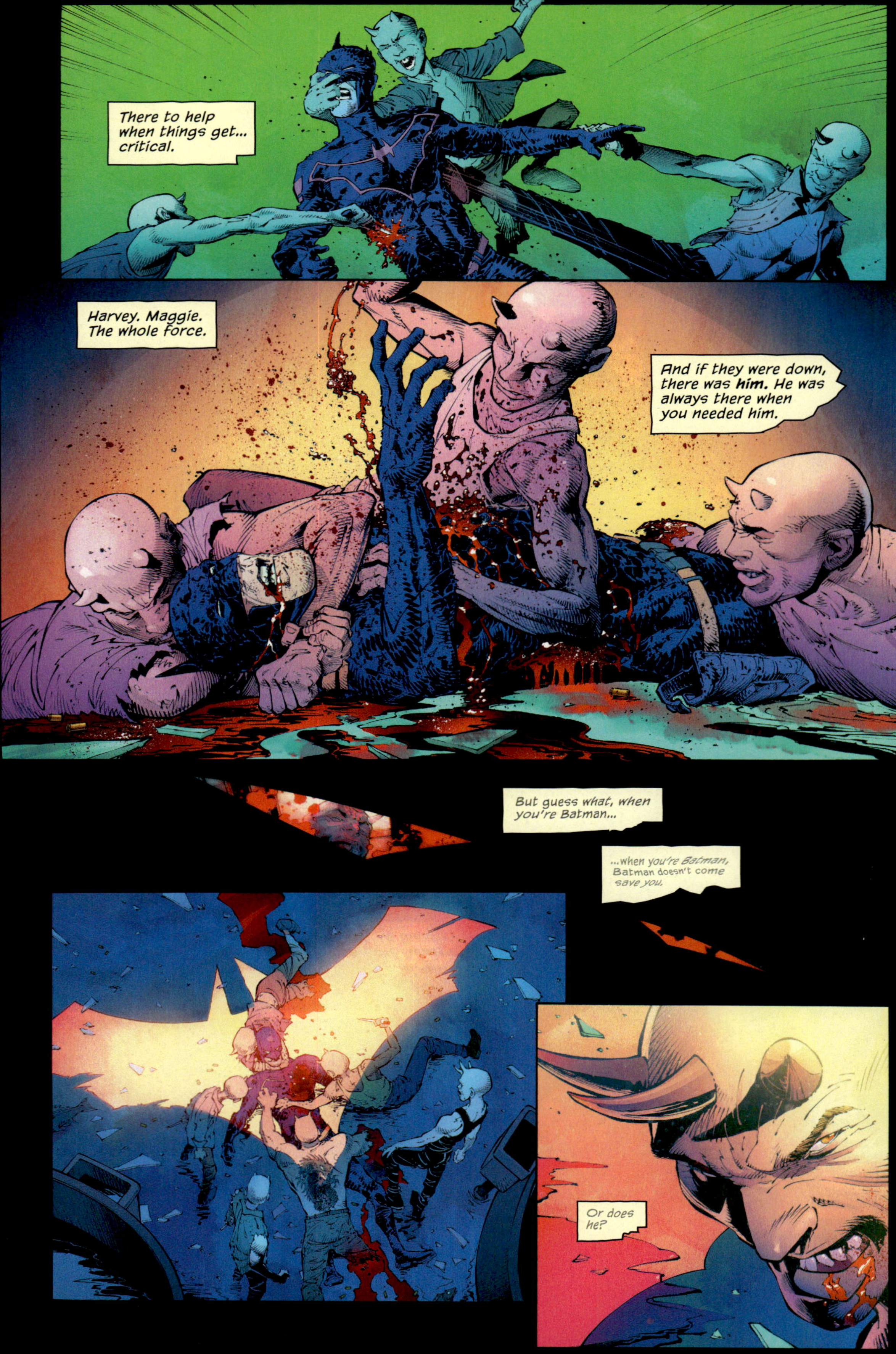
There to help when things get... critical.
Harvey. Maggie. The whole force.
And if they were down, there was **him.** He was always there when you needed him.
But guess what, when you're Batman...
...when you're *Batman,* Batman doesn't come save you.
Or does he?

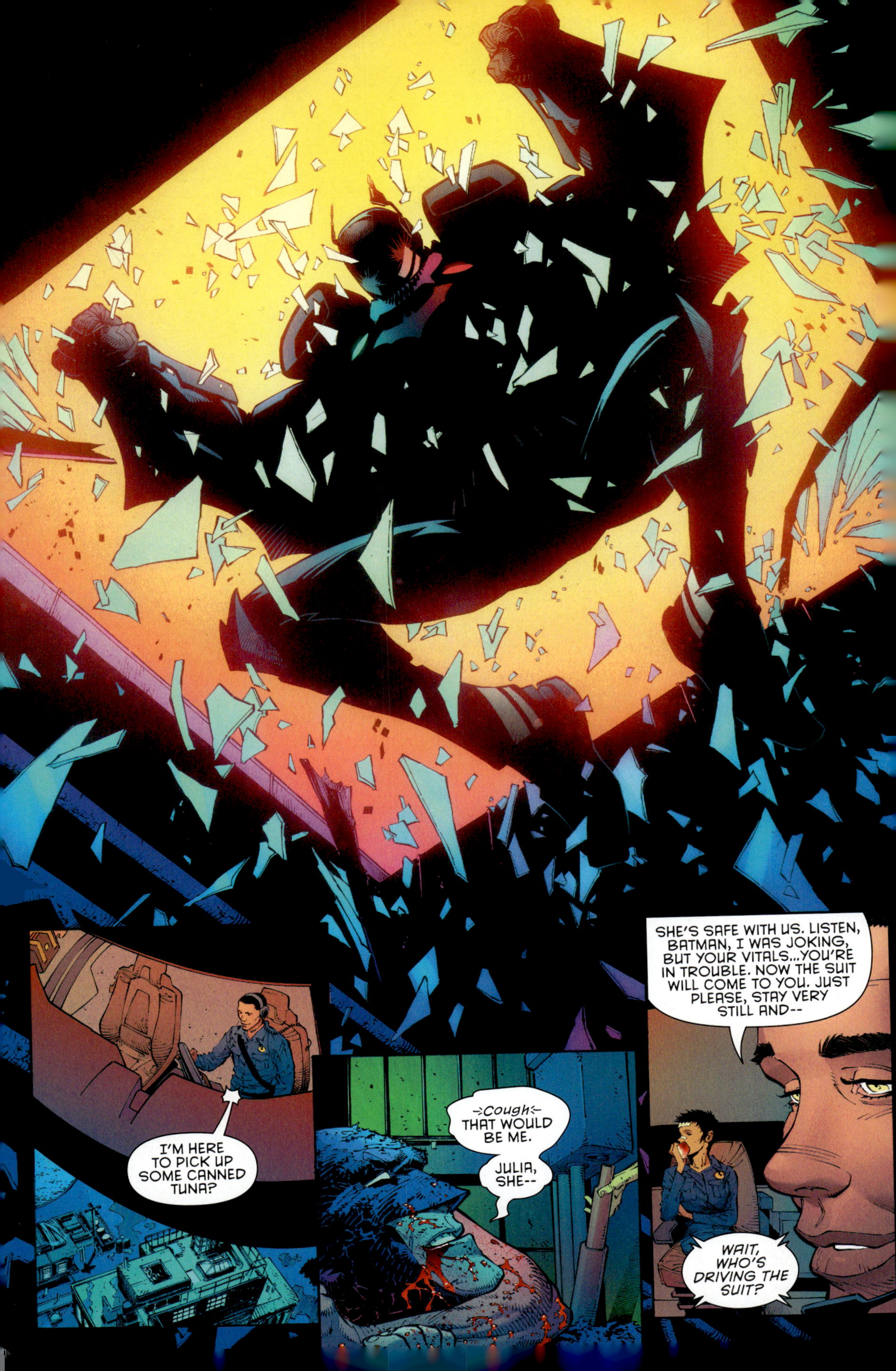
I'M HERE TO PICK UP SOME CANNED TUNA?
-Cough- THAT WOULD BE ME.
JULIA, SHE--
SHE'S SAFE WITH US. LISTEN, BATMAN, I WAS JOKING, BUT YOUR VITALS...YOU'RE IN TROUBLE. NOW THE SUIT WILL COME TO YOU. JUST PLEASE, STAY VERY STILL AND--
WAIT, WHO'S DRIVING THE SUIT?

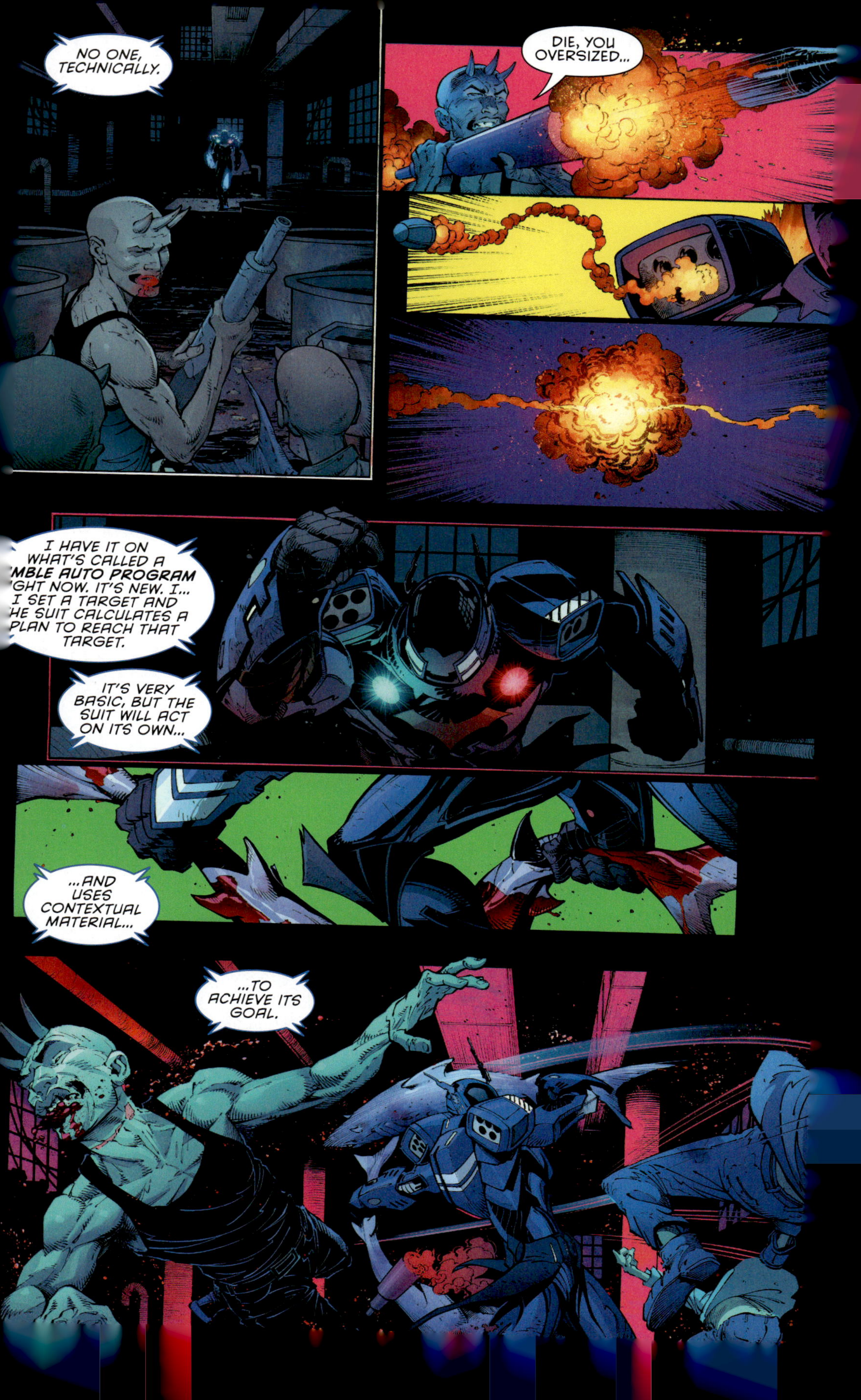
NO ONE, TECHNICALLY.
DIE, YOU OVERSIZED...
I HAVE IT ON WHAT'S CALLED A MBLE AUTO PROGRAM GHT NOW. IT'S NEW. I... I SET A TARGET AND HE SUIT CALCULATES A PLAN TO REACH THAT TARGET.
IT'S VERY BASIC, BUT THE SUIT WILL ACT ON ITS OWN...
...AND USES CONTEXTUAL MATERIAL...
...TO ACHIEVE ITS GOAL.

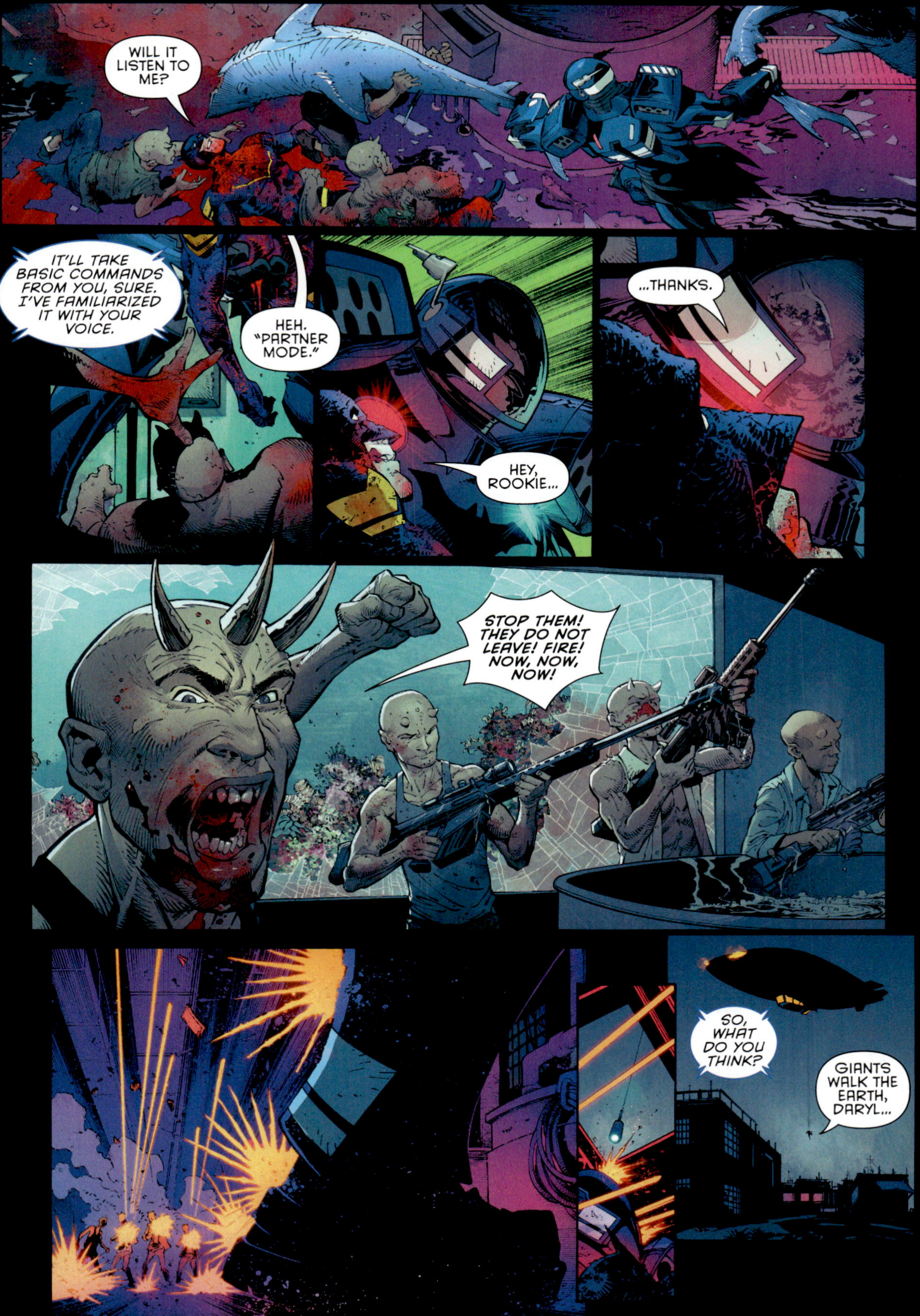
WILL IT LISTEN TO ME?
IT'LL TAKE BASIC COMMANDS FROM YOU, SURE. I'VE FAMILIARIZED IT WITH YOUR VOICE.
HEH. "PARTNER MODE."
HEY, ROOKIE...
...THANKS.
STOP THEM! THEY DO NOT LEAVE! FIRE! NOW, NOW, NOW!
SO, WHAT DO YOU THINK?
GIANTS WALK THE EARTH, DARYL...

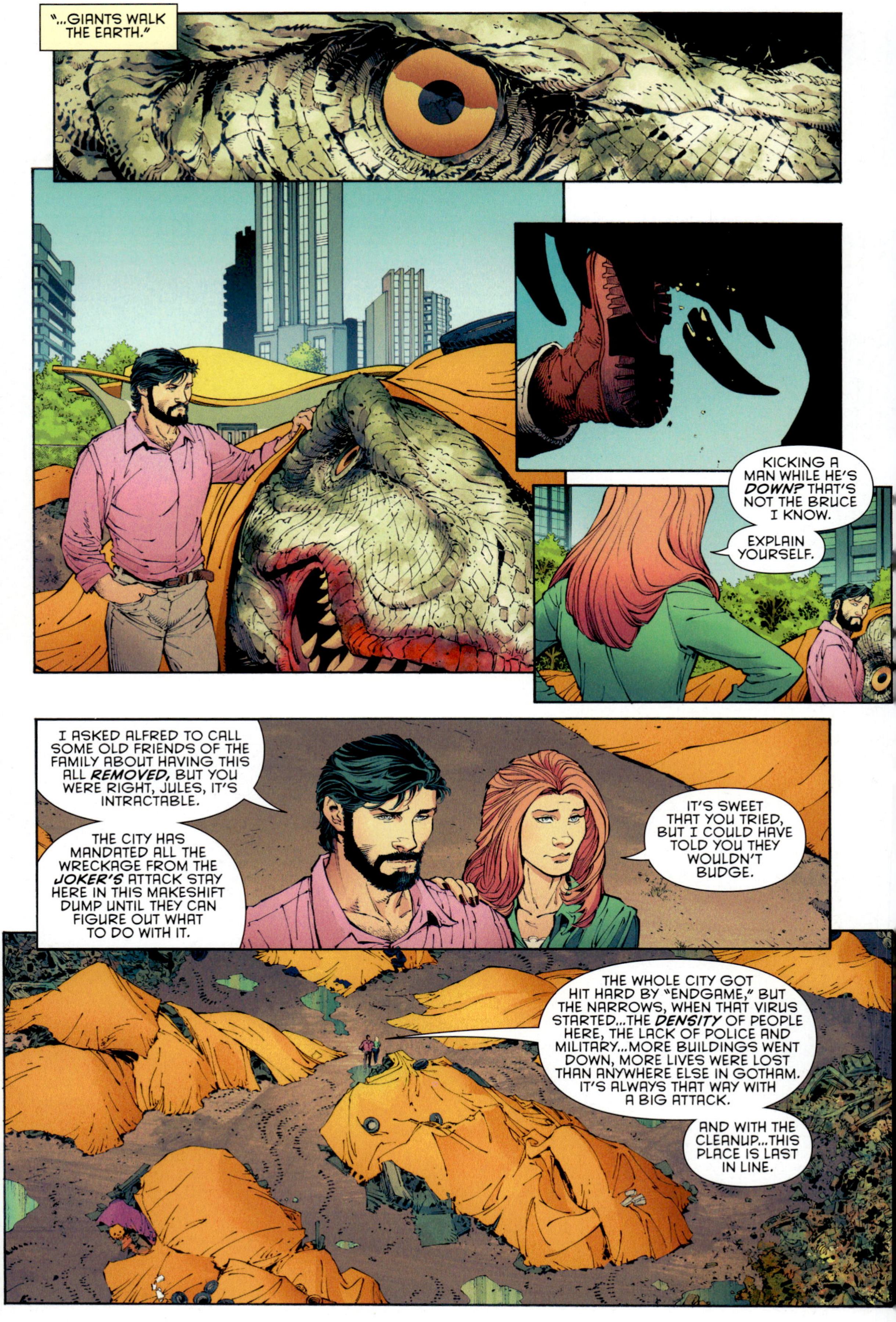
"...GIANTS WALK THE EARTH."
KICKING A MAN WHILE HE'S *DOWN?* THAT'S NOT THE BRUCE I KNOW.
EXPLAIN YOURSELF.
I ASKED ALFRED TO CALL SOME OLD FRIENDS OF THE FAMILY ABOUT HAVING THIS ALL *REMOVED,* BUT YOU WERE RIGHT, JULES, IT'S INTRACTABLE.
THE CITY HAS MANDATED ALL THE WRECKAGE FROM THE *JOKER'S* ATTACK STAY HERE IN THIS MAKESHIFT DUMP UNTIL THEY CAN FIGURE OUT WHAT TO DO WITH IT.
IT'S SWEET THAT YOU TRIED, BUT I COULD HAVE TOLD YOU THEY WOULDN'T BUDGE.
THE WHOLE CITY GOT HIT HARD BY "ENDGAME," BUT THE NARROWS, WHEN THAT VIRUS STARTED...THE *DENSITY* OF PEOPLE HERE, THE LACK OF POLICE AND MILITARY...MORE BUILDINGS WENT DOWN, MORE LIVES WERE LOST THAN ANYWHERE ELSE IN GOTHAM. IT'S ALWAYS THAT WAY WITH A BIG ATTACK.
AND WITH THE CLEANUP...THIS PLACE IS LAST IN LINE.

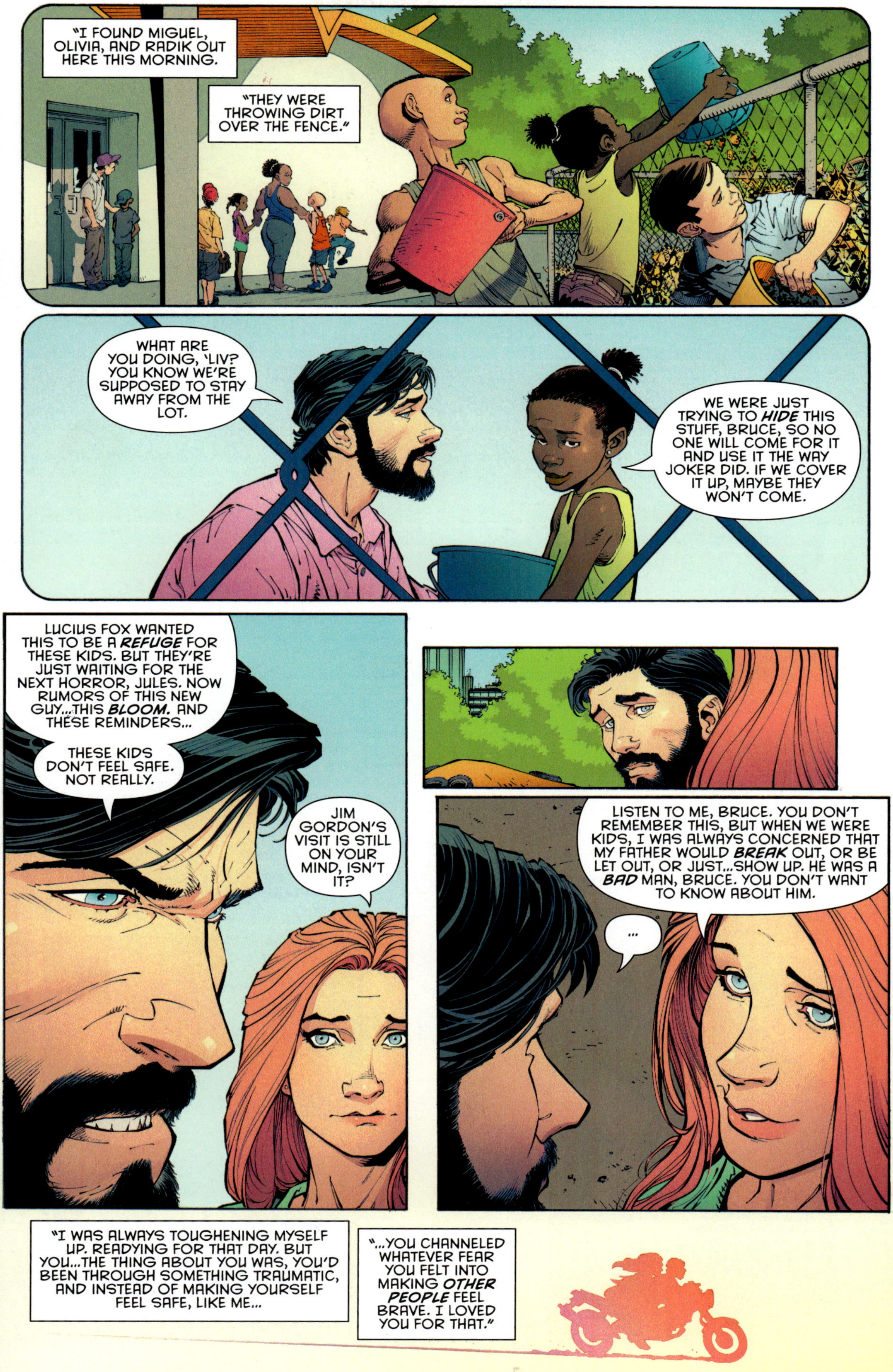
"I FOUND MIGUEL, OLIVIA, AND RADIK OUT HERE THIS MORNING.
"THEY WERE THROWING DIRT OVER THE FENCE."
WHAT ARE YOU DOING, 'LIV? YOU KNOW WE'RE SUPPOSED TO STAY AWAY FROM THE LOT.
WE WERE JUST TRYING TO HIDE THIS STUFF, BRUCE, SO NO ONE WILL COME FOR IT AND USE IT THE WAY JOKER DID. IF WE COVER IT UP, MAYBE THEY WON'T COME.
LUCIUS FOX WANTED THIS TO BE A REFUGE FOR THESE KIDS. BUT THEY'RE JUST WAITING FOR THE NEXT HORROR, JULES. NOW RUMORS OF THIS NEW GUY...THIS BLOOM. AND THESE REMINDERS...
THESE KIDS DON'T FEEL SAFE. NOT REALLY.
JIM GORDON'S VISIT IS STILL ON YOUR MIND, ISN'T IT?
LISTEN TO ME, BRUCE. YOU DON'T REMEMBER THIS, BUT WHEN WE WERE KIDS, I WAS ALWAYS CONCERNED THAT MY FATHER WOULD BREAK OUT, OR BE LET OUT, OR JUST...SHOW UP. HE WAS A BAD MAN, BRUCE. YOU DON'T WANT TO KNOW ABOUT HIM.
...
"I WAS ALWAYS TOUGHENING MYSELF UP. READYING FOR THAT DAY. BUT YOU...THE THING ABOUT YOU WAS, YOU'D BEEN THROUGH SOMETHING TRAUMATIC, AND INSTEAD OF MAKING YOURSELF FEEL SAFE, LIKE ME...
"...YOU CHANNELED WHATEVER FEAR YOU FELT INTO MAKING OTHER PEOPLE FEEL BRAVE. I LOVED YOU FOR THAT."

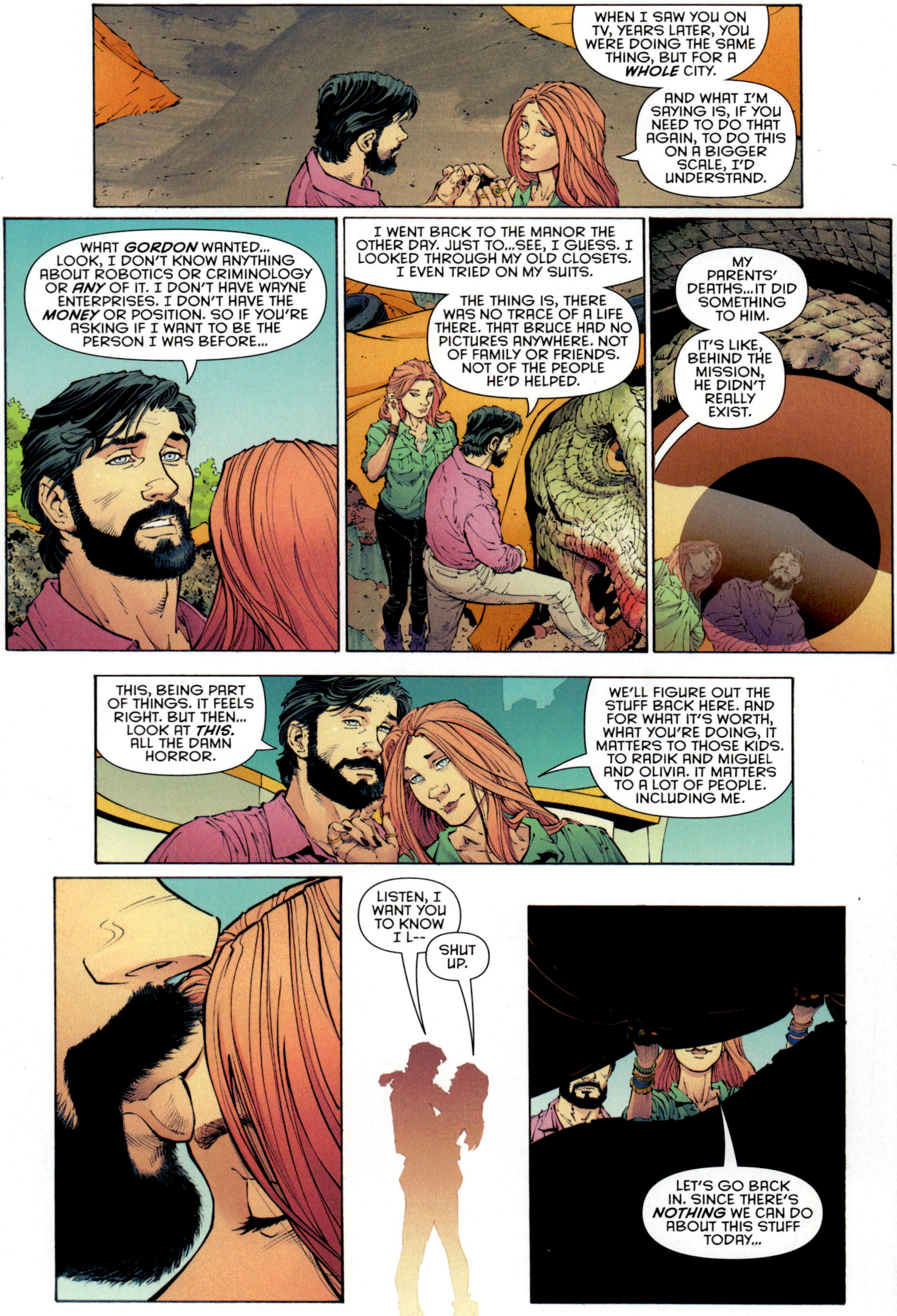
WHEN I SAW YOU ON TV, YEARS LATER, YOU WERE DOING THE SAME THING, BUT FOR A *WHOLE* CITY.
AND WHAT I'M SAYING IS, IF YOU NEED TO DO THAT AGAIN, TO DO THIS ON A BIGGER SCALE, I'D UNDERSTAND.
WHAT *GORDON* WANTED... LOOK, I DON'T KNOW ANYTHING ABOUT ROBOTICS OR CRIMINOLOGY OR *ANY* OF IT. I DON'T HAVE WAYNE ENTERPRISES. I DON'T HAVE THE *MONEY* OR POSITION. SO IF YOU'RE ASKING IF I WANT TO BE THE PERSON I WAS BEFORE...
I WENT BACK TO THE MANOR THE OTHER DAY. JUST TO...SEE, I GUESS. I LOOKED THROUGH MY OLD CLOSETS. I EVEN TRIED ON MY SUITS.
THE THING IS, THERE WAS NO TRACE OF A LIFE THERE. THAT BRUCE HAD NO PICTURES ANYWHERE. NOT OF FAMILY OR FRIENDS. NOT OF THE PEOPLE HE'D HELPED.
MY PARENTS' DEATHS...IT DID SOMETHING TO HIM.
IT'S LIKE, BEHIND THE MISSION, HE DIDN'T REALLY EXIST.
THIS, BEING PART OF THINGS. IT FEELS RIGHT. BUT THEN... LOOK AT *THIS.* ALL THE DAMN HORROR.
WE'LL FIGURE OUT THE STUFF BACK HERE. AND FOR WHAT IT'S WORTH, WHAT YOU'RE DOING, IT MATTERS TO THOSE KIDS. TO RADIK AND MIGUEL AND OLIVIA. IT MATTERS TO A LOT OF PEOPLE. INCLUDING ME.
LISTEN, I WANT YOU TO KNOW I L--
SHUT UP.
LET'S GO BACK IN. SINCE THERE'S *NOTHING* WE CAN DO ABOUT THIS STUFF TODAY...

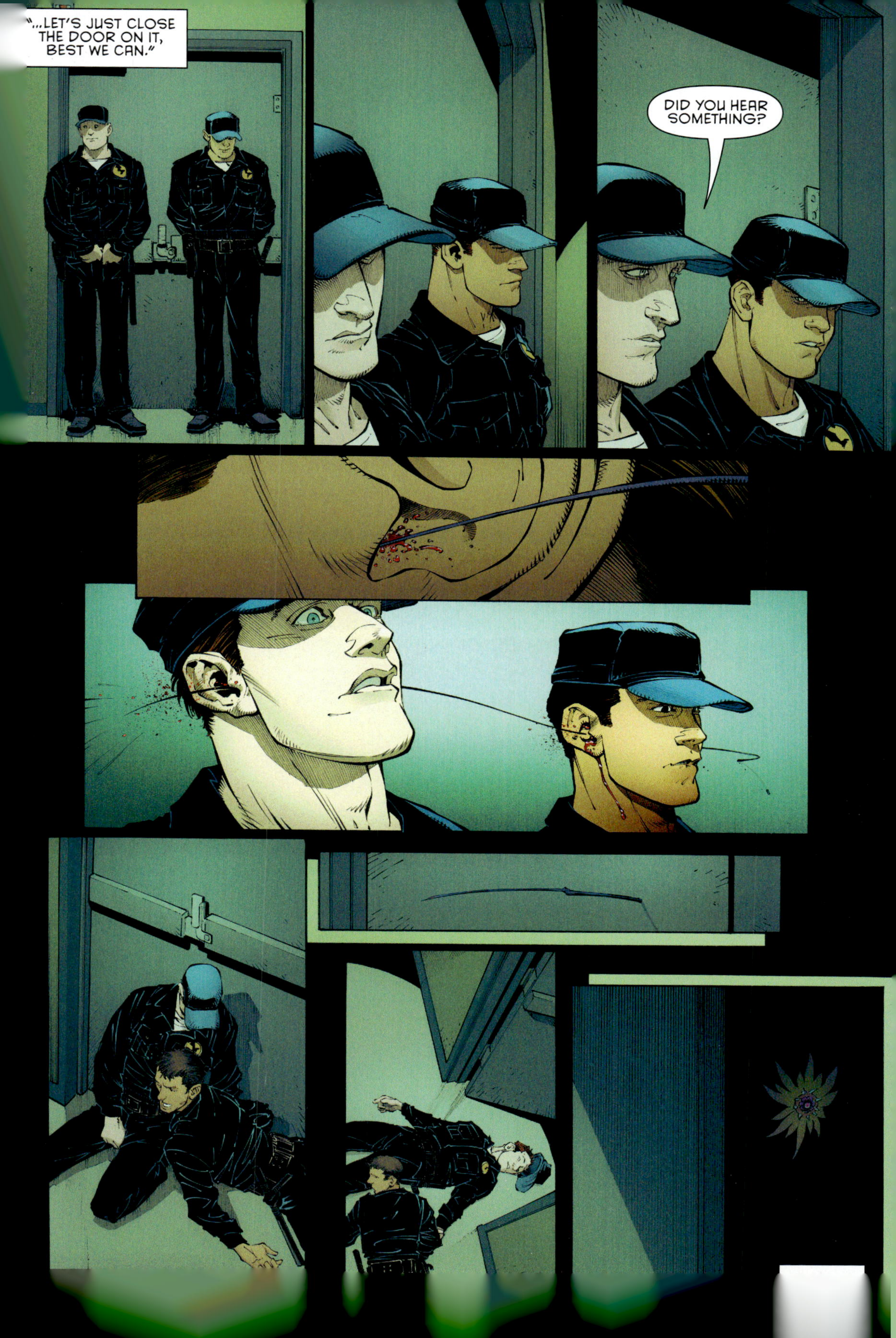
"...LET'S JUST CLOSE THE DOOR ON IT, BEST WE CAN."
DID YOU HEAR SOMETHING?

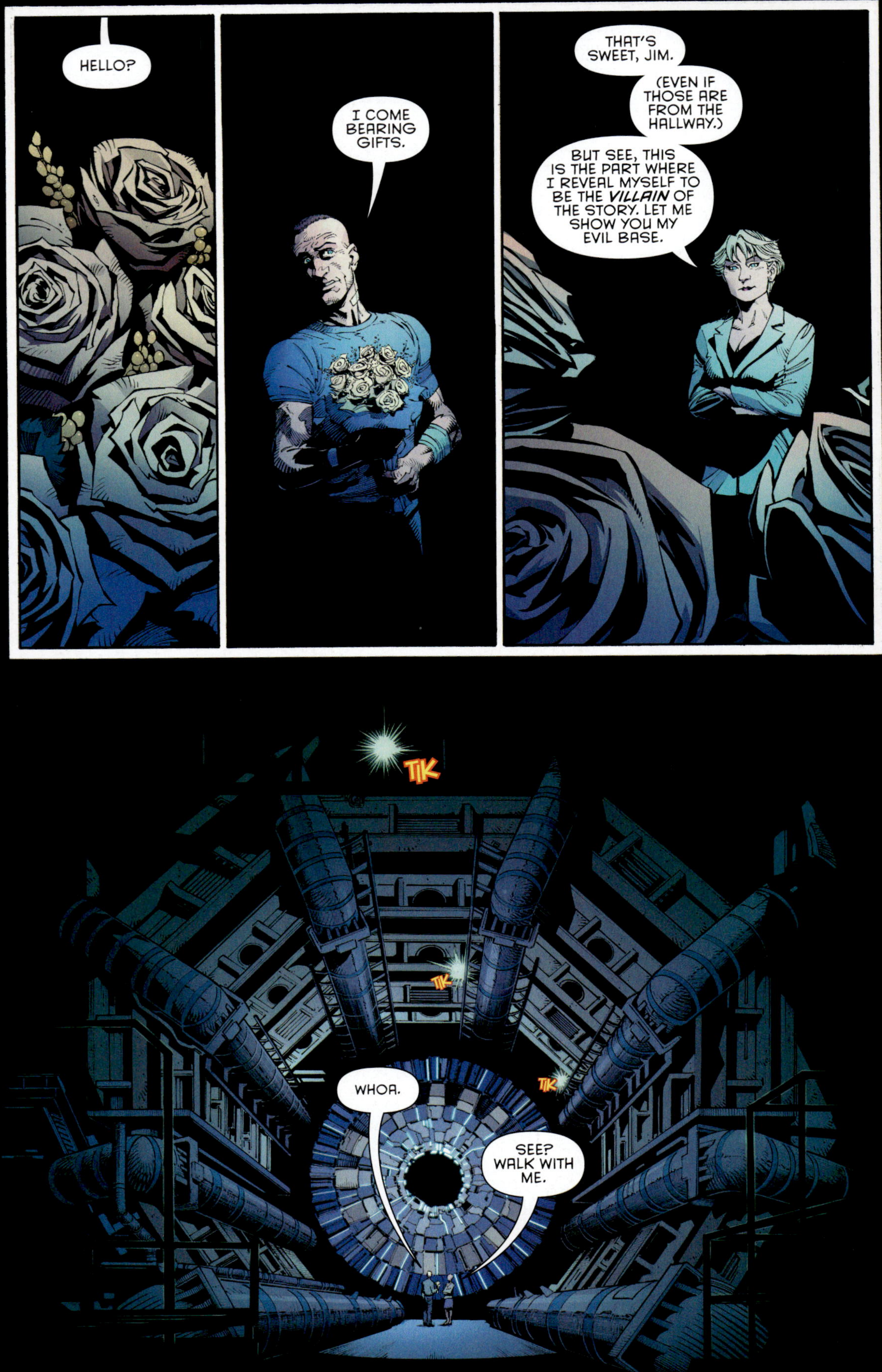
HELLO?
I COME BEARING GIFTS.
THAT'S SWEET, JIM.
(EVEN IF THOSE ARE FROM THE HALLWAY.)
BUT SEE, THIS IS THE PART WHERE I REVEAL MYSELF TO BE THE *VILLAIN* OF THE STORY. LET ME SHOW YOU MY EVIL BASE.
TIK
TIK
TIK
WHOA.
SEE? WALK WITH ME.

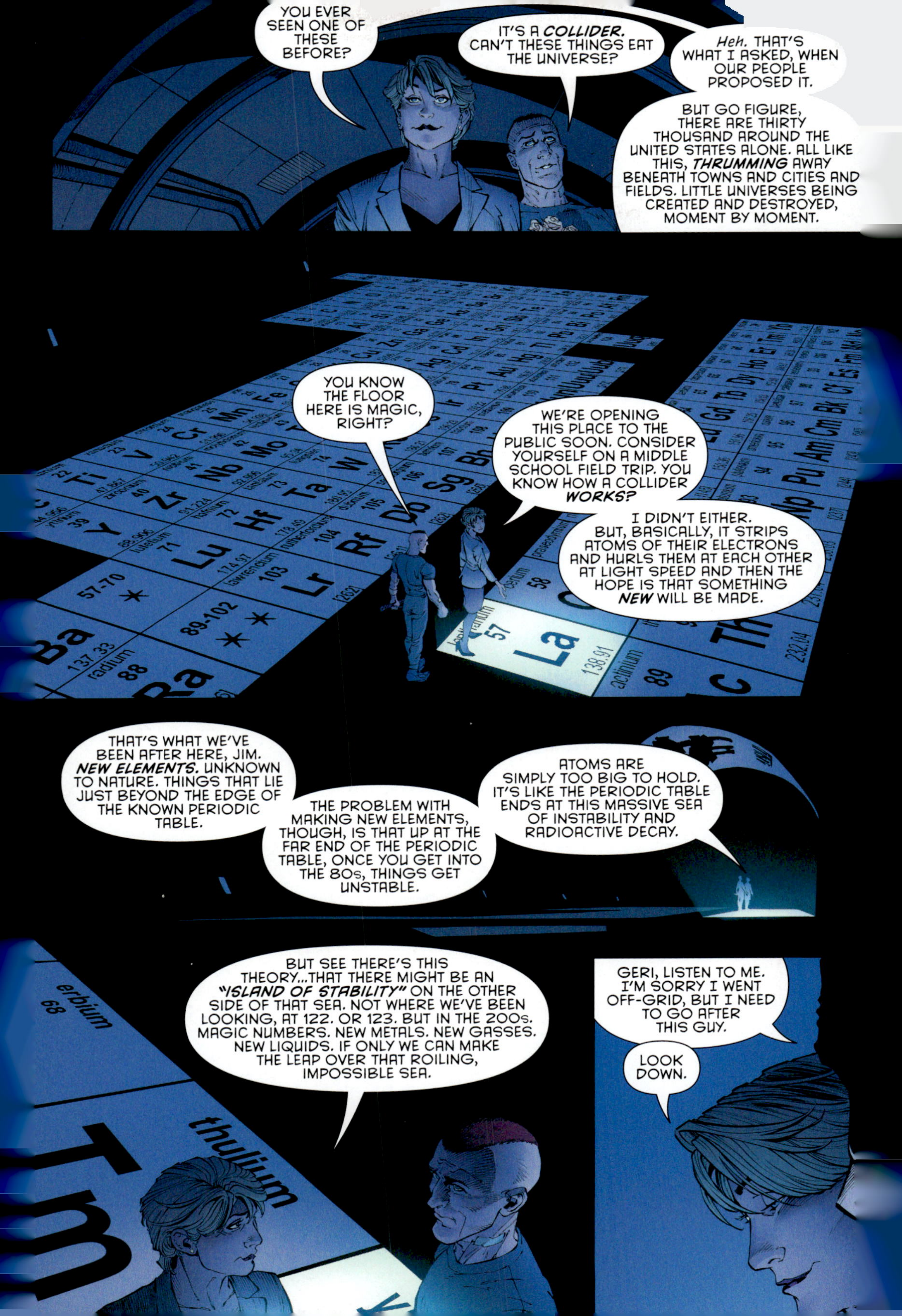
YOU EVER SEEN ONE OF THESE BEFORE?
IT'S A *COLLIDER.* CAN'T THESE THINGS EAT THE UNIVERSE?
Heh. THAT'S WHAT I ASKED, WHEN OUR PEOPLE PROPOSED IT.
BUT GO FIGURE, THERE ARE THIRTY THOUSAND AROUND THE UNITED STATES ALONE. ALL LIKE THIS, ***THRUMMING*** AWAY BENEATH TOWNS AND CITIES AND FIELDS. LITTLE UNIVERSES BEING CREATED AND DESTROYED, MOMENT BY MOMENT.
YOU KNOW THE FLOOR HERE IS MAGIC, RIGHT?
WE'RE OPENING THIS PLACE TO THE PUBLIC SOON. CONSIDER YOURSELF ON A MIDDLE SCHOOL FIELD TRIP. YOU KNOW HOW A COLLIDER ***WORKS?***
I DIDN'T EITHER. BUT, BASICALLY, IT STRIPS ATOMS OF THEIR ELECTRONS AND HURLS THEM AT EACH OTHER AT LIGHT SPEED AND THEN THE HOPE IS THAT SOMETHING ***NEW*** WILL BE MADE.
THAT'S WHAT WE'VE BEEN AFTER HERE, JIM. ***NEW ELEMENTS.*** UNKNOWN TO NATURE. THINGS THAT LIE JUST BEYOND THE EDGE OF THE KNOWN PERIODIC TABLE.
THE PROBLEM WITH MAKING NEW ELEMENTS, THOUGH, IS THAT UP AT THE FAR END OF THE PERIODIC TABLE, ONCE YOU GET INTO THE 80s, THINGS GET UNSTABLE.
ATOMS ARE SIMPLY TOO BIG TO HOLD. IT'S LIKE THE PERIODIC TABLE ENDS AT THIS MASSIVE SEA OF INSTABILITY AND RADIOACTIVE DECAY.
BUT SEE THERE'S THIS THEORY...THAT THERE MIGHT BE AN ***"ISLAND OF STABILITY"*** ON THE OTHER SIDE OF THAT SEA. NOT WHERE WE'VE BEEN LOOKING, AT 122. OR 123. BUT IN THE 200s. MAGIC NUMBERS. NEW METALS. NEW GASSES. NEW LIQUIDS. IF ONLY WE CAN MAKE THE LEAP OVER THAT ROILING, IMPOSSIBLE SEA.
GERI, LISTEN TO ME. I'M SORRY I WENT OFF-GRID, BUT I NEED TO GO AFTER THIS GUY.
LOOK DOWN.

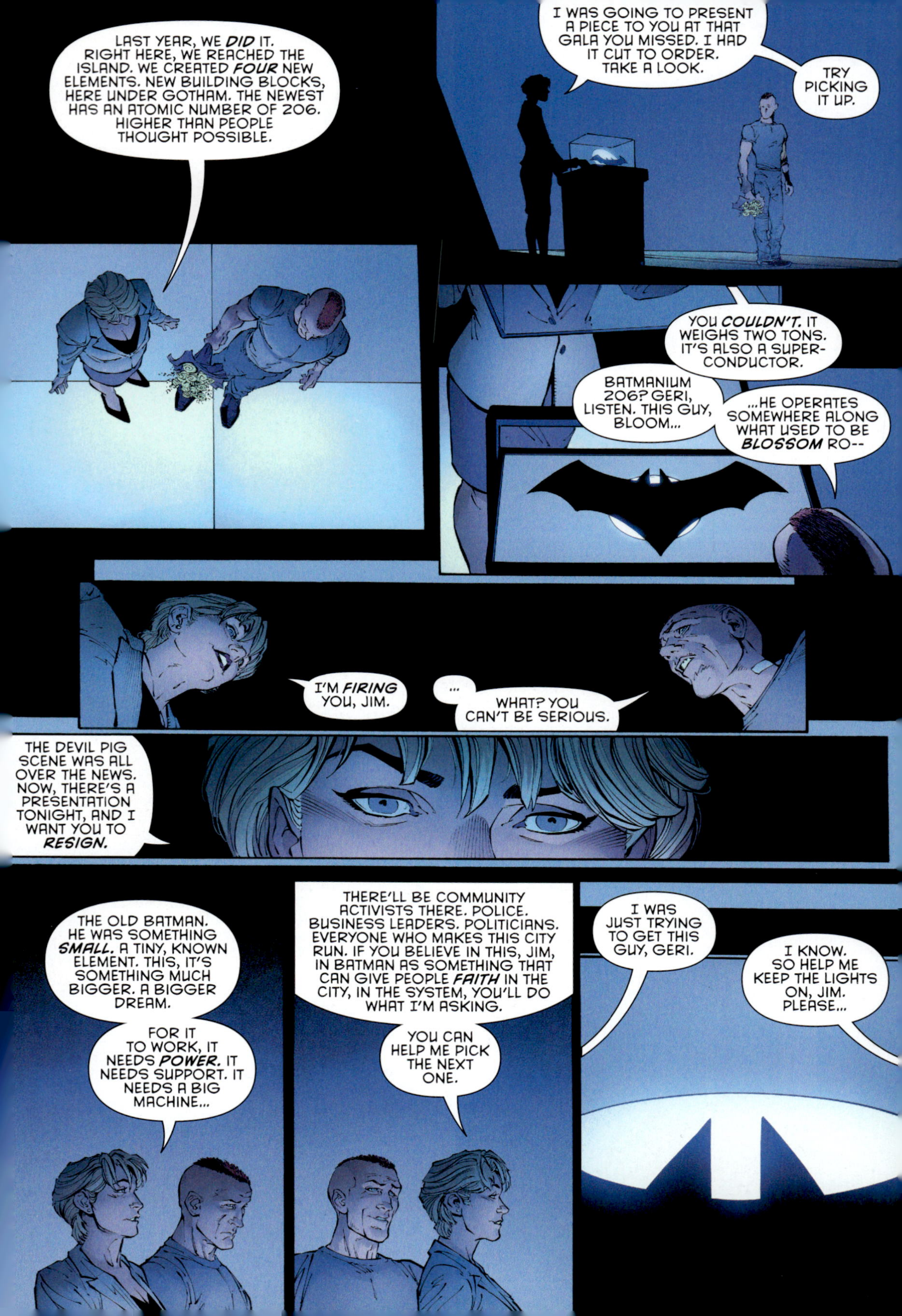

LAST YEAR, WE DID IT. RIGHT HERE, WE REACHED THE ISLAND. WE CREATED FOUR NEW ELEMENTS. NEW BUILDING BLOCKS, HERE UNDER GOTHAM. THE NEWEST HAS AN ATOMIC NUMBER OF 206. HIGHER THAN PEOPLE THOUGHT POSSIBLE.
I WAS GOING TO PRESENT A PIECE TO YOU AT THAT GALA YOU MISSED. I HAD IT CUT TO ORDER. TAKE A LOOK.
TRY PICKING IT UP.
YOU COULDN'T. IT WEIGHS TWO TONS. IT'S ALSO A SUPER-CONDUCTOR.
BATMANIUM 206? GERI, LISTEN. THIS GUY, BLOOM...
...HE OPERATES SOMEWHERE ALONG WHAT USED TO BE BLOSSOM RO--
I'M FIRING YOU, JIM.
...
WHAT? YOU CAN'T BE SERIOUS.
THE DEVIL PIG SCENE WAS ALL OVER THE NEWS. NOW, THERE'S A PRESENTATION TONIGHT, AND I WANT YOU TO RESIGN.
THE OLD BATMAN. HE WAS SOMETHING SMALL. A TINY, KNOWN ELEMENT. THIS, IT'S SOMETHING MUCH BIGGER. A BIGGER DREAM.
FOR IT TO WORK, IT NEEDS POWER. IT NEEDS SUPPORT. IT NEEDS A BIG MACHINE...
THERE'LL BE COMMUNITY ACTIVISTS THERE. POLICE. BUSINESS LEADERS. POLITICIANS. EVERYONE WHO MAKES THIS CITY RUN. IF YOU BELIEVE IN THIS, JIM, IN BATMAN AS SOMETHING THAT CAN GIVE PEOPLE FAITH IN THE CITY, IN THE SYSTEM, YOU'LL DO WHAT I'M ASKING.
YOU CAN HELP ME PICK THE NEXT ONE.
I WAS JUST TRYING TO GET THIS GUY, GERI.
I KNOW. SO HELP ME KEEP THE LIGHTS ON, JIM. PLEASE...

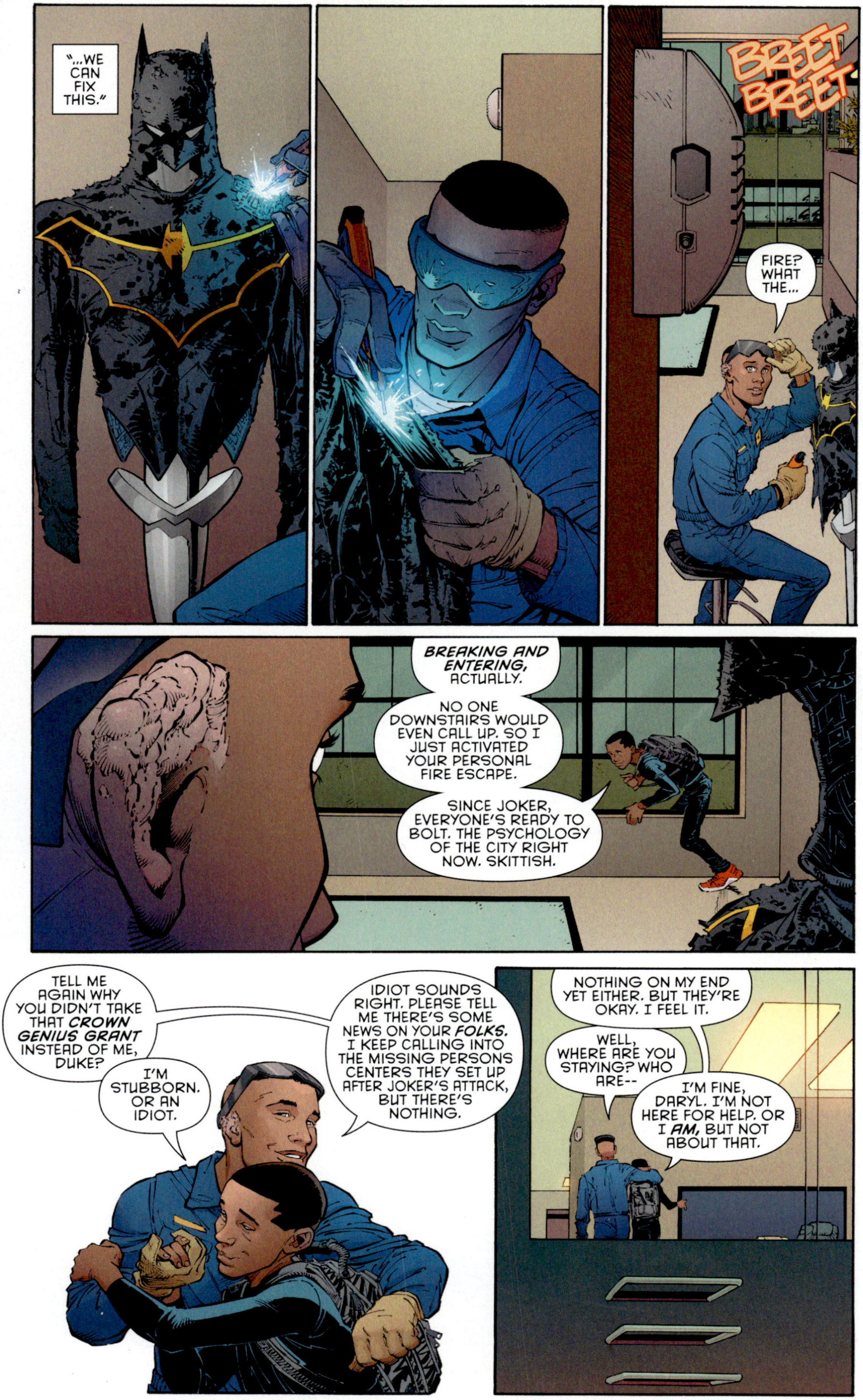

"...WE CAN FIX THIS."
BREET BREET
FIRE? WHAT THE...
BREAKING AND ENTERING, ACTUALLY.
NO ONE DOWNSTAIRS WOULD EVEN CALL UP. SO I JUST ACTIVATED YOUR PERSONAL FIRE ESCAPE.
SINCE JOKER, EVERYONE'S READY TO BOLT. THE PSYCHOLOGY OF THE CITY RIGHT NOW. SKITTISH.
TELL ME AGAIN WHY YOU DIDN'T TAKE THAT *CROWN GENIUS GRANT* INSTEAD OF ME, DUKE?
I'M STUBBORN. OR AN IDIOT.
IDIOT SOUNDS RIGHT. PLEASE TELL ME THERE'S SOME NEWS ON YOUR *FOLKS.* I KEEP CALLING INTO THE MISSING PERSONS CENTERS THEY SET UP AFTER JOKER'S ATTACK, BUT THERE'S NOTHING.
NOTHING ON MY END YET EITHER. BUT THEY'RE OKAY. I FEEL IT.
WELL, WHERE ARE YOU STAYING? WHO ARE--
I'M FINE, DARYL. I'M NOT HERE FOR HELP. OR I *AM,* BUT NOT ABOUT THAT.

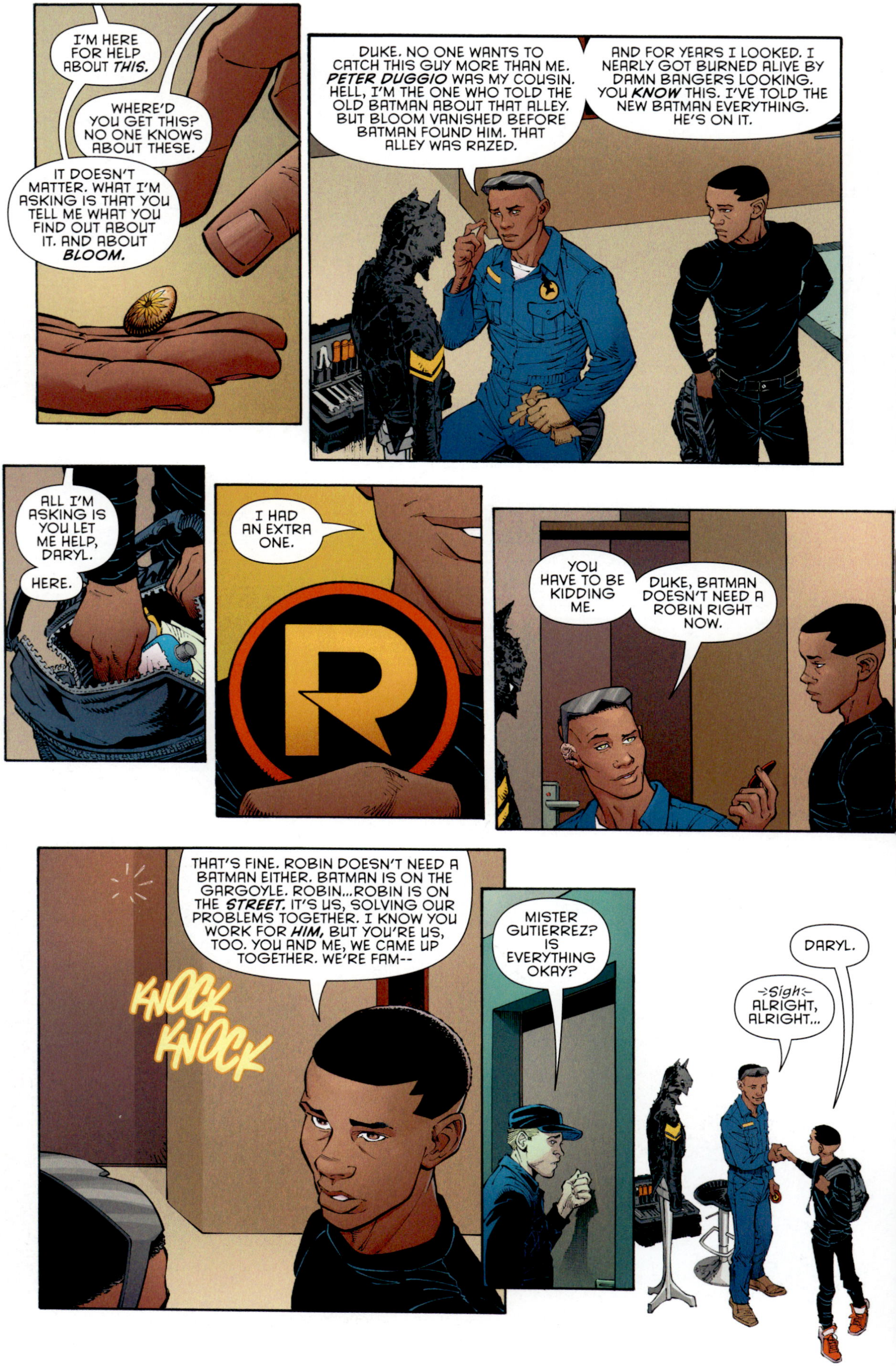
I'M HERE FOR HELP ABOUT *THIS.*
WHERE'D YOU GET THIS? NO ONE KNOWS ABOUT THESE.
IT DOESN'T MATTER. WHAT I'M ASKING IS THAT YOU TELL ME WHAT YOU FIND OUT ABOUT IT. AND ABOUT ***BLOOM.***
DUKE. NO ONE WANTS TO CATCH THIS GUY MORE THAN ME. ***PETER DUGGIO*** WAS MY COUSIN. HELL, I'M THE ONE WHO TOLD THE OLD BATMAN ABOUT THAT ALLEY. BUT BLOOM VANISHED BEFORE BATMAN FOUND HIM. THAT ALLEY WAS RAZED.
AND FOR YEARS I LOOKED. I NEARLY GOT BURNED ALIVE BY DAMN BANGERS LOOKING. YOU ***KNOW*** THIS. I'VE TOLD THE NEW BATMAN EVERYTHING. HE'S ON IT.
ALL I'M ASKING IS YOU LET ME HELP, DARYL.
HERE.
I HAD AN EXTRA ONE.
YOU HAVE TO BE KIDDING ME.
DUKE, BATMAN DOESN'T NEED A ROBIN RIGHT NOW.
THAT'S FINE. ROBIN DOESN'T NEED A BATMAN EITHER. BATMAN IS ON THE GARGOYLE. ROBIN...ROBIN IS ON THE ***STREET.*** IT'S US, SOLVING OUR PROBLEMS TOGETHER. I KNOW YOU WORK FOR ***HIM,*** BUT YOU'RE US, TOO. YOU AND ME, WE CAME UP TOGETHER. WE'RE FAM--
KNOCK KNOCK
MISTER GUTIERREZ? IS EVERYTHING OKAY?
DARYL.
Sigh ALRIGHT, ALRIGHT...

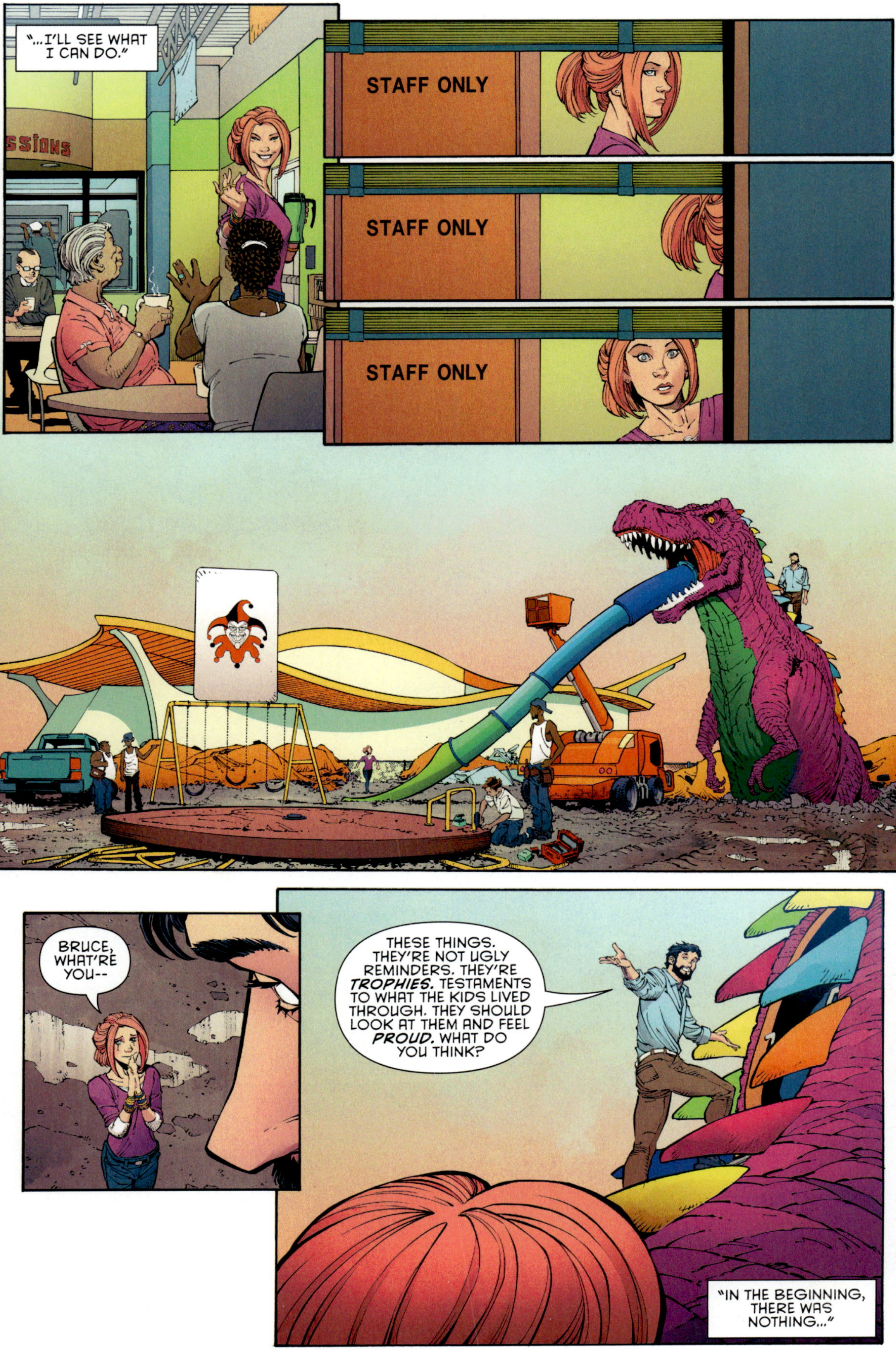
"...I'LL SEE WHAT I CAN DO."
SSIONS
STAFF ONLY
STAFF ONLY
STAFF ONLY
BRUCE, WHAT'RE YOU--
THESE THINGS. THEY'RE NOT UGLY REMINDERS. THEY'RE TROPHIES. TESTAMENTS TO WHAT THE KIDS LIVED THROUGH. THEY SHOULD LOOK AT THEM AND FEEL PROUD. WHAT DO YOU THINK?
"IN THE BEGINNING, THERE WAS NOTHING..."

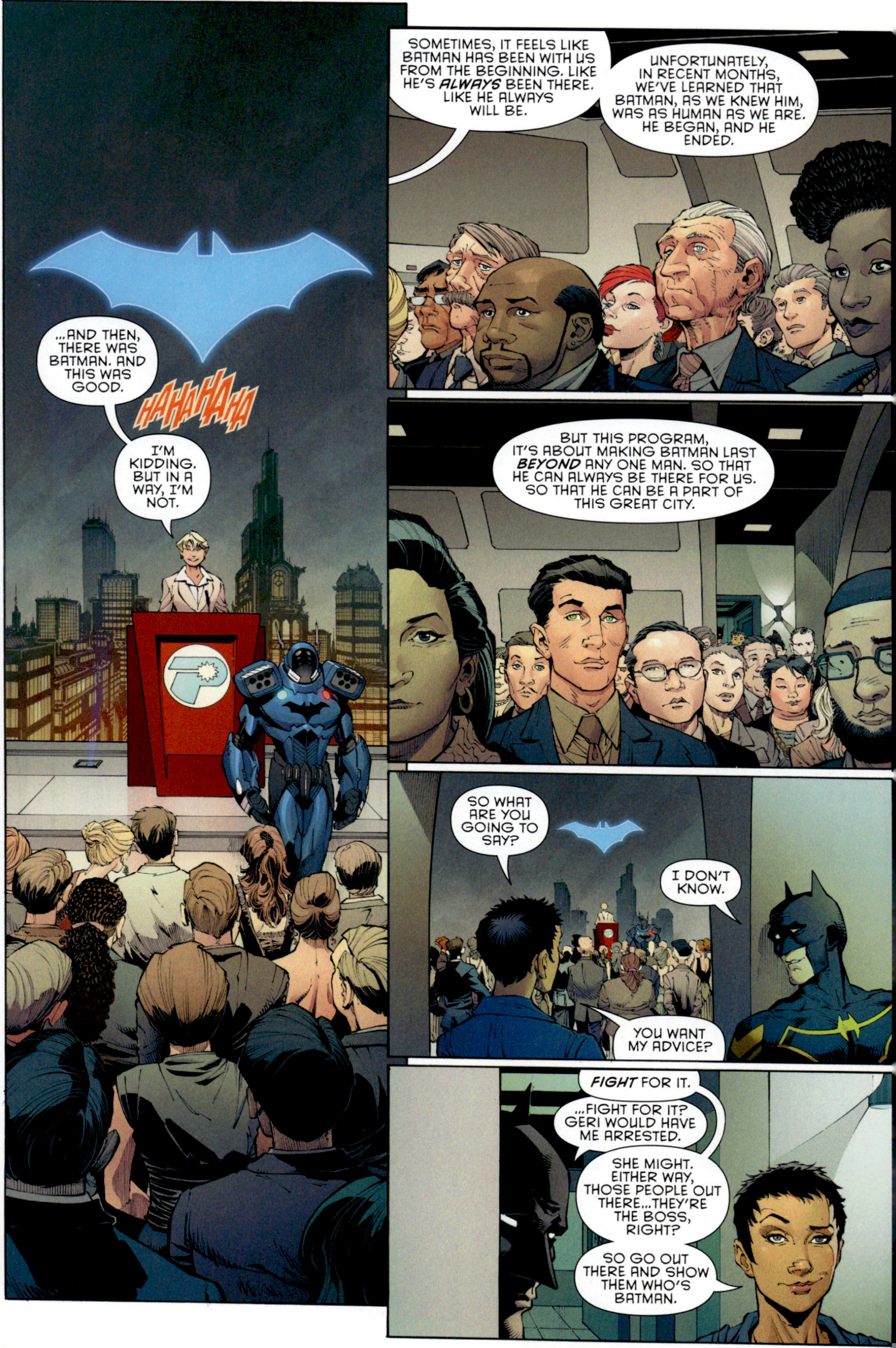
...AND THEN, THERE WAS BATMAN. AND THIS WAS GOOD.
HAHAHAHA
I'M KIDDING. BUT IN A WAY, I'M NOT.
SOMETIMES, IT FEELS LIKE BATMAN HAS BEEN WITH US FROM THE BEGINNING. LIKE HE'S *ALWAYS* BEEN THERE. LIKE HE ALWAYS WILL BE.
UNFORTUNATELY, IN RECENT MONTHS, WE'VE LEARNED THAT BATMAN, AS WE KNEW HIM, WAS AS HUMAN AS WE ARE. HE BEGAN, AND HE ENDED.
BUT THIS PROGRAM, IT'S ABOUT MAKING BATMAN LAST *BEYOND* ANY ONE MAN. SO THAT HE CAN ALWAYS BE THERE FOR US. SO THAT HE CAN BE A PART OF THIS GREAT CITY.
SO WHAT ARE YOU GOING TO SAY?
I DON'T KNOW.
YOU WANT MY ADVICE?
FIGHT FOR IT.
...FIGHT FOR IT? GERI WOULD HAVE ME ARRESTED.
SHE MIGHT. EITHER WAY, THOSE PEOPLE OUT THERE...THEY'RE THE BOSS, RIGHT?
SO GO OUT THERE AND SHOW THEM WHO'S BATMAN.

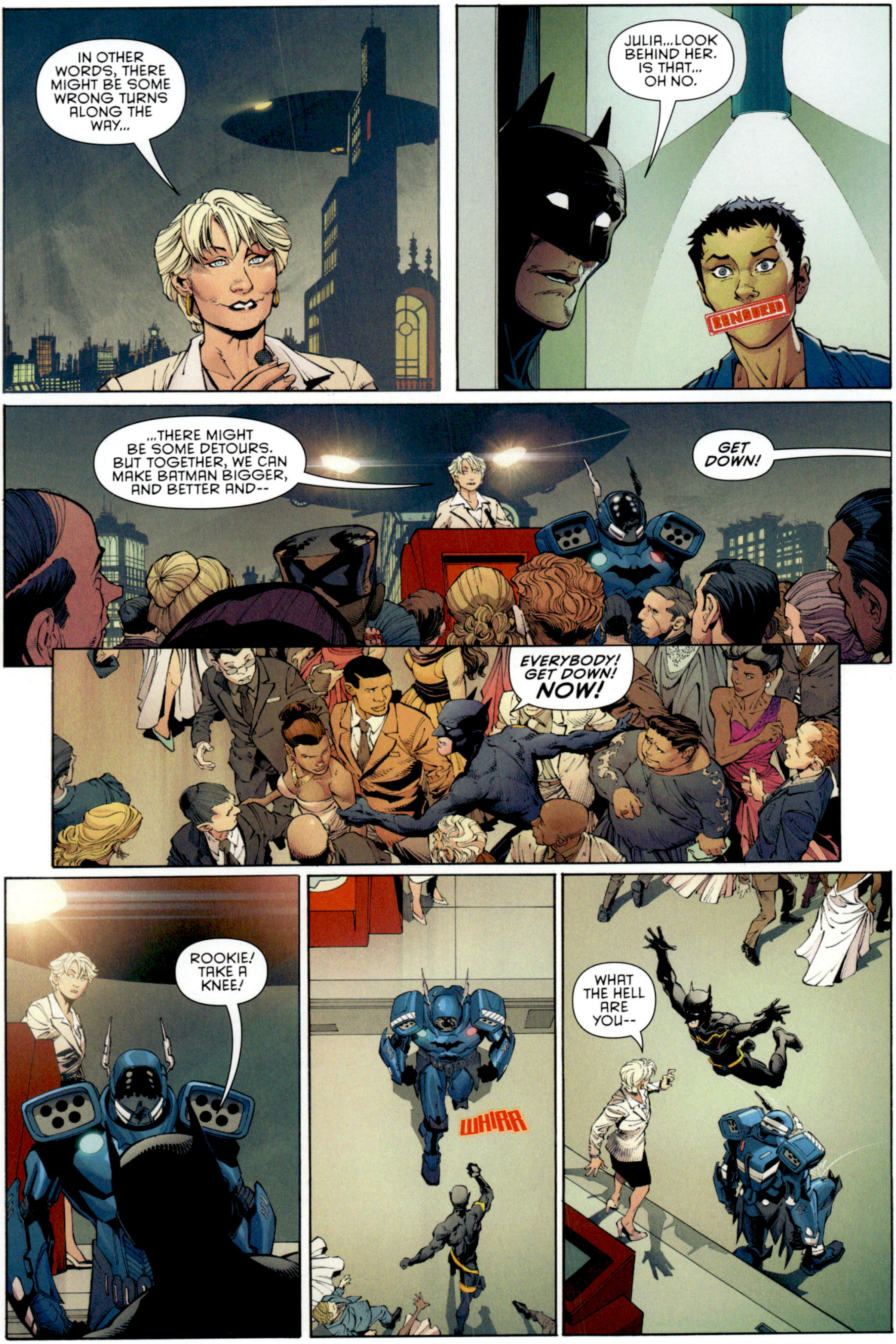
IN OTHER WORDS, THERE MIGHT BE SOME WRONG TURNS ALONG THE WAY...
JULIA...LOOK BEHIND HER. IS THAT... OH NO.
...THERE MIGHT BE SOME DETOURS. BUT TOGETHER, WE CAN MAKE BATMAN BIGGER, AND BETTER AND--
GET DOWN!
EVERYBODY! GET DOWN! NOW!
ROOKIE! TAKE A KNEE!
WHIRR
WHAT THE HELL ARE YOU--

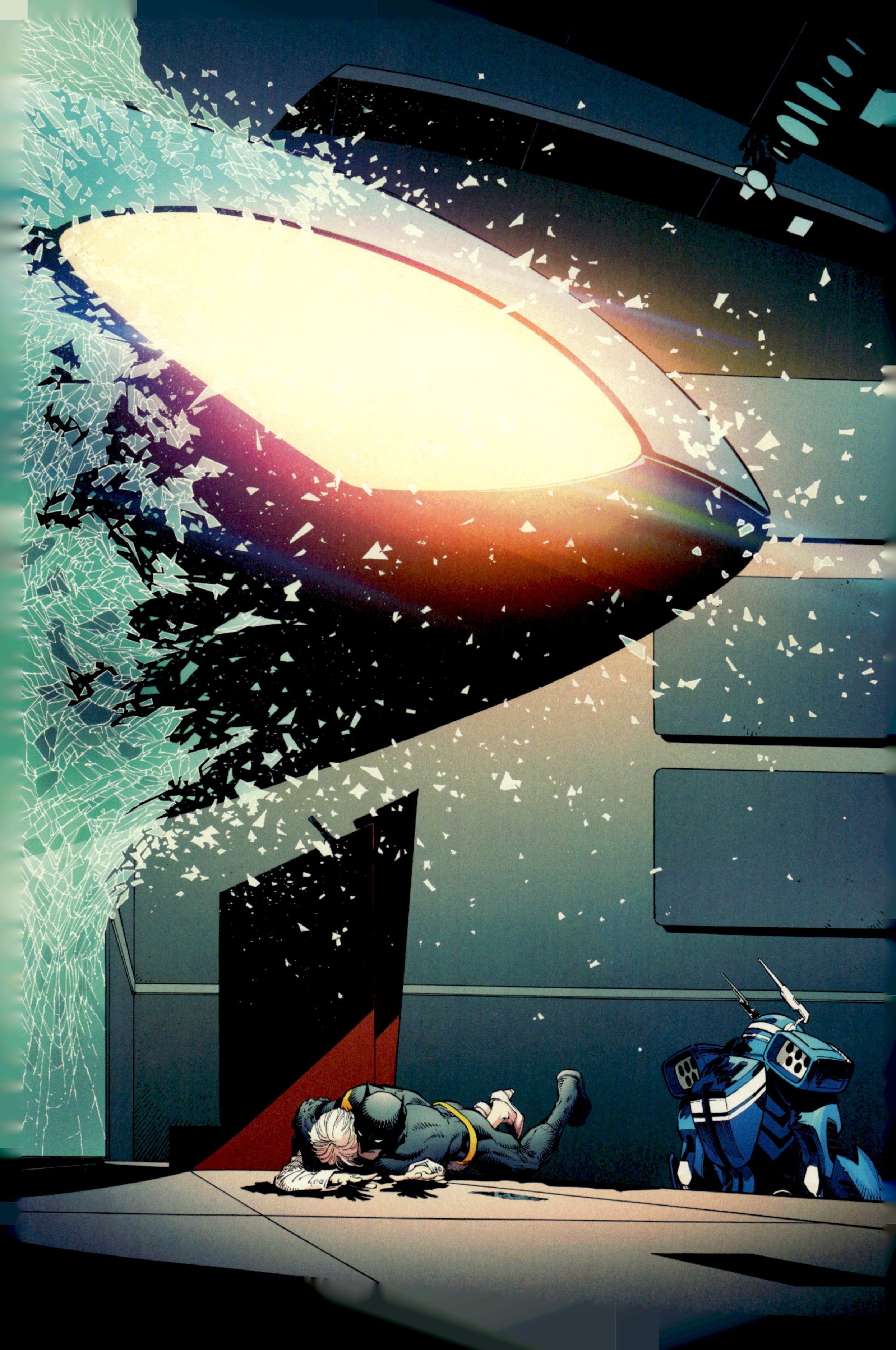

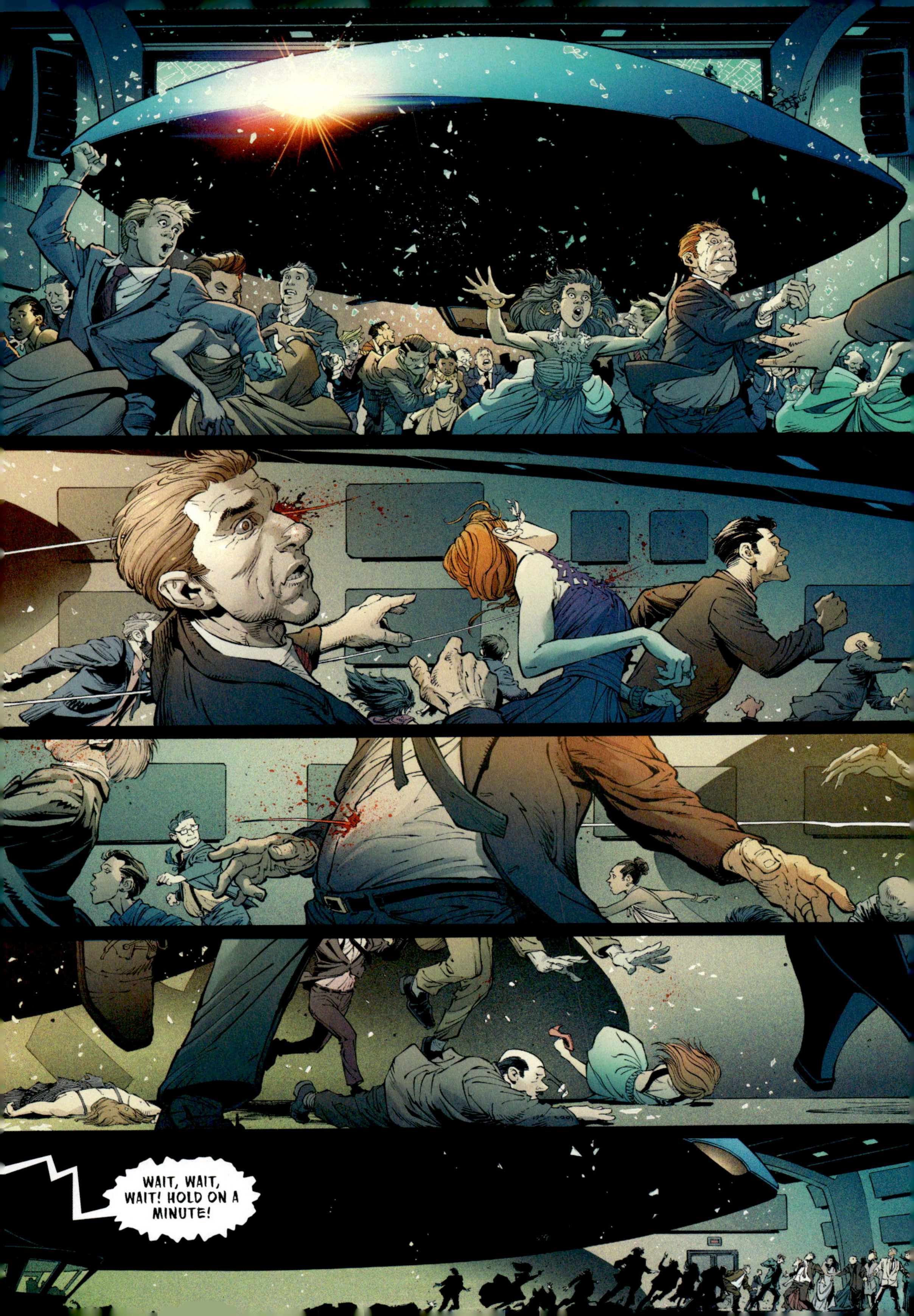
WAIT, WAIT, WAIT! HOLD ON A MINUTE!

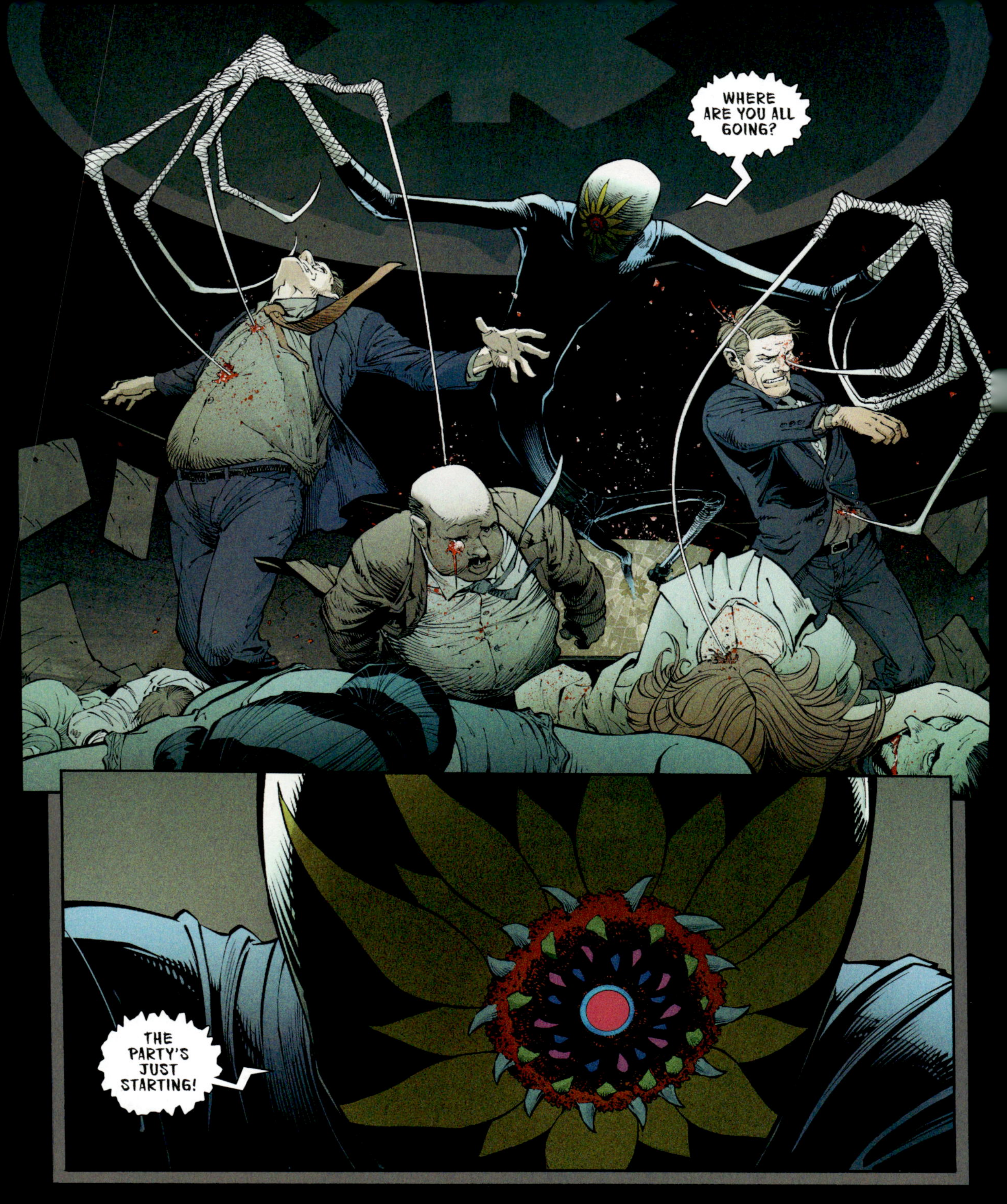
WHERE ARE YOU ALL GOING?
THE PARTY'S JUST STARTING!

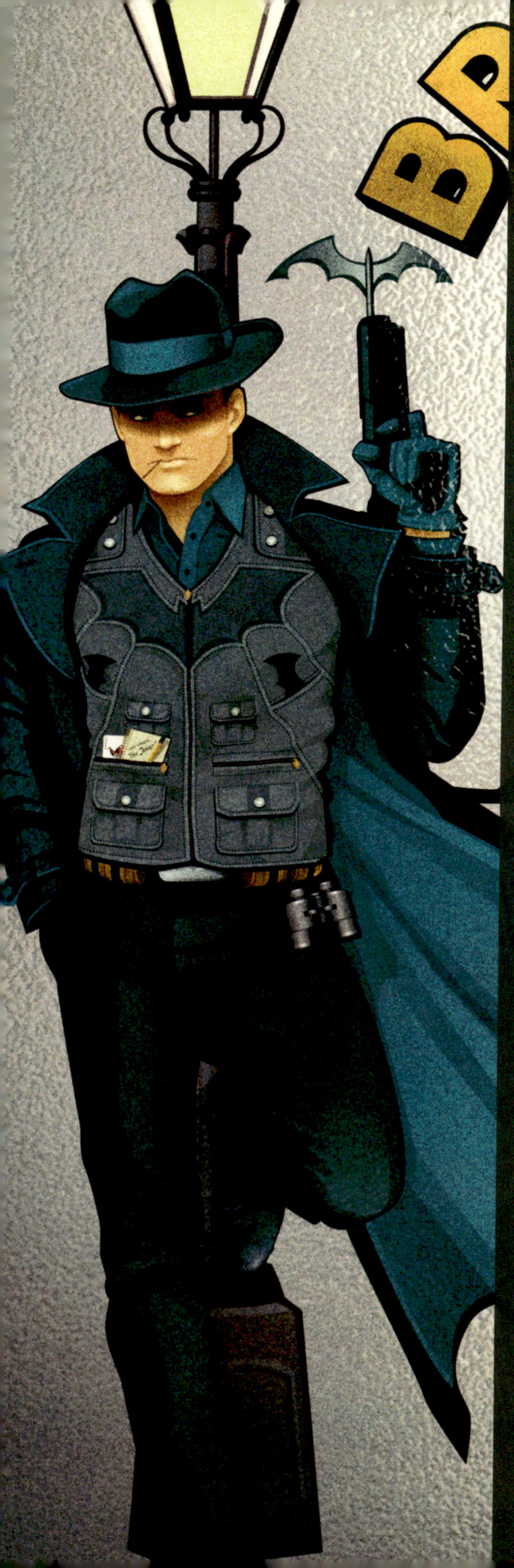

VARIANT COVER GALLERY

BATMAN #41
JOKER 75TH ANNIVERSARY VARIANT BY SEAN MURPHY & MATT HOLLINGSWORTH

BATMAN #42
TEEN TITANS GO! VARIANT BY DAN HIPP

BATMAN #43
BOMBSHELLS VARIANT BY ANT LUCIA

BATMAN #44
GREEN LANTERN 75TH ANNIVERSARY VARIANT BY TONY S. DANIEL & TOMEU MOREY

BATMAN #45
MONSTER VARIANT BY ANDY KUBERT & BRAD ANDERSON

BATMAN #43
LA MOLE COMIC CON VARIANT BY GREG CAPULLO

BATMAN #41
SAN DIEGO COMIC-CON VARIANT BY GREG CAPULLO

BATMAN #44
BALTIMORE COMIC-CON VARIANT BY JOCK

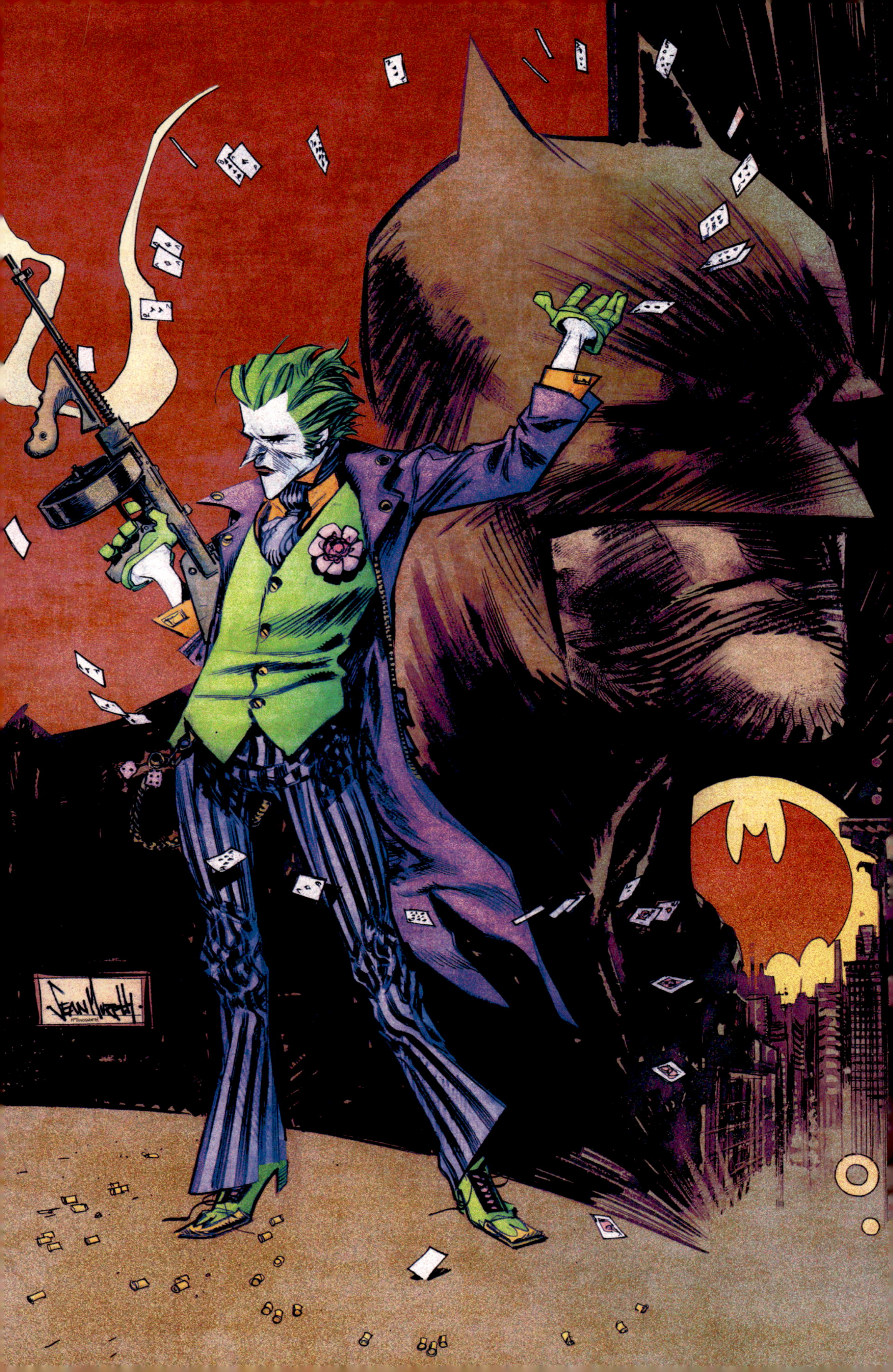

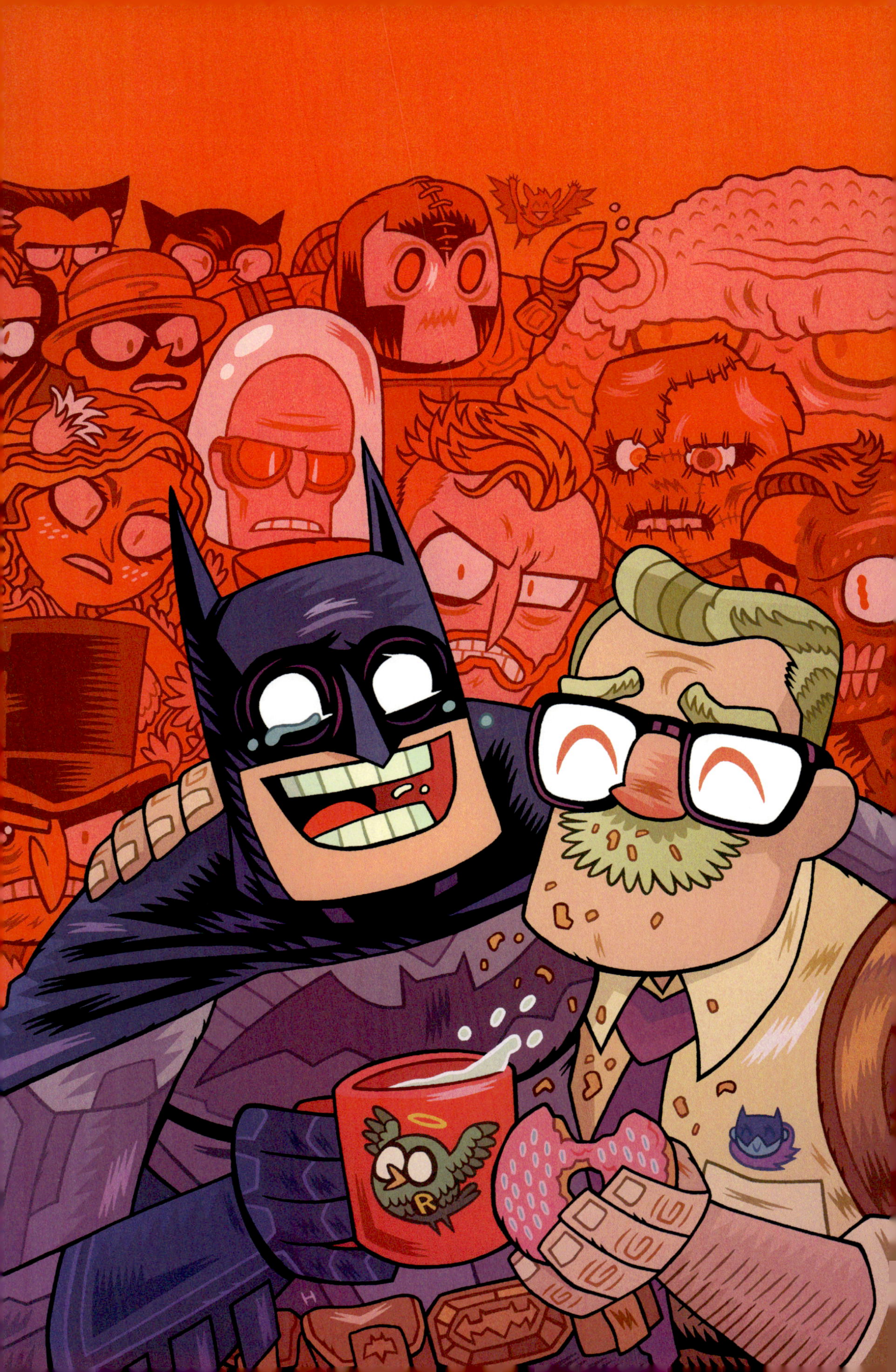

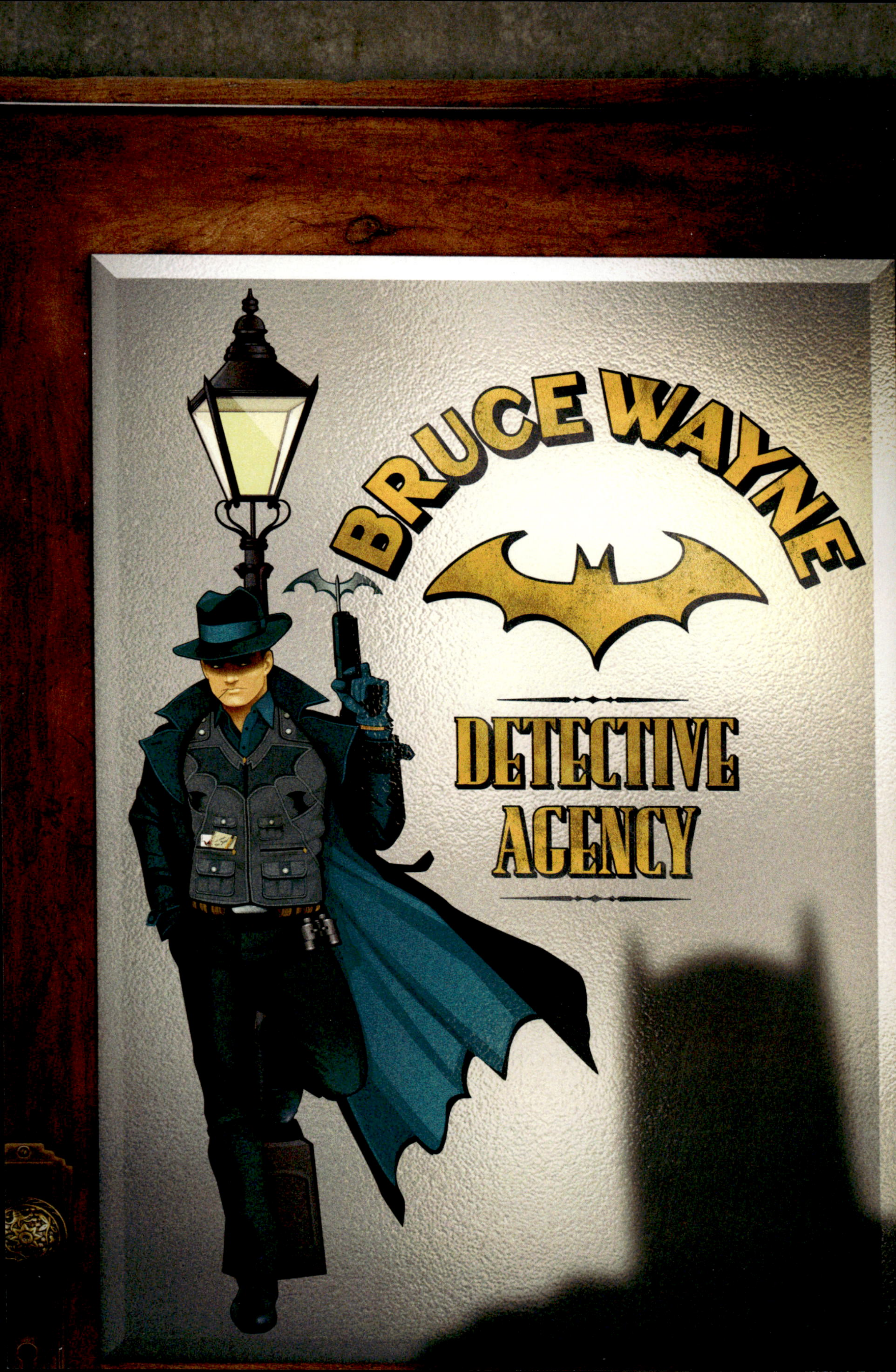
BRUCE WAYNE
DETECTIVE AGENCY

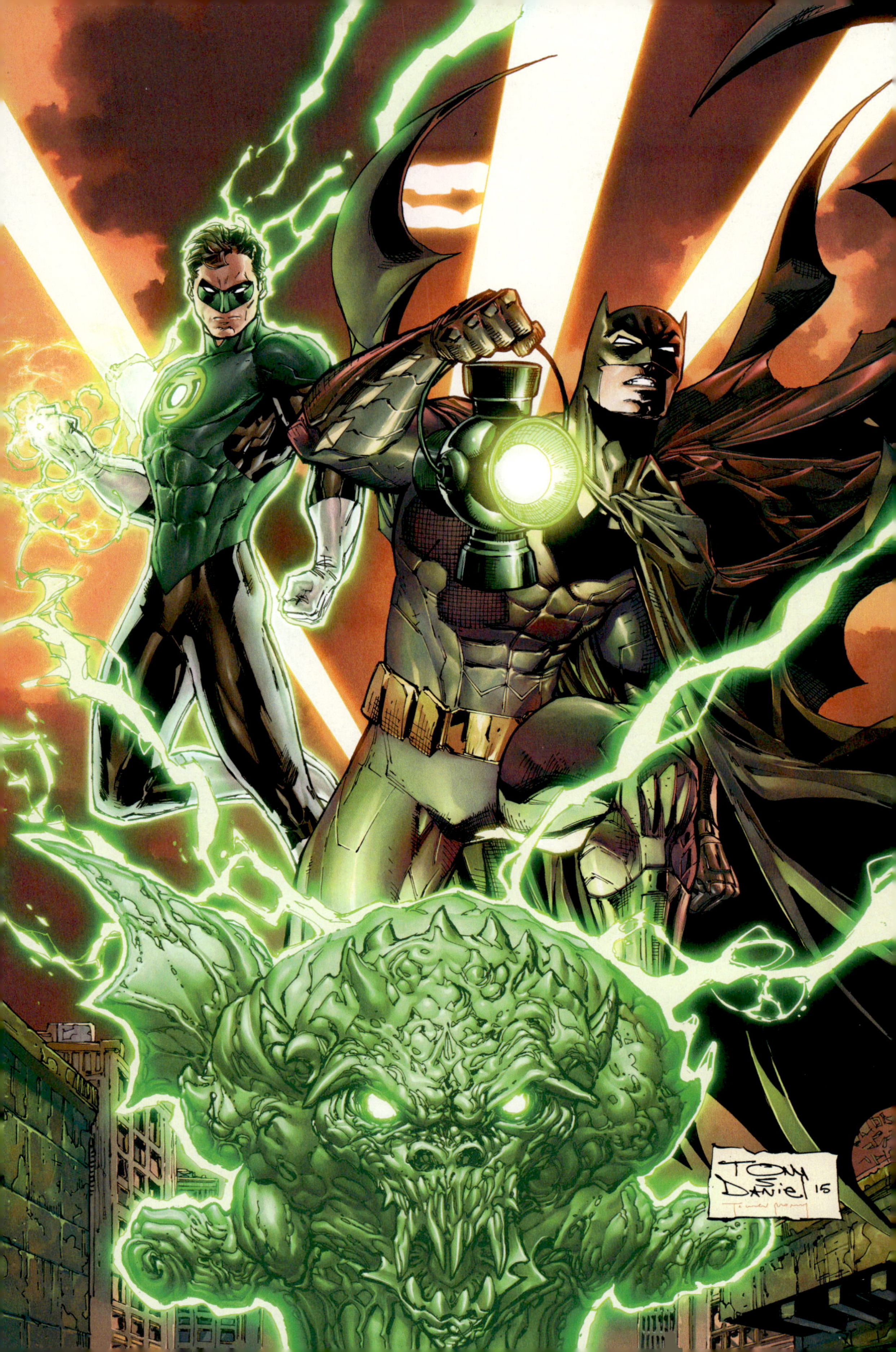
TONY S DANIEL 15

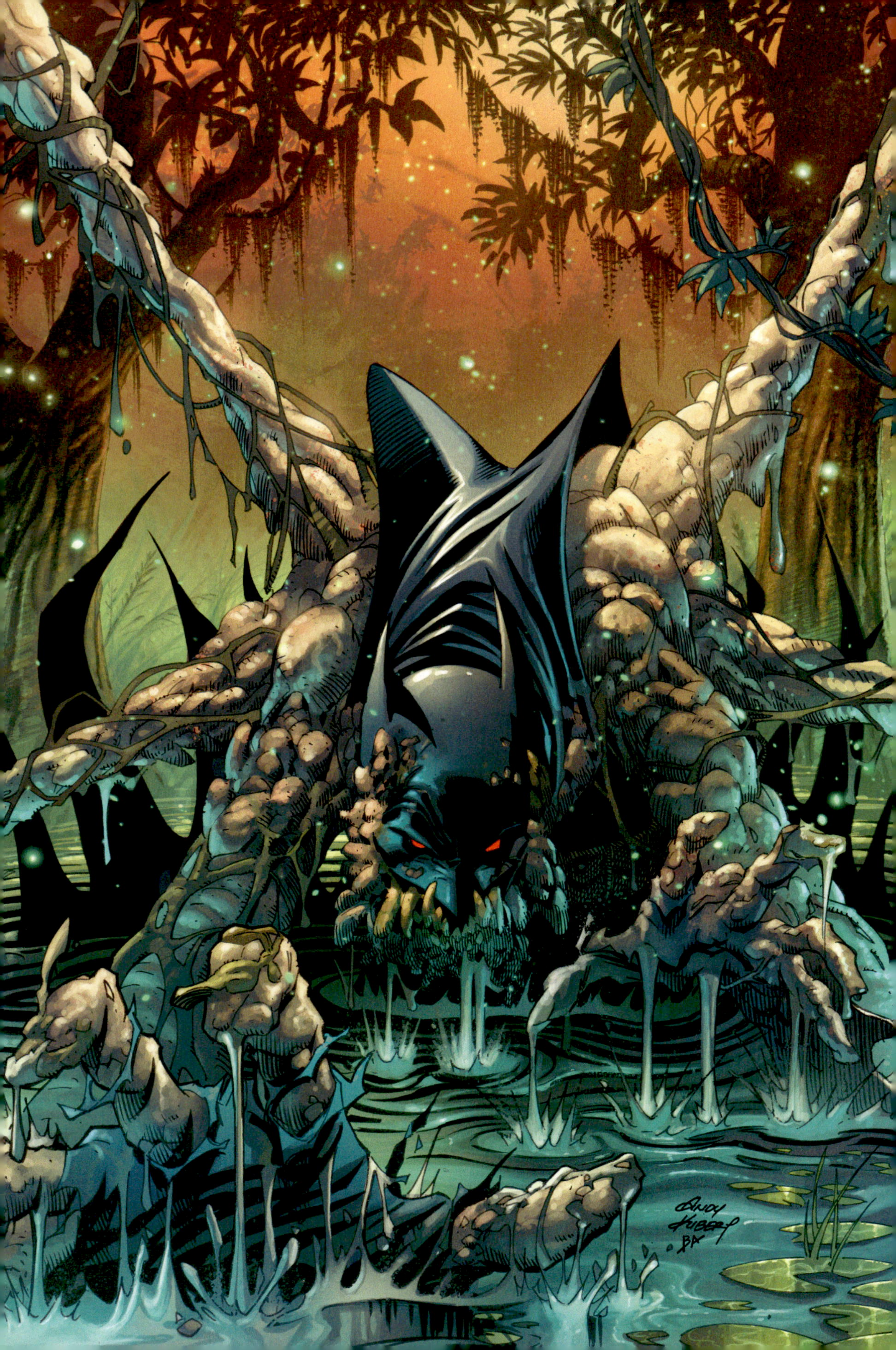
ANDY KUBERT
BA

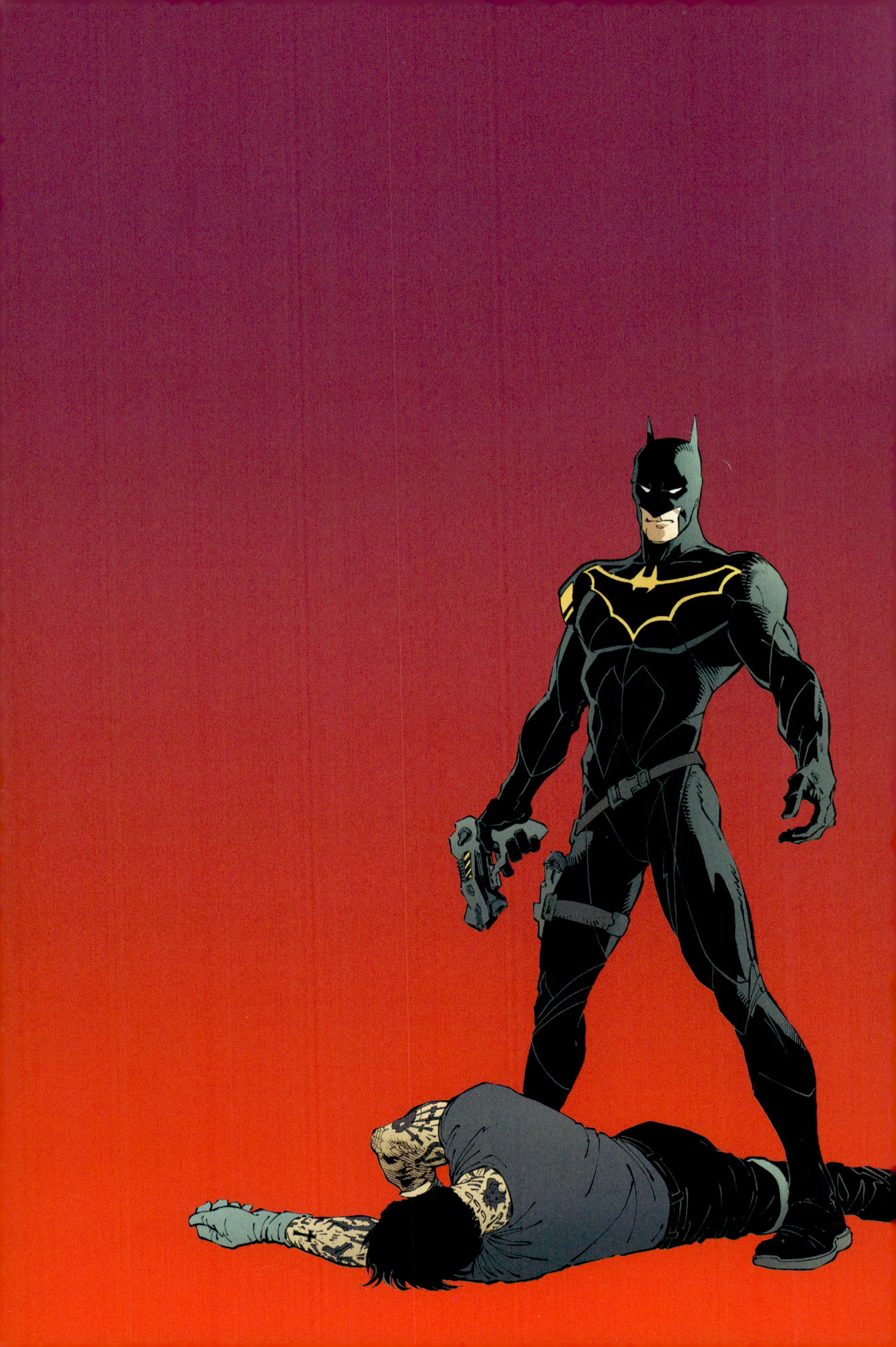

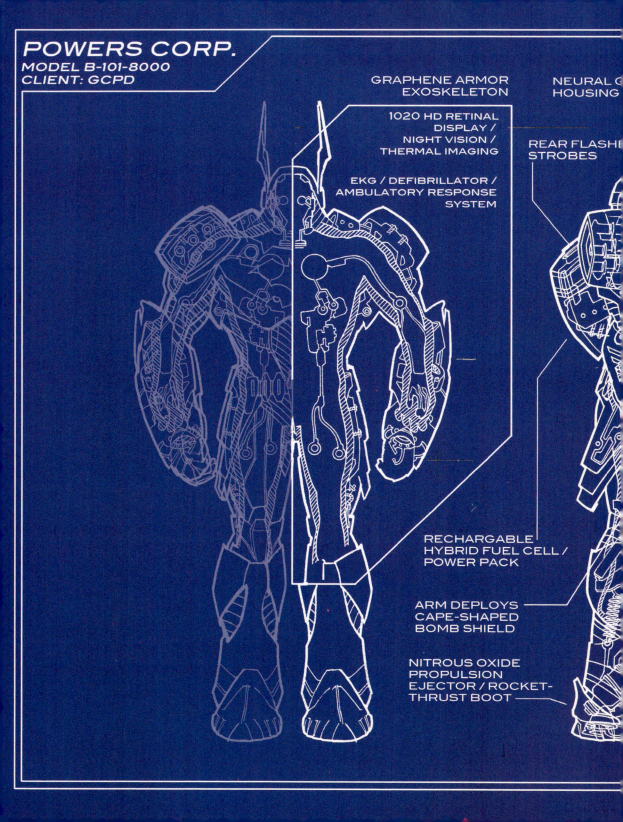

POWERS CORP.
MODEL B-101-8000
CLIENT: GCPD

GRAPHENE ARMOR
EXOSKELETON

NEURAL [] HOUSING

1020 HD RETINAL
DISPLAY /
NIGHT VISION /
THERMAL IMAGING

REAR FLASHE[]
STROBES

EKG / DEFIBRILLATOR /
AMBULATORY RESPONSE
SYSTEM

RECHARGABLE
HYBRID FUEL CELL /
POWER PACK

ARM DEPLOYS
CAPE-SHAPED
BOMB SHIELD

NITROUS OXIDE
PROPULSION
EJECTOR / ROCKET-
THRUST BOOT

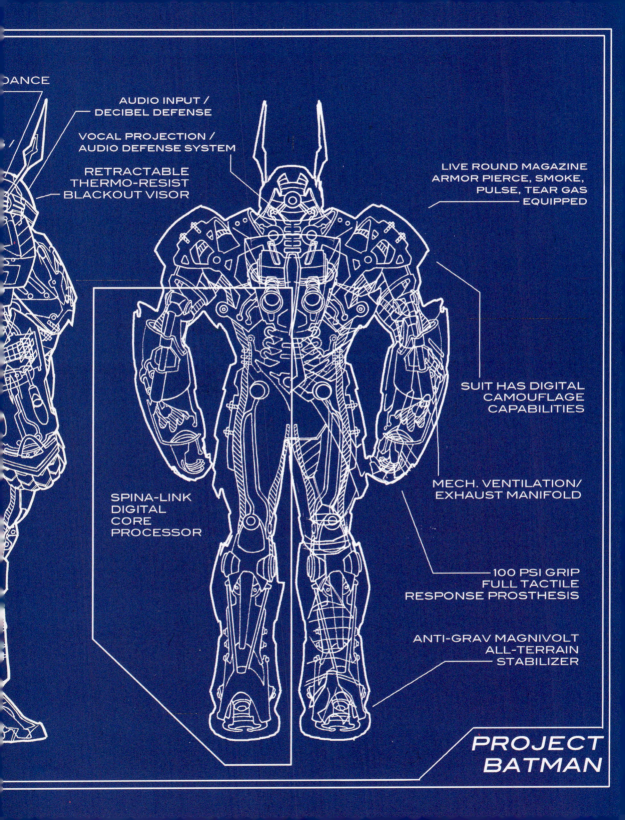

DANCE

AUDIO INPUT /
DECIBEL DEFENSE

VOCAL PROJECTION /
AUDIO DEFENSE SYSTEM

RETRACTABLE
THERMO-RESIST
BLACKOUT VISOR

LIVE ROUND MAGAZINE
ARMOR PIERCE, SMOKE,
PULSE, TEAR GAS
EQUIPPED

SUIT HAS DIGITAL
CAMOUFLAGE
CAPABILITIES

SPINA-LINK
DIGITAL
CORE
PROCESSOR

MECH. VENTILATION/
EXHAUST MANIFOLD

100 PSI GRIP
FULL TACTILE
RESPONSE PROSTHESIS

ANTI-GRAV MAGNIVOLT
ALL-TERRAIN
STABILIZER

PROJECT
BATMAN

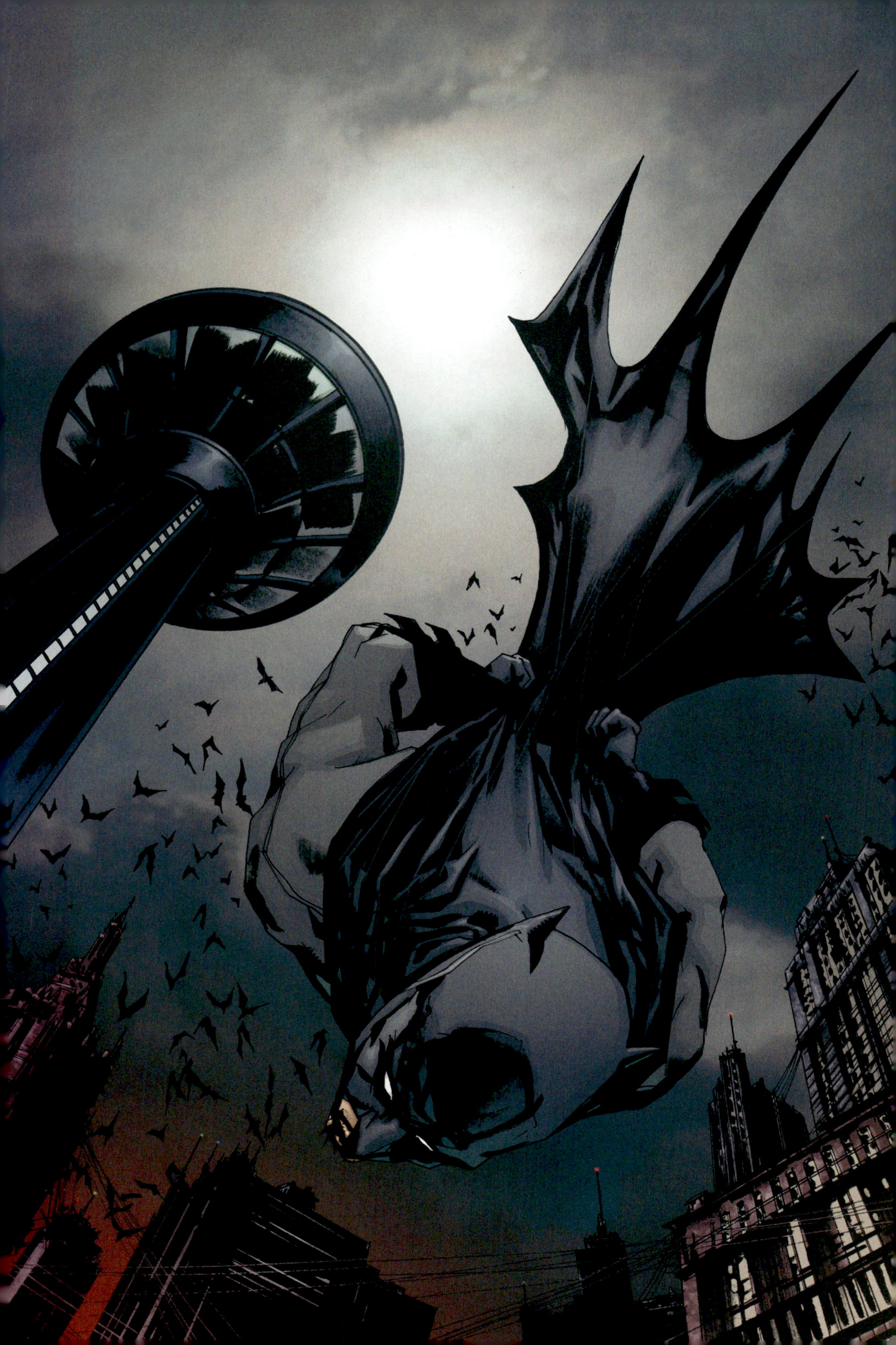

GCPD
Retract
Retract

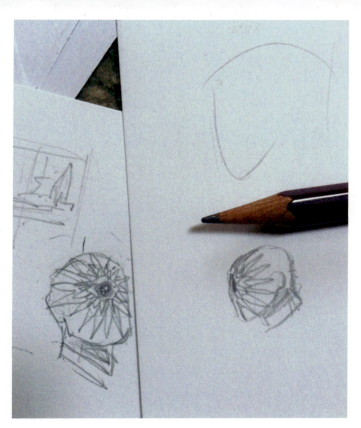

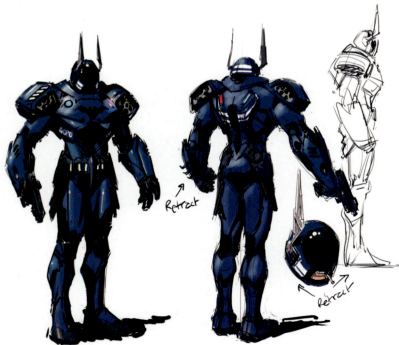

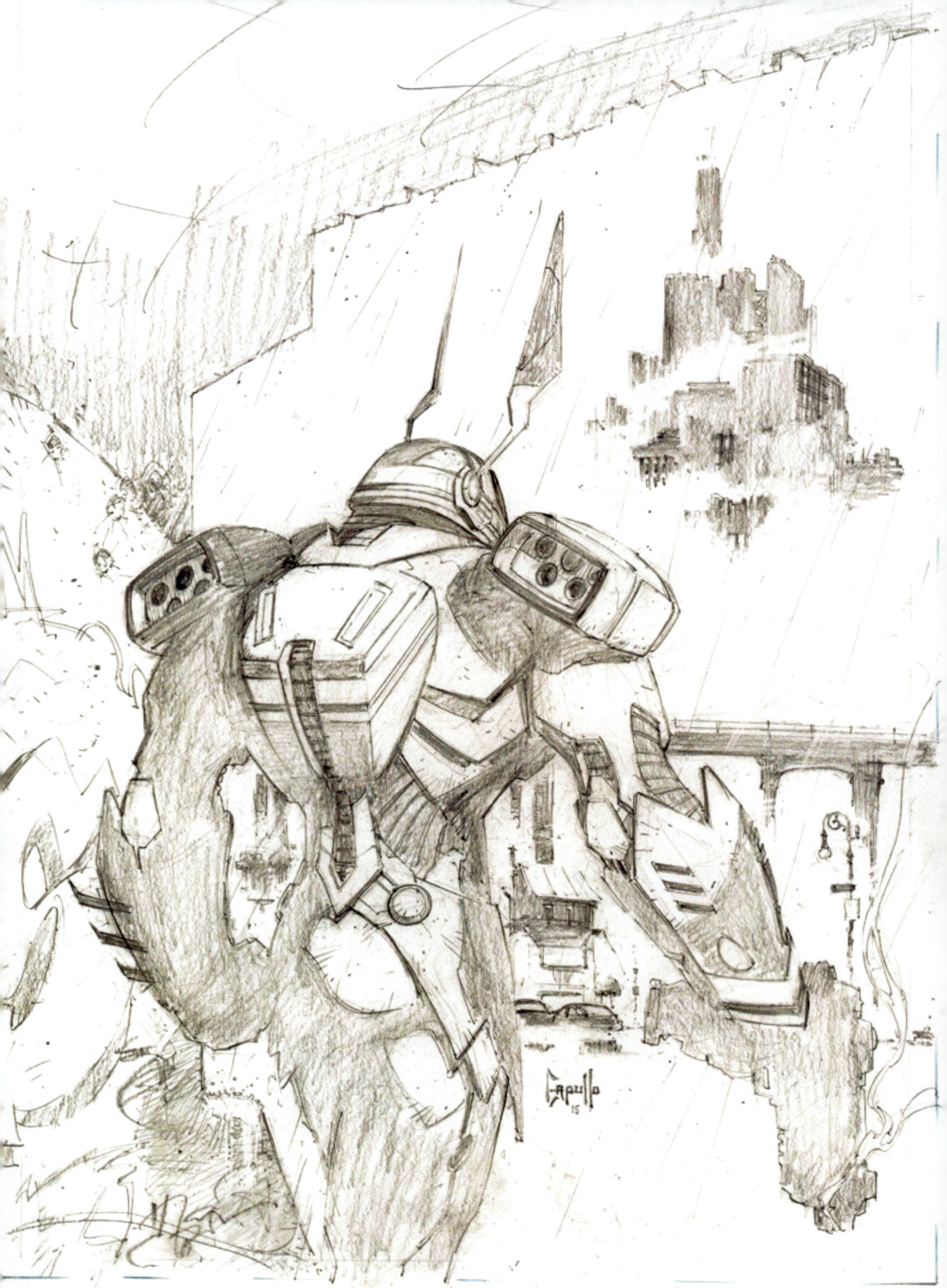
Capullo
15

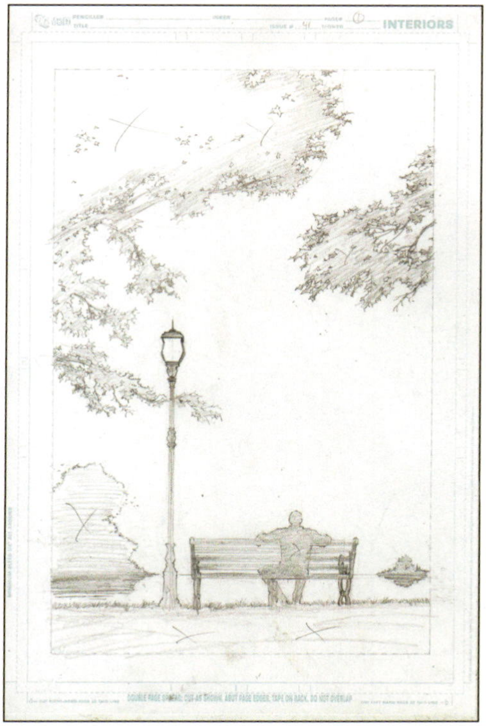
INTERIORS
DOUBLE PAGE SPREAD: CUT AS SHOWN, ABUT PAGE EDGES, TAPE ON BACK, DO NOT OVERLAP

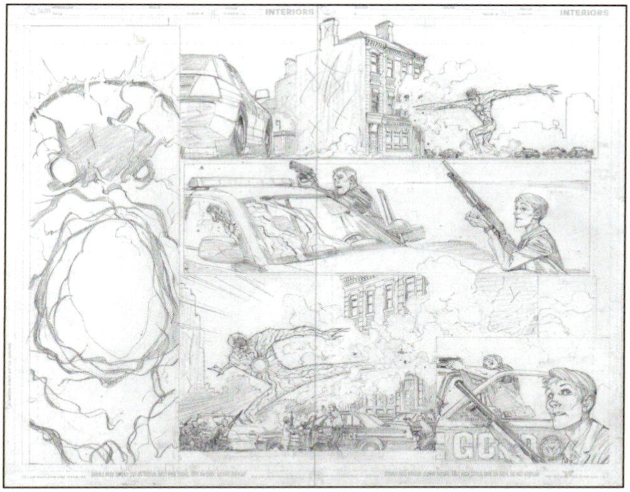
INTERIORS
INTERIORS

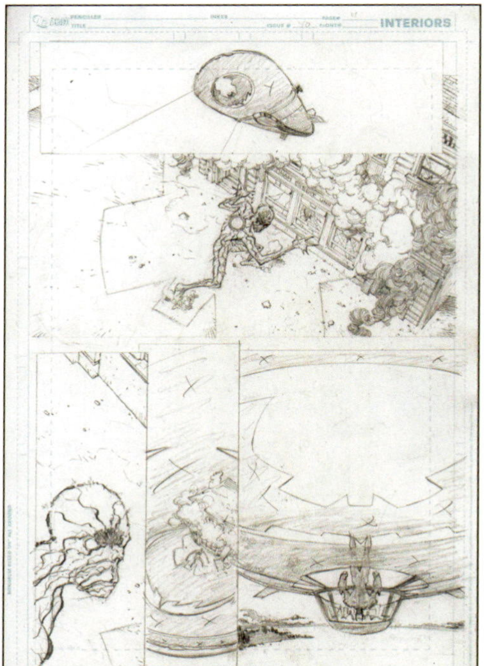
INTERIORS
DOUBLE PAGE SPREAD: CUT AS SHOWN, ABUT PAGE EDGES, TAPE ON BACK, DO NOT OVERLAP

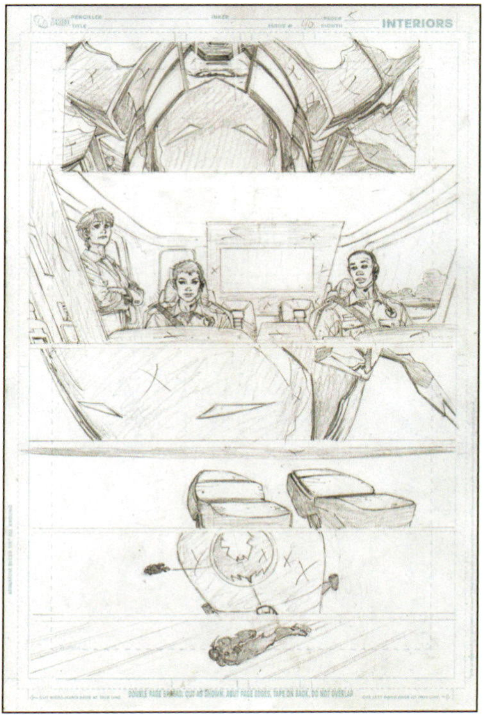
INTERIORS
DOUBLE PAGE SPREAD: CUT AS SHOWN, ABUT PAGE EDGES, TAPE ON BACK, DO NOT OVERLAP

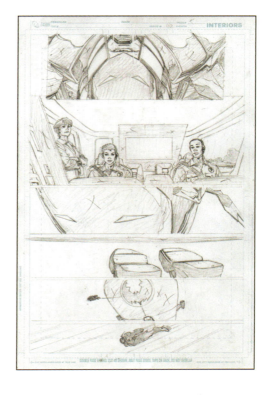

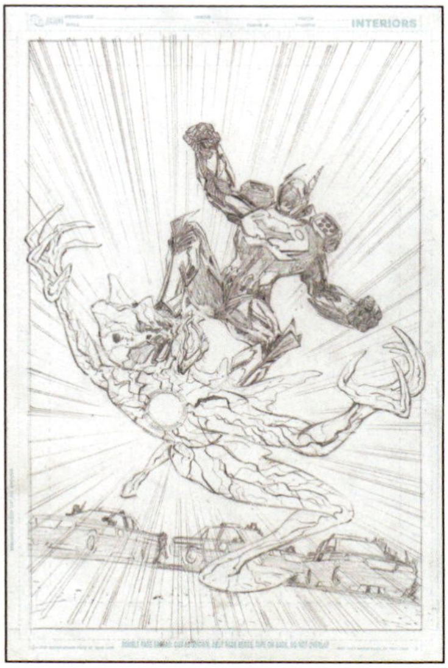
INTERIORS
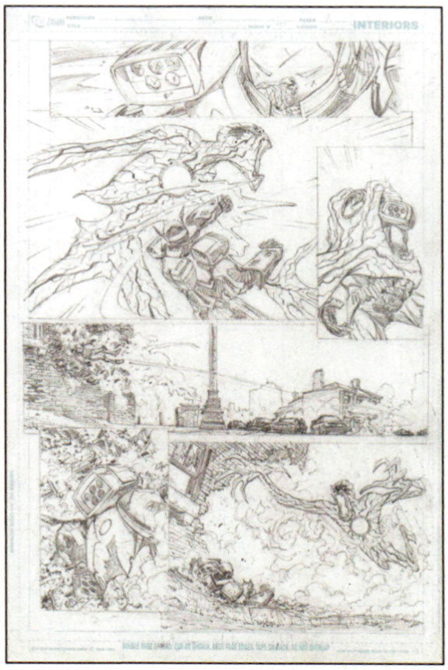
INTERIORS
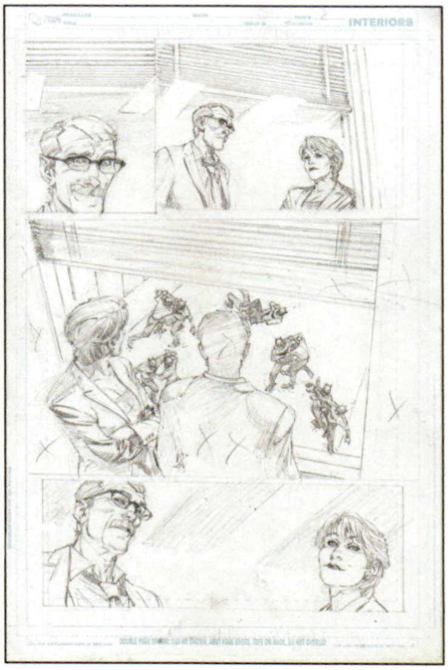
INTERIORS
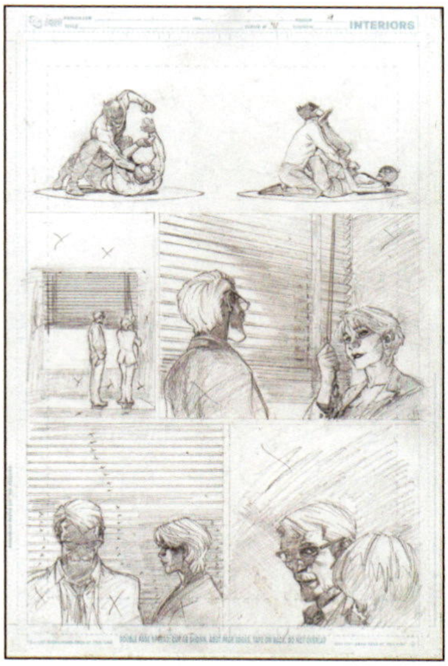
INTERIORS
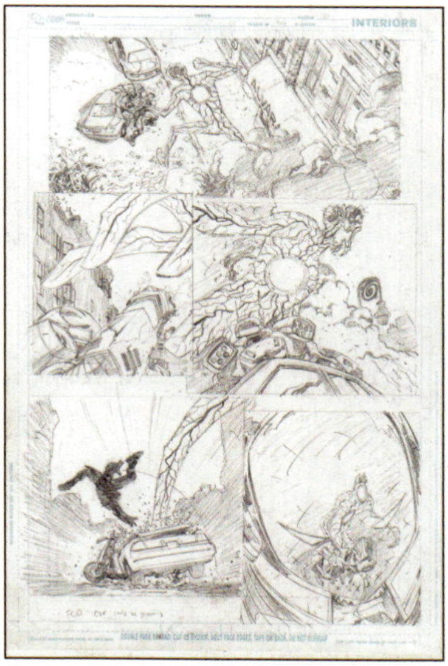
INTERIORS
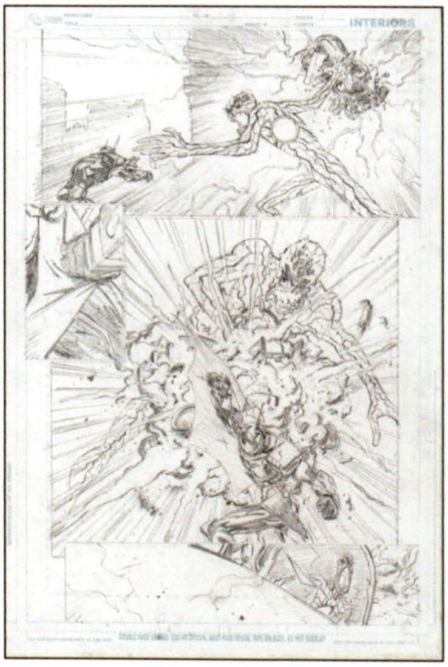
INTERIORS

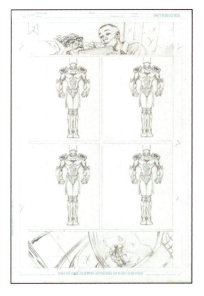

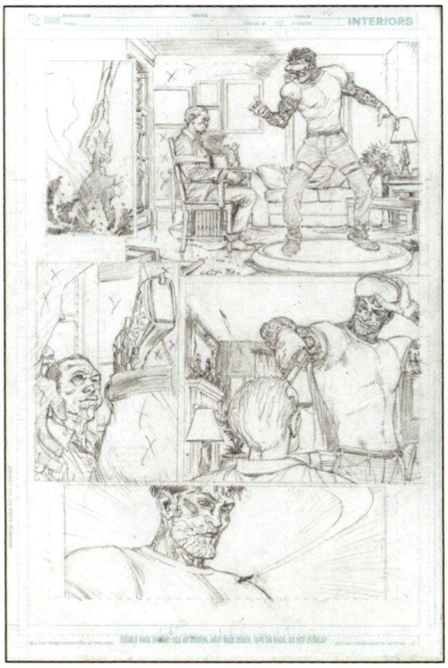
INTERIORS

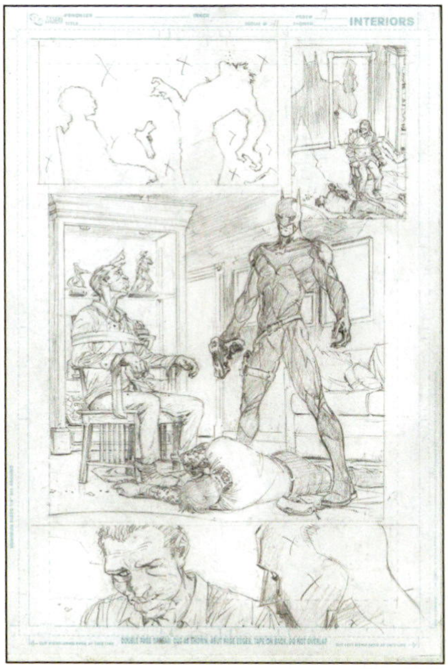
INTERIORS

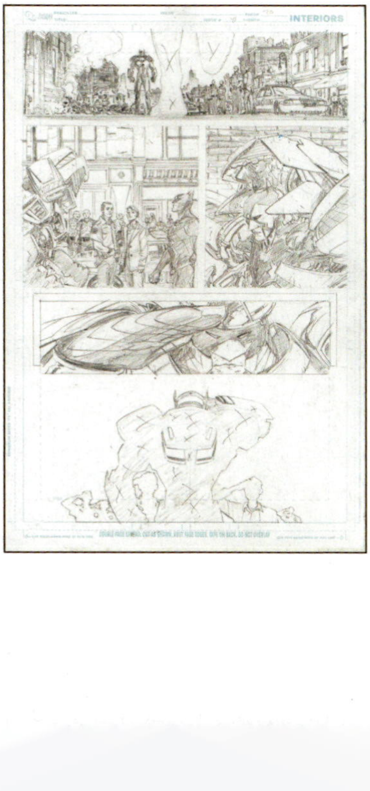
INTERIORS

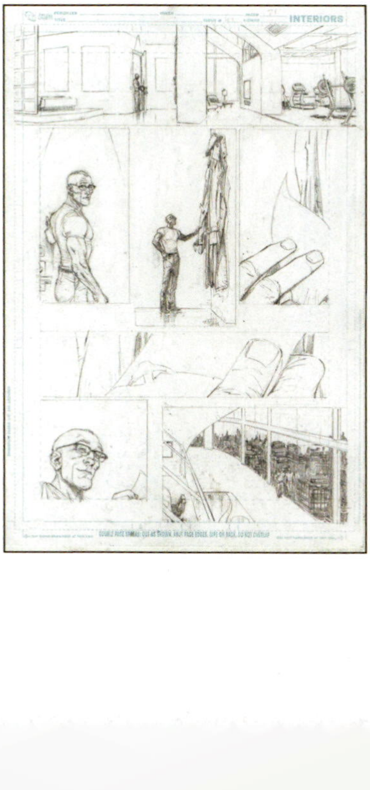
INTERIORS

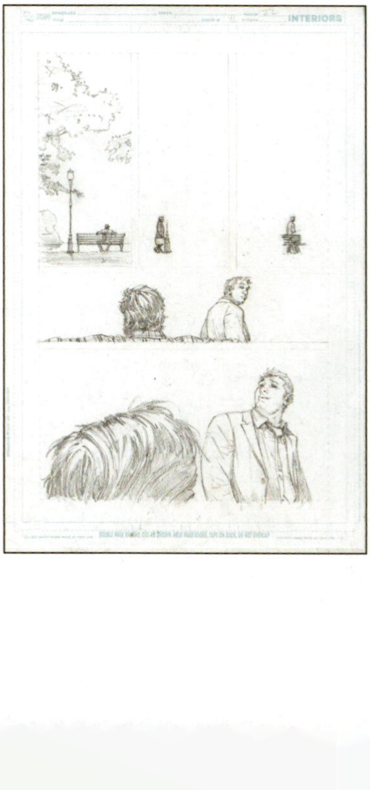
INTERIORS

"[Writer Scott Snyder] pulls from the oldest aspects of the Batman myth, combines it with sinister-comic elements from the series' best period, and gives the whole thing terrific forward-spin."—ENTERTAINMENT WEEKLY

START AT THE BEGINNING!

BATMAN VOLUME 1: THE COURT OF OWLS

BATMAN VOL. 2: THE CITY OF OWLS

with SCOTT SNYDER and GREG CAPULLO

BATMAN VOL. 3: DEATH OF THE FAMILY

with SCOTT SNYDER and GREG CAPULLO

BATMAN: NIGHT OF THE OWLS

with SCOTT SNYDER and GREG CAPULLO

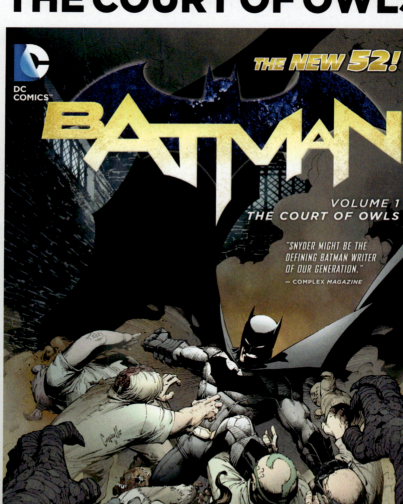

THE NEW 52!

DC COMICS™

BATMAN

VOLUME 1
THE COURT OF OWLS

"SNYDER MIGHT BE THE DEFINING BATMAN WRITER OF OUR GENERATION."
— COMPLEX MAGAZINE

SCOTT **SNYDER** GREG **CAPULLO** JONATHAN **GLAPION**

"Combines the real world elements that have made the Christopher Nolan movies so successful with stylized visuals that only the comic medium can provide."
—COMPLEX MAGAZINE

MUST-READ TALES OF THE DARK KNIGHT!

BATMAN
EARTH ONE: VOL. 1
GEOFF JOHNS & GARY FRANK

BATMAN VOL. 3:
DEATH OF THE FAMILY

by SCOTT SNYDER &
GREG CAPULLO

BATMAN: KNIGHTFALL
VOLS. 1-3

BATMAN:
NO MAN'S LAND
VOLS. 1-4

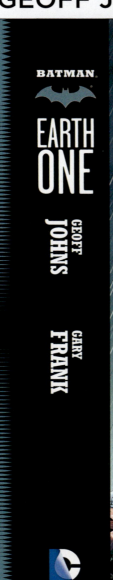

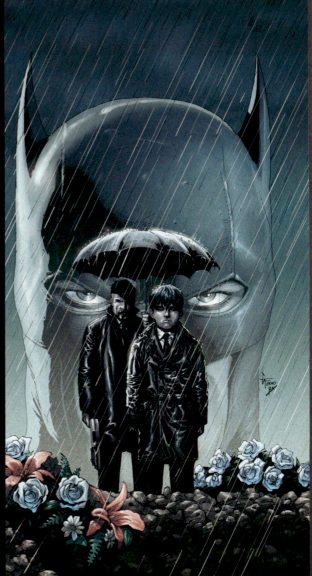

BATMAN

EARTH
ONE

GEOFF
JOHNS

GARY
FRANK

DC
COMICS™

DC COMICS™

FROM THE CREATOR OF *300* and *SIN CITY*
FRANK MILLER
with KLAUS JANSON

BATMAN:
THE DARK KNIGHT
STRIKES AGAIN

BATMAN: YEAR ONE
DELUXE EDITION

with DAVID MAZZUCCHELLI

ALL-STAR BATMAN
& ROBIN, THE BOY
WONDER VOL. 1

with JIM LEE

BATMAN: THE DARK KNIGHT RETURNS

FRANK MILLER
with KLAUS JANSON and LYNN VARLEY